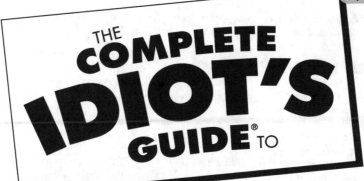

Communism

by Rodney Carlisle, Ph.D.
with James H. Lide, Ph.D.

ALPHA

A Pearson Education Company

For Loretta and Deborah, whose support allowed us to stay out of the shopping malls and at the computer keyboards over the Christmas season.

Copyright © 2002 by Rodney Carlisle

International Standard Book Number: 0-02-864314-3
Library of Congress Catalog Card Number: 2002102218

04   03   02   8   7   6   5   4   3   2   1

Interpretation of the printing code: The rightmost number of the first series of numbers is the year of the book's printing; the rightmost number of the second series of numbers is the number of the book's printing. For example, a printing code of 02-1 shows that the first printing occurred in 2002.

Printed in the United States of America

Publisher: *Marie Butler-Knight*
Product Manager: *Phil Kitchel*
Managing Editor: *Jennifer Chisholm*
Acquisitions Editor: *Randy Ladenheim-Gil*
Development Editor: *Tom Stevens*
Production Editor: *Kathy Bidwell*
Copy Editor: *Anja Mutic-Blessing*
Illustrator: *Chris Eliopoulos*
Cover/Book Designer: *Trina Wurst*
Indexer: *Brad Herriman*
Layout: *Stacey Richwine-DeRome*

Corporate and Government Sales: *1-800-382-3419 or corpsales@pearsontechgroup.com*
International Sales and Distribution: *Kit Kemper, 317-581-3665*
Marketing and Publicity: *Dawn Werk, 317-581-3722*

Contents at a Glance

Appendixes

Contents

14 Mao Zedong and the Communist Revolution in China   191

15 The Communist Party and the Cold War   207

Foreword

Communism and communists are central to the history of the twentieth century. When the socialist movement split at the end of World War I between a democratic socialist wing and a Leninist wing calling itself communist, communist parties sprang up in nearly every country in the world. Communist governments seized power in an arc of nations from the middle of Europe stretching east to the Pacific and south to the South China Sea with outposts in Africa and Latin America as well. Nations flying communism's red banner included the Union of Soviet Socialist Republics, the world's largest nation, and the People's Republic of China, the most populous. The USSR, equipped with nuclear-armed intercontinental ballistic missiles, atomic submarines, and the world's most powerful land army, was one of the world's two superpowers. And the long military stalemate between the USSR and the United States repeatedly threatened a civilization-destroying nuclear Armageddon. While the third world war never broke out, the Cold War consumed trillions of dollars in military expenditure, and more than a million persons died in scores of large and small proxy wars fought in Asia, Africa, and Latin America.

Communism inspired millions with the idea that by their political will and in accordance with Marxist laws of history, they could transform the world. The exploitation of man by man would end, economic security and material abundance would be guaranteed, and the chief source of social injustice—class conflict—would be abolished along with capitalism, racism, colonialism, and imperialism. Universal brotherhood would be swiftly achieved in a world in which communists ruled. Communist ideals attracted hundreds of thousands of revolutionaries who devoted their lives to the movement, won the backing of a share of the intellectual elite, and attracted millions to communist-led labor unions and political groups. For much of the last century, millions expected, its opponents feared, and its many intellectual supporters confidently predicted that communism would sweep the globe.

It did not, and it's now more history than threat, although communists still rule in China, North Korea, and a few other places. Communism failed its promise because, as this volume details, in practice the idealism of communism translated into ruthlessness, cruelty, and oppression combined with economic failure. Every communist government that gained power did so by force of arms rather than by democratic means. All created one-party tyrannies that denied free speech, free press, independent trade unions, and freedom of religion and attempted to destroy civil life outside communist control. Communists with conscious malice murdered tens of millions of innocent persons by mass political executions, police state terror, deprivation in harsh prison labor camps, and politically induced famines. All communist states also failed to achieve prosperity, and their standard of living fell well behind that of free market economies.

This volume presents in an authoritative and comprehensive form communism's perplexing combination of soaring humanitarian idealism, Promethean attempt to create a socialist utopia, degeneration into mass murder and political tyranny, and ultimate social and economic collapse.

—John Earl Haynes

Co-author of *The Secret World of American Communism* and historical adviser to the International Computerization of the Communist International Archives project

Introduction

For most of the twentieth century, communism was a word to be hated and feared or an ideal to be loved and pursued. Communists, anarchists, socialists, and others shared a vision of an end to wealth and poverty, the arrival of a classless society, and the final elimination of government itself. They organized political parties and labor unions. The more impatient ones planned, and sometimes won, revolutions.

Communism was a set of ideas to completely reshape society, and communists were men and women who worked to put those ideas into action. The ideas came together from diverse sources in the nineteenth century. There had always been the wealthy and the poor, but the quickening pace of technical progress appeared to be widening the gap, not narrowing it. Social thinkers like Karl Marx and less well-known writers like Henri St. Simon, Robert Owen, Pierre Proudhon, Emma Goldman, and Peter Kropotkin were all troubled by what they saw happening. Marx himself developed a "scientific" analysis of human history of the world that predicted that a socialist society was the inevitable outcome of the forces of history. In the late 1900s, socialists and anarchists in Europe and America put together the First and Second International organizations to share ideas and support.

Following the dozens of ideas, the hundreds of leaders, and the wide variety of related socialist and social-democratic thinkers into the twentieth century is pretty tough without a roadmap. But if you focus on a few key places, you can see the patterns.

In the United States, socialist parties led by men like Eugene Debs formed around 1900 while impatient and radical labor leaders such as Bill Haywood set up the IWW—the Industrial Workers of the World. In Britain, some intellectuals shaped their ideas around a go-slow approach, with George Bernard Shaw and H.G. Wells supporting the Fabian Society. Around 1900 British trade unionists and social democrats established the Labour Party.

In Russia, a minority of radical social democrats following Marx's ideas and led by V. I. Lenin called themselves the majority, or "Bolshevik," faction. Believing that a disciplined and centrally led corps of revolutionaries could bring about socialism, they won control of the remnants of the Russian Empire at the end of the First World War. One of their first moves after gaining power in Russia was to reestablish their party as the Communist Party and to finance like-minded radical socialist groups in other countries through a new Communist International. This Third International worked with small groups of socialists in country after country, using money from the new Soviet state to advance their cause. However, the Third International insisted that Communists abroad support the goals of the Soviet Union as a nation, causing factional fights, disillusionment, and bloodshed.

While socialism had always been controversial, the techniques of the communist parties of the 1920s and 1930s caused an uproar. Opponents of socialism had always included most successful business people, the wealthy, landowners, and much of the middle class. But the Russian Communist Party made many new enemies when they began funding particular socialist factions in the United States, Britain, Germany, and the rest of Europe. It was hard enough being a radical in those countries, but with some radicals on the payroll of Moscow, workers, labor leaders, and socialist politicians became outraged. On the one hand, the Third International tried to take over their groups. On the other hand, money from Moscow made Communist Party leaders the equivalent of paid foreign agents.

Some countries responded very quickly by outlawing communists as unregistered foreign and subversive agents. In other countries, such as Britain and America, communists were barely tolerated by the governments while earning the hostility of other socialists, labor leaders, and much of the general public. Meanwhile, Joseph Stalin emerged as the leader of the Soviet Union, using brutal police powers to suppress opponents and ensure that the Communist Party remained under his control.

When the Nazis came to power in Germany in 1933, Adolf Hitler began arresting not only communists but socialists as well, to destroy all opponents to his rule. Stunned by his success, Moscow adopted a new approach in the mid 1930s, aligning with other socialist groups and labor leaders, establishing a Popular Front against the fascists and Nazis. The communist parties, however, always sought to control and direct the coalitions through which they worked.

At the end of World War II, with the destruction of Nazi Germany and its Axis allies, communism appeared ready to move on to the rest of the world. The resulting Cold War, led by two "superpowers," the United States and the Soviet Union, was not only a struggle between two powerful nations. Its other side was a conflict between the version of socialism represented by the Soviet Union and the American and Western vision of free societies. But that simple view of late twentieth-century history might obscure many series of complications.

During the Cold War, communist parties—some linked directly to the Soviet Union, and others more independent—worked to seize power in Eastern Europe, Latin America, Africa, and Asia. In 1956, Nikita Khrushchev announced that Stalin had gone too far to build up his personal power, but the Soviet Union continued to use its power, including tanks and troops, to suppress those who disagreed too sharply with official doctrine. Meanwhile, the Soviet system became more and more bureaucratic and inefficient.

The communist parties of Yugoslavia, China, and some other countries made it clear that they would not take orders from Moscow. When the burden of military support by the Soviets for communist governments in Eastern Europe became too heavy in the 1980s, the Soviet leader Mikhail Gorbachev announced he would withdraw the troops. Within a couple of years, elections and rebellions threw out one communist regime after another. The Cold War began to wind down.

The Soviet Union itself dissolved in December 1991, and by the end of the century only a handful of nations still had governments dominated by communist parties. Despite the failure of the Soviet Communist Party to capture and control socialism, variations and aspects of socialist thought survived more widely.

The Complete Idiot's Guide to Communism will not explain everything there is to know about communism, but it will cover this core story and give you enough information to find your way through the tangles on the Left that are a big part of twentieth-century world history.

Part 1, "From Community to Communism," takes us through the ideas of the nineteenth-century socialists, including Karl Marx as well as a wide range of other thinkers and the movements they started that lasted into the early twentieth century.

Part 2, "Mother Russia," shows how the Bolsheviks took charge of the revolutionary situation in Russia, and how three leaders shaped communism there: Lenin, Stalin, and Trotsky.

Part 3, "Making Friends and Enemies," begins with the formation of the Third International and shows how the communists made some allies and lots more opponents, particularly in the United States. Then, in the Spanish Civil War and later in World War II, communists fought desperately to defeat the Nazis. With America and Britain as allies, the Soviet Union emerged bloodied from World War II but with prospects to spread communist doctrine and power to Europe and beyond.

Part 4, "Communist Expansion and the Cold War," shows some of the successes and failures of the Soviet Union in winning over the rest of the world to support its version of socialism. They had some strategic victories. But there was trouble in paradise, as country after country in their orbit began to define its own path to socialism or sought to abandon it altogether. The fights over who was "correct" in understanding Marx cost literally millions of lives.

Part 5, "From Advance to Retreat," takes us on a tour of the developing world, where the appeal of the communist message made some headway. Then we look at how, in Mother Russia, the system began to break down and the Cold War came to a quick end, leaving only a few remnants around the world following a Marxist-Leninist form of socialism like the one the communists had supported.

Extras

In addition to the main story, with photographs and maps, *The Complete Idiot's Guide to Communism* has some other types of information. You'll find quotations from supporters and opponents, definitions of specialized terms, anecdotes and trivia, and explorations of communist politics.

Voices

This feature includes contemporary statements, mostly from communists themselves, that shed light on personalities, strategies, ideas, and concepts.

Notes on the Left

These notes provide details of some of the twists and turns of socialist and communist politics. We had to put a few of them on the "right" side of the page. Sorry, Karl.

Red Words

Communists and their opponents had to think up a lot of jargon to describe their tactics and concepts, and here you'll find definitions of key words. Do you know the difference between an "opportunist" and a "leftist deviationist"? You will. We also put the language together in a glossary at the end, in case you miss the definition where it shows up in the book.

Vignettes

Despite the fact that communists and their opponents took themselves *very* seriously, like everyone else, their lives were touched by the bizarre, the human side, and the twists of fate. We capture some of them here.

Acknowledgments

The authors collaborated on writing this work, with Carlisle writing about communal thinkers and socialists, the United States, Britain, and Eastern Europe. Lide wrote about Marx and Russia, China, and the Third World. We checked each other's work and tried to draw from the most objective sources we could find. We've listed some of the best works in the bibliography.

We received support and help in the project from several sources. Elizabeth Knappman of New England Publishing Associates assisted in planning the work. Philip Cantelon, President of History Associates Incorporated, provided encouragement and some gracious prodding. Professor Joseph Held, noted expert on Eastern Europe and the author of a number of works in the area, read and commented on several chapters. Tom Stevens, editor at Alpha Books, made numerous suggestions that helped a great deal.

Trademarks

All terms mentioned in this book that are known to be or are suspected of being trademarks or service marks have been appropriately capitalized. Alpha Books and Pearson Education, Inc., cannot attest to the accuracy of this information. Use of a term in this book should not be regarded as affecting the validity of any trademark or service mark.

Part 1

From Community to Communism

If you've ever wondered about why the words "community," "communal," "commune," and "communism" all seem to stem from the same root but carry such different connotations, you've got the right book. In this part, we look at early experiments in communal living in America in the nineteenth century. You've heard of Karl Marx, but did you know that anarchists, syndicalists, and socialists all had similar ideas of how to restructure the economies and governments of the world? While they all agreed that producers should get more of what they produced, they argued about how and how fast the changes should happen. By the early twentieth century, organized political parties and labor unions were set up around each of these concepts in Europe, Russia, and America.

Communes and Communities

In This Chapter

◆ Communes around the world

◆ Nineteenth-century American communes

◆ Communes, socialism, and communism

In this chapter, we see the variety of *communes* that developed in the United States in the nineteenth century.

The general population of the country felt ambivalent about these numerous small social experiments. On the one hand, the communes seemed like little ideal communities in which greed and hardship so common in the rapidly industrializing society appeared to diminish. Some of the communes became prosperous and comfortable for the members.

On the other hand, the loss of individual freedom of making decisions over even minute personal matters seemed distasteful in a society that more and more championed individual initiative and achievement. Some of the new communes challenged basic family values and sexual mores. Some communities raised children in common, rather than in families, while others were celibate. A few experimented with varieties of companionate and temporary marriage, shocking the staid middle-class values of many, and drawing a sort of prurient and leering interest from others. In many of the short-lived communes, living conditions were pretty bad, with scarce food and fuel and poor housing.

We see that the term "communism," which was first used in the United States in reference to these scattered experimental villages, took on many connotations. For writers and readers in the general public, "communism" was something that suggested fascinating promise and at the same time a radical sacrifice of important values.

Roots of Communes

Nineteenth-century Americans and Europeans found the changes of rapid industrialization disturbing. The new systems of mills and railroads involved large employers who did not personally know employees, workmen who did not own their tools, and wage-labor and piecework payment. The growing enterprises yielded a host of other social consequences that were negative, even frightening. Where once there had been community, there was now anonymity. Where once people had known who produced the goods they consumed, they were now made in distant factories, transported by unknown carriers on land or water. Price and market systems began to be substituted for human relations.

Some idealists and ideologues thought of schemes that would restore what they believed was the lost sense of community, and published a variety of works suggesting either vague or specific plans for ideal little *utopias*. But even before such books were read and had much influence, small groups of like-minded individuals, often united by religion, established specific communities, or *communes*. Usually the communities held their land in common and shared the proceeds of their work.

> **Red Words**
>
> **Utopias.** In 1516, the British philosopher Thomas More published a fanciful novel describing an ideal society, titled *Utopia*. Since then, idealized planned societies have been called utopias, and a scheme for setting one up has been called utopian.
>
> **Commune.** In the nineteenth-century United States, the term described religious and non-religious experimental communities that shared ownership of land and the earnings from work.

Estimates of the number of such communities in the United States established in the eighteenth and nineteenth centuries vary considerably, but may have been around 130, scattered from New York and New England through the American Midwest, with some in Oregon and California. More than half were founded in the 20 years between 1840 and 1860, the year before the Civil War broke out.

Notes on the Left _____

Around the world there have been a wide variety of communes. In pre-industrial societies, many types of shared property holdings meet the definition of commune. For example, in present-day Mexico, the *ejidos* are Indian communities that hold land in common, and they are sometimes called "communes" in English. European village lands used for pasturage before the coming of modern agriculture were also often held in common and the term "commune" has been used to describe such holdings.

The nineteenth-century communes established in the United States on the basis of social ideals or shared religious identity incorporated socialist concepts. American communes went by many names, but Charles Nordhoff, a journalist who wrote a summary of them in the late nineteenth century, called these communes "Communistic Societies." In the twentieth century, when the word "communistic" implied for most readers an affiliation with the Soviet-dominated Communist International, a new edition of *American Communistic Societies* was published under the title *American Utopias*.

In 1870, John Noyes, himself an advocate of communal living, published a compilation of such experiments called *American Socialisms*. The issue of defining these experimental communitarian colonies that sought to find an alternative to the capitalist price, wage, and market system seemed to confuse participants and later writers who reported on them.

Throughout the world in the nineteenth and twentieth centuries, there was a number of communes representing a wide variety of religious and nonreligious planned communities. In Israel, the kibbutz movement reflected some of the same socialist ideals of the American experiments. In India, Mahatma Gandhi's followers often lived in communes known as ashrams. A convenient term adopted by historians for the ideology behind all such communes was "communitarian socialism."

Religious Origins

The first of the utopian experiments in the United States was set up by religious groups. Some of the communities and colonies vanished after a few years, while others dropped their idealistic goals and plans and transformed into more conventional towns. A few even converted their economic enterprise into a more or less ordinary corporation with stockholders. Very few survived on their original scheme for decades. *Sectarian* communes, held together by a shared faith, tended to outlast the communes built purely on nonreligious economic theories.

Red Words _____

Sectarian. Small religious groups that break away from mainstream religion are called sects, and their members sectarian.

Looking back at such communes from the viewpoint of the twentieth and twenty-first centuries, the experiments seemed less like efforts to build steps toward a future society than efforts to preserve or move back to a pre-industrial arrangement. Yet at the time, those living in such communities and especially visitors viewed them as path-finding plans suited to the future. Famous visitors included the economist Friedrich List, the British novelist Charles Dickens, and the noted writer Alexis de Tocqueville. Such tourists saw the communes as promising experiments suggesting how society might be organized in the future, not as escapes from modernity into an idealized past. The visitors and many of the participants viewed the communities as a force for reform and change in society.

Voices

Harriet Martineau, a British visitor to America, was impressed by Shaker and German sect communes in 1834. She considered that such experiments might serve as the basis for a broader socialist society. Somewhat of a snob, Martineau believed that Europeans could do a better job than the Americans at building an ideal society:

> If such external provision, with a great amount of accumulated wealth besides, is the result of co-operation and community of property among an ignorant, conceited, inert society like this, what might not the same principles of association achieve among a more intelligent set of people, stimulated by education?

Neither Revolutionists nor Gradualists, but a Bit of Both

The mind-set of the communitarian movement was neither revolutionary nor gradualist. The participants wanted to change society and change it immediately, so they could hardly be called gradualist. On the other hand, they sought to change it by example and constructive action, rather than by attempting to overthrow the existing social structure, as a revolutionist would do.

Perhaps the communitarian alternative appealed in part because the French Revolution had produced bloody excesses and had ultimately failed to establish a new order in Europe, disillusioning many in the promise of revolution. On the other hand, a slow approach through legislative reform seemed almost impossible, as the social problems generated by industrialism outstripped the mechanisms of government to deal with them.

Many communitarians were inspired by a religious sense—that they belonged to a special, chosen people who could create a more perfect society within a larger imperfect society. It is sometimes surprising to the modern observer to realize that communitarians did not think of themselves as impractical dreamers. Rather, they believed their societies were based on solid principles, tested out and demonstrated on a small scale to prove their practicality.

Voices _____

Parke Godwin, writing on the American version of Charles Fourier's ideas, said:

> Our plans are revolutionary .... But the revolution they contemplate is not violent, nor unjust, nor destructive .... Fourier's doctrine possesses a particular value to our minds because it seems to us to be Universal and consequently Reconciling and Pacific. It is both conservative and radical.

Although now remembered as a sort of quaint sidelight on the mainstream of American history, the dozens of communities and their thousands of members had an influence and an impact in mid-nineteenth century American life far greater than their numbers might suggest. Along with reform issues such as the abolition of slavery, education, prison reform, and temperance, the social experiments of the communes and the "communists" who lived in them provided fascinating reading and discussion topics across America.

Voices _____

William McClure, a settler at New Harmony, believed in the social experiment concept, arguing that it was far less dangerous to the total society than a broader revolution would be. He said:

> Each township might experiment on every thing that could conduce to the comfort and happiness, without interfering with the interests of their neighbors; thereby reducing all political, moral, or religious experiments to their simplicity, facility and utility of mechanism, [as found in] manufactures and all the useful arts; that is, that a failure could only hurt the contrivers and executors of the speculation, forcing them to nullify their mistakes and guaranteeing them against a perseverance in error.

Religious Utopias

Many of the religious communes in the United States had roots that went well back into history. Some sprang from the ideas and activities of religious reform groups that had risen in Europe, particularly in the region from Switzerland and Bohemia down the Rhine River, through the Netherlands. A sort of religious borderland between the Protestant and Catholic regions of Europe, this broad area gave birth in the seventeenth and eighteenth centuries to a wide variety of radical religious ideas. Dissenters were often forced to migrate, and as a whole community, taking their belongings and beliefs to a new land. Sharing their resources to preserve the communities seemed a natural and practical idea, motivated by simple survival concerns rather than any economic or social ideology.

Pennsylvania Dutch

The so-called Pennsylvania Dutch were in fact a variety of German-speaking immigrants. The United Brethren or "Moravians," refugees from Bohemia and Moravia, settled in Saxony, and then many small groups migrated overseas. In the 1740s, Moravians established themselves in Pennsylvania and set up their own separate communitarian economy.

From the same general region in Europe, Dutch Mennonites settled in New York. Followers of Jean de Labadie, who began his career in Switzerland, developed a following in the Netherlands and brought a group that settled in Maryland. A group of German followers of the mystic Johann Zimmerman settled in Germantown Pennsylvania, now a district of Philadelphia. Another group of Germans settled near Ephrata, Pennsylvania. The Moravians spread to several locations in Pennsylvania and to colonies in Georgia and North Carolina.

Rapp, Rappites, and the Separatists of Zoar

Father George Rapp led a group from Germany to western Pennsylvania, finally settling in a community called Economy Pennsylvania, down river from Pittsburgh. Perhaps because of their location on a westward migration route, the Rappites soon attracted attention from travelers passing through.

The British poet Lord Byron heard of the Rappites from a variety of European visitors and incorporated satire of the Rappites in one of his works. Like many other sectarian communities, the Rappites were split by factionalism and offshoot groups settled as far afield as Louisiana. One faction group set up a community with shared property, calling themselves the Society of Separatists of Zoar.

A religious group, the Separatists of Zoar, was very practical in its business practices. Before breaking up, the group established a woolen factory, flour mills, a sawmill, a planing-mill and machine shop. They had a tannery, a dye-house, and a large country store and hotel at their village in Tuscarawas County, Ohio, about halfway between Pittsburgh and Cleveland.

Notes on the Left

The Separatists of Zoar called themselves "Separatists" because, as they said in their Constitution, "We separate ourselves from all ecclesiastical connections and constitutions, because true Christian life requires no sectarianism, while set forms and ceremonies cause sectarian divisions."

The Separatists of Zoar had a hard time sustaining membership through a second generation, however, because they believed "Complete virginity or entire cessation of sexual commerce is more commendable than marriage." Although the Zoarites did permit marriage, some other groups, like the Shakers, were completely celibate and acquired children only through adoption.

The Zoarites and most of the other religious communes required that when a member joined, he or she would deposit any existing funds they had with the commune. In some societies, those probationers who were not finally accepted could get a refund.

Shakers

Famous for their contributions to American furniture and architectural styles, the Shakers set up many individual communities. Starting from a small group founded by Ann Lee in Britain, the Shakers immigrated to America immediately before the American Revolution. In 1776, they established a community near Albany, New York.

The Shakers regarded themselves as a collective body of Christians separated from the world. From the Mother Church in New York state, the Shakers established communities in Massachusetts and Connecticut, and later in Ohio (Shaker Heights outside of Cleveland) and Kentucky, and even later in Georgia and Florida. Other groups imitated the Shakers, establishing small religious colonies in Vermont and New York.

Spreading of Shaker Ideas to Non-Shakers

Gradually through the early nineteenth century, the Shakers attracted a lot of interest, in part because they were English-speaking and hospitable to visitors, writers, journalists, and idealists of one kind or another. In their writings, both visitors and Shakers alike often gave more emphasis to the economic concepts of shared ownership and equal rights and privileges of their members than to their religious teachings.

Serious writers and thinkers studied the Shaker plans. Timothy Dwight, President of Yale, and Yale chemistry professor Benjamin Silliman both wrote of the Shaker ideas and system. Edward Everett, a Harvard professor of Greek, published a long study of the Shaker system in 1823. Travel authors, popular newspaper writers, and novelists took up the publicity, including James Fenimore Cooper and Nathaniel Hawthorne.

Amana Communities

A group called the True Inspiration Congregations migrated to the United States from Germany in 1842, first settling near Buffalo, New York. The original inspiration for their religion can be traced back to the early 1700s in Germany. By the 1820s, under the leadership of Christian Metz, the then scattered followers gathered at Armenburg, where in 1842 Metz led the emigration to the United States.

In 1855, the groups began to move to Iowa, where land was plentiful. There, they established a group of villages some seventy miles west of Davenport. By the early 1870s, there were more than 1,450 members, living in seven small towns known as the Amana colonies.

They managed farms and developed a variety of manufactures to achieve self-sufficiency and to bring in income. The Amana communities became so well off that they could afford to send funds to Germany to cover the transportation costs of new members.

Voices

Charles Nordhoff wrote of the Amana settlers:

> They were not communists in Germany, and did not, I was told, when they first emigrated, intend to live in community. Among those who came over in the first year were some families who had been accustomed to labor in factories. To these the agricultural life was unpleasant, and it was thought advisable to set up a woolen factory to give them employment. ... Seeing that some of the brethren did not take kindly to agricultural labor, and that if they insisted upon a purely agricultural settlement they would lose many of their people, they determined that each should as far as possible have employment at the work to which he was accustomed. They began to build workshops ....

At Amana, the settlers established a woolen mill, saw mills, and a tannery. The society was governed by an elected group of thirteen trustees, who in turn chose a president of the society. The trustees managed the finances, and all property was held in common.

As word of the Amana communities spread, they received offers to join from many admirers, but accepted very few. A trickle came from Germany and Switzerland and a few from other existing communities among the Pennsylvania Dutch. New members were accepted on probation for two years.

Voices

Nordhoff found the Amana settlers pretty happy, and attributed it to a quality of the German national character. He said:

> I think I noticed at Amana, and elsewhere among the German communistic societies, a satisfaction in their lives, a pride in the equality which the communal system secures, and also in the conscious surrender of the individual will to the general good, which is not so clearly and satisfactorily felt among other nationalities.

Founding of Nonreligious Communes

Through religious conversion, geographical movement, and the constant attention in the press and in books, the ideas of the sectarian communitarians spread through the United States. Soon, a number of communities were founded by *secular* groups.

Secular groups without any religious identification found inspiration and ideas in the religious experiments. There was plenty of crossover between communities, as Rappite communities sometimes included a few Shakers and Shakers settled in completely secular communities.

Sometimes, when a secular community failed, Shakers would win converts from the broken-up community and the remnants would move to an established Shaker village. In these varied ways, the communitarian tradition survived and was transmitted, crossing lines between religions and between religious and nonreligious groups.

Red Words

Secular. Ideas or groups that are entirely nonreligious are known as secular. The New Harmony, Brook Farm, and Oneida communities, as well as another two dozen that followed the concepts of Charles Fourier, were secular communes.

Many communes not held together by a common religion broke up relatively quickly, although a few lasted for decades. Several of the very short-lived communes attracted attention, some because of the well-known teachers, writers, and international visitors who reported on the communes in books and articles.

Notes on the Left

Several historians have drawn up charts tracing the known migration of individuals from one commune to another in mid-nineteenth century America. Brook Farm drew members from three other settlements, and before and after it disbanded, contributed to another three communities. The North American Phalanx drew members from six other communes, and contributed to seven. The graphic representation of these and many other exchanges resembles two or three spider webs overlaid. With the movement of people, ideas flowed from one community to another, so that saying that one or another commune represents the ideas of a single particular writer became very difficult, and in some cases, impossible.

Among the dozens of communities, a few became quite famous through the writings of residents and visitors. New Harmony, Brook Farm, and Oneida attracted the most attention, although newspaper discussion about all of the communities and their ideas further popularized the concept and stimulated recruiting.

New Harmony

Robert Owen, a well-known British social planner whose ideas and experiments influenced many others, visited the United States from 1824 to 1825. After meeting and discussing his ideas and those of many American community planners, he closely examined a Rappite community at Harmonie, Indiana. Owen arranged to purchase the property and established New Harmony in 1825. Although the community suffered an economic collapse within two years, it became famous because dozens of writers, journalists, and intellectuals of all kinds visited and reported on the experiment.

Robert Owen's model community in New Harmony, Indiana, encouraged communal living in group houses such as the one pictured here.

(Library of Congress)

Brook Farm

First established in 1841 on the edge of Boston, Massachusetts, as the Brook Farm Institute of Agriculture and Education, this community soon reorganized as the Brook Farm Association for Industry and Education. The founder, George Ripley, had visited the German religious community of Zoar, and wanted to emulate the plan among English-speaking Americans. Nathaniel Hawthorne, who wrote of Brook Farm and publicized it, had earlier visited the Shakers.

Later, influenced by the ideas and schemes of the French planner François Fourier, Ripley's commune was renamed the Brook Farm Phalanx. At least 27 other communities set up by Americans, more or less tried to implement the ideas of Fourier.

Later scholars who have uncovered the correspondence, publications, and migration from one commune to another, have traced the flow of ideas among the different communities. By the mid 1840s, the commune development had become what we would now call a "movement" with various leaders, thousands of followers, and lots of public discussion of the pros and cons.

Oneida

One of the most controversial and most discussed of the communes was Oneida, founded by John Humphrey Noyes in November 1847 in upstate New York. Brook Farm had just closed, and Noyes himself believed that his community benefited by carrying on existing ideas.

Noyes and his followers held that long-term marriage was inappropriate, and at Oneida, couples were approved by committee, usually with one partner much older than the other. After several months, the couple would be dissolved, and the partners would hook up with others.

In a period when discussion of sexual matters was taboo, detailed public description of the Oneida arrangements, in the guise of discussing this social experiment, found avid readership. When word of their sexual scheme spread, the community received hundreds of applications, mostly from men, that had to be carefully screened. Most were rejected.

Noyes later wrote *History of American Socialisms*, providing many details of his community and the communitarian movement more broadly. He looked for patterns and connections, and tried to explain what he thought were the underlying lessons of the movement. He, like many other American writers, appeared more concerned with the psychological and moral consequences of communal living than with the economic alternative represented by sharing resources and work.

Vignettes
Noyes at Oneida and some other communitarians believed that self-criticism and group pressure could cure physical ills. Noyes reported that one Harriet Hall, who had been diagnosed by two doctors with an incurable disease 20 years before, had grown perfectly healthy, and "was trotting around," while both doctors had died. In 1853, the community's newspaper reported one case of "S.P." who had a bad cold and a "run of fever." She "tried the criticism-cure, and was immediately relieved."
Skeptical visitors, such as Charles Nordhoff, wondered whether the cures derived from the criticism sessions and the power of will as Noyes suggested, or whether the patients might have recovered in any case.

Oneida survived for decades, developing shops and inventions and deriving a good income from the sale of silk-spinning and measuring equipment. Calling themselves "Perfectionists," the Oneida community developed a system of public self-criticism that anticipated the techniques of group therapy. By the mid 1870s, visitors were impressed with the orderly life, the confession sessions, the prosperity of the settlement, and the inventiveness and ingenuity of the Oneida shops.

Legacies

Many of the communities, like Robert Owen's New Harmony, collapsed after just a few months or years, while others surprised their critics by growing prosperous and lasting for years. Eventually a few, such as Amana and Oneida, closed down as communes and their factories were reorganized under corporate ownership, continuing to produce highly respected products into the twentieth and twenty-first centuries. However, for most, the legacy was much less tangible.

Through the mid-nineteenth century, the term "communist" had come to take on several implications. For conservatives, it connoted impractical ideas, radical attack on the family, destruction of individualism, and the elimination of private property. For many people with a radical temperament, some of those very same connotations suggesting deep change seemed positive. Radicals especially liked the idealistic pursuit of a new and more just society that would eliminate social injustice and bring equal prosperity to all. By the 1890s, the term "communist" carried both these negative and positive overtones and undertones as it moved into the vocabulary of the ordinary person.

The ideas and ideals spread in many ways. The American writer Edward Bellamy, who had been attracted to the ideas of the communitarians in his youth, published an influential novel, *Looking Backward*, in 1888, that forecast a socialist utopian society, based on economic equality, but with the preservation of Victorian family values. In his novel, he predicted that over the 112 years between 1888 and the year 2000, America would convert corporations into nationally owned enterprises, through nationalization. His gradual approach to socialism through that process attracted followers known as *nationalists*.

Red Words

Nationalists. In most common usage, a nationalist is someone who believes strongly in the national superiority of his own nation. Nationalists are often conservative defenders of their own nation against foreign or international invasion, or even influence. However, for a period in the 1890s in the United States, the term had a different meaning. In that time and place, a "nationalist" was a supporter of the ideas of Edward Bellamy, believing that gradual nationalization or government ownership of industry would convert the United States into a socialist utopia within 100 years.

Bellamy's ideas soon spread through a network of fan clubs, known as Nationalist clubs. Bellamy and his readers and fans hoped to achieve gradual transformation to the type of socialist society he envisioned. Some of his followers became influential in the Populist and Progressive movements in the United States, moving the concept of nationalization as steps toward socialism into the mainstream of American politics.

The Least You Need to Know

♦ Early utopian communities, such as the Shakers and the Amana villages, were formed by religious communities of immigrants.

♦ Several nonreligious communities prospered although most failed quickly.

♦ Ideas and plans circulated among the communities, and were influenced by the writings of Fourier, Owen, and others.

♦ For conservatives, the communities gave "communism" a bad name.

♦ For radicals, the communes left a legacy of utopian optimism.

Chapter 2

Marx and Engels

In This Chapter

- Karl Marx's life and career
- The class struggle and its role in history
- Marx's critique of capitalism
- Marx's revolutionary prophecies

During the first half of the nineteenth century, Europe underwent a dramatic change. With the spread of industrialization, much of the world was turned upside down. Noble families who had once earned great wealth from their agricultural estates now seemed to be in decline. In their place arose new groups of factory owners and traders who made enormous fortunes. Capital was king, and those who controlled it became richer at the expense of the rest of society. Vast numbers of rural poor were leaving their homes in the countryside and moving to work in the cities, where most became even poorer. Europe was racked by uncertainty and chaos, which often broke out into bloody revolution.

Many writers and thinkers at the time tried to explain what was happening to their society, but none was more influential than Karl Marx. Combining theories of economics, history, and philosophy, Marx's work provided a concrete explanation for the changes that were occurring. But this only partially accounts for his devoted following. More important, Marx also had a clear message of hope for the future. His theories not only explained why Europe was experiencing such changes, but they also contained a prophecy that the current age of capitalism was destined to be replaced by a new society in which the workers would rule. This chapter examines Marx's life and thought.

The Life and Times of Karl Marx

For a man who gave birth to the world's most influential revolutionary movement, Karl Marx led a fairly uneventful life. He was a thinker and a writer, not a man of action. He spent the majority of his life in relative seclusion, working on his numerous books, most of which he never finished.

With a few minor exceptions, Marx avoided direct involvement in radical politics, preferring to spend his days living quietly in what we would now call a comfortable middle-class household. His rather ordinary bourgeois lifestyle, and his profession as a scholar, journalist, and author hardly meshed with what most people think of as a hotheaded revolutionary. His one brief attempt to organize a mass revolutionary movement ended in dismal failure. Yet, the power of his words was to shake much of the world down to its foundations.

Marx's Early Life

Karl Marx was born in 1818 in Trier, a small town in the Rhineland region of Germany, which at that time was part of the state of Prussia. His family was relatively well off. His father was a lawyer and descendent from a long line of prominent rabbis in the Jewish community of Trier. Shortly before Marx was born, his father converted to Christianity because of government regulations that prevented Jews from carrying out certain legal activities.

Marx attended the local high school in Trier and graduated with high grades in Greek and Latin but, ironically, very low grades in history and mathematics. In 1835, he entered the University of Bonn to study law in line with his father's wishes. However, Marx showed little aptitude for his legal studies and did poorly in Bonn. After a year, he transferred to the University of Berlin.

Vignettes
Marx's early academic career was far from stellar. He was arrested several times for disorderly conduct and public drunkenness. He also fought a duel against another student and was almost arrested for possessing illegal weapons because he used pistols rather than swords. At the University of Berlin, he ran into trouble with the administrators for associating with a circle of young radicals, announcing that he had become an atheist, and criticizing the authoritarian Prussian government.

Marx's experience at the University of Berlin was in many ways the defining period of his life. At that time, the University was a center for *left-wing* thinkers. Marx became exposed to a heady mixture of radical philosophies and revolutionary ideas that had been fermenting in Germany since being introduced by the French Revolution almost forty years previously. Much to the disappointment of his family, Marx began studying philosophy and history in addition to the law. However, when his father died in 1838, Marx abandoned his legal studies and switched completely to philosophy, earning a doctorate from the University of Jena in 1841.

Red Words

By the mid 1800s, the term **left-wing** was being used to identify political ideologies which called for radical changes in the organization and structure of society. The term originated during the French Revolution of 1789–1799. In the National Assembly, which eventually overthrew the French monarchy, the most radical members tended to sit on the left side of the room while more conservative members sat on the right side.

Marx's Career in Journalism

Upon receiving his doctorate, Marx hoped to find a teaching position at one of Germany's many universities. However, his adoption of radical philosophies made this impossible. Instead, he decided to embark on a career in journalism and began editing a paper that was owned by a liberal businessman in Cologne. Marx wrote a series of articles calling for freedom of the press and freedom of religion that attracted the attention of local government censors, and the paper was shut down in 1843.

Although out of work, Marx decided to marry his high school sweetheart, who was the daughter of the mayor of Trier. Together, he and his new wife Jenny moved to Paris. Marx wrote articles for various radical journals, studied the revolutionary ideas of socialists such as Pierre Proudhon and anarchists such as Mikhael Bakunin, and began mapping out his own theories on history, economics, and politics. While in Paris, Marx also met Friedrich Engels, another German exile who would become a life-long friend and would later have a significant influence on the formulation of Marxist ideology.

In 1845, Marx was expelled from Paris by French government officials and moved to Belgium, where he would live for the next three years. While in Belgium, Marx and Engels founded a Communist Correspondence Committee to try and link different radical groups of French, German, and Belgian socialists together around a common set of theories and ideas. This was a difficult challenge as the socialist movement at this point included numerous organizations, espousing a huge variety of overlapping and often conflicting viewpoints.

Friedrich Engels, shown here, helped Karl Marx draft many of his most influential writings.

(National Archive)

Notes on the Left

Friedrich Engels (1820–1895) was the son of a German textile manufacturer who also owned a branch facility in Manchester, England. While working at the Manchester factory, Engels witnessed firsthand the terrible plight of English factory workers, and the experience had a profound impact on him.

Engels first met Karl Marx in Paris in 1844 and started a close collaboration that would last until Marx's death four decades later. Engels played a significant role in helping Marx formulate his ideas and edit his writings. Engels also helped popularize Marx, particularly after Marx's death in 1883, making his work more accessible to a wider audience.

In 1847, the Communist League, one such group made up of German exiles in France and Great Britain, asked Marx to formulate a set of principles to guide their organization. Marx completed the task in January 1848 with the publication of *The Communist Manifesto*. This landmark document encapsulated his developing ideas on history, the political nature of class struggle, and the revolutionary future of the workers. *The Communist Manifesto* would eventually become the "Declaration of Independence" of the international communist movement. However, its publication was immediately overshadowed by other events, as cities across Europe erupted into revolution.

Voices

First published in 1848, Marx's *The Communist Manifesto* has become one of the best known and most influential political treatises ever written. The following is an excerpt:

A spectre is haunting Europe—the spectre of communism …

The history of all hitherto existing society is the history of class struggles …

The modern bourgeois society that has sprouted from the ruins of feudal society has not done away with class antagonism. It has but established new classes, new conditions of oppression, new forms of struggle in place of old ones …

The immediate aim of the Communists is the same as that of all other proletarian parties: Formation of the proletariat into a class, overthrow of the bourgeois supremacy, conquest of the political power by the proletariat …

The Communists disdain to conceal their views and aims. They openly declare that their aims can be attained only by the forcible overthrow of all existing conditions. Let the ruling classes tremble at a communist revolution. The proletarians have nothing to lose but their chains. They have a world to win.

Workers of the world unite!

Marx was little more than an observer during the revolutions which broke out in Paris, Brussels, Berlin and Vienna during the spring and summer of 1848. After the French king abdicated, Marx traveled to Paris at the invitation of the new provisional, republican government. When revolution spread to Germany in March 1848, Marx moved on to Cologne, where he began editing a new newspaper in support of the political reforms being demanded by German liberals.

However, the revolutions of 1848 did have a considerable impact on Marx, as they did on all radical thinkers at the time. Initially, Marx called for working class movements to cooperate with middle-class liberals. Not until early 1849 did he begin advocating that workers pursue their own, more radical political agendas. But by then, the tide of revolutionary change had turned. As the new governments in Europe began cracking down on working class groups, Marx was once again forced to leave Germany. He returned to Paris in May 1849, but was almost immediately expelled. With nowhere else willing to accept him, Marx went into exile in London, where he was to remain for the rest of his life.

For working class movements, the revolutions of 1848 were ultimately a disaster. For example, once the new republican government in France had solidified its hold on the country, it used army troops to massacre thousands of workers who had begun striking to demand lower food prices and other economic benefits.

Notes on the Left _____

Known as the "year of the barricades," 1848 represented a distinct watershed in the history of Western Europe. With the exception of Great Britain, almost every major country experienced a revolutionary upheaval. In France, workers overthrew the reigning monarchy and replaced it with a republican government based on universal male suffrage. Individual states throughout Germany erupted into turmoil, while a national convention of liberals met in Frankfurt and asked the King of Prussia to unify the country under a constitutional monarchy. In Austria-Hungary, workers seized control of Vienna and forced the government to flee.

The revolutions of 1848 did result in significant political changes, including the spread of universal male suffrage in many countries. New constitutions placed constraints on government power, and many states enacted other political reforms such as increased freedom of the press and religion.

By the end of 1848, most governments had restored order and severally repressed working class organizations. The lesson learned by Marx and other revolutionary leaders was that workers could not rely on political reforms to solve their problems and could not cooperate with middle-class groups who were only interested in such political reforms.

Marx's London Exile

Marx's first years in London were very difficult. He was chronically short of money, and the family was evicted several times before finally settling in a small, three-room apartment in one of the more unfashionable parts of the city. Marx attempted to continue working as a journalist and started another radical newspaper as well as contributing to Horace Greeley's paper the *New York Tribune*.

Marx also published a series of articles on the events in France during 1848, eventually released as a publication entitled *The Class Struggle in France*. However, Marx fell out with several working class groups, including the Communist League, and remained isolated from political movements for most of the 1850s.

Marx's fortunes did not significantly improve until the early 1860s, when his mother died and left him a small endowment. He was able to move his family to a much better house in the Maitland Park district of London. In 1864, he also returned to politics by participating in the International Working Man's Association, a group formed by French, German, and Italian workers, which would eventually become known as the First International.

Vignettes

Marx and his wife had several children, although most of them died at a young age during the family's most poverty-stricken years in the early and mid 1850s. Marx also had an illegitimate son after an affair with his household maid. Marx's friend Friedrich Engels, who had a reputation as a womanizer, agreed to claim that he was the father in order to protect Marx. One of Marx's legitimate daughters died shortly before he did, and his one surviving daughter committed suicide in 1898. His illegitimate son eventually became a mechanic in London and died in 1929 without ever knowing the real identity of his father.

In 1867, Marx published the first volume of his most significant work, *Das Kapital*, a mammoth historical and economic analysis of capitalism. The work initially received little reaction, and few of the 1,000 copies printed for the first edition were sold. But Marx's reputation among radical groups began to grow in the late 1860s. It grew even more in the early 1870s, especially after French police reports claimed that Marx had been behind the revolutionary movement in Paris which led to the formation of the Paris Commune in 1870 (see Chapter 3, "Arise, Ye Workers of the World!"). One year after the Paris Commune was bloodily repressed by government troops, Marx's *Das Kapital* was reprinted in Germany and also translated for publication in France.

During the last 10 years of his life, Marx suffered from severe health problems and published relatively little. Although he began work on a second volume of *Das Kapital*, it was never completed. Following the collapse of the First International in 1872 because of disputes between Marx and other factions within the movement, he also largely retired from active politics. His wife Jenny died after a long illness in 1881, and Marx followed her in 1883. He was buried in London's Highgate Cemetery.

 **Voices**

Marx's graveside eulogy was presented by Friedrich Engels. He said:

An immeasurable loss has been sustained both by the militant proletariat of Europe and America, and by historical science, in the death of this man .... Just as Darwin discovered the law of development of organic nature, so Marx discovered the law of development of human history .... But that is not all. Marx also discovered the special law of motion governing the present-day capitalist mode of production and the bourgeois society that this mode of production has created .... Marx was before all else a revolutionist. His real mission in life was to contribute, in one way or another, to the overthrow of capitalist society .... His name will endure through the ages, and so shall his work!

Marx's Theory of History

The heart of Marx's contribution to communism lies in his analysis of history. Marx took a set of principles that had been developed by the German philosopher Georg Hegel and adapted them into an extraordinarily powerful tool for understanding the past. Although he never used the term himself, his theoretical approach became known as "dialectical materialism."

Notes on the Left

Georg Hegel (1770–1831) formulated a philosophy that saw reality as the product of a dynamic interaction among various conceptual systems. He called this process "the dialectic" and argued that it was driven by a mystical "Absolute Reality," the combination of all of these conceptual systems. As history progressed, human beings would be able to understand more and more of this "Absolute Reality."

However, Hegel was no revolutionary. Because he believed that things were always progressing forward, he argued that current governments represented the closest ideal to his "Absolute Reality" possible at this stage of human development. As he put it, "the State is the Divine idea as it exists on earth." He further suggested that individuals could only really achieve their maximum self-worth by working for the state.

In some regards, therefore, Hegel was the founding father of the two most important political movements of the twentieth century. His notion of the dialectic, as developed by Marx, became a critical part of communist theory. His ideas on the importance of the state evolved into the conservative nationalism expressed by Nazism and Fascism. As some scholars have suggested, the fight between Nazi Germany and Communist Russia during World War II really represented a battle between right-wing and left-wing Hegelians.

Marx's Concept of Dialectical Materialism

Marx's dialectical materialism incorporated two critical ideas. The first is his notion that the most important factor governing history is the way in which different human beings secure their livelihood, and how they manage to support themselves and their families. Marx referred to this as the "means of production."

In primitive societies, the means of production were limited to natural resources and each individual's innate skill. In more complex societies, however, the means of production was also determined by relationships between people. According to Marx, these relationships were often exploitative, so that individuals who owned the means of production could live off the labor of those who did not.

In total, Marx identified five general types of societies—primitive, slave, feudal, capitalist, and socialist—each defined by how the means of production are owned. History, in Marx's view, was the story of how societies evolved from one type to another, or from one predominate means of production to another. Hence, Marx's view of history was materialistic. He argued that laws, religious beliefs, cultural attitudes, and morals all reflected the underlying productive forces at work in that society. This is what Engels meant when he suggested that Marx had discovered "the law of development of human history."

Marx on the Class Struggle

The second central idea in Marx's theory of history was the notion that the evolution from one type of society to another could never be smooth and uneventful. The reason for this was simple—those who owned the means of the production in one type of society had a vested interest in maintaining the existing system. Marx referred to such a group as a *class*. Those who had developed a new means of production and would, therefore, be in a different *class*, would have to fight in order to change the defining characteristics of their society.

Red Words

Marx was never very precise on what he meant by the term **class**. However, he described several different types in his works. These include the nobility, which was the ruling class in feudal societies that controlled agrarian means of production. Nobles owned the land and had rights over peasants, who were required to work for them. In capitalist societies, the ruling class was the bourgeoisie (often referred to as the middle class), that owned capital in the form of factories, industrial machinery, or financial assets. Workers, or the proletariat, were those who earned their livelihood by selling their labor to capitalists and working in factories. Marx also used the term *lumpenproletariat* for the poorer elements of society who were not actually workers, such as small shop owners, peddlers, and even petty criminals.

Therefore, as Marx put it in *The Communist Manifesto*, "The history of all hitherto existing society is the history of class struggles." As a society progressed from one mode of production to another, elements from the old ruling class would clash with the new groups who had discovered a better means of production.

Eventually, a new ruling class would be formed that reflected this new means of production. Marx called this the *dialectic* process. Not all societies and all countries were at the same stages in the evolution from one system to another, but all would go through essentially the same process.

> **Red Words** _____
>
> Marx's notion of the **dialectic** was taken directly from Hegel. Hegel suggested that concepts developed through the interaction of one idea (a thesis) with another (antithesis). The two combined together form a third concept (synthesis). Marx took Hegel's theory of the dialectic and applied it to the practical, everyday world of material events that made up history. Because Hegel's ideas were based on abstract principles rather than material reality, Marx's dialectic materialism is often described as having "turned Hegel upside down."

According to Marx, therefore, the revolutionary upheavals which affected Europe from the French Revolution of 1789 to the massive uprisings of 1848 represented the struggle of the bourgeoisie to overcome the nobility. Having unlocked a new means of production through industrialization and the development of capitalism, the bourgeoisie were attempting to overthrow the feudal system and seize power from the older ruling class. This struggle played out in the form of debates over democracy, representative government, or political reforms. But the real source of conflict was the clash between capitalist and agrarian means of production.

Marx's Economic Analysis

Marx was not the first person to develop a radical critique of the capitalist system. Other socialist thinkers had expounded on the notion that capitalism failed to account for the real value of the human labor which went into the manufacture of goods. What Marx did achieve, however, was the first concrete analysis of how capitalism managed to strip the extra value from workers to those who owned the capital.

Marx never fully developed his economic theories. Although *Das Kapital*, which was published in 1871, is a depressingly long and complex work, it was only the first volume of what was intended to be a three-volume publication. *Das Kapital* does outline Marx's basic approach, but Marx himself acknowledged that his economic theories still needed considerable improvement.

Like other critics of capitalism, Marx's starting point was the argument that only labor contributed to the value of a good. Using natural resources and their innate skills, workers improved an object. That improvement reflected the added value. To those who suggested that capitalists also added to the value by supplying machinery to help the worker make his improvements, Marx replied that machinery was only a form of saved-up labor.

Marx pointed out that the price of a good does not necessarily represent the true labor value of that good. Classical economists and defenders of capitalism had assumed that the price of something was determined by how much labor went into producing it. Marx suggested this was nonsense. Because capital owners were in a superior position of power over their employees, they could offer whatever wages they pleased. What capitalists were really buying from their workers, he argued, was not a specific amount of labor to produce a specific item, but the absolute control over all labor from that worker for a set period of time. Marx referred to this as "labor power."

Workers sold their labor power for a fixed wage. However, capitalists tried to drive this wage as low as possible, which was determined by the minimum amount the worker needed to support himself and his family. In most cases, the value produced by the worker exceeded the minimum amount he needed to stay alive, and this excess amount went into the pockets of capitalist owners as profits, which Marx referred to as "surplus value." According to Marx, this was nothing more than theft.

Notes on the Left

The economic theories laid out by Marx in *Das Kapital* are difficult reading at best. At times, Marx's writing is almost impenetrable, and there are numerous logical problems in his analysis. For example, Marx argued that all value is determined by labor, and profits are nothing more than surplus value stolen by capitalist owners. Therefore, according to Marx's theory, profits should fall as new technologies were adopted that would enable factory owners to employ less labor. However, this obviously did not happen in reality, as Marx himself recognized. Marx planned to address this problem and others in future publications, but he died before completing the work.

The Inescapable Proletarian Revolution

Taken together, Marx's understanding of history and analysis of capitalism led him to the conclusion that capitalism was doomed. Although the bourgeoisie could cooperate as a class to overthrow feudalism and protect the capitalist means of production, Marx argued that they were trapped by the mechanics of the capitalist system. No matter what capitalists did, their intense competition for profits would inevitably result in the destruction of their class. This, in turn, would pave the way for workers to seize control and establish a socialist mode of production.

Marx developed three iron laws that he claimed guided economic development under a capitalist system:

1. The Law of Capitalist Accumulation dictated that competition among capitalists would force each to try and use more and more machinery and less labor in order to

maximize production. Because labor alone produced value, capitalists would have less surplus-value to extract and accordingly fewer profits. (Marx recognized that this argument had some logical problems, but he insisted that these could be resolved eventually.)

2. The Law of the Concentration of Capital maintained that the number of capitalists will decrease as the more inefficient factory owners are driven into bankruptcy. Just as natural selection ensured that only the strongest survived in nature, capitalism dictated that only the best and most ruthless capitalists would stay in business. Those that survived would control larger and larger amounts of capital, eventually forming enormous monopolies. Those that failed would have no other choice but to join the ranks of the working class.

3. The Law of Increasing Misery suggested that workers would invariably get worse off. As they increased in number, the mass of unemployed laborers would drive down wages to the point where workers could no longer survive on what they were earning. In order to try and protect their profits, capitalists would force workers to work longer and longer days. And the more miserable workers became, the more likely they were to revolt and overthrow the capitalist system.

> ## " " Voices
>
> *Marx's Das Kapital* summarized why a revolt of the working class was inevitable. He wrote:
>
> Along with the constantly diminishing number of magnates of capital, who usurp and monopolize all advantages of this process of transformation, grows the mass of misery, oppression, slavery, degradation, and exploitation; but with this too grows the revolt of the working class .... The monopoly of capital becomes a fetter upon the mode of production .... The knell of capitalist private property sounds. The expropriators are expropriated.

For critics and opponents of capitalism, Marx brought great news. Marx appeared to have unraveled the mechanics of the capitalist system and identified a set of internal flaws that would eventually lead to capitalism destroying itself. The triumph of bourgeois democracy during the revolutions of 1848, which at first glance appeared to be a defeat for the working class, was simply a stepping stone on the path to the final victory of the proletariat. The role of the communist movement, therefore, was to guide the industrial proletariat along this path.

The only area of disagreement left to communists was how quickly the final victory of the proletariat could be achieved. Marx suggested that in each case: the victory of the bourgeoisie would have to come first, and that capitalism would have to be fully developed to the point that a large mass of revolutionally minded industrial workers had been formed. During the late 1800s and early 1900s, Marx's followers would argue bitterly over exactly what this meant and whether there were ways of moving the process along faster.

The Least You Need to Know

◆ Marx did not invent socialism or communism, but he did provide it with a solid theoretical foundation that made it much more attractive to a wider audience.

◆ Marx presented a materialistic view of history as being nothing more than a story of class struggles.

◆ Marx saw the revolutionary upheavals in Europe, from the French Revolution of 1788 to the events of 1848, as the fight of the industrial bourgeoisie to overthrow the feudal nobility.

◆ Marx insisted that capitalism was doomed to failure because its own internal contradictions led to the formation of a working class proletariat that would inevitably rise up and overthrow the capitalist system.

Chapter 3

Arise, Ye Workers of the World!

In This Chapter

- ◆ Communism becomes a revolutionary force
- ◆ Bloody revolution and bloodier repression in the Paris Commune
- ◆ International efforts to unite working class movements
- ◆ Varieties of working class protests

This chapter examines the development of working class movements during the last decades of the nineteenth century. After the failure of working class uprisings during the tumultuous years of 1848 and 1849, the age of big revolution appeared to be over. With one notable exception, the Paris Commune of 1871, there were no large-scale working class revolts anywhere in Western Europe until after the First World War. The forces of repression exercised by the existing governments, with their control of police forces and the army, were simply too powerful.

However, the potential for revolutionary upheaval simmered. With the spread of industrialization, the number of workers increased until they represented a majority of the population in many countries. The development of capitalism, although seemingly unstoppable, was far from smooth. Periodic depressions and economic crises kept most workers on the edge of poverty. As workers responded with strikes, demonstrations and public protests, many of which ended in violence, Western society often seemed poised on the brink of further uprisings.

The challenge for working class movements during this period was finding the best way to prepare for the revolution that most expected although few could agree on how or when it would occur. The theories developed by Karl Marx seemed to provide a clear picture for capitalism's eventual overthrow that many found enormously compelling. But there were other revolutionary movements with different goals and strategies for achieving them. The last decades of the nineteenth century saw several attempts to unify all working class movements into a single worldwide force. But, as we will see, all ended in failure.

The First International

In the early 1860s, groups of French, British, and German workers began meeting informally in London to explore ways of cooperating. Among the topics discussed were ways of preventing the import of cheap foreign labor as well as efforts to support Polish revolutionaries who were attempting to end Tsarist Russia's control of their country. At a meeting in September 1864, delegates from across Europe voted to create an International Federation of Working Men. Karl Marx, who by this time had developed a significant international reputation through his revolutionary writings (see Chapter 2, "Marx and Engels"), became a member of the International's executive committee.

Notes on the Left

Although today we often think of nationalism as being a more conservative and traditional ideology, during the mid 1800s there was often a close alliance between nationalist groups and the working class movement. Many revolutionaries drew a parallel between national independence and individual liberty. Early English socialists, such as Robert Owen, were avid supporters of Greek nationalism during Greece's struggle to obtain independence from the Ottoman Empire in the 1820s. The Italian nationalist Giuseppe Mazzini, who played a major role in unifying Italy and ending Austro-Hungarian domination in the 1850s and 1860s, was also involved in the First International. This same alliance between nationalism and revolutionary ideology would later appear during the twentieth century when many colonial independence movements in Asia and Africa declared themselves to be socialist or communist.

At the International's second meeting, which took place in Geneva, Switzerland, in 1865, the delegates voted to adopt a set of provisional rules that had been drafted by Marx. The rules broadly outlined the goal of the International, which was to create "a central medium of communication and cooperation" for the working class movements that presently existed in different countries. The International would take steps to keep all working class associations informed of events going on elsewhere. In order to build as unified a movement as possible, the International would try to encourage disassociated local working class groups in each country to unite themselves into a single national movement. The rules also called for the establishment of a Central Council, to be based in London, and a general congress that would meet once a year.

The provisional rules themselves did not clearly indicate that the International had the revolutionary aim of overthrowing existing governments. In fact, not all groups represented in the International necessarily shared this goal. However, Marx made every effort to convince the Central Council to accept as much of his doctrine as possible. In fact, his inaugural address to the Geneva meeting called upon the working classes to "conquer political power." His address ended with the same revolutionary slogan that appeared in *The Communist Manifesto* written almost 20 years earlier: "Proletarians of all countries unite."

Voices

Marx's inaugural address to the International Federation of Working Men's general congress in 1865 was a far cry from an open call for armed insurrection. However, it did include revolutionary language that frightened many government officials:

> It is a great fact that the misery of the working masses has not diminished from 1848 to 1864, and yet this period is unrivalled for the development of industry and the growth of commerce .... After the failure of the revolutions of 1848, all party organizations and party journals of the working class were, on the Continent, crushed by the iron hand of force ... and the short-lived dreams of emancipation vanished before an epoch of industrial fever, moral miasma, and political reaction.

The First International held annual meetings for the next several years and attracted a sizeable following. The number of dues-paying members by the end of the 1860s was around 800,000, although it was allied to millions of workers through its connections to various movements across Europe and America. The International also had some success in encouraging cooperation and convincing groups in one country to support strikes being carried out by workers in another.

However, the effort to unify working class groups proved far easier on paper than in practice. By and large, English representatives were more concerned with increasing the power of trade unions and using that power to secure immediate reforms in the workplace. German working class groups were split between supporters of Marx and supporters of Ferdinand Lassalle, who advocated cooperation with middle-class groups seeking to achieve political reforms. French representatives were greatly influenced by anarchist beliefs that made them resist any effort to centralize the working class movement under the control of any single organization, such as the International itself.

These divisions became most apparent when the First International faced its first real challenge: the war between France and Prussia in 1870. Ostensibly, the general goals of the International made it opposed to any conflicts that threatened to undermine the international solidarity of workers. However, Marx initially supported Prussia, hoping that the war would result in the unification of Germany, which in turn would help create a unified German working class movement. The war ended with the complete defeat of France, which soon collapsed into revolutionary turmoil as workers in Paris announced the formation of the Paris Commune.

Notes on the Left

In the mid 1800s, Germany was not a single country but was divided into numerous smaller states, principalities, towns, and regions. The largest and most important was Prussia, with its capital in Berlin. During the revolutions of 1848, German liberals had attempted to unify Germany from below, that is, by a mass movement rather than by agreements of the leaders of the constituent states. They asked the Prussian king, Friedrich Wilhelm I, to become head of a constitutional monarchy similar to that of England. However, he refused the offer because it would have required him to accept liberal reforms and constraints on his power.

Between 1848 and 1870, Germany was eventually unified under the Prussian monarchy. The key architect of German unification was the archconservative Prussian chancellor, Otto von Bismarck. Bismarck was adamantly opposed to any concessions to liberal reformers and, especially, to the growing German working class movement. After the defeat of France by Prussia in 1870, Wilhelm I of Prussia was crowned Kaiser of Imperial Germany. However, the new regime was far more autocratic than that envisioned by German liberals in 1848.

The Paris Commune

The Franco-Prussian War of 1870 was a catastrophe for France. Louis Napoleon, a relative of France's great military ruler Napoleon Bonaparte, had ruled the country ever since the revolutionary upheavals of 1848 had overthrown the French monarchy. Louis Napoleon insisted on leading his troops himself. However, he proved to be a far less impressive military leader than his famous relative, and the French forces were quickly surrounded and destroyed by the Prussian army in September 1870. Louis Napoleon abdicated and went into exile, and French republicans announced the formation of a new democratic government.

Although the French army had been defeated, Prussian forces had not yet captured Paris. While the new republican government, which was based in the city of Tours, attempted to sign a humiliating peace treaty, Prussian troops laid siege to Paris from September 1870 to January 1871. They were resisted by a republican National Guard that was strongly supported by workers in the city. When Paris finally fell and France signed a treaty with Germany, many workers felt betrayed by the new republican government.

In March 1871, the government became concerned about the presence of an armed and potentially radical force in Paris and decided to disband the National Guard. The Parisian workers responded by throwing up barricades and announcing the formation of a revolutionary government, now known as the Paris Commune. The Commune declared that it represented all of France and denounced the republican government as traitors and enemies of the working class.

Vignettes

European society was deeply shocked by the events of the Paris Commune. Newspapers were full of accounts describing the many terrible deeds carried out by the communards, including the murder of clergy and the destruction of churches in Paris. However, one of the most shocking stories was that of the *petrolistes,* women fighters on the barricades who used gasoline as their weapon to attack government troops and burn down buildings.

The Paris Commune government included many different radical groups, ranging from socialists to anarchists. They were largely united only in their opposition to the republican government. Despite its name, the Commune was not connected in any way to Marx. In fact, he had advised French workers earlier to accept the republican government and not use the defeat of Louis Napoleon as an opportunity for open rebellion. However, once the Commune was established and fighting broke out, Marx was quick to defend the Commune and describe it as allied with the aims of the First International.

For many years after its defeat, the Paris Commune continued to inspire revolutionary feelings in France. Two of the last surviving participants are shown here in a photo taken during communist rallies in the 1930s at the site where thousands of communards were executed.

(National Archives)

Notes on the Left _____

Many of the executions carried out by government troops took place in a cemetery on the outskirts of Paris called Père Lachaise. Hundreds of communards were shot along a wall, which would eventually become an important pilgrimage spot for French radicals. However, the Père Lachaise cemetery is better known as the site of many beautiful tombs and gravestones, and as the final resting place for many famous celebrities, such as singer Edith Piaf, playwright Oscar Wilde, and rock star Jim Morrison.

The conflict between the Paris Commune and the French republican government was a long and bloody affair. Government troops laid siege to the city from March to May 1871, and the fighting claimed thousands of lives and was marked by many atrocities on both sides. When the Commune was finally suppressed on May 28, government forces immediately embarked on a savage repression of the communards, in which 20,000 people were arrested and thousands more were summarily executed.

The events of the Paris Commune had a dramatic impact around the world. For existing governments, the affair highlighted the lingering danger of working class revolt that had appeared as diminishing since the upheavals of 1848. Some working class groups were appalled at the bloodshed and took steps to distance themselves from more radical movements. For others, however, the destruction of the Commune by the French republican government demonstrated that no amount of political reforms or democratic changes could alter the fact that bourgeois governments were invariably hostile to workers.

The Collapse of the First International

The outbreak of war between France and Prussia and the subsequent suppression of the Paris Commune greatly undermined the cohesion of the First International. However, its final death knell came as a result of a bitter conflict between Marx and Mikhael Bakunin, a leading Russian anarchist revolutionary. Bakunin accepted many of Marx's arguments regarding the evils of capitalism. He had actually undertaken the first translation of Marx's *The Communist Manifesto* into Russian. As an anarchist, however, Bakunin was also extremely suspicious of Marx's efforts to dominate the working class movement.

Bakunin had been a member of the International, but in 1867 Marx had expelled him from the organization. Nonetheless, in 1869, Bakunin attended the annual congress of the International and succeeded in dominating the proceedings. After the congress voted to reject several proposals advanced by Marx, who did not attend the meeting, Marx became convinced that Bakunin was attempting to seize control. Marx did attend the next meeting, which was not held until 1872 because of the Franco-Prussian War, and he again succeeded in having Bakunin expelled from the International.

🗨 **Voices** _____

Writing in 1871, Bakunin recalled his first meeting with Marx, which had taken place shortly after the founding of the First International. Bakunin remarked:

Marx was then much more advanced than I was, and he still remains today incomparably more advanced than I—as far as learning is concerned .... There was, however, never any frank intimacy between us—our temperaments did not permit it. He called me a sentimental idealist, and he was right; I called him vain, perfidious and sly, and I was right too.

Because Bakunin still held a great deal of influence over many of the International's members, Marx took the extraordinary step of arranging a move of the International's headquarters from Europe to the United States. Isolated from the working class movements in Europe—few workers could afford the price of a lengthy transatlantic voyage—the First International quickly fell apart and was finally dissolved in 1876.

The Second International

The ignominious collapse of the First International left many working class groups reluctant to make another attempt at creating an international organization. During much of the 1870s, police repression, especially in France, made any form of radical political activity difficult. Moreover, Marx himself was opposed to any such international movement, arguing that it would "fade away in stale, generalized banalities." He maintained this position until his death in 1883.

However, working class movements within different countries made considerable progress during the 1870s and 1880s. By the late 1880s, socialist parties in France, Germany, the United States, and Great Britain had begun to achieve electoral success at the polls and some had representatives in national parliaments. The time appeared ripe for another effort to unify nationally based movements into an international body.

In 1889, two international workers' congresses were held in Paris, one made up of Marxist supporters and one consisting of non-Marxists. After a lengthy debate, the two agreed to merge into a single organization, the Second International. The formation of the new International was announced on July 14, 1889, exactly 100 years after the storming of the Bastille in Paris launched the beginning of the French Revolution.

The Second International was a loosely organized body made up of several different affiliated groups. In many ways, it was a less overtly revolutionary organization than the First International had been. Although the International theoretically adopted many of Marx's arguments about the nature of class struggle and the need for workers to control the means of production, it stopped short of calling for revolution. Many of the groups affiliated with it were, in fact, more willing to follow the reformist path toward improvement of working conditions rather than seeking to overthrow existing governments.

Notes on the Left

The Western world experienced an unprecedented economic boom during the last decades of the nineteenth century. Although there were periodic downturns, the general picture was one of continual growth. In Germany, for example, steel production increased by a factor of 10 between 1880 and 1900. New industries, such as chemical production, were established through Europe and America. Even Russia, long considered the economic backwater of Europe, doubled its industrial output in the 1890s. Most European countries were also able to tap into new sources of wealth by seizing control of large parts of Asia and Africa. Contrary to Marx's predictions, workers benefited during this economic boom as wages increased, prices dropped, living conditions improved, and governments became willing to implement social reforms.

In part, reform was a more attractive goal than revolution because the events of the Paris Commune had demonstrated just how violent and bloody revolution could be. Moreover, reform also appeared to work. During the last decades of the nineteenth century, worker's lives were becoming demonstrably better. Rapid development of industry during this period led to increased demand for labor, and wages rose significantly. At the same time, prices dropped considerably as mass-produced goods became less expensive and international trade led to the import of cheaper food from around the world.

The willingness of working class movements to try to reform existing governments from within rather than seeking their destruction also had tangible political benefits. As socialist parties in Europe began achieving electoral success, they became increasingly powerful in some of the national assemblies. In some countries, such gains in political power led to a variety of social reforms on issues such as workers' pensions, the length of the working day, public health and housing, and workplace safety.

By the early 1900s, socialist representatives had even taken up positions in some national governments. This step led to some difficult internal debates over whether or not representatives of working class movements should cooperate with bourgeois authorities. However, it did seem increasingly possible that the democratic process might actually lead to significant political changes without the need to resort to revolutionary activity.

The Second International also differed from its predecessor in that it was a much less highly centralized organization. Affiliated groups were not required to adopt a particular ideology or doctrine. The only principle that all were expected to follow was the idea that the International should not allow national wars or conflicts to undermine working class solidarity. The Second International also lacked any kind of central council comparable to the one dominated by Marx which had exercised control over the First International.

The loosely organized nature of the Second International may have contributed to its success on one level. For, it never suffered from the kinds of internal disputes that had crippled and ultimately destroyed the First International. The Second International continued to meet every few years from 1889 up until 1914. However, it failed to do much other than provide a means for working class representatives from different countries to gather and exchange ideas every once in a while.

Vignettes
Up until 1914, many socialists in Europe were convinced that war would be impossible because workers from every country would go on strike to prevent it. The French socialist Jean Jaurès, for example, refused to believe that French workers would allow themselves to be drafted for the military. When workers in France overwhelmingly and enthusiastically supported taking up arms against Germany in World War I, Jaurès was shattered. He argued that the war was caused by the capitalist system, and all capitalist governments, including that of France, were equally responsible for the conflict. However, he had few supporters and was assassinated shortly after the war began.

In its primary aim of promoting international cooperation among various national working class groups, the Second International failed miserably. At the International Congress in 1907, the delegates unanimously agreed to resist growing international tensions and pledged to use any threat of war as an opportunity to "hasten the destruction of the domination of the capitalist class." When war finally broke out in 1914, however, most working class movements in each country uniformly voted to support their governments in the conflict. This abject failure completely destroyed the credibility of the Second International, and it collapsed soon afterward.

Varieties of Working Class Movements

By the early 1900s, the widely varying working class movements and ideologies had begun to coalesce into three general types: socialism, anarchism, and Marxism. All shared the same overall aim of ending capitalist exploitation and promoting a more cooperative and egalitarian society. However, they differed sharply in strategy and outlook, ranging from those who were willing to follow a more gradual path toward social change to those who advocated immediate revolutionary action. In addition, trade union movements won many members, but for the most part such groups worked within the system of capitalism, seeking specific improvements in wages, hours, and working conditions. Unlike the trade unions, socialists, anarchists, and Marxists were all dedicated to bringing capitalism to an end.

The distinctions between these movements were never clearly drawn or defined. Each movement shared many overlapping beliefs, and suffered from numerous internal divisions.

Moreover, individual groups within these movements often adopted similar names that made it confusing for workers to clearly understand how they differed from one another.

Socialists

Socialists comprised the largest and most successful working class movement during the last decades of the nineteenth century. In general, they accepted Marx's theory of the class struggle and, in many cases, acknowledged that the capitalist system would eventually have to be overthrown by force. Also, most called for a future in which workers would own the means of production.

However, socialists advocated a strategy of using reform to achieve most of these goals. In particular, socialists put most of their energy into the political process, taking part in elections and trying to work within the system. Socialists also worked closely with the trade union movement and saw it as an important means of improving workers' lives. Socialists became deeply divided over the issue of how far they could cooperate with bourgeois governments to achieve reform, but most accepted some level of collaboration.

Notes on the Left

Unlike the American political system, most European countries followed a parliamentary model in which governments were formed from whichever party had the largest number of elected representatives. In many cases, this resulted in coalition governments being formed by several different groups that together represented a majority in the national assembly. As socialist parties became increasingly successful, some left-wing middle-class political parties began turning to them for support in forming governments. By the early 1900s, the coalition principle had resulted in socialists accepting some government ministerial positions. In essence, they were able to achieve some degree of political power without resorting to revolution.

The political strategy had various degrees of success. In Germany, the Social Democratic Party made considerable electoral gains during the early 1900s, and by 1912, it controlled almost one third of the seats in the German Reichstag. Ostensibly, the German Social Democratic Party adopted Marxism as its guiding ideology in 1891. However, some leading members, such as Eduard Bernstein, advocated a policy of *revisionism* that opposed the revolutionary components of Marxism. Instead, Bernstein called for a more gradual policy of trying to convince middle-class groups of the need for reform.

Likewise, English socialists such as the Fabians also advocated a gradual approach of cooperating with the political process and raising social consciousness through education (see Chapter 5, "Socialist Parties"). French socialist parties also achieved impressive electoral success, and in 1897, a socialist representative accepted a ministerial position in a bourgeois-led government.

Red Words

As envisioned by Bernstein, **revisionism** was not so much a complete rejection of Marxism as it was a recognition that his philosophical outlook was outdated. What may have made sense during the early years of industrialization no longer applied, now that workers were becoming better off, contrary to Marx's predictions. Bernstein suggested that reforms were possible by working with middle-class groups with a shared sense of moral responsibility for improving society as a whole. Naturally, Marxists denounced Bernstein as a weak-minded apologist at best and, at worst, a traitor to the working class movement. For pure Marxists, revisionism was a dirty word.

Anarchists

Like Marxism, anarchism developed in response to the widespread social upheavals during the nineteenth century. But where Marx blamed this social upheaval on the rise of capitalism, anarchist thinkers blamed all organizations that they believed tried to limit personal liberty. For anarchists, that meant the church, the state, the factory, the army, and any other government or social institution.

Vignettes

America's most famous anarchist was Emma Goldman. Born in 1868 in Lithuania, she moved to the United States with her family at a young age and became a factory worker in Rochester, New York. She first made her mark during worker protests in the 1880s, when she and her lover Alexander Berkman attempted to assassinate a leading industrialist. After her release from prison, she toured the United States speaking on such issues as women's rights, sexual equality, and birth control, which she saw as being an integral part of anarchism's call for complete freedom in all aspects of human behavior. She founded the journal *Mother Earth* in 1906 but had to flee the United States after speaking against America's decision to enter World War I. Goldman traveled to Russia after the Bolshevik Revolution; however, she was very critical of the new regime's efforts to consolidate power. She remained influential in anarchist circles until her death in 1940.

Anarchism never developed into a fully unified movement, as any such organized movement was anathema to the anarchist creed. Organizing anarchists was almost a contradiction in terms. However, leading anarchists, such as Bakunin, were enormously influential in many parts of Europe, including France, Italy, Spain, and Russia, as well as the United States.

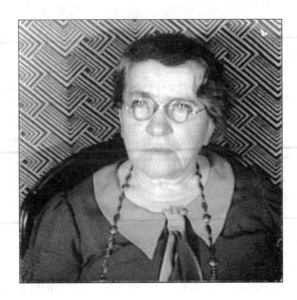

America's most famous anarchist, Emma Goldman was forced to spend the last years of her life in exile because of her radical attacks on the U.S. government. She was equally critical of the Soviet Union's communist regime.

(Library of Congress)

Marxists

Although Marxism was not the dominant working class ideology by the early 1900s, the Marxist movement was the most highly organized and disciplined. The key distinction between Marxists and other socialists was whether reform alone could achieve the eventual triumph of the working class movement. More dogmatic Marxists argued that reforms only served to disguise the true extent of capitalist exploitation. As such, they believed reforms only delayed the development of working class consciousness and should be rejected outright.

As a general rule, Marxism was most influential in those countries where working class movements were most excluded from involvement in the political process. Accordingly, Marxism was especially strong in Germany and Russia, where both the German Social Democratic Party and the Russian Social Democratic Party adopted Marxism as their official ideology.

The Least You Need to Know

- The First International failed because of internal disputes between Marx and Bakunin.
- The Paris Commune was suppressed after a bloody conflict and came to symbolize the worst excesses of revolutionary upheaval as well as government repression.
- The Second International was largely ineffectual and failed to promote international solidarity among working class movements in different countries.
- By the early 1900s, the working class movement had broadly organized itself into socialist, anarchist, and communist groups, which shared many of the same aims but differed over how best to achieve them.

4

The IWW and Anarcho-Syndicalism

In This Chapter

♦ American and European roots of the Industrial Workers of the World

♦ Unions and strikes

♦ Anti-war and free speech

♦ Arrests and persecutions

♦ IWW and the formation of the Communist Party (USA)

In this chapter we look at the Wobblies, the Industrial Workers of the World (IWW). A radical labor union organized in 1906 in the United States, its greatest influence was during its first 13 years. After 1919, the IWW shrank to a shadow organization.

The ideology of the IWW followed the ideas of anarcho-syndicalists, who believed that through syndicates or unions, the masses should take control over the economy, making government redundant. Like anarchists, they believed that the state should vanish once capitalism was replaced, but also held that the path to that goal would be through militant unions. Following Proudhon, both anarcho-syndicalists and anarchists believed that if socialism were controlled by the state, "socialism of the barracks" would replace capitalism. Hence the search for other ways to organize society in some sort of federation of self-governing and self-owned enterprises.

We also look at some of the colorful leaders of this movement, examine some of the major strikes that the union supported, and take a look at the causes of its decline in the 1920s.

Formation of the IWW

The IWW came into being from a meeting held in Chicago in 1905, attended by more than 200 socialists and trade unionists. The new union sought to recruit unskilled workers, often overlooked by the trade unions organized in the American Federation of Labor (AFL) since 1885. The AFL had focused on a *trade or craft union* approach, while the IWW attempted to organize on the basis of an *industrial union* approach.

Red Words

Trade or craft union. The American Federation of Labor organized workers by a particular trade or craft. Thus in one large factory, the mechanics and carpenters would each belong to locals of their craft. However, many of the unskilled "operatives" who worked machines might go unorganized.

Industrial union. The industrial union approach was to organize all workers in a particular industry, whatever their craft or trade, into a single union. When the IWW began to organize, they aimed for "One Big Union," with separate sections by industry.

Setting up industrial unions incorporating unskilled workers would be difficult even in a culturally or ethnically homogeneous society. It was especially difficult in the United States at the turn of the twentieth century, where a great proportion of unskilled workers was comprised of recent immigrants, speaking quite a number of languages. The IWW had to find recruiters who could speak the varied languages of the target population. Even though most of the first organizers of the IWW were Anglo-American, the organization soon flourished with leaders and recruiters fluent in Italian, Spanish, German, and other languages.

First Leaders

Among the delegates to the founding convention were William Haywood, secretary of the Western Federation of Miners. Over six-feet tall, and known as Big Bill Haywood, he remained the leader of the union until its decline. Other delegates included Eugene V.

Debs, leader of the Socialist Party and founder of the American Railway Workers Union. Debs ran for the presidency of the United States on the Socialist ticket, winning 94,000 votes in 1900 and about 400,000 in 1904. Mary Harris (Mother) Jones was another important figure, an organizer of coal miners and textile workers.

Daniel De Leon, leader of the Socialist Labor Party, claimed to have been born in the Dutch island of Curaçao and had been educated in Europe. Moving to the United States at the age of 20 in 1872, he earned a law degree from Columbia University. De Leon read Edward Bellamy's *Looking Backward* and had been active in the New York Nationalist clubs that followed Bellamy's idea of a gradual transition to socialism. In 1891, he joined the Socialist Labor Party, largely built on immigrant groups in New York, but by 1900, that party lost members to Deb's organization.

Notes on the Left

European anarcho-syndicalists had developed theoretical views of how unions could replace both corporate structures and government. As in other "isms," American followers of radical thought tended to be less theoretical and more interested in organization and building a following.

Some of the Europeans stressed the need for revolutionary tactics. The French philosopher Georges Sorel advocated the general strike and sabotage of factories, which he saw as techniques of direct action. In Flanders, when workers wanted to disrupt a textile factory, they would toss a few wooden shoes, or sabots, into the works. Hence "sabotage." Bill Haywood of the IWW spoke in favor of sabotage, scaring off the more conservative labor leaders.

Other leaders who attended the founding meeting of the IWW included William Trautmann, editor of a German-language newspaper for the United Brewery Workers and Charles O. Sherman, secretary of the United Metal Workers. The rest of the founders came from a variety of anarchist, socialist, and union organizations.

The ideas of the new union represented a shifting mix of concepts borrowed from Marx, Bakunin, Sorel, Bellamy, and Charles Darwin. Many social thinkers, on both the conservative and radical ends of the spectrum of ideas, attempted to apply Darwin's concept of evolution to society itself. Perhaps a new social arrangement would adapt better to economic conditions, surviving as the old society became extinct.

But the anarcho-syndicalism of the IWW was not so much a specific ideology, or a clear-cut set of principles, but a typically American mixture of radical ideas that challenged capitalism.

Early Factionalism

Like the predecessor socialist and anarchist groups of the 1880s and 1890s, the IWW immediately faced internal disputes. De Leon, apparently attempting to convert the union into a recruiting ground for his political party, earned the animosity of Western groups that wanted to focus on union activity, not ideology and politics.

After bitter squabbles that lasted through 1907 and 1908, De Leon departed and set up what he called the "real" IWW in Detroit, in 1908. That organization existed largely on paper. Because the IWW had decided to abandon politics, De Leon accused them of being bums and anarchists.

A few years later, in 1911, the Western Federation of Miners left the IWW and joined the AFL. Later, the core leaders of the remaining IWW fell into disagreements over legal tactics in court cases, further weakening and splitting the organization.

Voices

The IWW rewrote the preamble to its union constitution in 1908, including some fiery language that showed they were different from socialists who wanted to work through the political machinery:

The working class and the employing class have nothing in common. There can be no peace so long as hunger and want are found among millions of working people, and the few, who make up the employing class, have all the good things of life. Between these two classes a struggle must go on until the workers of the world organize as a class, take possession of the earth and the machinery of production, and abolish the wage system. ... It is the historic mission of the working class to do away with capitalism.

IWW Tactics

Although the IWW, by European standards, had no clear or single ideology, and by the standards of American socialists like Daniel De Leon and Eugene Debs, no clear political approach, the organization was intensely creative in its tactics.

The union adopted or invented a number of practices that set them apart from most existing unions. They believed in direct action and inspired membership with songs, speeches, rallies, and striking art in the form of cartoons, posters, and stickers. They reveled in strikes, quickly moving leaders and organizers into towns where unorganized workers had spontaneously walked off their jobs in protest over a grievance.

The IWW celebrated the Marxist Labor Day on May 1, rather than following the American practice of taking off the first Monday in September. When they held a strike, they accepted a settlement, but refused to sign labor contracts, regarding them as interference with the unconditional right to strike. Some of their literature suggested that eventually, a mass strike in all the industries at once would bring capitalism to an end.

Haywood advocated sabotage in a general way. A 1915 sticker depicted a large wooden shoe, or sabot, with the quotation from Haywood that said: "Sabotage means to push back, pull out, or break off the fangs of Capitalism." Such statements angered other labor leaders and political socialists, but Haywood avoided making specific suggestions for sabotage that could be construed as inciting criminal action. His stand appeared to be rhetorical, to clarify and define the difference between himself and other leftist labor leaders.

Between 1905 and 1917, the IWW participated in over 150 strikes. While many were small, some involved thousands of strikers and lasted for several months. The most notable were the Goldfield, Nevada strike of miners in 1906 and 1907, the Lawrence, Massachusetts, strike of 1912, the Paterson, New Jersey silkworkers' strike of 1913, lumber workers' strikes in Arkansas and Louisiana in 1913, and the Mesabi Range iron workers' strike of 1916.

Notes on the Left

Big Bill Haywood became a celebrity in the first decade of the twentieth century. In 1906, shortly after participating in the founding the IWW, Haywood was accused of the bombing murder of Frank Steunenberg, the former governor of Idaho. Haywood was more or less kidnapped from Colorado and taken to Idaho for trial, where he was defended by Clarence Darrow.

While in prison, Haywood ran for governor of Colorado on the Socialist ticket. After his acquittal of the murder charges in July 1907, Haywood went on a lecture tour, charging admission and giving the funds to the Socialist Party. He represented the American Socialist Party at two meetings of the Second International.

At some of the strikes, the IWW experimented with different ideas of how to make their point or win support. In Schenectady, New York, in 1906, they occupied a plant in what may have been the first "sit-down" strike. Over and over, they organized foreign-language groups with bilingual spokesmen who could translate speeches, keep non-English speakers informed, and engage them in strike organization and leadership.

They set up women's groups, held pageants, published a *Little Red Song Book*, and pioneered in mass picketing with linked arms to prevent strike-breaking workers from getting access to the work site. In Lawrence, Massachusetts, they worked out a tactic of sending strikers' children to live with temporary foster parents among sympathizers, relieving the families of childcare and freeing them up for picketing and at the same time, reducing their household expenses for the duration of the strike.

Lawrence, Massachusetts

In 1912, when the textile workers at several different factories in Lawrence discovered that they had suffered a pay-cut, hundreds walked off the job. The companies had cut the pay because a state law reduced the allowable maximum hours of work per week, and almost all of the workers were paid on a piecework basis. In other words, their pay depended on their output, and with fewer hours worked, their pay envelopes shrank. The IWW immediately sent in organizers to help the strike, and they soon worked through more than 20 language groups.

Mass marches to prevent the factories from bringing in strikebreaking workers had some success, but the Governor ordered state militia to keep order. The emplacement of machine guns and sandbags gave the small city the appearance of a war zone.

In order to win sympathy, strike organizers sent groups of workers' children to live out of town, as "refugees from the class war." One group, temporarily received into New York socialist foster homes, marched in a parade to rally support for the strike. Bearing American flags and singing labor songs, they showed their solidarity.

Two of the IWW leaders of the strike, Joe Ettor and Arturo Giovannitti, were arrested on trumped-up murder charges, but the union replaced them with Bill Haywood and Elizabeth Gurley Flynn. Meanwhile, the AFL United Textile Workers opposed the strike, and its leader declared that Lawrence was a revolution, not a strike.

Notes on the Left

Elizabeth Gurley Flynn was a colorful leader of the IWW. She was the daughter of Irish immigrants, and grew up in poverty in the Bronx section of New York. An attractive and slight woman, she commanded huge audiences. Known as the "Rebel Girl," so named by the IWW songwriter Joe Hill, she was a great orator.

In 1912, Flynn became the lifetime companion and lover to Carlo Tresca, a free-lance revolutionary writer and journalist, who helped arrange the release of Ettor and Giovannitti from jail. Disagreements over negotiating pleas in various cases of arrested IWW leaders, between Tresca and Flynn on the one hand, and Haywood on the other, led to one of several later splits in the organization.

Flynn went on to become a member of the Communist Party of the United States. She died in 1964 in Moscow while attending a Soviet Communist Party congress as chairman of the American Communist Party.

The tactic of the children's exodus infuriated the local authorities in Lawrence so much that town police, positioned at the railroad station, used their billy clubs to break up a group of mothers and children attempting to leave. The image of police brutality against the mothers and their kids gave the factory owners such bad press all over the United States and internationally that stockholders and executives began to insist that the textile mill managers make concessions.

> ## Voices
>
> At the conclusion of his trial on trumped-up charges of murder in Lawrence, Antonio Giovannitti addressed the jury:
>
>> And if it be that these hearts of ours must be stilled on the same death chair and by the same current of fire that has destroyed the life of the wife-murderer and the patricide and parricide, then I say that tomorrow we shall pass into a greater judgment, that tomorrow we shall go from your presence where history shall give its last word to us.
>
> Both Ettor and Giovannitti were acquitted.

In the end, the Lawrence strikers won a wage increase for 275,000 textile workers in New England. Although the IWW ranks had swollen with thousands of members in Lawrence, the union did not build a permanent organization on the basis of the strike.

Paterson, New Jersey

Since the mid 1890s, a number of Italian anarchists had settled in Paterson, New Jersey. There, an Italian-language newspaper, *La Questione Sociale*, attracted followers among the silk weavers and dyers. The newspaper reflected current ideas of French and Italian anarchists, among them Errico Malatesta, a protégé of Mikhael Bakunin. Supporters brought in several famous anarchist speakers, including Emma Goldman and Peter Kropotkin, on his tour of the United States.

The local anarchists believed in group rather than individual action, and participated in several strikes in Paterson. After a strike that bogged down, three speakers addressed a mass meeting on June 17, 1902, speaking in German, English, and Italian. In fiery rhetoric, they urged a *general strike*. After the meeting, a riot ensued, with shots fired, several injuries, and damage to a mill. Martial law was declared, the strike was smashed, and the leaders imprisoned. However, the IWW led a smaller successful strike against the Victoria Silk Mill in 1905.

Red Words _____

In the United States, **general strike** refers to a strike across several enterprises, usually in the same city. Thus the strikes in Lawrence (1912) and Paterson (1913) were general strikes in this sense of the word. Internationally, the term is usually used to refer to a strike in which all of the workers in all industries in a city or a whole nation go on strike.

A general strike in Seattle, Washington, and one in Winnipeg, Canada, both in 1919, and another in San Francisco, California, in 1934, represented cases of such a widespread, citywide general strike. In Latin America, general strikes frequently bring a whole nation to a standstill as transport workers join others in a political protest.

In 1913, Haywood, Carlo Tresca, and Elizabeth Gurley Flynn came to Paterson and joined in organizing a strike that had broken out spontaneously over the issue of work assignments. The mill management had increased the number of looms attended by each worker from two to four.

Flynn held some women-only meetings, and a number of local women rose to positions of leadership in the strike. John Reed, a young writer living in Greenwich Village in Lower Manhattan, organized a pageant regarding the strike. Over 1,000 strikers performed in the pageant held in Madison Square Garden on June 7, 1913. The pageant emphasized the strike itself as training for the eventual management of society, an IWW goal and an idea at the heart of anarcho-syndicalism.

The pageant, with its support from writers and other Greenwich Village intellectuals, as well as a full audience at the Garden, put the strike in the national limelight. Nevertheless, the strike failed, and Flynn blamed socialists, Reed, the pageant, and to an extent, Bill Haywood, for the failure.

Free Speech

One of the tactics of the Industrial Workers of the World was to send organizers and speakers to downtown districts across the country, where day-workers would "shape up" for possible recruitment by agricultural labor contractors or others looking for menial labor at the lowest possible rate. The "labor sharks," who rounded up the men, were the special target of *Wobbly* wrath.

Literally standing on soapboxes (soap was shipped in sturdy wooden boxes in the first decades of the twentieth century), IWW speakers would harangue the gathered laborers. Angry employers often called in the police who simply rounded up the speakers and threw them in jail. In about 30 different episodes between 1907 and 1917, IWW agitators were arrested, then protested their arrest and used a First Amendment defense in court. Some got off, but most served time. Many were beaten by vigilantes. While most middle-class journalists and attorneys objected to the speakers' message, a few, like Roger Baldwin, the founder of the American Civil Liberties Union, came to their defense for the right to speak out.

Red Words

In a story that smacked of what we now call an urban legend, the IWW ended up being known as **Wobblies,** because of a difficulty in pronunciation. A Chinese American worker was challenged at one of the strikes in the West, and he insisted he was a member of the union. "What union?" his accosters asked. "I-wobble-wobble," he answered. The name stuck and was used with pride by members of the union thereafter.

The free speech effort reached its peak in 1909. The City of Spokane, Washington, tried to put a stop to the street agitation by the IWW against the system of labor sharks who recruited the day laborers. However, when the city arrested the speakers, more came to speak, from all over the West, some traveling in the bitter cold by railroad boxcar.

Before the fight was over, more than 400 speakers had been arrested and crowded into makeshift unheated jail cells through the winter. The prisoners would be marched daily to another location, given a cold shower, and then marched back. The sentences and jail conditions outraged non-IWW sympathizers, just as the police brutality against the women in Lawrence had done.

Frank Little, one IWW speaker in Spokane, testified at his trial that he had been reading aloud from the Declaration of Independence when arrested. Like others, he was given 30 days in jail for the offense. In 1917, Frank Little was lynched by vigilantes in Butte, Montana.

Vignettes

In 1909, Elizabeth Gurley Flynn, 19 years old at the time, was arrested in Spokane during the Free Speech fights. The prosecutor was enraged when the jury found a fellow speaker, Charley Filigno, guilty but declared Flynn not guilty.

The prosecutor asked the jury foreman, "What in hell do you fellows mean by acquitting the most guilty, and convicting the man, far less guilty?"

The foreman answered, "She ain't a criminal, Fred, an' you know it. If you think this jury, or any jury is goin' to send that pretty Irish girl to jail merely for being bighearted and idealistic, to mix with all those whores and crooks down at the pen, you've got another guess comin'."

Eventually, the city of Spokane had to free the prisoners, and it also reformed the labor shark arrangements. The IWW had achieved a victory of sorts and had demonstrated a technique that would become a standby for later generations of civil disobedience in the United States: packing the jails with activists whose worst offense was exercising their rights.

IWW During WWI

Although the AFL took up a pledge not to hold strikes after the United States entered World War I in April 1917, the IWW encouraged strikes as a means to oppose the war. After about five months, the U.S. Justice Department raided IWW offices across the United States, and served warrants for the arrest of more than 200 IWW leaders. More than 90 were tried in Chicago, with heavy federal sentences and fines. The government portrayed their ideology and their strikes as treason.

On November 11, 1919, a group of American Legion members broke into a local IWW meeting hall in Centralia, Washington. They destroyed the office, beat up some of the members, and then lynched Wesley Everett. Seven other IWW members were then arrested and sentenced to long jail terms. This outrageous act also won wide sympathy for the plight of the IWW members. The episode was incorporated in the novel *1919*, by John Dos Passos.

IWW in Decline

After the mass arrests of leadership in 1917, the organization suffered. Flynn and Tesca argued for plea-bargaining and accepting amnesty, while Haywood wanted to continue to fight through the courts. The internal disagreement over tactics grew more and more bitter, with recriminations on both sides.

Public hostility over the union's anti-war stand led to dozens of raids on IWW halls, similar to the one in Centralia, but not resulting in deaths. Nevertheless, between American Legion and vigilante harassment and Justice Department arrests, membership declined.

In 1920, the American Communist Party formed, and IWW members were invited to join. Some were attracted to the idea, including Flynn and Haywood. However, as the policies of the Soviet Communist Party became clearer in the 1920s, most of the old Wobblies dropped out of the party.

Haywood's tactic of fighting through the courts on appeal of the sedition convictions bogged down, and in March 1921, he jumped bail and fled to Moscow. He stayed there, published a memoir, and died in 1928. He was buried in the Kremlin wall alongside other revolutionary heroes.

Legacy of the Wobblies

The short-lived IWW left a mark on the American left. As the concept of anarcho-syndicalism died away in America, some of the specific tactics of the Wobblies found their way into the mainstream labor movement. Several members who joined in the later years made sure to preserve pamphlets, documents, artwork, and other publications and thus capture the history. These collections provided material for later scholars and helped feed a nostalgic approach to radicalism that became popular in later decades.

More specifically, the IWW emphasis on industrial unionism bore fruit in the 1930s with the formation of the Committee on Industrial Organization inside the AFL. It then split off to form the independent Congress of Industrial Organizations (CIO), from 1936 to 1955, when the unions reunited in the combined AFL-CIO. Some of the early CIO leaders were former IWW members, and the principle of reaching out to the unskilled, to women, and to the ethnically diverse became a hallmark of CIO organizing. In its early years, the CIO used sit-down strikes and mass picketing, tactics first demonstrated by the Wobblies.

The IWW's vigorous exercise of First Amendment rights, and winning support for free speech, even among those disagreeing with the content of the speeches, all found later echoes in student and civil rights movements of the 1960s.

Some of the methods that had once been regarded as revolutionary moved into the mainstream. However, the core idea of an anarcho-syndicalist approach to replacing capitalism with a union-managed economy almost entirely died out in the United States.

The Least You Need to Know

◆ The IWW members believed in One Big Union, and an industrial union organizing principle.

◆ The IWW adopted new union tactics including free speech campaigns, mass picketing, and packing jails.

◆ IWW organizers targeted the unskilled, immigrants, and women, when most unions did not.

◆ Bill Haywood, Elizabeth Gurley Flynn, and several others moved into the Communist Party after its creation.

◆ IWW as a movement died in the 1920s.

◆ The IWW left a legacy of vigorous labor art and music, as well as tactics of direct action.

Chapter 5

Socialist Parties

In This Chapter

- ◆ Growth of socialist parties
- ◆ Factions and splits in U.S. socialism
- ◆ Socialists react to Bolshevism
- ◆ National styles: Britain, United States, and Sweden

In this chapter we look at how socialism developed in the last years of the nineteenth century and the first two decades of the twentieth century. We especially focus on socialists in the United States, and how they reacted to overseas developments. When a branch of Russian socialists, calling themselves Bolsheviks, and then communists, struck out on a path of revolution rather than gradual change, socialists elsewhere, including the United States, had to decide how to react.

A movement that was already divided over big issues (such as whether to operate through political parties or labor unions, or through both), as well as over many differences of personality and tactics, found itself facing a new divisive issue: whether and how to cooperate with the Bolsheviks. After the success of the Bolshevik seizure of power in Russia, the American socialist movement was torn into even smaller competing factions.

Early Socialists in the United States

Through the 1880s and the 1890s, socialists in the United States followed several different pathways. The Socialist Labor Party (SLP), founded in 1877, incorporated largely immigrant socialists, mostly German, who had read or been influenced by Marx. Led after 1890 by Daniel De Leon, the party attracted many who were interested in the overthrow of the capitalist system, but De Leon's advocacy of such an overthrow was coupled with his insistence on using the electoral process and working through a political party. The contradiction between "overthrow" and "politics" made some SLP members doubtful of his leadership, but his control of the party through a group of loyal supporters remained strong.

The SLP ran candidates with some success. From 1878 through 1879, the party elected an Illinois state senator, three representatives, and four Chicago City councilmen. The city candidates stood for a program of municipal ownership of utilities, a concept later emulated by many more mainstream progressive candidates in the early twentieth century.

In 1880, the SLP decided to support the Greenback party (a group advocating monetary inflation as a solution to the problems of the debtor class), and some dedicated Marxist members of the SLP dropped out. The Greenback nominee for the presidency, James Weaver, polled about 308,000 votes nationally.

The SLP also worked through labor unions during that same period. SLP members participated in the formation of the Federated Order of Trades and Labor Unions, founded in 1881, but soon that group decided to stay out of politics, leaving many of the SLP members disaffected. In 1885, the union changed its name to the American Federation of Labor (AFL) and moved away from politics in the direction of *bread and butter unionism*.

Red Words

Bread and butter unionism was the technique advocated by AFL leader Samuel Gompers, former head of the Cigar Makers Union. While earlier groups, including the Knights of Labor and some specific trade unions, had supported political action, Gompers focused on staying out of politics and simply negotiating an increase in wages and hours worked, as well as better job conditions. He used holding out strikes as a threat when negotiations did not result in gains. Marxists saw such "bread and butter" gains as destructive of the revolutionary spirit, and as outright cooperation with the capitalist system.

SLP members with an interest in revolutionary socialism were disappointed with both the political emphasis of the party and its limited success among labor unions. Some drifted into support of the anarchist movement.

Notes on the Left

In the 1890s, Edward Bellamy's *Looking Backward* attracted many American-born enthusiasts in nationalist clubs. Bellamy's prediction that American society would transform from capitalism to socialism through government nationalization of industries attracted those of a more moderate temperament. At first, the nationalist clubs in Boston won very limited support, but as such clubs reorganized around the United States in 1891, Bellamy himself gave them more support, speaking and touring the local groups. He died in 1898, and many so-called nationalists joined others in the new Socialist Party after that.

Victor Berger

Meanwhile, some of those disaffected from the SLP sought another political framework. Victor Berger (1860–1929), an immigrant to the United States from the Austro-Hungarian Empire, became a leader of some of the former SLP members. He had studied at universities in Vienna and Budapest, before coming to the United States in 1878, and settling in Milwaukee. He became a language teacher and worked as a journalist on a number of both German and English newspapers. Berger joined the SLP in 1889.

After briefly supporting the Populist Party in the early 1890s, Berger was a founding member of the Social Democratic Party (SDP) in 1898. He felt that Marxist principles needed some modification in the face of changing political and economic conditions, and like De Leon, thought that the path to socialism lay through the ballot box. In Milwaukee, the SDP remained a local force, with victories in elections to city council, and with an SDP mayor in the periods between 1910–1912 and 1916–1940.

The Social Democratic Party held a convention in Indianapolis on March 8, 1900, and nominated Eugene V. Debs, who had founded the American Railway Union, as candidate for president of the United States. The Socialist Labor Party convened in New York and nominated Joseph P. Maloney for president. Of course, these minor candidates were hardly noticed in the final vote count. Debs received about 94,000 votes, although Republican William McKinley defeated Democrat William Jennings Bryan by a vote of 7.2 million to 6.3 million.

Socialist Party

The Socialist Party (SP) in the United States was formed in 1901 out of a variety of groups, including dissidents who left the SLP, followers of Eugene Debs, and branches of the Social Democratic Party like the one led by Victor Berger in Milwaukee. The active membership of the Socialist Party in 1901 may have been in the range of 5,000 to 10,000 total. Nevertheless, in the first decade of the twentieth century, the Socialist Party grew rapidly, far outdistancing the SLP. By 1912, dues-paying SP members increased to 118,000, and in 1912, Eugene Debs won 897,000 votes in the presidential election.

Debs's vote tally as a socialist in the 1912 election was a high-water mark for the party, representing 6 percent of the total vote cast in that election. Woodrow Wilson, a reform Democrat, won against the Republican William Howard Taft. Theodore Roosevelt, who served as president from 1901 through 1909, bolted from the Republican Party and ran on a newly created Progressive Party ticket in 1912, splitting the Republican vote.

The vote tally in the 1912 election is shown in the following table.

1912 Presidential Votes

Candidate	Party	Vote	Percent
Woodrow Wilson	Democrat	6,286,000	42
Theodore Roosevelt	Progressive	4,126,000	28
William Howard Taft	Republican	3,484,000	24
Eugene Debs	Socialist	897,000	6

Because of the American system of Electoral College voting, Wilson was the clear winner in the election, with 435 electoral votes, against 88 for Roosevelt and only 8 for Taft. Debs's vote, a minority in every state where it was cast, earned no electoral votes. Even so, since Wilson, Roosevelt and Debs all stood for reform of one kind or another, the election encouraged the socialists.

Vignettes

Victor Berger, running on the Socialist Party ticket, was elected to Congress in 1910. Although elected a total of six times, he only served four terms!

Berger served from 1911 through 1913 after winning the 1910 election. He was elected again to serve in the 66th Congress (1919–1921), but the House of Representatives declared him ineligible because he had opposed the entrance of the United States into World War I. The seat was declared vacant, so he ran again and was denied the same seat in the same congress. That made his third electoral victory. He was, however, elected and he served in the next three congresses, the 68th through the 70th, from March 1923 through March 1929.

The socialists made other gains in 1912, suggesting that the party might be on its way to becoming a major force in American politics. More than 1,000 socialists were elected to office in that year, including more than 300 city council members, more than 50 city mayors, and state legislators scattered across the country. Even in the American Federation of Labor, which officially opposed the socialist political platform, a socialist won a third of the votes for the presidency of the union in 1912.

There were other signs that the SP had gained strength. By 1912, there were 5 English-language socialist daily newspapers and 8 foreign-language dailies. In addition, there were almost 300 English and foreign-language weekly newspapers. By 1912, most members of the SP were American-born and English-speaking, with a minority of foreign-language groups.

Notes on the Left

The socialist press was vigorous in the United States around 1912. The *Jewish Daily Forward* reached a circulation of 200,000 in the decade between 1910 and 1920, thus becoming the largest Yiddish publication in the world.

The *Appeal to Reason*, published from 1895 to 1922, was a weekly socialist news-paper out of Girard, Kansas. It obtained a regular prepaid circulation of more than 760,000 in 1913, with some special issues selling over 4 million. Over 80,000 men and women sold subscriptions and left off sample copies at hotels and union halls. The *Appeal* carried items written by Marx and Engels, Jack London, Eugene Debs, and dozens of other well-known writers of the era.

Some other socialist papers and magazines of the period included: *Rebel*, in Halletsville, Texas, with 25,000 readers, *National Rip-Saw*, in St. Louis, with 150,000 readers, Slovakian *Rovnast Ludu* in Chicago, with almost 10,000 readers, and *Christian Socialist*, also in Chicago, with about 20,000 readers.

Within the SP, various wings and factions represented somewhat different emphases. In Wisconsin, the SP took a practical, reform approach, including support for municipal ownership of utilities, strong public health regulations, and an end to corruption. By putting off the realization of a socialist society to the distant future and concentrating on here-and-now reforms, the leaders of the Wisconsin SP did not seem so different from other Progressive Era politicians in the Democratic Party, the Republican Party, and the breakaway Progressive Party, led by Theodore Roosevelt and Robert La Follette in the period from 1912 through 1916.

Elsewhere, socialists joined in supporting the IWW, and more radical members rankled under the overall conservative approach of the SP. However, Socialist Party leadership and the socialist periodicals tended not to be doctrinaire, not opposing local leadership in either political and union activity and appearing to encourage the adoption of policies and programs suited to a local following. The socialist newspapers and magazines tended to welcome writings by Marxists and non-Marxists alike. The SP broad, umbrella organization was both a strength and a weakness, however.

The ill-defined doctrine of the SP allowed all sorts of Marxists and others who believed in some form of socialist state in the future to join together in one group. Yet, when the SP was called upon to take a single stand on a particular issue, the various factions would take hard positions, opposing each other and trying to swing the party as a whole to its viewpoint and control its resources.

Although the majority of the SP membership was American-born and English-speaking, by 1915 the party included many immigrants through 14 separate foreign-language federations. The federations included local branches, incorporating not only larger groups, such as Germans and French, but smaller groups of Finns, Latvians, Russians, and others. The national viewpoints of these groups were another source of potential disunion.

SLP Membership

The SLP, by contrast to the broader-based SP, shrank during the first decades of the twentieth century. The SLP insisted on strict adherence to a party line, at first under Daniel De Leon, and after his death in 1914, under the leadership of Arnold Peterson. Peterson held the position of national secretary of the small group from 1914 until 1969.

Peterson followed in De Leon's footsteps, expelling individual members, and even whole branches when they did not conform to SLP doctrine. Over the years, SLP candidates would win between 15,000 and 50,000 votes in presidential elections, in 12 to 23 states. On the whole, the SLP tended to include more foreign-born and foreign-language-speaking members than did the SP. With the formation of the Communist Party in the 1920s, many SLP members left the organization to join the new party.

Notes on the Left

In the United States, Marxist and Marxist-influenced parties, unions, and groups appeared to flourish around the end of the nineteenth and beginning of the twentieth century.

The membership often overlapped. These were the main groups:

- Socialist Labor Party (SLP)—radical but political, founded 1877, largely immigrant
- Nationalist Clubs—gradualist, founded 1889, followers of Edward Bellamy, merged into SP after 1901
- Social Democratic Party (SDP)—reformist, founded 1898, remained independent but worked with SP
- Socialist Party (SP)—reformist to radical, founded 1901, largely native-born
- Industrial Workers of the World (IWW)—syndicalist, founded 1905

Meanwhile, in Europe

In Germany, the Social Democratic Party got 4.15 million votes, about one third of the total cast, and elected 110 members to the German parliament in 1912. Smaller social democratic and socialist parties in other European countries at the time had some success with individual elections in France, Italy, Belgium, Great Britain, Scandinavia, and even in the Austro-Hungarian Empire.

Russia

In Russia, the Social Democratic Party split between a more radical branch, headed by Lenin, calling themselves Bolsheviks, and a more moderate branch, called Mensheviks. A Social Revolutionary Party also included many revolutionary socialists. Under the autocratic regime of the Russian tsar, many outspoken socialist leaders of all types were imprisoned, exiled to Siberia, or left the country entirely as voluntary political exiles (see Chapter 6, "The Russian Revolution").

Scandinavia

In the Scandinavian countries (Sweden, Norway, Denmark, and Iceland), many socialists endorsed the type of cooperativism that had been put forward as an alternative by the Britisher Robert Owen and the American Josiah Warren. The *Rochdale* pattern of consumer cooperatives, with members receiving dividends on both their quantity of purchases and on their investments, spread widely through Scandinavia.

Red Words

Rochdale cooperatives. In 1844, on Toad Lane in the British textile town of Rochdale, a small group of 28 workers known as the Equitable Pioneers opened a shop. The principle that made the shop work was the concept of a dividend on purchases, as well as an interest in the share capital of the store. The Rochdale Pioneers sold goods at market prices and returned the profit to members in proportion to each member's total value of purchases at the shop. Dozens of new shops opened, and by 1875, there were over 8,000 members of such co-ops in Britain.

Cooperativism meshed with other reforms in the Scandinavian countries. Coupled with some nationalization of major industries, innovations in adult education, and reforms such as setting up state-funded ombudsmen to handle individual problems with the government, as well as strong social welfare legislation, these countries developed what many called a "Middle Way" between Marxist socialism and capitalism. The Scandinavian model was difficult to export, however, since each of the countries had features not found elsewhere: few immigrants and a high degree of ethnic and cultural homogeneity, extremely high literacy rates, and long-standing commitment to parliamentary democracy.

British Fabianism

In Britain, a form of gradual socialism known as *Fabianism* took hold, influencing mainstream politics well into the twentieth century.

Red Words

The **Fabians** first organized in Britain in January 1884. The Fabian Society was named in honor of the Roman general Fabius who was known for his strategy of patience and delay in fighting against Hannibal.

Over the two decades following their formation in 1884, the Fabians attracted notables, including Sidney and Beatrice Webb, Annie Besant (an early leader of the religious movement Theosophy), George Bernard Shaw, H.G. Wells, and Ramsay MacDonald, among many others. The Webbs, Shaw, and others wrote a number of articles, included in a work called *Fabian Essays*, capturing their ideal of the gradual evolution of society's institutions.

The Fabians argued that, from the beginning of the industrial revolution, economic individualism had only been an abstract ideal. In fact, government had to be involved in regulation and limitation of business, and socialism was a logical extension of the pattern of economic control already in place.

In several regards, Fabian socialism differed from Marxist socialism. Perhaps the biggest difference was the gradualism of the Fabians, suggesting that society would naturally evolve into a form of economic cooperation, although many Marxists also believed that socialism would be achieved gradually. The Fabians believed that the general public, through education and enlightenment, would accept the idea of transformation to socialism.

Fabians also departed from Marxists on theoretical grounds in a number of areas. Instead of the labor theory of value favored by Marx and many other socialists, the Fabians criticized the capitalist view of value by suggesting that products had a "utility value." They were also attracted by the writings of Henry George, the American writer who suggested that land values and rents, being socially created, should not accrue to the individual in the form of wealth. For the Fabians, social injustice grew from the incorrect distribution of wealth, based on capital investment and land values. Such benefits should be spread among workers and the total society, since they developed out of social progress and not out of individual achievement.

Annie Besant focused on the issue of motivation to work in a socialist society. She pointed out that a socialist society could fire workers as easily as a capitalist society, and this negative incentive would remain. Pressure from fellow workers would keep the slacker in line. Other motives, such as the desire to excel, to be creative, to work for individual achievement, to gain social approval, and to improve oneself, would all take hold and make people share the load in a socialist society.

Fabians argued that the community should own the means of production, but that individuals should own the means of consumption. Without providing a detailed prescription of how to attain that goal, most Fabians agreed that major industries and utilities, such as railroads, should be owned by the total community, but they left the question of how land and smaller enterprises would be owned and managed to socioeconomic evolution.

The Fabian Society remained extremely influential in the British Labour Party. In 1945, the Labour Party had 400 seats in Parliament, and almost two thirds of those members were also members of the Fabian Society. As a doctrine of gradual change, and with its endorsement of many of the principles of individualism, Fabianism was a doctrine well-suited to the British culture, temperament, and political structure.

Socialists and World War I

Internationally, members of various socialist parties believed that international working class solidarity would prevent a widespread general European war. The Second International, or Socialist International, meeting in 1912 called for a revolution by the working classes of all potential belligerent nations to stop a world war should one break out.

Vignettes
In July and August 1914, the *New Times*, the voice of socialism in Minnesota, reiterated the proposition that a European war was almost impossible because of working class solidarity. When German socialist deputies voted for declaring war in August 1914, the *New Times* at first denied it could be true. Later, the paper reported incorrect rumors that the Kaiser had to execute some socialist members and coerce others to get the socialist vote for the war. The reality, of national feeling being stronger than international working class solidarity, was tough to believe.

The United States entered the First World War in April 1917, after German decisions to cut off food and fuel supplies to Britain through submarine sinking of American ships. The Industrial Workers of the World came out explicitly against U.S. participation in the war, and William Haywood continued to urge sabotage in general terms. The IWW refused to join the AFL in pledging no strikes for the duration of the war. When incidents of sabotage against American munition plants did occur, apparently arranged by German agents, Congress passed the 1918 Sedition Act, leading to the suppression of the IWW and arrest of hundreds of IWW members.

The Socialist Party took a more mixed stand. Most of the socialist newspapers in the United States opposed the war, but did not endorse sabotage. Many had their postal mailing privileges revoked, which led to the closure of some newspapers and magazines. Individual SP members who urged resistance to the war or to the draft were jailed, including Eugene Debs.

Feelings over the question of participation in World War I were too strong to gloss over with a compromise, umbrella position. The American SP started to break up over this issue, reflecting the factional divisions that had simmered below the surface for years.

With the suppression of newspapers, and the decline of the influence of moderate leaders in the Socialist Party, signs that the radicals within the party wanted to form their own organizations began to surface. In 1915, before U.S. entry into the War, while the European powers were becoming bogged down in trench warfare, a group called the Socialist Propaganda League of Boston openly called for a new international organization. They urged that it bring together anti-war, revolutionary socialist parties to replace the moderate Second International. Similar movements elsewhere in the socialist world spelled the end of the Second International by 1917.

Others on the "left wing" of the American Socialist Party indicated their dissatisfaction with the moderation and mild anti-war sentiments of the majority of the SP. Such leaders and spokesmen included Louis Fraina, an Italian-born revolutionary socialist who emphasized a syndicalist approach. Louis Boudin, a Russian Jewish immigrant and leading theoretician of Marxism, took a similar stand. Another was S. J. Rutgers, a Dutch anarcho-syndicalist living in the United States, who was active in the Socialist Propaganda League. At a meeting in 1917, temporarily exiled Russian leaders Nikolai Bukharin and Leon Trotsky (an independent revolutionary not yet aligned with the Bolshevik group under Lenin), met with Rutgers, Fraina, and others to plan a new radical newspaper under Fraina's leadership.

The SP split took more serious form in April 1917, right after the United States joined in the First World War. Although the SP leaders, including Victor Berger, endorsed an anti-war proposition stating their "unalterable opposition" to the war, the radicals wanted to go further. Although 140 delegates voted to endorse the resolution, 31 favored a left-wing alternative put forward by Boudin.

Berger, Debs, and the "old guard" of the party made it clear that they supported conscientious objectors to the draft, but not sabotage or any other direct action against the war effort. Increasingly, this position frustrated the more radical members of the party.

American SP Reactions to Bolshevism

Divisions over the war came to a head in 1918. In New York, several socialist city aldermen voted to support the sale of war bonds, and the left wing of the party denounced them. When party leadership blocked an effort to officially consider charges against the aldermen, the left-wing delegates walked out of the party to form their own organization.

The leader and publisher of this group's newspaper, the *New York Communist*, was John Reed. In August 1919, Reed and others were formally expelled from a convention of the Socialist Party held in Chicago.

Reed came from an upper-class American background, and had graduated from Harvard in 1910. He had moved into the bohemian lifestyle of Greenwich Village in Lower Manhattan and become involved in a number of causes on the left, including organizing the pageant for the 1913 Paterson IWW strike. He went to Mexico and wrote about the Mexican Revolution guerilla forces of Pancho Villa. He visited Russia during the Bolshevik revolution and became entranced with their position. Reed was catapulted into fame in 1919 with the publication of his firsthand report on the Bolshevik revolution, *Ten Days That Shook the World*. Years later, a romanticized version of John Reed's life was presented in the popular movie *Reds*.

Voices

"Adventure it was, and one of the most marvelous mankind ever embarked upon, sweeping into history at the head of the toiling masses and staking everything on their vast and simple desires."

—John Reed, *Ten Days That Shook the World,* 1919

The division over how to react to the Bolsheviks severely strained the American Socialist Party. Seven of the language federations hoped to be able to swing the Socialist Party into an endorsement of the Bolsheviks in 1919. The seven groups were all Eastern European: Russian, Polish, Hungarian, Yugoslav, Latvian, Lithuanian, and Ukrainian.

The trouble brewed into a major split by mid 1919. The central leadership of the Socialist Party expelled the whole "left wing," including the seven language federations, the whole state organizations in Massachusetts, Michigan, and Ohio, and altogether, about two thirds of the membership. The Socialist Party umbrella could no longer simultaneously cover both the radical and moderate wings.

The expelled groups themselves divided over a variety of issues, and the early factionalism of the party that became the Communist Party of the United States of America (CPUSA) reflected the complicated in-fighting of the expelled groups and others (see Chapter 9, "The Communist Party in the U.S. and Britain in the 1920s").

Socialism Diminished, Continues

The expulsion of the radical groups supporting the Bolshevik revolution in one way or another left the Socialist Party a mere shadow of its former self. Further crises and divisions in the early 1920s made it clear that this version of Marxism, with its roots in the campaigns of Americans like Bellamy and Debs would remain pretty small, although its total membership would often exceed that of the Communist Party in later years.

Despite the fact that the party survived, it did so in pockets. One pocket remained in Milwaukee, with its long-standing allegiance to Victor Berger and the SDP tradition. Some of the ethnic federations remained loyal to the SP, notably the Slovenians, who feared the growth of the Soviet Union. In New York, the Rand School, founded in 1910, remained part of the Socialist Party apparatus for a few years.

Notes on the Left

The Rand School was founded in 1902, as a workers' school. Gradually, it evolved into a more conventional adult-education institution. Algernon Lee, a moderate socialist and a member of the New York City Board of Aldermen in the period from 1918 to 1922, remained head of the School from 1909 to the 1950s. At its peak years, between 1910 and 1920, the Rand School enrolled about 5,000 students each year. It was briefly investigated for subversive activities in 1919, for publishing an anti-war pamphlet.

After lawsuits, the School fought off governmental attempts to confiscate its property. With the split among socialists following the Russian Revolution, it remained under the control of the moderate, anti-Soviet wing of the American Socialist Party during the 1920s, and became independent of the party after 1932. Later, the School was partially funded by a resort in Pennsylvania, the Tamiment Camp. In the 1950s, the Rand School was dissolved.

The Socialist Party remained a minor party on the American scene in later years. In 1924, the SP supported a third-party effort of Robert M. La Follette to run for president on the Progressive Party ticket. Working with groups in the Farmer Labor Party and with support from the AFL, La Follette polled 4.8 million votes, losing to Calvin Coolidge, the Republican, with 15.7 million. The Democratic candidate in that election, John Davis, polled 8.3 million.

This 1924 "fusion" effort left the SP demoralized. However, the party was somewhat revived under the leadership of Norman Thomas in 1928. Thomas remained a candidate for the presidency on the Socialist Party ticket over the next five presidential elections!

In the 1936 election, many socialists defected from the party and worked through the American Labor Party to support Franklin Roosevelt.

Thomas faced continual factionalism through the 1930s and 1940s, and the Socialist Party never regained the strength, unity, or electoral attraction that it held in 1912 under Eugene Debs. Briefly in the period 1936–1938, followers of Leon Trotsky joined the Socialist Party, then withdrew, drawing away many of the young members who enrolled in that period.

Notes on the Left

Norman Thomas, candidate for president, ran altogether six times. Although never winning any Electoral College votes, his minority candidacy always won more votes than any other Marxist candidacy in the United States.

Socialism in a Democracy

In retrospect, it is clear that in the United States, the political path to power chosen by the Socialist Party never had much chance of success. The British Fabians, by contrast, did not establish a separate party but worked by winning over Labour Party politicians to their ideals. Scandinavian advocates of social democracy also tended to work through politics and through independent cooperativism. In Russia, the struggle between Marxists advocating control through politics or through revolution was bitter, with eventual victory going to Lenin and his followers.

The American Socialist Party tried to field its own candidates in almost every major election between 1904 and the 1980s. With the exception of a few local posts and an occasional member of Congress, the political effort was doomed to failure in twentieth-century America.

The Least You Need to Know

◆ The Socialist Party in the United States tended to be dominated by English-speaking native-born Americans, in contrast to the Socialist Labor Party.

◆ European socialist movements took on different national characters in Russia, Scandinavia, and Britain.

◆ The U.S. Socialist Party believed in achieving the goals of a socialized society through politics and the electoral process.

◆ Although it opposed the U.S. entry into World War I, the Socialist Party supported conscientious objectors to the draft rather than strikes and sabotage.

- The U.S. Socialist Party split over whether to support the Russian Revolution, with the left wing of the party splitting off to become part of the new Communist Party in the United States.

- Norman Thomas ran as a socialist for president of the United States in every election from 1928 through 1948, never polling as many votes as Debs had done in 1912.

Part 2

Mother Russia

Russia, communism, and Bolshevism are synonymous. Right? Wrong. It turned out that one branch of the social democratic parties formed in the early twentieth century in Russia wanted to achieve socialism with a revolution. Although they were a minority, they were led by a brilliant political strategist, V. I. Lenin, who won them the name of Bolshevik (or majority, in English).

In this part, we look at the situation in Russia and then at the tactics, techniques, and ideas of the three men who made the revolution and established the Soviet Union: Lenin, Stalin, and Trotsky. We see how Stalin solidified power by using murder, torture, prison camps, purges, and show trials.

Chapter 6

The Russian Revolution

In This Chapter

◆ Two revolutions in Russia
◆ The communist seizure of power
◆ The role of V. I. Lenin
◆ Russian Civil War and foreign intervention

The Russian Revolution was one of the most important events of the twentieth century. It was the first example of a successful communist uprising, and the formation of the Soviet Union as a communist state had an enormous impact on the rest of the world. For some, the new communist regime symbolized the greatest hope of mankind. For others, the Soviet Union came to represent the worst imaginable tyranny. In this chapter we look at how the Russian Revolution began and how the communists seized power afterward.

The Tsarist Regime

Russia was the most authoritarian and backward nation in Europe during the late nineteenth century. The country was headed by an emperor known as the Tsar (sometimes spelled Czar), but the ruling Romanov dynasty stayed in power only because there appeared to be very few alternatives. Although some attempts were made to modernize the country and reform the government, they progressed at a snail's pace. Tsar Nicholas II, who ascended the throne in

1894, stubbornly resisted any changes that might have weakened his position or that of the Russian aristocracy.

The Russian parliament, the Duma, had very little power. Moreover, most members of the Duma came from wealthy backgrounds, with peasants and workers hardly represented at all. While Russian peasants had been given some freedom in the 1860s, many still lived in pitiful conditions and at the mercy of the local land-owning nobility whose fields they farmed. The country was very poor, and efforts by peasants and workers to protest their living conditions or demand political reforms were always punished extremely harshly.

Notes on the Left

In 1904, Russia went to war against Japan over land disputes in the Far East. Although everyone expected Russia to win quickly, the Japanese won a series of startling victories. Many Russians began to protest against rising food prices and the government's efforts to conscript more people into the military. On Sunday, January 9, 1905, a large crowd of 150,000 people gathered in front of the Tsar's palace in St. Petersburg to present him with a petition of grievances. The government responded by sending in army troops, who dispersed the crowd and killed more than 1,000 protestors. The massacre is remembered as "Bloody Sunday." The event convinced many Russians that there was no hope for reform, and only a complete revolution could bring about any change.

Reformers and Revolutionaries in Russia

There were several different opposition groups in Russia that wanted to end the Tsarist regime. These included liberal middle-class parties that called for political reforms. A central goal was to increase the importance of the Duma and impose a constitution that would limit the power of the Tsar. Another important movement was the large, though unorganized, group of social revolutionaries who were primarily interested in land reforms and social changes that would improve the plight of Russian peasants. Finally, there was the Social Democratic Party that had adopted Marxist ideology and demanded a complete overthrow of the Tsarist state and the formation of a communist regime.

In many ways, Russia was a country ripe for revolution by the early 1900s. However, according to Marxist theory, it should have been the last country in Europe that was ready for a communist revolution. Marx had predicted that the revolution would begin in the most industrially advanced countries where capitalism had reached the final stage of its development. At the time, the vast majority of Russians still lived in rural areas and worked in agriculture. Russian peasants were primarily interested in only one thing—land reform, which would break up the large estates and allow each peasant to farm his own individual plot.

The number of industrial workers was growing rapidly in Russia, but there were still far fewer of them than in countries like England, France, or Germany. Most Russian revolutionaries openly admitted that they would not live to see the birth of communism in their country. They could not have been more wrong.

V. I. Lenin

V. I. Lenin, the father of the Soviet Union, was born in 1870 into a Russian middle-class family. His real name was Vladimir Ilyich Ulyanov, but like many revolutionaries, he adopted a new name. Lenin was well educated and began training as a lawyer. However, after his brother was executed in 1887 for attempting to assassinate the Tsar, Lenin became a full-time revolutionary.

He began organizing working class Marxist groups in St. Petersburg and was eventually arrested by the police and sent to Siberia. Upon his release in 1900, he went into exile to Switzerland.

Head of the Russian Bolshevik Party, Vladimir Ilyich Lenin oversaw the communist revolution in Russia and became the first leader of the Soviet Union.

(National Archives)

While in exile, Lenin became a leading member of the Russian Social Democratic Party, as well as an influential writer and thinker. He rejected any attempt to adopt what he called "economism." Some social democrats believed that the party should focus on helping industrial workers improve their status rather than trying to bring about a revolution. This was a strategy that had been somewhat successful in places like England, France, and Germany, where trade unions had fought for better pay and working conditions.

But for Lenin, such a goal was nothing less than treason to the communist cause. Communists, he argued, could not just try to help workers. They had to be a separate group that would devote all its efforts to bringing about the revolution. In effect, he rejected all the gradualist approaches of politics and union work in favor of revolution.

Voices

In a pamphlet called *What Is to Be Done?* published in 1902, Lenin harshly criticized other Russian revolutionaries for being disorganized and too focused on trade-union politics. He wrote:

> Economists are forever lapsing from Social-Democracy into trade unionism. The political struggle of Social-Democracy is far more extensive and complex than the economic struggle of the workers against the employers and the government .... [T]he organizations of revolutionaries must consist first, foremost and mainly of people who make revolutionary activity their profession .... Such an organization must of necessity be not too extensive and as secret as possible.

Lenin also insisted that Russia was a special case and could not follow the same path to communism that Marx had prophesized for other countries in Europe. In particular, Lenin argued that the Russian middle-class was too small and weak to carry out the initial bourgeois political revolution that Marx claimed was a necessary first step before the working classes could launch their own revolution.

Instead, he suggested that a highly disciplined and devoted group could act as a revolutionary vanguard and take power directly in Russia, bypassing the country's bourgeois stage of development. Lenin recognized that this vanguard had to be ready to use force in order to impose socialism on the Russian masses not yet ready to accept it.

However, not all Russian revolutionaries agreed with Lenin's thinking. At a series of conferences held in London and Brussels in 1903, the Social Democratic Party found itself hopelessly split into two wings. Lenin insisted upon making the party a small, highly centralized group controlled from the top. Others wanted the party to be broader, with more room for internal disagreements and local autonomy.

Bolsheviks: The Minority Known as the Majority

Lenin succeeded in attracting a majority of the party delegates at the 1903 conferences. From that point onward, Lenin's followers referred to themselves as *Bolsheviks*, the Russian word for "majority." Those socialists who opposed Lenin came to be known as *Mensheviks*, the Russian word for "minority." In fact, Lenin did not always enjoy the support of the Social Democratic Party's majority, and in 1912 the Bolsheviks formally left the Social Democratic Party and formed their own movement.

In fact, it was a little ironic that the Russian term for "majority" became attached to the party that believed in a small, dedicated core of revolutionaries who were anything but a majority.

Lenin believed that the communists could seize power in Russia because the entire capitalist world was on the brink of collapse. During the last decades of the nineteenth century, all industrialized nations, including Russia and the United States, had become involved in a great scramble to collect as many colonies as possible. By the early 1900s, almost every part of the world was under the control of one industrialized country or another.

Lenin argued that the cause of this imperialist expansion was a crisis in capitalism. He maintained that capitalism was starting to find it more and more difficult to make profits at home, so it embarked on a period of colonial expansion to make profits abroad. But sooner or later, he added, capitalism would run out of places to go.

When the First World War began in 1914, Lenin believed that the final death knell for capitalism had rung. However, even he did not foresee that Russia would be the first country to go.

Red Words _____

Bolsheviks were followers of Lenin who believed that the communist movement in Russia had to be a small, secretive, and highly centralized party. **Mensheviks** were also communists, but they believed the movement should be more open and less tightly controlled.

The First Revolution in Russia, March 1917

In August 1914, Russia declared war against Germany and entered the First World War. Although the Bolsheviks and some other revolutionary groups called for a general strike, most Russian workers and peasants initially supported the war. Within a few years, however, everything would change.

Despite a few early military successes, the war began to go very poorly for the Russians. The army was led by incompetent officers, and casualty figures on the front lines soon reached horrific numbers. Moreover, the Tsarist government proved completely incapable of handling the demands of running a full-scale war effort. By early 1917, the regime had become completely discredited and had all but collapsed.

Notes on the Left _____

Life at the Tsarist court in St. Petersburg became increasingly bizarre during the war. The wife of Nicholas II, Tsarina Alexandra, fell under the spell of a self-proclaimed holy man called Gregori Rasputin. Known as the "Mad Monk," Rasputin claimed that he possessed mystical powers and could heal the Tsar's son, who suffered from a rare disease. Rasputin became very influential at the court and began interfering with government offices. In 1916, a group of Russian nobles decided to remove Rasputin by assassinating him. It was not an easy job, and Rasputin had to be poisoned, shot, stabbed, beaten with a club, and then finally drowned.

The March (or February) Revolution

The first revolution in Russia broke out in March 1917. It came as a complete surprise to everyone, Lenin and the Bolsheviks most of all. The revolution started in the form of protests against food prices in St. Petersburg (which had been renamed Petrograd at the beginning of the war to sound less German). These protests were largely spontaneous, but they quickly grew and spread after army troops mutinied and refused to put down the crowds. Workers and soldiers in Petrograd announced the formation of a local *soviet*, or workers' council, which refused to recognize the leadership of the Tsar.

> **Notes on the Left**
>
> In 1917, Russia still used an old-style Gregorian calendar. Since most of Europe had long since switched to a new, updated calendar, this resulted in the annoying problem of Russian dates not being the same as those in other countries and differing by a little more than two weeks. According to the Russian calendar, the March 1917 revolution actually occurred in February and is often referred to as the February Revolution. Likewise, the Bolshevik seizure of power in November 1917 is often referred to as the October Revolution.

> **Red Words**
>
> In Russian, **soviet** means workers' council or commune. Soviets were local groups of workers and soldiers that formed during revolutionary periods.

At the same time, more moderate middle-class liberals in the Duma also began calling for a sweeping reform in the Tsar's government. Tsar Nicholas II responded by dismissing the Duma, but the Duma refused to go. Under pressure from the Petrograd Soviet, the Duma formed a provisional government and began calling for the Tsar to step down. After hearing from his generals that the frontline troops were on the verge of mutiny, Tsar Nicholas II abdicated on March 17, 1917. Without much fuss or fanfare, the revolution in Russia that many predicted would never happen, had just occurred.

Of course, this was not a communist revolution. Lenin and most other Russian revolutionaries were not even in the country and had no idea of what was taking place. In many ways, it appeared to be the bourgeois, middle-class political revolution that Marx had predicted.

Prince Lvov and Alexander Kerensky

The provisional government was headed by a liberal nobleman, Prince Lvov, but also included the socialist Alexander Kerensky, who was a supporter of the Social Revolutionary Party. The government called for new elections, without universal suffrage. It also planned to meet in order to decide upon a new constitution for the country. In normal times, the provisional government might have successfully formed a new middle-class regime in Russia, as had occurred elsewhere in Europe.

However, the government made a couple of terrible mistakes. First, it decided not to do anything about land reform. Although the government announced that it would consider giving land to the peasants, it did not take any immediate steps toward doing so. The broken promise had the result of alienating Russian peasants, many of whom decided to start grabbing land with or without the government's support.

Moreover, the provisional government decided to stay in the war. This was an even more serious mistake. In June 1917, it launched a new offensive against Germany, which soon became a complete disaster, with many army officers refusing to recognize the government's orders.

Meanwhile, the Petrograd Soviet announced that all military units should form their own soldiers' soviets and elect new officers. In the resulting confusion, hundreds of thousands of troops began to simply leave the front and go home. Army discipline completely collapsed, and the provisional government found itself severely shaken.

The Bolshevik Seizure of Power, 1917

The Russian revolution in March 1917 caught Lenin by surprise. At that point he was still living in Switzerland, where he had spent most of the war. Lenin immediately made plans to return to Russia. He did so with the help of the German government, which allowed him to cross Germany in a special train. By the time Lenin arrived in Petrograd in April 1917, the revolution had already occurred and the new provisional government had assumed control. However, he immediately announced that the Bolshevik Party would support the Petrograd Soviet, believing it would be a true revolutionary government.

Notes on the Left

When Lenin decided to return to Russia from Switzerland in March 1917, he faced the difficult problem of how to get there. Switzerland was surrounded by countries at war with Russia. So Lenin asked the German government for help. After secret negotiations, the German government agreed to allow Lenin to pass through its territory in a specially sealed train that would travel directly from Switzerland to Petrograd. The Germans recognized that Lenin's presence in Russia would help undermine the new government. Lenin arrived safely, but his means of travel did raise some suspicions. Many Russian revolutionaries believed that he was a German spy.

Lenin understood the situation in Russia perfectly. He recognized that most Russian workers and peasants were not yet ready to embrace the idea of forming a communist regime. So, he took the pragmatic step of simplifying Bolshevik ideology to three basic ideas: Land, Peace, and Bread. He called for land to be distributed freely between peasants and demanded the immediate end of the war. He also called for workers to take control of all factories and for all power to be transferred from provisional government to the Petrograd Soviet. This simple message attracted the support of many revolutionaries in Petrograd, and the Bolsheviks began to become more influential.

Lenin Miscalculates

However, the growing support led Lenin to make a serious miscalculation. After the failure of the provisional government military offensive in June 1917, the Bolsheviks attempted a mass uprising against the government. It was poorly planned and quickly failed. Many Bolsheviks were arrested, and Lenin had to flee to Finland to avoid being imprisoned himself. In response to the uprising, Prince Lvov resigned from the provisional government, and the socialist Alexander Kerensky became its leader. To many, it appeared as though the Bolsheviks had missed their chance.

July Days in Petrograd. Lenin's first attempt to seize power in July 1917 was a failure, and government troops easily dispersed the Bolshevik supporters. He planned more carefully before making his second, successful effort in November 1917.

(National Archives)

However, Kerensky found it impossible to build a stable government. Conservative elements in the provisional government demanded that he continue the war and put down the Petrograd Soviet and all other opposition to the new regime. Revolutionary elements insisted that the war should end immediately and the government should begin the social reforms it had promised. As a result, Kerensky had difficulties appeasing either side and ended up doing nothing.

The key turning point came in September 1917 when the army commander General Kornilov decided to solve the problem by marching on Petrograd and using his troops against the Petrograd Soviet. Kornilov's plot failed when his troops refused to move into the city, but the provisional government became completely discredited. This opened the door for Lenin's return.

Notes on the Left

Sailors from the Kronstadt naval base near Petrograd were to play a tragic role in the Russian Revolution. In November 1917, they provided vital support to the Bolshevik uprising by marching on the city and using the warship *Aurora* to shell troops from the provisional government. However, the sailors were not Bolsheviks. Many, in fact, were anarchists who became very suspicious of Lenin's efforts to establish a Bolshevik dictatorship.

Four years later, in February 1921, many of these same sailors attempted to overthrow Lenin. The uprising was put down savagely and many of the sailors were executed. The suppression of this Kronstadt Revolt led many anarchists and anarchist sympathizers in the West to turn against Lenin and Soviet communism.

The November Revolution

Over the next few weeks, the Bolsheviks gathered more and more support within Petrograd. By late September 1917, they commanded a majority within the Petrograd Soviet for the first time; in July only 10 percent of the Soviet had been Bolshevik supporters. On the night of November 6, Bolshevik supporters seized key points throughout the city of Petrograd. The uprising was planned and organized by Leon Trotsky, who proved to be one of the most able members of the Bolshevik Party.

The uprising was also aided by mutineers from a nearby naval base who sailed the warship *Aurora* upriver and bombarded the Winter Palace, which housed the offices of the provisional government. Kerensky fled into exile, and Lenin announced that he was the head of a new Council of People's Commissioners, which had replaced the defunct provisional government.

Voices

After the Bolsheviks succeeded in overthrowing Kerensky's government, they still had to deal with other, more moderate revolutionary groups in Petrograd that did not support all of Lenin's plans. At a meeting of the Petrograd Soviet held on the same night the Bolshevik uprising began, several of these groups attempted to force Lenin to come to a compromise. Leon Trotsky angrily denounced these efforts, declaring "Your role is played out. Go where you belong from now on—into the trash can of history."

The Russian Civil War, 1918–1920

Unfortunately for Lenin, announcing that he was the head of Russia's new government was not the same thing as actually being in control of the entire country. Although the Bolsheviks now enjoyed widespread support, they were by no means the most popular party and there were many anti-Bolshevik forces scattered throughout the rest of the Russian Empire. Moreover, the country was still at war.

Although Lenin announced that he wanted peace, Germany and Austro-Hungary saw little reason to stop fighting now that Russia was in such chaos, and their armies soon advanced deep into Russian territory. At the same time, the Russian Empire began to fall apart as far-flung provinces in the east and south declared themselves independent. Over the next two years, Lenin and the Bolshevik Party were embroiled in a desperate struggle to cement their hold on the country.

As a first step, Lenin had to make sure that he was not threatened by other revolutionary groups, many of whom enjoyed far more popular support than the Bolsheviks did. Only a few short weeks after the Bolshevik uprising, Russia held a popular election. The election had been planned by the old provisional government with the idea of forming a Constituent Assembly, which would decide what the new government should be. The Constituent Assembly met in January 1918.

Although nine million people voted for Bolshevik deputies, more than twice as many voted for Kerensky's Social Revolutionary Party. The Bolsheviks solved this problem by simply declaring the Constituent Assembly dissolved and using Bolshevik troops to disperse its members. As an extra step, Lenin also moved the capital from Petrograd to Moscow, which was more firmly under Bolshevik control.

Lenin also took two other steps to make sure that the Bolsheviks would stay in power. First, he created a new Red Army under the leadership of Leon Trotsky. The Red Army was made up entirely of soldiers and officers devoted to the Bolshevik cause. The formation of a military force under Bolshevik control freed Lenin from the threat of a military uprising against his regime. Second, Lenin also created a new police force, which would be able to move against all political enemies. His secret police organization, the *Cheka*, arrested thousands of political opponents.

The Bolsheviks' first step in their military campaign was to end the fighting with Germany and Austro-Hungary. In March 1918, the new government signed the humiliating Treaty of Brest-Litovsk, which ended the war but at the cost of surrendering large parts of the old Russian Empire. However, the peace treaty did give the Bolsheviks time to move against their internal enemies. Over the next few years, the Red Army fought across all of Russia on a variety of fronts, from the Ukraine in the west to Siberia in the east, in a terrible civil war that claimed hundreds of thousands of lives.

Notes on the Left

Lenin recognized that the Bolsheviks could only stay in power if they were not afraid to use force against their political opponents. In December 1917, he established an Extraordinary All-Russian Commission of Struggle Against Counterrevolution, Speculation, and Sabotage (or Cheka, as it was known by its initials in Russian) to act as a secret police force. Headed by Feliks Dzerzhinsky, the Cheka used terror and brutality to intimidate all those who opposed the Bolshevik Party. In many ways, the Cheka was worse than the old Tsarist police. During the first years of the Bolshevik regime, tens of thousands of Russians were arrested, killed, or exiled. The Cheka would eventually become the KGB.

The Russian Civil War was a confusing conflict that pitted the Bolsheviks against a wide variety of foreign and domestic foes. Many of the early campaigns were fought against armies led by army generals bent on overthrowing the Bolshevik regime and returning the monarchy, a struggle that continued even after Tsar Nicholas II and his entire family were executed by Bolsheviks in July 1918.

The Red Army also fought against foreign powers that had decided to intervene in Russia during the chaos. These included troops from the newly created country of Poland, as well as American, French, British, and Japanese expeditionary forces that invaded different parts of the country in late 1918 and early 1919. Finally, the Bolshevik government also launched assaults to conquer back many of the outlying areas of the old Tsarist empire that had tried to declare themselves independent during the chaos of the Russian Revolution.

Notes on the Left

During the Russian Civil War, several foreign countries launched secret invasions of Russia in the hopes of destabilizing the newly established Bolshevik regime. In June 1918, British and French forces landed at Archangel in the north of Russia, and were later joined by American troops. Additional Allied forces landed in Odessa in southern Russia, while Japanese and American troops also intervened in Siberia. Perhaps the most interesting foreign group that became involved in the Russian Civil War was a division of 45,000 Czech soldiers who had been fighting for the Tsarist army and found themselves stranded far from home when the revolution broke out. The Czech division fought its way all across Russia to the Pacific Ocean.

By late 1919, most foreign forces had been withdrawn. However, the Allied decision to intervene in the Russian Civil War convinced Lenin that the capitalist governments in France, England, Germany, and America would stop at nothing to bring down the Bolshevik regime.

Although with a tremendous toll in human lives, the Red Army emerged victorious from the Russian Civil War by 1920. Anti-Bolshevik forces were far too disunited and disorganized to put up any further resistance. Fighting would continue for several more years, especially in the Far East, but the Bolsheviks eventually succeeded in assuming control over most of Russia. Lenin could now move forward with creating a new communist society in Russia.

The Least You Need to Know

- ◆ Despite being the most backward country in Europe, Russia experienced the first successful communist revolution.
- ◆ Lenin was a follower of Marx but believed that a small and dedicated communist party could seize power in Russia, even though the country as a whole was not yet ready for communism.
- ◆ The fall of the Tsarist regime in March 1917 was the result of general unhappiness over the war and not of any kind of communist uprising.
- ◆ The Bolshevik Party eventually seized power in November 1917, because it was willing to use force and violence to win.
- ◆ After seizing power, the Bolsheviks had to fight a long civil war against a variety of enemies, including foreign troops, before they stabilized their hold on the entire country.

Lenin and the Communist Regime

In This Chapter

- ◆ The communist regime in Russia
- ◆ Economic policies and plans
- ◆ Formation of the Third International
- ◆ The death of Lenin and struggles for succession

In the first few years following the Bolshevik Revolution in Russia, the new regime was engaged in a fierce struggle for its life. Surrounded by enemies from abroad and battling against enemies at home, the Bolshevik Party had little opportunity to think through exactly what kind of communist state it wanted to create. Since it was the first successful communist revolution, Lenin and his supporters had no clear model to follow.

Although Marx had provided a general idea of how communism was supposed to work, putting these ideas into practice proved to be far more challenging than most had imagined. Lenin had to balance his ideological beliefs with the pragmatic needs of a government at war with almost everyone. This chapter explores Lenin's efforts to build a communist state in Russia and shows how he built a tightly centralized regime. It also examines the difficulties that followed his death, as his supporters fought among themselves over who would become the next ruler of Russia.

Instruments of Communist Rule

Marx believed that communism would eventually result in the "withering away of the state." With the creation of a workers' paradise, there would be no need for government agencies, state officials, police, bureaucracies, or any of the other trappings of capitalist governments. But the experience of Russia under communism turned out to be the exact opposite. In their effort to maintain control of Russia and impose communism on its people, the Bolsheviks created an extensive system of governing institutions that weighed heavily on the lives of every Russian, as well as the peoples of other nations and ethnic regions of the Russian Empire, brought into the Soviet Union.

Notes on the Left

Growth of the Communist Party in Soviet Union

Year	Number of Members
1917	70,000
1918	200,000
1930	2 million
1933	3.5 million
1938	1.9 million
1940	3 million

The Party

The most important of these powerful institutions was the Communist Party itself. In 1918, the Bolsheviks officially renamed themselves the All-Russian Communist Party to indicate that they were legitimate rulers of the entire former Russian Empire. All other political parties were banned, and the Communist Party was the only group permitted to organize and operate. At that point, the Party had around 200,000 members, while the population of the Soviet territory as a whole was well over 150 million people.

In theory, Party membership was open to all. However, applicants were carefully screened to eliminate those who came from the wrong background or seemed ambivalent about supporting the new regime. Members were expected to study the principles of Marxism-Leninism religiously. They were also expected to follow the Bolshevik ideal of absolute obedience to the Party at all times.

Whatever the Party decided had to be followed without question or debate. The principle of a vanguard party, run through democratic centralism, meant unswerving obedience to the policies set by leadership. It was centralized, all right, but not what would be called democratic in the West. Despite the harsh discipline, many Russians were eager to join the Party during the first years of the regime. By 1930, Party membership had reached more than two million.

Voices

At the All-Russian Communist Party Congress in 1921, Lenin announced that the Red Army had driven all hostile forces from Russia. But he warned that the enemies of communism were waiting to attack again, so the Party could show no signs of weakness and allow no internal debate or dispute:

> Our efforts should be more united and harmonious than ever before; there should not be the slightest trace of factionalism .... That is the only condition on which we shall accomplish the immense tasks that confront us .... [T]he end of this Congress must find our Party stronger, more harmonious, and more sincerely united than ever before.

The Russian Communist Party ostensibly held general congresses every few years to discuss issues facing the movement and to develop plans for the future. In practice, however, the congresses did little more than rubber-stamp policies that had already been established by a Central Committee made up of 100–150 prominent members. The heart of the Central Committee was the *Politburo*, or Political Bureau, a group of approximately a dozen leaders who represented the ultimate power within the Party. The head of the entire Party was the general secretary, a position that eventually came to be the most important office in the Soviet Union.

The Government

Although the Communist Party was the most important organization in Russia, it was not technically the government. Rather, the Party operated as a parallel organization alongside the government. A constitution adopted in 1918 created a federal system in which each town and village elected members of a local soviet or council. These local soviets elected members of a provincial soviet, which in turn elected members of a regional soviet.

In 1922, these regional soviets were united into the Union of Soviet Socialist Republics (USSR, or Soviet Union), which represented the entire region of the old Russian Empire, stretching from Poland to the Pacific Ocean. The Union-Wide Congress of Soviets, made up of representatives from each regional soviet, acted as the central law-making body for the country. Later, constitutional changes provided modifications to this system and introduced some democratic practices. For example, voters were permitted to select members of the regional soviets directly through secret ballot.

Red Words

The **Politburo** was the central policy-making office in communist Russia. The abbreviation for "political bureau" in Russian, the Politburo was responsible for deciding everything, from foreign affairs to domestic economic policies. Its size varied at different times but was usually made up of around a dozen members, selected by the Central Committee of the Russian Communist Party.

Notes on the Left

The Union of Soviet Socialist Republics is usually abbreviated in English as USSR. Russian, however, is written in the Cyrillic alphabet, which uses different letters. In Russian, the USSR is abbreviated as CCCP.

Red Words

The **Kremlin** is an ancient walled center in Moscow. After Lenin moved the capital of Russia to Moscow in 1918, the Kremlin became the central government office in the Soviet Union. In the rest of the world, journalists and political observers often used the term "Kremlin" as a synonym or piece of jargon to refer to the Soviet government as a whole.

However, the governing system always remained tightly controlled by the Communist Party. Government officials did not necessarily have to be members of the party. And, in some cases, local ones were not. However, few officials survived for long if they were not willing to toe the party line when asked. All high-ranking officials were invariably party members, and the close link between the Communist Party and the government eliminated any distinction between the two at this level. For all practical purposes, power flowed from the top down, and communist officials working in the *Kremlin* made the most important policy decisions.

The Army and the Police

The Communist Party maintained its hold on the Soviet Union through controlling two other critical institutions. The first was the Red Army, which was founded by Leon Trotsky immediately after the Russian Revolution. Trotsky did a very good job in creating the efficient and disciplined army that led the communists to victory in the Russian Civil War.

Trotsky also took steps to ensure that the Red Army would remain completely faithful to the Communist Party. Party membership was required for high-ranking officers. In addition, all military units had special political officers, called commissars, who made sure that the troops were indoctrinated with communist ideology.

The final instrument of communist control in Russia was the secret police. Originally established in December 1917 as the Cheka (the Russian abbreviation for All-Russian Commission of Struggle Against Counterrevolution, Speculation, and Sabotage), the Soviet secret police acted swiftly and brutally to eliminate all opposition to Lenin and the communist regime. Under the leadership of Feliks Dzerzhinsky, the Cheka became the most feared agency in Russia. The organization would go through several name changes over the next decades.

In 1922, the Cheka became the United State Political Administration (OGPU) and was renamed the People's Commissariat for Internal Affairs (NKVD) in 1934. It eventually became the Committee for State Security (KGB) after the Second World War. Despite these name changes, however, its essential function remained the same. Secret police agents used terror, assassination, arbitrary arrest, and exile to intimidate all those identified as enemies of the Communist Party. In later years, the KGB became an instrument for ensuring Party control in other countries (see Chapter 17, "Trouble in Paradise").

A Giant Leap Backward: Lenin's New Economic Policy

Military demands during the Russian Civil War made it impossible for Lenin to organize any kind of formal communist system in Russia. Instead, the Bolsheviks practiced what they called "war communism." War communism was little more than organized plunder, in which the largest factories were placed directly under communist control. To feed the workers who produced military goods, the new government announced that all peasants were required to supply food directly to the cities under communist control. When peasants began to hoard food for themselves, military units were sent to the countryside to requisition agricultural surpluses directly from the farms. However, the result of war communism was an almost complete economic collapse. Industrial production fell sharply, and peasants were producing only a little more than half as much food as before the revolution. In addition, military enforcement of war communism created huge unrest throughout the rural areas.

The New Economic Policy

In 1921, Lenin announced a radical change. Explaining that Russia had tried to create a communist system too quickly, he suggested the country should adopt a New Economic Policy (NEP). What was striking about the NEP was that it wasn't really "new," but instead represented a compromise between socialism and capitalism. While Marxist ideology called for workers' control of all means of production, under the NEP only the "commanding heights" of the economy were owned by the state. These included transportation, banks, and heavy industries like steel production. However, private ownership of smaller enterprises, like stores and restaurants, was permitted.

Furthermore, under the NEP, land ownership laws were changed to allow more productive peasants to expand their individual, private holdings. Free trade between urban and rural areas was encouraged, and the communist regime reached out to foreign capitalists who could provide the investment and expertise to modernize Russia's industry. Some of the more radical communists at home and abroad were stunned that Lenin endorsed all these compromises with private property, capitalism, and the market system.

> **Voices**
>
> In a report to a special committee of the Communist Party in 1921, Lenin admitted:
>
> The New Economic Policy means substituting a tax for the requisitioning of food; it means reverting to capitalism to a considerable extent …. Concessions to foreign capitalists … and leading enterprises to private capitalists definitely means restoring capitalism, and this is part and parcel of the New Economic Policy.

Profiteers and Kulaks

Lenin clearly intended that the New Economic Policy should be a temporary measure. He referred to it as a strategic retreat from socialism, made necessary by the need to rebuild the Soviet economy weakened by three years of warfare and a series of famines and droughts. The NEP demonstrated Lenin's pragmatism, for he recognized that it would require the Communist Party to compromise its Marxist values. The NEP resulted in the rise of a new class of businessmen who made profits from the trade between urban and rural areas.

> **Red Words**
>
> **Kulaks** were a class of more prosperous peasants who owned larger farms than the small plots tilled by most peasants. Under the NEP, Kulaks greatly expanded their holdings by buying land from other peasants.

The NEP also saw the growth of the *Kulak* peasant class of independent farmers who took advantage of the new regulations and free market opportunities to acquire large landholdings. To many devoted communists, it appeared as though the NEP had allowed capitalism to return to Russia. Despite some rumbles on the left, however, the NEP was successful in revitalizing the Soviet economy, and production levels began to climb back to what they had been before the Revolution.

> **Notes on the Left**
>
> Under the NEP, the Soviet Union made efforts to make Russia a more attractive place for foreign investment, which was a pretty tough job. Not only had the new regime defaulted on all its foreign debts, but the Communist Party also openly declared that its aim was the worldwide destruction of the capitalist system. Hardly the sort of public relations to encourage American stockbrokers! Despite this, some international companies did decide to do business with their sworn enemies. Ford Motor Company opened up a tractor factory in Russia. Other American businessmen, such as Armand Hammer, who later became head of Occidental Petroleum, and Tom Watson, founder of IBM, also had extensive dealings with the Soviet Union in the 1920s.

Soviet Foreign Policy and the Third International

Another great challenge facing the Soviet Union in the early 1920s was its relationship with the rest of the world. In the early days after the Revolution, the question of foreign policy seemed unimportant to Lenin and most other communist leaders. During the First World War, Lenin had argued that the conflict represented a final desperate effort by capitalism to stay in power. Marx's writings clearly indicated that a communist revolution could not be successful unless it was universal and included all industrialized nations. Accordingly, Lenin was convinced that Russia was simply the first country in which the forces of capitalism had been routed, and he expected that revolutions would soon break out everywhere else as well.

Exporting Bolshevism

By early 1919, there were signs that this might be happening. The end of the First World War brought chaos and unrest throughout Europe. In Germany, groups of soldiers and sailors mutinied and formed local soviets, modeled after what took place in Russia. A short-lived Bavarian Socialist Republic appeared to be a harbinger of a wider transformation. In Hungary, the communist Bela Kun seized power and declared the country a socialist republic. There were pro-Bolshevik demonstrations in France, England, and the United States. But these revolutionary signs subsided and the socialist regimes were soon overthrown. When the worldwide communist uprising failed to materialize, communist leaders in the Soviet Union decided it was time to help along the world revolution.

In March 1919, Lenin announced the formation of the Third International, often referred to as the *Comintern*. The Third International openly challenged what Lenin saw as the outdated and impotent policies adopted by socialist groups throughout the rest of the world.

Red Words

The **Comintern,** from the Russian for "Communist International," was the international organization of communist parties that supported the new regime in Russia. The Comintern was largely financed and directed by the Soviet Union. During the period from 1920 to 1943, the Comintern controlled, or sought to control, the communist parties of the world. Sometimes the terms "Third International" and "Comintern" were used interchangeably.

Under the Second International, which continued to meet up until the beginning of the First World War, working class groups had argued endlessly and bitterly among themselves over obscure ideological differences, minor tactical disagreements, and often focused on personality differences among leaders. Socialism had gone in many different directions, with constant squabbling among the factions. The Third International was planned as something completely different. Controlled and directed by officials in Moscow, its aim was nothing less than the exportation of a revolutionary model that the Bolsheviks had already successfully demonstrated.

Organizing the Comintern

At the first major meeting of the Third International, held in 1920, delegates representing 37 countries endorsed a general set of Twenty-one Points drafted by Lenin. The Twenty-one Points provided ironclad rules for the behavior of communist parties outside of Russia who wished to join the International. Members had to pledge to always work toward fomenting a violent overthrow of the existing governments in their countries. All communist parties had to call themselves "communist" and repudiate any alliance with "reformist socialism," which set out to improve working class conditions by cooperating with bourgeois governments.

Elections, parliamentary organizations, and other democratic institutions were to be utilized only to help in the destruction of the existing government system. Above all else, communist parties throughout the world had to agree to follow all instructions from the central executive of the Third International. From 1919 until 1927, the head of the Third International was Gregori Zinoviev, a leading Bolshevik and close associate of Lenin.

Voices

Article 17 of Lenin's Twenty-one Points for admission into the Third International clearly outlined his call for centralized control of the international communist movement:

All decisions of the Communist International's congresses and of its Executive Committee are binding on all affiliated parties. Operating in conditions of acute civil war, the Communist International must be far more centralized than the Second International was.

Throughout the 1920s and 1930s, the Third International acted as an extension of Soviet foreign policy. Communists from around the world traveled to Russia for training and indoctrination in Marxist-Leninist ideology. The Soviet Union also sent agents to advise communist movements in numerous countries, including China and the United States. In 1924, letters from Zinoviev to British workers openly called upon them to provoke a revolution. Publication of the "Zinoviev letters" caused a rift with Great Britain, which had only just recognized the Soviet Union as the legitimate regime in Russia, and it led to a victory of the Conservative Party in British elections (see Chapter 9, "The Communist Party in the U.S. and Britain in the 1920s").

In many cases, the fear of Soviet efforts to export Bolshevik ideas far outweighed any real threat to the governments in other countries. However, apprehension about the "Red Menace" provoked strong reactions throughout the rest of the world and played a key role in the rise of anti-Bolshevik parties, such as the Fascist Party in Italy and the National Socialist, or Nazi, Party in Germany.

The Death of Lenin and the Struggle for Succession

In 1922, Lenin suffered the first of a series of debilitating strokes that would eventually lead to his premature death in January 1924, at the age of 54. The Communist Party soon created a personality cult celebrating his leadership and his role as the father of the Soviet Union.

During his last years in power, Lenin, shown here, suffered a series of strokes that eventually left him incapacitated. His death in 1924 plunged the Soviet Union into a political crisis over who should succeed him.

(National Archives)

Lenin's embalmed body was placed on display at the Kremlin in Moscow, and communists from around the world began making pilgrimages to the site. Petrograd, which had been called St. Petersburg before the First World War, was renamed again as Leningrad. Communists soon took to placing Lenin's writings on an equal footing with those of Marx, so that the expression "Marxist-Leninist" came to represent the mainstream of communist ideology as defined by the Third International.

Lenin's casket was carried by most of the leading members of the Russian Communist Party, including Joseph Stalin (at far left with head bowed). All the other pallbearers were eventually killed off during Stalin's purges in the 1930s.

(National Archives)

However, many of Lenin's revolutionary comrades did not always agree with his policies. The years immediately after his death saw bitter struggles for succession and redefining of policies.

The Problem of Succession

While Lenin was universally acknowledged as the undisputed head of the Soviet Union during his lifetime, there was no clear indication that he had chosen a successor. There were plenty of candidates, but the Communist Party lacked an established mechanism for choosing one. The struggle played on the surface as a debate over ideology, but the basic issue was how to decide who would take up the reigns of power.

At the time of Lenin's death, the leading candidate appeared to be Leon Trotsky. His revolutionary credentials were solid. It was Trotsky who had organized and orchestrated the November 1917 uprising, which had first brought the Bolsheviks to power in Russia. As head of the Red Army, he had played a key role in defeating communism's enemies during the Russian Civil War. A brilliant orator and only slightly less well-known than Lenin himself, Trotsky seemed poised to take his place as leader of the Communist Party, and by extension, of the Soviet Union.

Vignettes
Trotsky's real name was Lev Davidovich Bronstein. He became a Marxist at a very young age and was arrested numerous times for revolutionary activity. In 1900, he was exiled to Siberia by the Tsarist government. However, Trotsky escaped from Siberia by forging a passport with the name of the policeman who had first imprisoned him. He then adopted that name—Leon Trotsky—as his revolutionary pseudonym.

Leon Trotsky

Trotsky was one of the members of the Communist Party who had criticized Lenin's decision to retreat from socialism in 1921 and adopt the New Economic Policy. After Lenin's death, Trotsky set out to bring the Soviet Union back to what he saw as its true revolutionary path. He railed against the policies that had allowed the growth of bourgeois traders and Kulak landowners. Instead, he demanded that the Soviet Union embark on an immediate push for rapid industrialization in which all aspects of the economy, including agricultural production, would be centrally controlled by the state. Trotsky also accused the Communist Party of having become stagnant and complacent since it seized power. He advocated a policy of what he called "permanent revolution," in which the movement would aggressively push forward on all fronts at all times.

However, Trotsky made a serious miscalculation. Although he had many supporters, he failed to recognize that the Soviet Union was no longer a revolutionary government. It was an established state, complete with a well-entrenched bureaucracy. The kind of fervent revolutionary oratory that had served him so well in rousing workers and soldiers to join the Bolshevik cause proved less convincing to the communists who were now acting as government officials. The real source of power in the Soviet Union lay not with the revolutionary masses, but with the administrators who ran the Party. And in 1924, it was Joseph Stalin who controlled the administrators.

Joseph Stalin

Joseph Stalin is one of the most intriguing and complex figures in twentieth-century history. Born in the province of Georgia in 1879, he was the son of a shoemaker. Unlike many of the other Bolshevik leaders, he remained in Russia during most of the early 1900s and helped run the party newspaper, *Pravda*. Although he played a relatively minor role in the Russian Revolution, he was widely respected as an administrator and served as the People's Commissar for Nationalities. In this role, he was responsible for solving the difficult problem of dealing with the variety of ethnic groups that had been ruled under the Russian Empire, and then in the Soviet Union. The position enabled him to make close contacts with communists from throughout the country, and in 1922, he was elected general secretary of the Communist Party Central Committee.

Vignettes
Stalin's real name was Joseph Vissarionovich Dzhugashvili. At the age of 15, he began studying for the priesthood at a seminary in the Caucasus region. However, Stalin became a convert to Marxism and was expelled from the seminary. After experimenting with several other choices, including "Koba" (the name of a famous outlaw in Georgia), he adopted the name Stalin in 1913. Stalin is a Russian abbreviation for "a man of steel."

Stalin possessed a remarkable sense of political intrigue and used his position as Communist Party general secretary to build a power base among the party membership. He maintained a detailed list of contacts throughout the Party, and leading members began referring to him as "Comrade Card Index." As general secretary, he was responsible for making appointments to Party offices, controlling who was assigned to Party committees, and regulating Party congresses. Although Lenin had begun to become suspicious about Stalin's consolidation of power, his death in 1924 left Stalin in control of most of the rank and file membership of the Party.

Voices _____

Only a few days before his death, Lenin drafted a letter to the Communist Party Congress warning it about Stalin and his possible conflict with Trotsky:

Comrade Stalin, having become Secretary-General, has unlimited authority concentrated in his hands, and I am not sure whether he will always be capable of using that authority with sufficient caution. Comrade Trotsky, on the other hand, ... is personally perhaps the most capable man in the present C.C. [Central Committee], but he has displayed excessive self-assurance and shown excessive preoccupation with the purely administrative side of the work. These two qualities of the two outstanding leaders of the present Central Committee can inadvertently lead to a split, and if our Party does not take steps to avert this, the split may come unexpectedly.

Stalin accused Trotsky and his supporters of "leftist deviation." Dismissing Trotsky's proposals as fanciful, Stalin argued that the New Economic Policy had to be continued, since Russia was not yet ready for full communism. In addition, he maintained that Russia needed to strive for "socialism in one country" rather than foment revolutionary activity around the world. In a more serious charge, Stalin also accused Trotsky of breaking Party discipline by encouraging dissent and disagreement, an accusation that placed Trotsky in a very difficult position. Any attempt to respond to Stalin appeared to violate the doctrine of absolute Party loyalty and obedience that was engrained into every member.

Stalin Eliminates the Competition

Step by step, Stalin was able to strip away Trotsky's power. In 1924, Trotsky was removed as head of the Red Army. Over the next few years, Stalin patiently and methodically expanded his influence among the Party membership and limited that of Trotsky. In 1926, Trotsky was removed from the Politburo. At the Party Congress in 1927, Stalin orchestrated a vote calling for the expulsion of Trotsky from the Party Central Committee. The vote was supported by 95 percent of the Party. Trotsky and his supporters, including Zinoviev, lost their positions and were eventually expelled from the Party. Trotsky was exiled to Siberia, and the following year fled the Soviet Union, never to return.

By 1928, Stalin was the undisputed leader. In a pattern that was to be followed over the next decades of his rule, Stalin immediately set out to erase any reference to Trotsky or his contribution to the communist revolution in the Soviet Union.

The Least You Need to Know

- The Communist Party maintained absolute control over the Soviet Union by banning all other parties and ensuring that all high-ranking government officials had to be Party members.

- The Red Army or the Soviet secret police eliminated any potential threat to the Party's control.

- Lenin adopted the New Economic Policy, with aspects of capitalism, in order to rebuild Russia's economy after years of decline.

- The Third International, or Comintern, became an instrument of Soviet foreign policy, as communist parties around the world were forced to protect the regime in Russia.

- Stalin used his position as general secretary of the Communist Party to become ruler of the Soviet Union after Lenin's death.

Chapter 8

Stalin and the Purges

In This Chapter

- ◆ The career of Joseph Stalin
- ◆ "Socialism in one country" and the Third International
- ◆ The Great Leap Forward and agricultural collectivization
- ◆ Purges and show trials

The figure of Joseph Stalin cast a long shadow on the history of the twentieth century. Between his rise to power in the mid 1920s and his death in 1953, Stalin ruled the Soviet Union with an iron fist. His reign represented both the greatest triumph of communism and, at the same time, its greatest tragedy. Stalin led the Soviet Union to victory when it was invaded by Nazi Germany in the Second World War. During his reign, the Soviet Union made great progress in industrial development and agricultural expansion. Under Stalin's leadership, the Soviet Union was transformed from a backward and isolated country into a military and economic superpower whose claim for global hegemony was challenged only by the United States. For many observers, such progress seemed to demonstrate that communism could actually work.

However, this transformation came at an enormous cost. Stalin often behaved like a paranoid megalomaniac and ruled as a brutal dictator who had absolutely no qualms about using terror to intimidate his enemies, both real and imaginary. He came to power by systematically isolating and killing all potential rivals to his position as leader of the Communist Party, and maintained his control by keeping party members in line through periodic purges, thus weeding out all those who might oppose him.

For the population as a whole, the Stalinist regime was characterized by an almost unimaginable repression in which millions of Soviet citizens were imprisoned, exiled, and executed. This chapter examines both of these aspects of communist rule in the Soviet Union during the Stalinist era.

Stalin's Life and Ideology

It is difficult to understand Stalin's career and his behavior as head of the Soviet Union. Stalin left few writings that provide any clear sense of his personal feelings or thoughts. Unlike Lenin, Stalin was no theoretician and made little contribution to Marxist ideology. Some scholars have simply dismissed him as a madman who was only interested in power, and there is ample evidence to support this view.

But there certainly was an internal logic to his madness. Perhaps the best way of understanding Stalin's life is to see him as a devoted Russian nationalist determined to make the Soviet Union a great power regardless of the cost, and to hold on to personal power in the process.

Although he became a totalitarian dictator, Joseph Stalin could be charismatic and charming, as shown by this photo taken during his exile in Siberia shortly before the Russian Revolution.

(National Archives)

Stalin's Early Life

Ironically, Stalin was not, in fact, Russian. His real name was Joseph Vissarionovich Dzhugashvili. He was born in 1879 in Georgia, a separate province in the Caucasus region along Russia's southern border, which had been conquered by the Russian Imperial government in the late 1700s. Unlike many of the other Bolshevik leaders, Stalin's family came from very humble origins. His father was a shoemaker who had been born into a peasant family.

Stalin was initially educated in church schools and attended a theological seminary in Tiflis, the Georgian capital, during the late 1890s. History would have been very different if Stalin had continued his religious studies; however, he showed little promise for a career in priesthood. Instead, he joined a Marxist student group and was eventually expelled from the seminary in 1899. He later reported that he had become a Marxist because of his family's "social position" and "the harsh intolerance and Jesuitical discipline" that characterized his school days.

Stalin the Revolutionary

Stalin began his revolutionary career as a writer for Marxist newspapers in Georgia and adopted the pseudonym of "Koba," a famous Georgian bandit. He became a follower of Lenin when the Russian Social Democratic Party split into Bolshevik and Menshevik wings in 1903 (see Chapter 6, "The Russian Revolution"). For the next several years he served as a Bolshevik organizer in Georgia and earned a reputation for himself by helping to orchestrate a series of daring bank robberies to raise money for the Bolshevik cause.

Notes on the Left

During the political chaos that gripped Russia during the years 1905 through 1907, Bolshevik groups in Georgia and other parts of the Caucasus region launched a guerrilla campaign against the Tsarist government. Stalin's exact role in these attacks is unclear, although he appears to have been only an administrator and not to have taken part in the fighting himself. However, the campaign was harshly criticized by leading Russian communists during a party congress attended by Stalin in 1907. Trotsky, who was far more famous and influential than Stalin at this point, dismissed the attacks as amateurish affairs and little more than petty criminal acts. It was the beginning of the personal conflict between Stalin and Trotsky that would culminate in their bitter fight over who was to succeed Lenin following his death in 1924.

Unlike many other Bolshevik leaders, Stalin remained in Russia during most of the early 1900s. He only left the country on a handful of occasions to attend Bolshevik meetings in Europe, and was also captured by police and sent to Siberia several times. He complained that Bolshevik leaders in exile had become "aloof" from the reality of revolutionary feeling in Russia. However, he did attract the attention of Lenin, who recognized Stalin's administrative ability and nominated him to the Bolshevik Party Central Committee in 1912. Stalin appears to have adopted the name "Stalin," which means "a man of steel," about the same time. However, in early 1913, he was again arrested by the police and spent the next four years exiled in Siberia.

Vignettes

In February 1913, Stalin was arrested after being tricked by a fellow Bolshevik named Malinovsky who was in the pay of the Tsarist police. Malinovsky invited Stalin to attend a music festival in St. Petersburg. While at the festival, Stalin sensed a trap and tried to escape by disguising himself with a woman's coat. However, he was captured by police agents and sent to Siberia for imprisonment. The incident may have contributed to Stalin's paranoid fear of betrayal from within the Communist Party after he came to power.

Stalin the Administrator

Following the fall of the Tsar in February 1917, Stalin returned to St. Petersburg and played a minor role in the November 1917 revolution that eventually brought the Bolshevik Party to power. During the early years of Lenin's rule, Stalin served as the People's Commissar for Nationalities. As a Georgian, he had the right background for speaking on what policies the Bolshevik Party should adopt toward the numerous different nationalities and ethnic groups that made up the former Russian Empire. He used the position to gain enormous influence over rank-and-file communists throughout the Soviet Union. During the Russian Civil War, he helped direct campaigns to extend Bolshevik control throughout the old Tsarist empire, including an invasion of Georgia to topple the non-Bolshevik revolutionary government that had seized power after the collapse of the old regime.

Stalin also began playing a key administrative role in both the Soviet government and the Communist Party. In 1919, he was appointed Commissar of the Workers' and Peasants' Inspectorate, an agency established to eliminate corruption and inefficiency in the Russian civil service. He was also appointed to the Politburo, the central policy-making body of the Russian Communist Party, where he took on the responsibility for coordinating between the Politburo and the rest of the Party organizations. Dismissed by other Politburo members as being suited only for such "practical" jobs, Stalin proved to be a tireless and capable administrator.

In April 1922, Stalin was elected to the position of General Secretary of the Communist Party. Only a few weeks later, Lenin suffered the first of a series of strokes that would eventually lead to his death. With Lenin forced to retire from any active role in governing the country, the Soviet Union experienced a power vacuum. Stalin quickly used the situation to his advantage. He formed an alliance with two other members of the Politburo, Gregori Zinoviev and Leo Kamenev, to assume *de facto* leadership of the Party. However, he continued to build himself an unassailable power base as General Secretary of the Party after Lenin's death in January 1924. Over the next four years, he moved first against Leon Trotsky and then against his former allies Zinoviev and Kamenev, before eventually seizing complete control of the entire Communist Party.

Notes on the Left

In late 1922, shortly after suffering the first of his series of strokes, Lenin dictated a final will that laid out his concerns about the future of the Communist Party. A postscript in the will singled out Stalin as being the greatest threat to the Party and suggested that he be removed as General Secretary. Lenin began making plans to dismiss Stalin from his influential positions.

However, in March 1923 Lenin suffered a final stroke that left him completely incapacitated. Lenin's will was kept secret until May 1924, when it was read to the Communist Party Central Committee. Stalin appeared doomed but was saved by Zinoviev, who convinced the Central Committee not to release the will publicly. Stalin repaid Zinoviev by moving against him three years later, expelling him from the Politburo, and eventually executing him in 1936.

Socialism in One Country

The one idea that Stalin did contribute to Marxist thought was the notion that a socialist state could be achieved in one country without a worldwide Marxist revolution. Marx himself was quite clear on this issue. He insisted that no individual working class uprising could be successful unless it occurred during a universal revolution that cut across all national boundaries. Otherwise, Marx argued, bourgeois governments from surrounding countries would intervene to protect the capitalist system.

Of course, according to Marx's original theories, Russia should never have experienced a proletarian revolution in the first place. In 1917, Russia was still primarily an agrarian country, had very limited industrial development, and its working class was far too small. Just as Marx was wrong in predicting where a communist revolution would first occur, he was also wrong in arguing that such an isolated revolution was doomed to quick failure.

Stalin presented his theory of "socialism in one country" in a work titled *Problems of Leninism*, published in the fall of 1924. His primary goal was to undermine Trotsky, who advocated a theory of "permanent revolution" and argued that the Bolshevik movement could not stop at achieving victory in Russia, but had to export communism throughout the industrialized world. In *Problems of Leninism*, Stalin argued the opposite.

The most important goal of the Russian Communist Party, Stalin maintained, was to build up socialism in Russia, and that this was possible despite the hostility of the Soviet Union's foreign enemies. Stalin did not abandon the idea of encouraging revolutionary movements in other countries, but he insisted that the best way to do so was building socialism in the Soviet Union first.

Voices

"The principle task of socialism—the organization of socialist production—has still to be fulfilled. Can this task be fulfilled, can the final victory of socialism be achieved in one country without the joint efforts of the proletarians in several advanced countries? No, it cannot."

A few months later Stalin reversed himself, withdrew the pamphlet and argued that "socialism in one country" was possible. In his *Problems of Leninism*, Stalin described Trotsky's theories as a betrayal of Lenin. He added: "… the victory of socialism in one country …is quite possible and probable … Lack of faith in the strength and capacities of our revolution, lack of faith in the strength and capacity of the Russian proletariat— that is what lies at the root of the theory of 'permanent revolution.'"

—Stalin, *Foundations of Leninism*, 1924

Stalin's argument for socialism in one country was not exactly an example of theoretical brilliance. As a writer, he paled in comparison to Lenin, or Trotsky for that matter. Stalin's work is full of internal inconsistencies; only a few months previously he himself had argued that the socialism in one country was not possible. But Stalin's message was an attractive one for rank-and-file members of the Communist Party. He accused Trotsky and other opponents of being "panic mongers" who refused to believe in the "creative force" of the Russian Revolution.

The ideological debate over the concept of *socialism in one country* provided a stage for the more personal conflict between Stalin and Trotsky. Their theoretical differences were played out in articles they wrote for Party newspapers and speeches they gave during Party meetings, but the real issue at stake was deciding who was going to lead the Party, and through the Party, the whole Soviet Union.

Expelling Trotsky

At the annual Communist Party conference in 1925, Stalin won the first round when the Party voted to endorse his plan to focus on developing socialism in the Soviet Union rather than exporting worldwide revolution. With the help of his allies Zinoviev and Kamenev, Stalin was able to begin stripping Trotsky of power and, in 1926, he expelled Trotsky from the Politburo.

Notes on the Left

The fight between Stalin and Trotsky between 1922 and 1929 was more than a simple power struggle. At its heart was an ideological debate over the future of the socialism in the Soviet Union. Trotsky remained convinced that the Bolshevik regime was doomed unless its neighbors experienced their own working class revolutions. And he despaired over the way that the Russian Communist Party had been taken over by bureaucrats loyal to Stalin. After he was exiled from the Soviet Union, Trotsky tried to build an anti-Stalinist revolutionary movement known as the Fourth International, but he never had much success. He eventually fled to Mexico, where he was assassinated in 1940 by a Soviet agent.

However, Stalin was not about to let himself become dependent on support from any one source. As soon as he eliminated Trotsky as a potential threat, he found new allies and immediately turned on Zinoviev and Kamenev. Stalin's new supporters came from the right wing of the Communist Party that pushed to continue Lenin's policy of economic liberalization, the New Economic Policy (NEP). They included Alexei Rykov, Nikolai Bukharin, and Mikhael Tomsky, all of whom accepted Stalin's arguments about the need to focus on building up socialism in Russia and who also believed that moving cautiously toward implementation of a fully socialist economy is the best way to achieve this.

Vignettes

Stalin took many steps to eliminate Trotsky and his supporters from their positions within the Communist Party. In 1925, he arranged to have Trotsky removed as head of the Red Army and replaced by Mikhael Frunze, a supporter of Zinoviev. However, Frunze became seriously ill, and his doctors disagreed over whether an operation might save him. The Politburo intervened and ordered Frunze to undergo surgery. Frunze agreed, but died on the operating table. Stalin then arranged to have one of his supporters named the new head of the Red Army. Trotsky later accused Stalin of having orchestrated the whole episode by convincing Frunze's doctors to insist on the operation.

Although they had supported Stalin in his fight with Trotsky, Zinoviev and Kamenev had great doubts about continuing the NEP. The NEP restricted communist control to the "commanding heights" of the economy, such as heavy industry and transportation. Other sectors, including agriculture, were allowed to operate in a more or less free market. This was not communism, but a limited form of state socialism, and Zinoviev and Kamenev pushed for a more aggressive creation of a full socialist economy.

Even though he fled into exile, Trotsky was not able to escape from Stalin. In 1940 he was assassinated—his body shown here—by a Soviet agent.

(Wide World Photo)

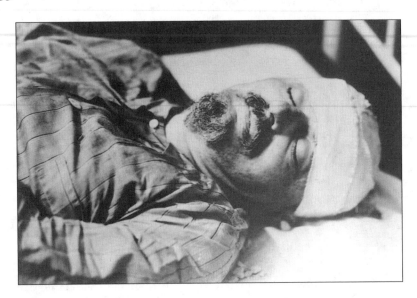

Zinoviev and Kamenev Out

However, Zinoviev and Kamenev found themselves isolated by Stalin's maneuvers. Their only potential supporter was Trotsky, whom they had just helped to get fired from his influential posts within the Party. In the spring of 1926, Zinoviev, Kamenev, and Trotsky attempted to form a united front against Stalin, warning that the communist state had been highjacked by a bureaucracy that threatened to undermine its revolutionary goals. By then, it was far too late. An overwhelming majority of 95 percent of the Communist Party membership voted to support Stalin against the "leftist deviants." In 1927, Stalin expelled Zinoviev, Kamenev, and Trotsky, first from the Communist Party Central Committee and then from the Party itself, which left him as the undisputed leader of the Soviet Union.

The Great Leap Forward

In 1928, only a few months after his victory against the "leftist deviation" of Trotsky, Kamenev, and Zinoviev, Stalin executed a remarkable 180-degree turn in his policies. He announced that the NEP had achieved its aim of stabilizing the Soviet economy, and the time was now ripe for what he referred to as a "Second Revolution."

The Second Revolution represented nothing less than a massive effort to convert the Soviet Union into a fully socialist state. Over the next decade, the NEP reforms were completely repudiated. The communist government assumed complete control over all aspects of the economy, launched a massive effort of industrial development, and embarked on a radical transformation of the country's agriculture through *collectivization* of peasant farms.

Ironically, Stalin used many of the same arguments against the NEP that had been voiced by Trotsky, Zinoviev, and Kamenev earlier. He maintained that the NEP, while necessary for rebuilding the Soviet economy after years or revolution and civil war, represented a retreat from the socialist path. He also argued that it had created a new class of petty bourgeois businessmen and allowed some peasant farmers to become rich at the expense of their poorer neighbors. These were precisely the complaints that had been raised by the "leftist deviants," and in presenting them Stalin put himself in conflict with his erstwhile right-wing supporters within the Communist Party, like Bukharin, Tomsky, and Rykov.

Red Words

The Soviet policy of **collectivization** called for land owned by individual peasants to be combined into a larger cooperative farm, known as a Kholkhoz. The aim was to increase agricultural production through economies of scale and use of mechanization. Many peasants resisted this process but, by the end of the 1930s, almost all agricultural land in the Soviet Union had been collectivized.

When viewed as an ideologue (or man motivated by a set of ideas), Stalin's actions made little sense. But many Western historians and observers were more cynical. They saw Stalin's apparent ideological about-face as a way of eliminating critics, first on his "left," with Zinoviev and Kamenev, and then on his "right." If his policy shifts were interpreted as tools of power-grabbing rather than a set of motivating ideas, his switch-around made good sense.

Voices

In a speech given to a special Communist Party meeting in early 1929, Stalin warned about the threat posed by his former right-wing allies who opposed his economic reforms:

Comrades, sad though it is, we have to record the fact that within our Party a separate Bukharin group has been formed, consisting of Bukharin, Tomsky and Rykov. The Party knew nothing of the existence of this group before …. Bukharin's group is a group of right deviators who advocate not the elimination, but the free development of capitalist elements in town and country.

In characteristic fashion, Stalin's first step was to isolate those he now identified as being "rightist deviants." In late 1928, he began removing other possible opponents from their Communist Party posts. Bukharin, Tomsky, and Rykov were fired from their government positions and then expelled from the Communist Party Politburo. By 1930, all remaining members of the Politburo were devoted followers of Stalin, and all leading government officials owed their positions to his support.

The Five-Year Plan

In April 1929, the Communist Party annual congress adopted Stalin's proposed Five-Year Plan for development of Soviet industry. The plan's goals were nothing short of stunning. Although it had taken 10 years for the Soviet Union to rebuild its economy back to where it had been before the revolution, Stalin announced that industrial output would increase by 250 percent. Agricultural production was to increase by 150 percent, with 20 percent of private peasant farms to be collectivized. Massive development projects were to be launched around the country, in an effort to increase electric power production by 400 percent.

> ### Notes on the Left
>
> In order to achieve the goals laid out in the Five-Year Plan, the communist regime had to assume direct control over all economic decisions. A central planning agency, known as Gosplan, determined what was to be produced and how these products were to be distributed. Gosplan also set prices and determined wages for workers. State control extended to every level of the economy, from how many shoelaces were manufactured to where new dams were constructed. These efforts demanded a huge increase in the number of government bureaucrats to monitor economic developments and guide the plan. The administrative framework established during this period would continue to control the Soviet economy until the collapse of the communist regime in the late 1980s.

The first Five-Year Plan achieved only limited success in its industrial goals. Industrial output certainly increased, and in some cases significantly, but it failed to reach the targets set by the plan. In certain key areas, such as iron and steel production, the goals laid out in the first Five-Year Plan were not to be achieved until the middle of the Second World War, almost 15 years later. There were also numerous mistakes, some of them almost laughable had they not also been a tragic waste of resources. Factories were established in places that had no power, while power plants were built in areas that had no factories. The pricing system set by the government could not keep up with changing demands. Some consumer goods became impossible to find, while others had to be stockpiled in warehouses for lack of buyers. It was an economic mess.

However, Stalin became convinced that he could oversee the transformation of the Soviet Union into an industrialized society. In some regards, this was a more important goal than any specific target for industrial production. When some Soviet economists and technicians raised concerns about the workings of the state economic planning system, Stalin dismissed them as being "rightist deviants" who failed to understand the broader importance of the program. In 1930, Stalin declared that he was "dizzy with success" over what the Five-Year Plan had accomplished, and in 1932, he declared (quite untruthfully) that the plan had achieved all its goals one year ahead of schedule. He also announced the adoption of a Second Five-Year Plan, to guide economic developments through 1937.

Voices

Stalin's emphasis on industrial development was clearly driven as much by nationalist concerns as Marxist ideology. In a famous speech given to Soviet managers in 1931, he said: "... the pace [of industrial development] must not be slackened. On the contrary, we must quicken it as much as is within our powers and possibilities .... To slacken the pace would mean to lag behind; and those who lag behind are beaten. We do not want to be beaten .... We are fifty or a hundred years behind the advanced countries. We must make good this lag in ten years. Either we do it or they will crush us."

Agricultural Collectivization

The agricultural goals of the first Five-Year Plan launched in 1928 were even more ambitious than those for industry. By the late 1920s, Soviet agriculture had largely returned to the levels it had reached before the First World War. However, many communist leaders were troubled by the rise of more prosperous middle-class peasants, known as *Kulaks*, who had taken advantage of the NEP reforms to expand their land holdings. Moreover, in the period from 1928 to 1929, the Soviet Union experienced a series of crop failures, which precipitated a grain crisis, as many peasant farmers began hoarding their harvest. Stalin's solution was a complete overhaul of the agricultural sector to encourage collectivization and eliminate the Kulaks as a class.

The collective farms established during the first five-year plan consisted of large plots of land, worked by groups of around 75 families. A family was allowed a small individual plot and could keep a few animals for its own use, but the bulk of the land and livestock was owned by the collective as a whole. Every member had to spend between 100 and 150 days per year working for the collective, and discipline was strictly enforced through fines and other punishments. All agricultural surpluses had to be handed over to the state, and any earnings were divided among the collective as a whole.

Collectivization of Soviet agriculture was achieved through a combination of force and inducement. Some poorer peasants were attracted by the possibility of getting access to government-provided tractors and other forms of technical assistance. However, many peasants resisted the program since it called for them to give up control of their land.

In theory, the decision to join the collective was supposed to be voluntary, but government officials in the countryside often had to resort to violence in order to impose collectivization on an unenthusiastic population. In 1930, the Soviet government also enacted laws allowing it to confiscate property owned by Kulaks, who were officially barred from joining collectives.

The result of collectivization was complete chaos in the countryside. By 1932, more than 75 percent of all arable land in the Soviet Union had been collectivized. The price in human terms was enormous. Between eight and ten million people were exiled to outlying parts of the Soviet Union, especially Siberia. Millions of other peasants died in a famine that gripped the Soviet Union from 1932 through 1933.

The Soviet government claimed all peasants were as enthusiastic about collectivization as the ones shown in this propaganda photo. The banner reads "Marching toward the fields. The Kulaks will be liquidated as a class."

(Wide World Photo)

Peasants forced to join collective farms reacted by destroying their machinery and livestock. Between 1929 and 1933, half of all horses and cattle in the Soviet Union, and more than two thirds of sheep and goats, were slaughtered. Agricultural production did not recover until well after the Second World War.

Notes on the Left _____

It is impossible to say for sure what was the human toll for the Soviet Union's collectivization program. Under Stalin's orders, government officials deliberately exacerbated the effects of the famine in 1932–1933 to destroy the Kulaks and encourage collectivization. Stalin himself admitted that as many as 10,000,000 (ten million) peasants may have died during this period, and that was one figure that Stalin was unlikely to exaggerate. Millions more were displaced from their homes and moved to other parts of the Soviet Union.

The Purges

The economic and social chaos which followed Stalin's Great Leap Forward left him in a vulnerable position. Many Communist Party members were dismayed at what had occurred during collectivization. As one communist military officer reported to a foreign journalist, "I worked in the underground against the Tsar and then I fought in the Civil war. Did I do all that in order that I should now surround villages with machine guns and order my men to fire indiscriminately into crowds of peasants?"

Vignettes
Stalin was enormously secretive about his private life, and especially about his family. He married twice, although little is known about his first wife who died only a few years after their marriage. He married his second wife, Nadezhda Alliluyeva, in 1919. She committed suicide in 1932, apparently after fighting with Stalin over his collectivization policies. His daughter, Svetlana Alliluyeva, defected to the United States in 1967.

In characteristic fashion, Stalin reacted to the critics of collectivization by launching a *purge* to eliminate all potential opposition from within the Communist Party. In truth, he faced little real threat. In 1929, he successfully convinced the Central Committee to order Trotsky expelled from the country. Former opponents, like Zinoviev, Kamenev, and Bukharin, recanted their views and were allowed back into the Party, although in minor positions and with little influence.

In December 1934, one of Stalin's closest supporters, Sergei Kirov, was assassinated in Leningrad. The murderer was a former associate of Zinoviev, although there is some evidence that Stalin himself might have ordered the killing. Stalin officially responded by announcing that his old enemies were planning to move against him. Thousands of former supporters of Trotsky and Zinoviev were arrested and deported to the *gulag* system in Siberia. Thousands more simply disappeared at the hands of the Soviet secret police.

> **Red Words** _____
>
> A **gulag** was a Soviet forced labor camp, in which prisoners were made to work on development projects such as road building, mining, or timber production. Conditions were so rough that literally millions of prisoners died in the camps. Originally established under the Tsarist regime, the gulag system was greatly expanded during the Soviet era and played an important role in industrializing parts of Siberia and other outlying regions of the Soviet Union. Because they were scattered about the map, a later Soviet dissident, Aleksandr Solzhenitzin, titled his exposé of the camps, *The Gulag Archipelago*.

In 1936, 16 prominent members of the Bolshevik old guard were put on trial, including Zinoviev and Kamenev. They all confessed to a variety of crimes and were convicted and executed. In the following year, another round of *show trials* eliminated more leading communist officials.

> **Red Words** _____
>
> During Stalin's purges of the Communist Party to eliminate opponents, a common practice was to hold a **show trial**. After a suspect was interrogated, usually with tortures such as sleep deprivation and beatings, he would be placed on public trial, often filmed. At the trials, the accused usually made abject confessions of their "errors," before being sentenced to death or long terms in prison camps. The show trials stunned communist sympathizers outside the Soviet Union, causing many to drop any affiliation with the Party.

Stalin also instigated a purge of the Red Army in which most of the general staff and almost half of the entire officer corps were killed. Finally, in 1938, Stalin's former enemies on the right, including Bukharin and Rykov, were also put on trial and sentenced to death.

By the time the purges ended, all of the Bolshevik old guard had been eliminated, along with almost 70 percent of the Communist Party Central Committee and thousands of other party members. According to later reports, more than 3.5 million people had been arrested and convicted of "counterrevolutionary activity" during this period, and almost 800,000 had been executed.

The purges had a catastrophic effect on the Communist Party, both within and outside the Soviet Union. The Party itself lost almost a million members. The destruction of most of its leadership left the country weakened and ill-prepared for the new challenges it faced from abroad. This was especially true in the case of the Red Army staff, as Stalin was to discover when Nazi Germany invaded the Soviet Union only a few years later. From Stalin's point of view, however, the purges and show trials had the positive effect of completely suppressing any potential opponents.

The purges and show trials convinced many foreign observers that Stalin had gone insane. Those who had supported the Bolshevik Revolution and admired Stalin's efforts to industrialize the country now concluded that Stalin was little more than a petty dictator who had perverted the communist movement for his own ends. They may have been right, except that his dictatorship was hardly "petty."

The Least You Need to Know

- Stalin was a ruthless politician who came to power by outmaneuvering his enemies, playing them off against each other, and then having them executed.
- Stalin was primarily interested in making the Soviet Union a powerful, modern state and advocated a policy of "socialism in one country."
- Under Stalin's leadership, the Soviet Union embarked on an intensive period of industrial expansion.
- During the period from 1928 to 1939, the Soviet Union transformed its agricultural sector by forcing peasant farmers to form collective farms, at an enormous human sacrifice of at least 10 million deaths.
- Stalin was so paranoid about threats from within the Communist Party that he purged hundreds of thousands of Party members during the 1930s.

Part  3

Making Friends and Enemies

Conservative politicians who claimed that the communists sought to dominate the world were just blowing smoke, right? Wrong again. One of the first achievements of the communists in Russia after the Bolshevik Revolution was to set up the Communist International, or "Comintern," and to get dedicated and loyal communist parties in other countries to go along with policies set in Moscow. It wasn't easy. Getting radicals in the United States, Britain, and the rest of the world to accept Moscow's rules was like herding cats.

Here we look closely at the communist parties in Britain and the United States during the 1920s and 1930s. We also look at how the communists in those and other countries fought against the Nazis and fascists in the Spanish Civil War (1936–1939). We wind up this part following the Soviet Union and the Communist Party through World War II.

The Communist Party in the U.S. and Britain in the 1920s

In This Chapter

◆ Communism outside of Russia in the 1920s

◆ Formation of the Communist Party in the United States

◆ British revelations of Comintern activity

◆ Recognition of the Soviet government

In this chapter we look at how the formation of the Third International, the Comintern, affected socialist groups outside of Russia. In particular, we examine the formation of communist parties in the United States. Stalin's victory over Leon Trotsky in the late 1920s, among other factors, gave focus to factionalism and splits in the overseas communist parties.

Meanwhile, the governments of the Western democracies, particularly Britain and the United States, were divided over the issue of whether to extend diplomatic recognition to the Soviet Union. On the one hand, the Soviets had established control over almost all of the old Tsarist empire and that reality was hard to ignore. On the other hand, the Soviet Union's commitment to world revolution and the destruction of capitalism made it difficult to recognize its government as a friendly nation among nations.

In this chapter we see how revelations of Moscow's funding agitation and propaganda in Britain and the British Empire delayed formal diplomatic recognition of the USSR. However, Lenin's New Economic Policy of cooperation with capitalism, and then Stalin's emphasis on " socialism in one country," made Russia a little more tolerable to the men in pin-striped suits in London and Washington. The apparent renunciation of world revolution as a doctrine and the expulsion of Trotsky also made Russia seem somewhat less threatening (see Chapter 7, "Lenin and the Communist Regime").

Birth Pangs of the CPUSA

In the spring of 1919, the Socialist Party in the United States already had severe splits within it. The issue of how to state the opposition to American participation in World War I had shown the division between moderates and radicals (see Chapter 5, "Socialist Parties"). The left wing of the socialists sought to steer their party toward supporting the Bolshevik cause, responding to the January 1919 invitation from Lenin to join in the forming of the Third International. Lenin invited 39 groups around the world to send delegates, including 4 in the United States: the IWW, the Socialist Labor Party (SLP), the SLP labor affiliate (called the Socialist Trades and Labor Alliance), and the left wing of the Socialist Party.

SP Splits over Third International

There were a lot of American socialists ready to side with the Bolsheviks in 1919, and for a while it appeared they could simply convert the SP into an American version of the Bolshevik Party. The Eastern European language federations and many radical socialists supported a Left Wing Council, and a party referendum to join the Comintern passed by a heavy vote, about ten to one. Even so, in May, the SP moderates who were in control of the party, expelled the pro-Bolshevik language federations, whole organizations in three states, and about two-thirds of the total party membership.

The expelled groups tried to organize a new, American Communist Party, but they faced further squabbling and break-ups. The expelled Michigan Socialist Party took the lead in calling for a national convention. In June 1919, the most radical socialist leaders, now expelled from their party, spoke at an organizing convention. Present were John Reed, the Harvard-educated journalist, as well as Benjamin Gitlow, Charles Ruthenberg, and James P. Cannon. This convention itself divided.

Reed and the other leaders argued for one more effort to take over the Socialist Party, but the Russian language federation walked out. They, and the other radical language federations, held out for an immediate formation of a new party. Those left in the meeting called for one last effort to take over the SP in August, and if that failed, to work toward a new Communist Party.

But even before the August meeting of the SP, the Michigan State socialists and the language federations went ahead with scheduling a formation convention for a communist party. Over the summer, they attracted some support from other socialists, but John Reed and Benjamin Gitlow continued to hold out and try to take over the SP rather than form a new party first.

Reed and Gitlow planned to take over the U.S. Socialist Party at its August meeting in the Chicago Machinists' Hall, by having supporters of their position pack the convention hall early. They discussed their plans in a Chicago barroom. Leaning over the bar, the bartender listened intently. He was a friend of the moderate SP members' leader, Adolph Germer, who was also the executive secretary of the Socialist Party. The bartender warned Germer of the Reed-Gitlow plot. Germer was ready for them and arrived at the Machinists' Hall even earlier. He had no compunctions about calling in the "capitalist police" to throw out the Reed-Gitlow supporters. The coup failed.

The day after the SP convention, Reed, Gitlow, and their supporters joined with other expelled socialists to form the Communist Labor Party (CLP). The 82 delegates were chaired by Alfred Wagecknecht, editor of *The Ohio Socialist*. The CLP named John Reed as an international delegate, and swore allegiance to the Comintern. However, some of the CLP's platform sounded more like the syndicalism of the IWW than the emerging Marxist-Leninist doctrine from Moscow.

Meanwhile, the foreign language federations that had been expelled from the Socialist Party planned their own convention in order to form another party.

Communist Party Factions

As soon as the language federations and others expelled from the Socialist Party met to form the American Communist Party (ACP), on September 1, they revealed three definable factions, or blocs. They appeared to divide as follows. One group of about 55 represented the language federations. A second, English-speaking group of 31, led by Louis Fraina, represented the Left Wing Council. The Michigan State Socialist Party represented the third faction with 20 delegates. They disagreed on the question of tactics in joining with the Communist Labor Party, that had been formed on August 31, but finally compromised on trying to negotiate a merger with that group. That plan did not work out.

The three factions also disagreed over what the manifesto of the ACP should say. The Michigan delegates wanted to indicate that the transition to socialism would take a while, but the manifesto ended up taking a far more radical tone.

The next summer, the whole Michigan party dropped out of the ACP and formed its own group, the Proletarian Party, that lingered on in isolation from other radical groups for years. The ACP remained based in its uncomfortable alliance of the foreign language federations that had been expelled from the SP and the Left Wing Council of radical expelled socialists.

" " **Voices**

"The world is on the verge of a new era. Europe is in revolt. The masses of Asia are stirring uneasily. Capitalism is in collapse. The workers of the world are seeing a new life and securing new courage. Out of the night of war is coming a new day .... Communism does not propose to capture the bourgeois parliamentary state, but to conquer and destroy it."

—The CPA manifesto, September 1919

With its strong reliance on the foreign language federations, the ACP differed from the CLP (headed by John Reed) by stressing its acceptance of immigrant strength. The ACP began a publication in English, *The Communist*, edited by Louis Fraina. Another leader was Charles Ruthenberg, son of German immigrants. Born in 1882 in Ohio, he had worked in various white-collar jobs. He had been jailed for anti-war activities as a socialist and headed the left wing of the Ohio SP.

Notes on the Left

The small group of the Proletarian Party, formed out of the Michigan State branch of the Socialist Party, never had more than 500 members, but eventually built locals in more than 30 cities, including San Francisco, Chicago, Detroit, and Rochester. Although the Proletarian Party endorsed the Comintern and its policies for some years, it remained fiercely independent. Other communists accused the Proletarian Party of "Menshevism," by which they apparently meant a willingness to accept bourgeois democracy for a while longer. Headed by John Keracher, the PP eventually petered out in the 1970s, after his death.

Small and Large Parties

All of the radical parties in the United States tended to exaggerate their strength. Trying to reconstruct the actual strength of the various factions in the formative period of turmoil is really hard to do. However, one solid estimate gives the following figures for late 1919:

Party	Membership
Communist Party of America made up of the following groups:	24,000
Russian Federation	7,000
Lithuanian Federation	4,400
Ukrainian Federation	4,000
Yugoslav Federation	2,200

Party	Membership
Polish Federation	1,700
Lettish-speaking	1,200
Yiddish-speaking	1,000
English-speaking	1,100
Miscellaneous	1,300–1,500
Communist Labor Party	10,000
Proletarian Party (formerly Mich. SP)	500–800

The radical parties tried to exaggerate their numbers, in order to impress themselves and each other. At the same time, their political enemies also exaggerated the importance and influence of these various small groups.

The First Red Scare

In the period from 1919 to 1922, there was a *Red Scare* in the United States, sometimes called the "First Red Scare," to distinguish it from the attack on the left in the 1940s and 1950s. Despite the fact that the left had been split over Bolshevism, thus nearly destroying the Socialist Party, and that the splitters were themselves split into smaller and smaller factions, conservatives in the American public and in the government grew worried over the possibility of a communist uprising.

Red Words

A **Red Scare** was an American political phenomenon, in which journalists, government leaders, and aspiring politicians made exaggerated claims that radicals endangered the safety of the American republic. The First Red Scare, in the period from 1919 to 1922, aimed at communists, the IWW, and anarchists. In the period from 1949 to 1959, another Red Scare focused primarily on whether or not communists were loyal to the United States during the Cold War. (See Chapter 16, "Communists in the U.S. Red Scare.")

Several events made such fears seem less like political paranoia and somewhat reasonable to U.S. authorities. Overseas, the victory of Bolshevism in the Russian Empire was consolidating. In 1918, the Bolshevik-leaning wing of the Finnish Social Democratic Party seized power in Finland. Short-lived socialist revolutions took place in Bavaria and Hungary. In Berlin in 1919, a socialist revolutionary group, the Sparticists, seized control and declared a workers' republic. In Ukraine, Georgia, and Latvia, Bolshevik-aligned revolutions seized power.

In the United States, a wave of strikes had a radical side. The Seattle general strike, lasting five days, grew out of a strike of 30,000 shipyard workers, supported by 30,000 more from all the AFL unions in the city. Winnipeg, Canada, also had a general strike in 1919. Boston was wracked by a strike of the city's police force, followed by some looting of stores. In September, 365,000 steel workers went on strike, followed soon after by almost 400,000 coal workers, members of the United Mine Workers.

The leading organizer of the steel strike was William Z. Foster. Foster had been an early member of the Socialist Party before joining the IWW in 1909, when he was active in the Spokane Free Speech fight. A self-taught intellectual, he learned French and German on his own, studied the writings of Marx in the original, and traveled around Europe, where he studied labor strategies. Foster left the IWW in 1911 over the issue of *dual unionism.*

Instead of setting up completely separate unions, Foster decided that the technique, advanced by some European syndicalists, of "boring from within" existing trade unions in order to convert them to radicalism was the best course of action. He established the Syndicalist League of North America in 1912.

Foster had considerable success with his tactic. In 1917, he worked with the Chicago Federation of Labor in a joint organizing drive among meatpacking workers, getting several hundred thousands to join. The AFL then supported Foster in organizing the steel industry. Even though the 1919 steel strike failed, his efforts in getting over 300,000 members into the union impressed the AFL.

In 1919, both the CPA and the CLP denounced Foster and the steel strike because the communist groups believed that workers should not be working for short-term goals within the capitalist system. But changing winds in Moscow would later alter Foster's fortunes.

Red Words

Dual unionism referred to the concept, advanced by the IWW, that workers should organize in revolutionary unions, rather than working through existing trade unions, thus setting up two union structures. William Z. Foster, and some other revolutionary labor leaders, believed in "boring from within," that is, advancing the revolutionary cause from within existing trade and industrial unions.

Such divisions and disagreements among radicals were lost on many on the outside of the movements. To Woodrow Wilson's Attorney General, A. Mitchell Palmer, it appeared that the strikes in Boston, in the steel and coal industries, and the general strike in Seattle were all part of a pattern, suggesting that "boring from within" had succeeded in revolutionizing the American working class.

Palmer Raids

In the fall of 1919, Attorney General Palmer rounded up hundreds of alien radicals. The raids focused on the IWW and various immigrant radicals. On November 7, simultaneous coordinated raids led to the arrest of hundreds of members of the Union of Russian Workers.

Then, on January 2, 1920, federal authorities took into custody some 2,700 suspected members of the Communist Party of America and the Communist Labor Party in 33 cities. The federal government deported those who were aliens and turned U.S. citizens over to the state governments, for prosecution under anti-revolutionary, "criminal syndicalist" laws.

On December 22, 1919, the U.S. transport ship *Buford* took 249 deportees, including Emma Goldman and Alexander Berkman, to Russia. The Labor Department insisted that future deportations be preceded by hearings, and an additional 600 or so radical aliens were deported after the hearing procedure was set up.

Local police supplemented the federal effort. In November 1919, New York police raided dozens of radical groups and arrested several hundred radicals. New York State prosecuted 75 of those arrested, including Charles Ruthenberg and Benjamin Gitlow.

Vigilante groups in the West rounded up IWW sympathizers and members, leading to the notorious lynching of Wesley Everett in Centralia, Washington, on November 11, 1919. However, by the end of 1920, the First Red Scare had spent its energies. Even so, the combined effect of internal factionalism, the Palmer raids, and the state and vigilante actions had weakened support for Bolshevism in the United States. The IWW was crippled and many of the communist leadership became convinced they should operate underground.

CPA and CLP In-Fighting

Gregori Zinoviev, head of the Third International in Moscow, urged that the two rival American communist parties get together under the name of the United Communist Party. Instead, the factionalism got more severe for a while.

The ACP itself split into two organizations in April 1920, with each group claiming the name American Communist Party. Most of the English-speaking members of the ACP joined a small group headed by Ruthenberg and Jay Lovestone. A larger group, headed by leaders from the Russian and the Yiddish federations, was made up almost entirely of non-English speakers. Then, about a month later, in May 1920, the Ruthenberg-Lovestone, English-speaking group of the ACP met with the leadership of the CLP, and following the Zinoviev suggestion, formed a new group called the United Communist Party (UCP). Thus, by May, there were once again two communist parties in the United States, the UCP and the CPA.

Meanwhile, CLP and CPA delegates had gone to Moscow, each seeking the blessing of the Third International. John Reed represented the CLP, while Louis Fraina represented the CPA. Russians, who knew Reed from his days as a favorable reporter on the 1917 revolutions, welcomed him. Fraina found himself tangled up with a secret U.S. government agent who denounced him to the Russians. After a struggle, Lenin personally cleared Fraina of the false charges.

The Comintern insisted that Fraina and Reed represent the American communist movement together and they dutifully cooperated and attended the second meeting of the Comintern, in July and August 1920. The Americans were thrown off guard by the fact that Lenin announced a new doctrine, which sounded like the old moderate wing of the American SP that had them both expelled. Lenin, in *Left-Wing Communism: An Infantile Disorder*, insisted that communist parties should operate within the democratic electoral systems in countries like the United States. He advocated working in elections, giving up revolutionary syndicalism in favor of working with, not against, unions like the AFL. Reed argued against the position.

Vignettes

In February and March 1920, Reed attempted to leave the Soviet Union by way of Finland. The Finnish police, who found him carrying gems and cash, arrested Reed on his way. The exact value remained in dispute, but was estimated by some sources at about $1.5 million. What this money was intended for was also in dispute. Since Reed was intercepted before Zinoviev had ordered the formation of the UCP, perhaps the Comintern hoped he would be able to use the funds to favor the CLP in its fight with the CPA. On the other hand, the money might have been intended for the official Soviet Government Information Bureau in the United States. Since Reed had clashed with Zinoviev over the issue of the role of revolutionary labor, it is even possible that the Comintern betrayed Reed to the Finns, and set him up to be busted. The money was confiscated, and Reed went back to Russia, with his mission, whatever it was, apparently foiled.

John Reed attended a conference in Baku, where he contracted typhus. He died in Moscow in October 1920 and was given a state funeral with a Red Army honor guard. He is buried in the Kremlin Wall with other revolutionary heroes.

The other American delegate to the 1920 Comintern meeting, Louis Fraina, soon dropped out of the Communist Party altogether. He adopted a new name, Lewis Corey, and became a professor of economics at Antioch College in Yellow Springs, Ohio, in the period from 1941 to 1951.

Struggling for Unity

Meanwhile, the Comintern's insistence on unity brought together the UCP and the foreign language groups still in the CPA. At a convention held in Woodstock, New York, in May 1921, the party agreed on the name Communist Party of America (CPA), divided the offices, and adopted the language of the Comintern's policy.

William Z. Foster attended a labor conference in Moscow in July 1921, and found that his concept of "boring from within" had won great support there. Lenin dictated that communists work within the mainstream labor movement, and abandon dual unionism. This meant that the IWW tactic was to be completely scrapped, but that Foster's method was officially endorsed.

Furthermore, Foster had always believed that majority rule in unions was a bad idea. Rather, he thought that the unions should be led by a militant minority. That concept sounded very much like Lenin's concept of a "revolutionary vanguard." After a few months in Moscow, Foster returned to the United States as a dedicated communist, loyal to the Comintern's line of thinking.

In the United States, communists faced the problem of whether to work aboveground as a legitimate party, which is what the Comintern wished. The problem with that approach was that, as revolutionaries, they might be subject to another round of arrests similar to those of the Red Scare in 1919–1920.

The temporary solution was a dual party organization. The American Communist Party continued to operate more or less underground, while a separate Workers Party of America, formed in December 1921, represented the aboveground organization. Having a legal, nonrevolutionary aboveground party allowed growth, with groups from the Finnish-language federation and the Yiddish federation joining.

 Notes on the Left

The first years of the Communist Party in the United States were hectic, and the party went through several reorganizations. Here is the abbreviated scorecard for the 1920s, showing its various names and some of the major leaders:

- Communist Labor Party (John Reed)—1919–1922
- Communist Party of America (Louis Fraina)—1919–1922
- United Communist Party becomes Communist Party of America (underground)—1922
- Workers Party of America (aboveground)—1921–1925
- Communist (Workers) Party (William Z. Foster)—1925–1929
- Communist Party of the United States of America (Earl Browder, William Z. Foster)—1929–1961

Disagreements over whether to operate aboveground or underground continued to divide American communists, and for a while it appeared they would break up into three or four parties over the issue. After continued disputes over aboveground versus underground activity in the period from 1922 to 1923, the aboveground Workers Party became the official, Comintern-recognized party. In 1925, it changed its name to the Workers (Communist) Party of America, and finally, in 1929, to the Communist Party USA, or CPUSA. Henceforth, the CPUSA would be the party officially recognized by the Comintern as the legitimate Communist Party in the United States.

Recognizing the USSR

At the same time that the Comintern worked to establish control over the communist parties in the United States and bring to an end the factionalism that divided the groups, it made similar efforts in other countries. The Comintern developed a party quite loyal to its direction in the Communist Party of Great Britain (CPGB), established in the summer of 1920. The Comintern apparently had high hopes that the strong labor movement in Britain would become a force for revolution in the early 1920s.

The British had established a strong code-breaking capacity during World War I and, by 1920, founded the Government Code & Cipher School (GC&CS). The GC&CS would later play a crucial part in cracking the codes used by the Germans in World War II.

However, in the early 1920s, the GC&CS was able to intercept and decipher a great many secret messages sent by the Comintern to supporters in Britain. Among these were evidence of funding provided by the Soviets to the socialist newspaper, the *Daily Herald*, under the editorship of George Lansbury.

Other messages, referring to the smuggling of jewelry and funds to the CPGB and pro-Bolshevik labor leaders, fed the concerns of conservative members of the intelligence community and the government that the "Red Menace" was growing more and more powerful and real. Evidence from decrypted messages that the Soviets hoped to work through Kabul, Afghanistan, to stimulate a Muslim insurrection in the vast British Empire holdings in Southern Asia (later the independent countries of Pakistan, India, Bangladesh, and Ceylon) further enraged British officials.

However, the British leadership was in a spot. If the evidence of the Soviet funding of activities in Britain were made public, GC&CS's ability to decipher Soviet messages would be compromised. Once the source of the information was known, the Soviets could adopt new, perhaps less easily deciphered codes.

Even so, the Prime Minister Lloyd George leaked to the press decrypted messages which showed that the *Herald* received Soviet aid in 1920. Leaders of the British Trade Union Council worked to oppose Soviet funding of specific labor leaders.

Despite suspicions of the Soviets, when Lenin announced the New Economic Policy, the British signed an Anglo-Soviet trade agreement in March 26, 1921. Even after the agreement, and a mutual pledge not to issue propaganda against each other, the Soviets continued to agitate against British control in India and to provide clandestine funds to pro-Bolshevik groups in Britain.

Members of the intelligence community were stunned when the Fabian socialist and Labour Party leader, James Ramsay MacDonald became Prime Minister on June 22, 1924, in a coalition government supported by the Liberal and Labour parties. Conservative fears seemed to be confirmed when MacDonald signed two further agreements with the Soviets, in early October 1924. The liberals withdrew their support for the MacDonald government, and a new election was scheduled.

Vignettes
On the basis of decrypted messages, the intelligence community carefully watched one CP member of parliament, LeStrange Malone. He was arrested and given a six-month jail term, after giving a speech suggesting that people like Winston Churchill and Lord Curzon, the British Foreign Minister, should be hanged from lampposts.

Over the next few weeks, another revelation stunned the British public, one that was popularly credited for bringing down the first MacDonald administration.

The Zinoviev Letter

In a letter dated September 15, Zinoviev, as head of the Comintern, instructed the CPGB to support ratification of Anglo-Soviet treaty, to intensify agitation and propaganda in the armed forces and prepare for a coming British revolution. The British intelligence services obtained the letter on October 10, 1924.

MacDonald was shown the intercepted Zinoviev Letter on October 16 and prepared a stiff note to the Russian delegation, protesting their duplicity in interfering in domestic British affairs and promoting revolution. On October 24, 1924, a few days before the scheduled British election, the Zinoviev Letter was leaked to the press, probably by one or more members of the intelligence community who hoped to discredit MacDonald.

The Soviets immediately claimed that the letter was a forgery. In fact, there were a number of forgers of Soviet documents, operating in Poland and Paris, who sold such documents to the press, thus trying to discredit the Soviet government. However, experts on the history of British intelligence believe that the published Zinoviev document was genuine. In any case, what it said was quite in line with the Comintern policy.

Despite MacDonald's protest to the Soviets, his government was perceived as "soft on Communism," because of the Zinoviev Letter, and the election went to the conservatives. In 1926, Britain suffered a brief general strike of transport workers and others, and further decrypted letters showed that the Soviets had hoped to make gains among the striking workers and spread resistance to the government and the military.

Vignettes

When the British Trade Union Council heard of the Zinoviev Letter, they were shocked. The Soviets invited a delegation to come to Moscow and look at the files of the Comintern and see that no such letter, or its stated policy of fomenting revolution in Britain, was in the files. When the delegation agreed to come, the Comintern officials spent three days and nights feverishly cleaning up the files, taking out any incriminating evidence.

The British union leaders went through the files and were satisfied. Later, one of the Comintern officials who had sanitized the records, Aino Kuusinen, recalled in his memoirs with some amusement, "After the delegation had left there was general relief and everyone had a good laugh over the fact that they had been able to pull the wool so easily over the Englishmen's eyes."

The Conservative Prime Minister Stanley Baldwin revealed such further Soviet communications in 1927, and broke off relations with the Soviets entirely. These revelations were convincing, and the Soviets did not even try to deny the authenticity of this round of documents. However, the British code-breaking system was fully compromised by the explicit publication of secret Soviet communications, and the Soviets adopted a much more difficult system of sending messages, rarely deciphered by the Bletchley Park code-breakers over the next decade.

In June 1929, MacDonald again became Prime Minister, and four months later, the British formally established full diplomatic recognition of the Soviet Union. By this time, apparently, the Soviet policy of aiding sympathetic communist parties and labor leaders in Britain and the United States had become so well-known that it had lost its shock value.

Diplomatic Recognition

As in the United States, British business interests wanted to keep the lines of communication with the Soviets open, so that the lucrative markets for equipment and machinery under the Soviet Five-Year Plans could be tapped. Furthermore, the expulsion of Leon Trotsky, the official rejection of the doctrine of a world revolution, and the building of "socialism in one country," all made the Soviet Union a little more palatable to both Britain and the United States.

One of the first diplomatic moves of the new Democratic administration of Franklin Roosevelt in the United States in 1933 was to extend recognition to the Soviet Union. Roosevelt was inaugurated in March 1933, and, on May 16, sent a message to the heads of 54 countries, urging military disarmament and a focus on economic recovery from the depression. Among the governments was the Soviet Union. Then, on October 10, Roosevelt asked the Soviet president to send an envoy to the United States. Maxim

Litvinov, Stalin's Commissar for Foreign Affairs, arrived on November 7, and the two countries formally exchanged notes on November 16, 1933.

As in the agreements with Britain, the Soviet Union promised not to interfere in U.S. domestic affairs and to abstain from propaganda. Furthermore, the Soviets promised to extend religious freedom and fair trials to any Americans in the Soviet Union, and to settle mutual debts. In fact, no settlement of the old Tsarist debts was ever made, and the Comintern continued directing the work of the Communist Party of the United States through the next decade.

The Least You Need to Know

- ◆ American socialists divided over whether to support the Bolsheviks.
- ◆ Factions among American pro-Bolshevik socialists prevented formal unification of the Communist Party of the United States until 1925.
- ◆ British code-breakers learned of Soviet funding and support for strikes and anti-government agitation in Britain.
- ◆ The revelation of the Zinoviev Letter, from the Comintern to British communists, brought down the MacDonald government in 1924.
- ◆ Britain officially recognized the Soviet Union in 1929, and the United States did so in 1933.

10

Come to the Party: CPUSA

In This Chapter

- ◆ Communist Party of United States in the 1930s
- ◆ United Front and Popular Front strategies
- ◆ Making enemies and making friends
- ◆ Comintern orders, American realities

In this chapter we see how the Communist Party of the United States (CPUSA) responded to the opportunities for recruitment that developed during the period of the Crash of 1929 and the Great Depression. We look at how the policies established by the Comintern in Moscow shaped the way the CPUSA worked with other groups on the left. The ouster of Trotsky from the Party and other early purges tended to leave the American Communist Party in disarray, and its methods often offended potential allies.

However, during the mid 1930s Moscow began to recognize that the threat of Nazi Germany was so serious that it would be wise to form political alliances not only with parties on the left, but also with the middle-class based reform parties. We see how the American communists responded to this change in strategy and began to win wider support, both aboveground and underground, among various groups in the United States. The methods that the Communist Party adopted, of working through a variety of organizations, some under direct party control, extended its influence quite far beyond its small total number of official members.

Obstacles to CP Growth

The Communist Party of the United States faced great obstacles in trying to win support throughout its history. Of course, in retrospect, it is easy to dismiss the party's efforts as naïve, misguided, and perhaps fundamentally ignorant of American conditions. After all, with the value of hindsight, it is clear that communists never had much of a chance of winning control of the United States, either through the electoral process or through building up a committed revolutionary party that would seize power.

Yet in the 1930s, communists thought they could get control, and so did others, ranging from leaders of the old left such as socialists through liberals and conservatives. Communist leaders really thought they had a chance of gaining power in the United States, and despite being hampered by policies and ideas dictated from Moscow that simply did not fit the American situation, they gained considerable influence and strength in the years 1929–1939.

Notes on the Left

During the early 1930s, the Communist Party of the United States changed its ethnic base. In 1930, the typical American communist was a young white man. Two thirds were foreign-born. The two largest ethnic groups were Finns (mostly in the upper Midwest), and Jews (mostly in New York). In fact, about a third of the party membership was concentrated in New York City. The attempt to recruit among some African Americans and broaden the ethnic base brought some gradual changes over the decade. By 1939, the majority of the party members were American-born.

Several developments in the 1930s made the prospect of taking over the United States seem less like a fantasy and more like a real possibility.

Stock Market Crash

In October 1929, the American stock market suffered a sharp drop in all stock prices, known as the Great Crash. Government and business tools for dealing with the overnight disappearance of paper value were inadequate to stop the sell-off. As a consequence, many investors in the market suffered. In that period, far fewer Americans held stock equity than 70 years later, but the impact of the Crash rippled through the whole economy. As the American capitalist system appeared to come apart at the seams, Marx's predictions seemed pertinent.

The collapse spread with corporate layoffs of workers, bank failures, and thousands of business bankruptcies over the next few years. As unemployment rose, consumer confidence and prices fell, leading in a cycle to further business failures and closures. State and local tax revenues dried up. As farm prices fell, farmers could not meet their mortgages on land and equipment, and foreclosures wiped out thousands of family farms.

Great Depression

The Great Depression reached its depths by 1933–1934, as local relief agencies simply ran out of funds to help the unemployed. Former working class families, now destitute, took to scavenging food from garbage heaps. Thousands of unemployed young men, some who had never held jobs, became hobos, riding railroad freight cars in search of work. The unemployed, outside of any unions, seemed a ripe field for developing a radical following.

The Great Depression struck not only in the United States, but across the industrialized world, throwing millions out of work in Canada, Britain, Germany and France. Within a few years, it seemed, capitalism had demonstrated that it could not survive its own cyclical ups and downs.

Radical alternatives and schemes caught on, winning followings. In Germany, Adolf Hitler was selected as Chancellor of the Weimar Republic in 1933, and quickly began the transformation of that nation to a fascist state. In February 1934, French fascists battled against police in Paris, leaving 15 people dead and 1,600 policemen injured.

Even in the United States, signs of popular discontent looked like potential for revolution.

Political Responses to Crisis

In the United States, Republican President Herbert Hoover, who took office in March 1929, only six months before the Crash, struggled to find a pathway through the economic crisis. Although a progressive republican, and highly experienced in government after serving eight years in the cabinets of presidents Harding and Coolidge, Hoover did not inspire confidence, either in the government or in the general population. His cautious style as a seasoned administrator and engineer, and his concern that reforms not undermine the independence of either business or state governments from federal control, lost him support, making a victory by a democratic candidate in the next election seem almost certain.

In 1932, Franklin Roosevelt, the liberal democratic governor of New York State, was elected president, taking office in March 1933, one month after Hitler took power in Germany. As far as the communists were concerned, both Hoover and Roosevelt represented the tools of the capitalist class.

 Voices

William Z. Foster, writing in the *Daily Worker* about the nomination of Roosevelt, said:

> First of all, let me say that the policy of Mr. Roosevelt's party is identical in all essentials with that of the Republican Party. The platform of the Republican Party could be adopted by the Democratic Party and they could get along very nicely with it. Or the candidate of the Democratic Party could run on the Republican Party ticket; Mr. Hoover could be a member of Mr. Roosevelt's cabinet or vice versa.

Although Roosevelt promised a "New Deal" in his nomination acceptance speech, and although his first three months as president saw many immediate relief measures passed, the Depression continued, and unemployment still deepened.

Among the reforms put in place by the Roosevelt administration was a set of rules stimulating labor organization. Membership in the AFL climbed, and organizers sought to bring the unorganized into expanding unions.

Notes on the Left

Roosevelt's first plan for economic recovery, the National Industrial Recovery Act (NIRA), included a provision, "Section 7a," prohibiting the dismissal of employees for union activity, and outlawing the "yellow dog contract" that required new employees to sign a pledge not to join a union. Although the NIRA was declared unconstitutional in 1935, the principles of Section 7a were incorporated in a new National Labor Relations Act. In this way, the reforms of the New Deal stimulated and protected labor organization, and union membership soared in the United States.

Despite the relief measures, the system set up under the NIRA had little success. By the middle of Roosevelt's first term, a wide variety of leaders advocated deeper reforms.

During the turbulent 1930s, the Communist Party sought, with some success, to gain membership and influence in the American labor movement.

(National Archives)

Communist Strategy in the Early 1930s

Through the early 1930s, the communists in America followed the Comintern line. According to Comintern policy, the world had entered the "Third Period," announced in 1928, during which radical groups, many based on a socialist appeal, would work with discontented members of the working class. These *social fascists* were false prophets, trying to subvert the proletariat's revolutionary energies and turning them to their own purposes.

Red Words

In the period from 1928 to 1934, the Comintern accused European and American socialists, labor leaders, and other popular leaders on the left of being **social fascists.** These groups would falsely promise change, the Comintern argued, with the real purpose of propping up capitalism in its last phases. Fascist regimes, based on popular support, but really designed to preserve capitalism, would emerge. They, in turn, would be easier to overthrow, once the working class recognized that they had been betrayed. Since many radical leaders also hated fascism, they found the communist charge of social fascism both hostile and insulting.

The technique of dealing with social fascists that the Comintern proposed was to penetrate their organizations, and win their followings away from their social fascist leaders to the Communist Party. Officials of the Communist Party used the label social fascist to attack and discredit a wide range of opponents, ranging from Norman Thomas, the leader of the Socialist Party, to liberal intellectuals like John Dewey and Oswald Garrison Villard, and the African American leader of the National Association of Colored People, W.E.B. Du Bois. Some were simply called "fascist," including labor leaders in the AFL.

The policy of criticizing liberals and radical leftists as social fascists was a recipe for disaster, it turned out. Rather than cooperating with socialists against the Nazi Party in Germany, the Communist Party there worked to undermine the stability of the government and to fight the socialists. The Comintern believed, quite wrongly, that once Hitler gained power, the working class would rally around the Communist Party, recognizing Hitler as an oppressive supporter of the old capitalist system. Working class people who had been duped by social fascists, they believed, would now come to join them in a genuine revolution of class against class to overthrow capitalism. As the Nazis in Germany used the power of the government to methodically suppress all political opposition, it gradually became clear to the Comintern that their concept was mistaken.

However, in the period from 1929 to 1934, the Comintern dictated that internationally, communist parties should work inside the other parties and popular groups on the left, forming a *united front from below*.

> **Red Words**
>
> In Comintern language in the early 1930s, a **united front from below** was not what it sounded like, for it was more divisive than unifying. The concept was that Communist Party workers should penetrate other parties, like the socialists, and working class groups, like labor unions, and recruit members and get them to join the Communist Party and accept its leadership and direction.

Splinters and Splits

The Comintern's policies were based on a Moscow perspective on European affairs, however mistaken that interpretation or perspective might be. Since the Comintern took the position that a single strategy was correct everywhere, what dictated the way the CPUSA should operate was the concept of the world's communist parties working through united fronts from below to undermine other parties of the left. In 1929, the American party was purged, and Jay Lovestone, who argued that American conditions dictated the adoption of a unique American approach and strategy, was expelled. Outside the party, he formed his own group of *Lovestoneites*.

With the expulsion of Leon Trotsky from Russia, small groups of revolutionary minded Trotskyites in the United States worked independently to win adherents to a revolutionary path. Meanwhile, Lovestoneites gathered a few adherents. While neither group was particularly large, the Communist Party spent lots of energy denouncing these renegade groups and warning against their doctrines.

Red Words

In 1929, Stalin personally ordered the expulsion of Jay Lovestone from the CPUSA. Lovestone and his followers, the so-called **Lovestoneites,** continued to make up a small Marxist group through the 1930s, active in unions. The Lovestoneites believed in working within the American system. Lovestone and his organizers worked with an anti-communist faction in the United Auto Workers, and another Lovestoneite, Charles Zimmerman, remained active in the International Ladies' Garment Workers Union.

With "left revisionists" following Trotsky out of the Party, and with those advocating a special American pathway to communism, independent of the Comintern and following Lovestone, the CPUSA was torn in two directions. Meanwhile, independent politicians, farm leaders, Marxist radicals, labor leaders and the Socialist Party appeared to be drawing new followers out of the discontents brought by the Great Depression.

With the Party torn by its expulsions, the Central Committee chose, with Moscow approval, a quiet and unassuming former accountant, Earl Browder, to be the secretary by 1932. Browder was born in 1891 in a poor family in Wichita, Kansas. He had worked as an errand boy and bookkeeper, while taking law courses by correspondence. He joined an AFL bookkeepers' union, opposed World War I, served time in prison, and then joined the militant wing of the Socialist Party. He attended a labor conference in Moscow in 1921, and remained a quiet worker in the Communist Party through the 1920s.

Head of the Communist Party of the United States from 1932 to 1946, Earl Browder led the party during its period of greatest strength.

(National Archives)

In 1927, American communist Earl Browder was visiting in Moscow, when he was added at the last minute to a delegation to Hankow, China, to a labor conference hosted by Chiang Kai-shek, at that time regarded as an ally by the Soviet Union. At the Pan-Pacific Trade Union Conference, the delegates arrived to be greeted by a banner proclaiming: "Welcome to the Earl of Browder." The Chinese hosts apparently assumed Browder was an English nobleman.

At first, many viewed Browder as an interim leader, but he brought some financial management to the Party's affairs and, perhaps influenced by Stalin's example, carefully promoted followers and demoted or expelled opponents among the party *cadres*.

Red Words

In the Communist Party, **cadres** were paid party workers. While the major parties had very small paid staffs, the Communist Party employed scores of people on small salaries and paid their expenses. Responsible to the Party's Central Committee, they could be fired, reassigned, or promoted at the discretion of the leadership. Through the cadres, the party could place paid organizers to work within unions or to establish separate labor unions, to organize political parties in particular cities or states, or to work in jobs usually held by volunteers in other organizations and clubs.

Although building a power base, and even a small cult of personality in the CPUSA, Browder was careful to adhere precisely to the party line established by the Comintern.

American Ferment

During the period when the Comintern dictated that world communist parties should undermine other groups on the left that they accused of social fascism, a wide variety of protests developed in the United States against the government. Late in Herbert Hoover's administration, a spontaneous movement of unemployed World War I veterans worked up a march on Washington, asking that a "bonus" on veterans' benefits be paid in cash immediately. These bonus marchers, the communists said, were social fascists.

As Roosevelt's reforms stimulated labor union growth, a wave of strikes swept the country. The Communist Party accused all the AFL leaders of being social fascists, especially those most prominently engaged in winning support, like John L. Lewis of the United Mine Workers.

Vignettes

In June 1932, some 20,000 veterans of World War I converged on Washington, demanding cash payment of a veterans' benefit bonus. Although some Communist Party members had helped start the idea, the movement was spontaneous and the Party could not keep control of the group. When some marchers occupied empty federal buildings, President Hoover had the military clear out the bonus encampments. General Douglas MacArthur led a small contingent that burned a shantytown the marchers had built on the Anacostia River.

Upton Sinclair

In 1934, in California, the Democratic Party nomination for the governorship was won by Upton Sinclair, a long-time socialist. Years before, his novel *The Jungle* had exposed conditions in meat-packing plants and contributed to the passage of the Pure Food and Drug Act of 1906. Sinclair had written a novel, *I, Governor of California*, published in 1934, predicting what he would do if elected. The novel and his platform as an actual candidate proposed a scheme called "End Poverty in California," or EPIC. Under EPIC, the state would foreclose idle industries, farms and ranches for back taxes, and then operate those enterprises, hiring the unemployed, who would receive credits to purchase items produced in other enterprises. In effect, a state-socialized economy would grow up alongside the existing capitalist economy.

In California, the local leadership of the Communist Party sought to work with Sinclair to help him get elected. Soon, however, the word came from the Comintern, and from the headquarters of the national Communist Party, that EPIC was another form of social fascism, and that Sinclair should get no support.

Meanwhile, conservative forces, represented particularly by the movie industry and five large-circulation newspapers owned by William Randolph Hearst, rallied to support the republican candidate. Sinclair was defeated.

Farm Holiday

Other popular movements received a similar cold shoulder from the Communist Party in the early 1930s. Over and over, fairly large movements began that attracted discontented groups, each treated as social fascists by the CPUSA.

In the Midwest, the Farm Holiday Association represented farmers hurting from drought, low commodity prices, and bank foreclosures. The basic plan advocated by Milo Reno, the leader of the Association, was to withhold products from market to drive up prices. More radical followers sometimes interfered with noncooperating farmers by stopping their trucks by force and destroying shipments.

Other farmers took up the practice of "penny auctions." Under this method, when a farm was being sold by a bank for nonpayment of mortgage, an intimidating group of farmers would bid a few cents for the farm, take title, and then turn the property back to the original farmer.

The communists tried to establish their own organizations among farmers, the Farmers National Relief Committee and the United Farmers League. But as communist leaders of these organizations were arrested one by one in various small protest actions, the two organizations had little success in winning converts. When the communist-led groups finally offered to work with the Farm Holiday Association, that organization was already in decline. Milo Reno refused their offer. According to reliable later estimates, of 6 million American farmers, about 1,200 became communists.

While other popular leaders attracted followings in the early 1930s, Browder made sure that the Communist Party continued to treat all such groups independent of the Party as social fascists or leftist deviationists.

Muste and Musteites

Leaders on the Marxist left who remained independent of the Communist Party received particular censure in Communist Party publications. One was Abraham Johannes Muste, known as A.J. Muste. Born in the Netherlands in 1885, he immigrated to the United States as a child with his parents. Brought up in a strictly religious home in Michigan, he trained for the ministry in the Dutch Reformed Church at Union Theological Seminary in New York. There he met a number of radical thinkers, including Norman Thomas.

Muste first attracted national attention in 1919, when he led a textile strike in Lawrence, Massachusetts, which lasted for 16 weeks. Unlike the IWW, who had trouble sustaining a group after a strike, Muste set up the independent Amalgamated Textile Workers of America and remained active in trying to unite small labor locals in textile factories in New England through the 1920s. He established Brookwood Labor College in Katonah, New York, and soon became an influential national figure in the labor movement in the 1920s. However, his criticisms of AFL leadership led him to organize a Conference for Progressive Labor Action. Refusing to join the Communist Party but following his own radical ideas, he established the American Workers Party.

The growth of Muste's following in the early 1930s angered Browder and the Communist Party. "Musteism" was another form of social fascism, they claimed. The American Workers Party (AWP), which remained on the scene from 1933 through 1935, claimed to be more radical than the socialists and more practical than the communists. Organizing among the unemployed, and successfully leading a strike against the Auto-Lite factory in Detroit in 1934, Muste's group appeared on the road to success. The AWP briefly merged with American Trotskyites and formed the Workers Party of America, but later Muste and many of his followers drifted out of that organization.

The CP Organizations

The Communist Party's influence, even though it was quite small during the early 1930s, spread far beyond its membership. Through a number of affiliated organizations, party cadres operated newspapers and magazines, held leadership positions in a few unions, and operated the John Reed Clubs as organizations of intellectuals.

International Labor Defense Fund

International Labor Defense Fund attracted national attention, as it raised money to defend nine black youths accused of raping two white girls. The Party, through its identification with the Scottsboro Boys, won some support among African Americans and white liberals concerned with minority civil rights.

Vignettes
The "Scottsboro Boys" were nine young black men accused of raping two white girls in a freight train near Paint Rock, Alabama. Arrested on March 25, 1931, they were tried without adequate legal counsel, and all but one sentenced to death. The communist-operated International Legal Defense (ILD) raised funds and engaged in a vicious battle against the National Association for the Advancement of Colored People (NAACP) for control of the appeal case.
The ILD hired a renowned criminal lawyer, Samuel Leibowitz, who eventually split with the ILD to form his own organization and rally support for the defendants. Eventually, the several rival defense groups began to work together and a compromise court decision resulted in the release of four defendants, while the other five served lengthy sentences.

Some of the party organizations were nominally independent, while others were well known as *front organizations*, continually and explicitly controlled by party cadres.

Red Words

In the United States, the Communist Party worked through numerous affiliated organizations, usually controlled by a few loyal cadres. Opponents on the left, and others familiar with the tactic, called these affiliated groups communist fronts or **front organizations.** The fronts ranged from small labor union locals or groups of locals, to special interest farmer, political advocacy, youth, and ethnic groups.

League Against War and Fascism

The most successful of the front organizations was the League Against War and Fascism, that was able to recruit thousands of members, many of them pacifists who had little in common with the Communist Party, although the League continued to be run by the Party. The League had its beginnings in a 1932 World Congress against Imperialist War, which was held in Amsterdam. Henri Barbusse, a noted French communist, chaired the Congress. About 2,000 people attended, with only about 830 of them announced communists. When delegates from the Congress returned to the United States to build an American Committee for Struggle Against War, both communists and socialists signed up.

However, when socialists insisted that non-communist groups be represented on the central arrangements committee for new meetings, they were disappointed. Of 52 organizations represented in the American League, 34 organizations were those controlled by communists. The socialists walked out in disgust.

When the dust settled, the American League Against War and Fascism, later called the American League for Peace and Democracy, represented a spectrum of organizations controlled by the Communist Party. Through its member organizations, the League claimed to represent several million members, but only about 9,000 unaffiliated individuals were members of the League alone. Since many of the membership lists of participating front groups overlapped, it was difficult to determine the actual total membership, but the Party control of the League represented the Party's greatest American triumph using the method of front organization.

Publications and Clubs

In the 1930s, the best-known American communist publications were the newspaper, the *Daily Worker* and the weekly news and opinion magazine, the *New Masses*. Both developed fairly large circulations during the 1930s.

The *Daily Worker* was started in Chicago in 1924, with funds raised from the communist-led language federation groups. Control of the paper was an indication of the shifting control of the Party itself during the factional struggles of the 1920s. In 1927, the paper relocated to New York and began a transition from a narrow party organ to a newspaper with a broader appeal to labor. With the infusion of some professional journalists, the paper gradually became more like a commercial newspaper.

Earl Browder installed one of his followers, Clarence Hathaway, as editor of the *Daily Worker*. Hathaway added comic strips and a sports page, and the paper's political cartoons soon became vibrant examples of that art form.

Some of its writers, like the black author Richard Wright and songwriter Woody Guthrie, later gained national fame far beyond the Communist Party. Daily circulation ran about

25,000 to 30,000, with an occasional weekend edition selling about 60,000. The paper remained a relatively faithful party organ until the mid 1950s, finally closing in 1957.

The *New Masses* began as a monthly magazine in 1926 and was converted to a weekly in January 1934. With roots in earlier radical publications like the *Masses* (1911–1917), the magazine published cartoons, literary contributions and commentary. Famous noncommunists and fellow travelers contributed articles and stories, including Ernest Hemingway, Richard Wright, James Agee, Langston Hughes, Erskine Caldwell, and Theodore Drieser. In the period from 1936 to 1939, the magazine focused on events of the Spanish Civil War (see Chapter 11, "Spanish Civil War: Loyal Communists and Rebel Conservatives"). The largest circulation attained was 25,000.

The John Reed Clubs were founded in New York in 1929, by the editors of the *New Masses*. The concept of the club was modeled on a Soviet system of literary studios for worker-correspondents. Using "Art as a Class Weapon," the clubs were supposed to stimulate the use of art and literature for a social purpose, rather than "art for art's sake" that had characterized the 1920s attitudes. Artists made posters and painted murals for meeting halls, taught classes in art and theater for workers, and members attended cultural meetings in Moscow.

The John Reed Clubs spread from New York to Chicago and to some smaller towns, with a reported total of 30 such local clubs and a total membership of about 1,200. Internal wrangling and party control kept the clubs embroiled in controversies, and they dissolved after 1935. One offspring of the dissolved clubs was the 1936 publication of an anti-Soviet magazine of the left, the *Partisan Review*.

From Isolation to Popular Front

From mid 1934, when the California CP at first attempted to work with Upton Sinclair, through late 1935, the American Communist Party began a transition from its strategy of united front from below and attacks on other leftist groups to a policy of conciliation with the groups. Many, like the Farm Holiday Association and the socialists, already burned by former clashes with the communists, rejected such advances. The new policy, officially known as the united front from above or the *Popular Front*, received official Comintern endorsement in August 1935, at the Comintern's Seventh World Congress held in Moscow.

Georgi Dimitroff (also spelled Dimitrov), a Bulgarian communist, had achieved international fame during a trial of communists accused of having set fire to the German parliament building, the Reichstag. His defiance of the Nazi leadership during the trial raised his stature to that of a leading opponent of fascism, recognized throughout Europe and America.

Red Words

The **Popular Front,** or united front, announced in August 1935 that the communist parties would work with other groups, labor leaders, and political parties to oppose fascism, or the threat of it rising. Popular Front governments took power in France and Spain with minority support from communist parties there. In the United States, American leaders began to interpret the Popular Front strategy to mean that communists could even support a candidate of one of the two major parties in specific elections. Later, some American writers suggested that Browder had anticipated the Popular Front strategy by a year or two. Others point out that Browder did not change tactics until after the Seventh Comintern World Congress of 1935, following Comintern policy carefully.

At the Seventh Congress, Dimitroff was elected general secretary of the Comintern, the first non-Russian to hold the post. In his speeches to the Congress, Dimitroff gave new stress to the concept of a united front. He and Wilhelm Pieck, a German spokesman, argued that communists should work with socialists to oppose fascists. In France, the anti-fascist alliances had gone further, to include non-Marxist and bourgeoisie-based political groups. Dimitroff endorsed the method, suggesting that there should be a "broad people's anti-fascist front on the basis of the proletarian united front." In effect, Dimitroff had announced the Popular Front.

Although based on, and intended as a reaction to, the situation in Europe, the Popular Front meant that American communists no longer had to act with such hostility to other groups on the left, but could work with them.

Dual Unionism Again

The Communist Party, in the spirit of the Popular Front, dropped its agitation for separate unions, and began to work with the AFL to help organize separate industrial unions through the Committee on Industrial Organizations. When that organizing group split off from the AFL in 1936 and formed its own Congress of Industrial Organizations (CIO), the CPUSA was confronted with a strange dilemma. In a doctrinaire way, it had just gone through denouncing dual unionism as part of its Popular Front strategy, but in order to remain active in its most promising union field, it had to go back to dual unionism.

Communist Party organizers worked in a number of CIO unions, including most notably the Steel Workers Organizing Committee, or SWOC. CP organizers also had success in gaining members and holding leadership positions in several maritime union groups, in the American Newspaper Guild, and in the Screen Writers Guild in Hollywood.

A Normal Party

From 1935 through 1939, the American Communist Party began to act much like other "normal" American political groups. It seemed that Lovestoneism, the political doctrine of following a uniquely American cultural pattern, once denounced as a complete heresy, was now in favor. Lovestone and his followers, however, were not welcomed back into the Party.

No longer were Roosevelt and his New Deal accused of trying to establish fascism. Rather, Browder and the CPUSA began to view Roosevelt as a barrier that kept the fascist threat at bay. Financial circles and right-wing politicians, like publisher William Randolph Hearst, were now seen as the basis of the fascist threat. Party cadres began to work within existing labor unions, rather than trying to establish communist-dominated separate unions. The communists downplayed their opposition to religion, and tried to build alliances with Catholic workers. The *Daily Worker* even serialized a novel written by Upton Sinclair, who was formerly criticized as a leading social fascist.

In the Popular Front as applied in the United States, the party cadres shifted their emphasis from organizing direct protests (from below) and taking over trade unions and rival political groups, to working through the traditional electoral process. Party districts and sections were reorganized to conform with electoral districts.

Notes on the Left

Although Earl Browder ran for president of the United States on the Communist Party ticket in 1936, he made it clear that he wanted to defeat the republican candidate, Alf Landon. Roosevelt's defeat would be a disaster, he said, allowing fascist forces to take control of America. It was a difficult path to follow, but it appeared to work. In some districts, local Communist Party candidates won more votes than Browder did on the national ticket, indicating that some Communist Party members took the hint and voted for Roosevelt. In the end, their small numbers made little difference, as Roosevelt won reelection by a vast landslide.

By 1938, Browder began a quiet shift of strategy to an even more cooperative form of the Popular Front, informally known as the Democratic Front. The policy goals of the Democratic Front sounded a lot less like the radical party of Lenin, and a lot more like a traditional American political party: "Jobs, Security, Democracy, Peace."

Despite the rough road through the 1930s, the CP had grown from about nine or ten thousand members at the beginning of the decade to more than sixty five thousand by the end of it. Furthermore, many of its new members were no longer immigrants or children of immigrants, but English-speaking, with some base in the working class.

Voices

The Central Committee of the Communist Party of the United States made its shift to the Democratic Front explicit. After attempting to unite with the small Farmer-Labor Party, the Central Committee passed a resolution showing the shift:

> Experience has shown that the People's Front cannot now be limited to the Farmer-Labor Party which is not yet acceptable to the most important forces essential to its success .... These forces, which still express themselves politically largely within and around the Democratic Party, are clearly ripe for inclusion in a broad People's Front movement that does not call upon them to split organizationally and to form now a new party.

Membership in the Party had become slightly respectable compared to its earlier reputation as a fringe group operating semi-legally and concerned with undermining every other group on the left. With its support of goals that sounded very much like those of the liberal wing of the Democratic Party in 1938 and 1939, for a brief period of time, it appeared that the Communist Party of the United States would move into the mainstream of American politics.

The Least You Need to Know

◆ The Communist Party in the United States followed the Comintern line (1928–1935) of rejecting alliances with other groups on the left.

◆ After alienating many left-wing groups and leaders, the Party switched to the Popular Front tactic in late 1935 that called for cooperation against fascism.

◆ The Communist Party worked through an extensive network of its own organizations and front organizations to win support, especially in the period from 1936 to 1939.

◆ By the end of the 1930s, the Communist Party actively supported many of the same goals as the Democratic Party.

Chapter 11

Spanish Civil War: Loyal Communists and Rebel Conservatives

In This Chapter

- ◆ Spanish Civil War's importance outside Spain
- ◆ Interveners: Nazis, fascists, and communists
- ◆ Americans and Canadians in Spain
- ◆ Challenges to the Popular Front

In this chapter we see how the Spanish Civil War, which broke out in 1936 and lasted until 1939, affected communist parties and other parties of the left in Europe and America. Although a "civil" war fought between two Spanish forces for control of the Spanish Republic, the war became an international confrontation.

We also look at how defense of the Republic (dominated by parties of the left, calling themselves *Loyalists*) against the *Insurgents* (the Spanish Army, supported by parties of the right) became a test of the Popular Front strategy across Europe and the rest of the world. Volunteers from communist parties and from other groups on the left came from Britain, Canada, and the United States to fight on the Loyalist side. And we see that Nazi Germany and fascist Italy provided support to the Insurgents.

For many of the idealistic young men who flocked to Spain to help the Loyalists, the experience was disillusioning. Some found out that the Popular Front, for which they fought, was dominated by the Communist Party, which took its orders from Moscow. Yet in Britain, Canada, and the United States, support for the cause in Spain provided a rallying point for many on the left.

Background to the War

Spain had been a monarchy for hundreds of years, since the time of Columbus, when Ferdinand and Isabella united the kingdoms of Leon and Castille. In the period 1923 to 1931, the monarchy had been under the control of the Army in the person of the dictator General Primo de Rivera. In 1931, the king abdicated and the Spanish Republic was established, along the lines of the parliamentary democracies of Britain and France.

Red Words

Loyalists. After the February 1936 elections in Spain, the government was controlled by the Popular Front, including the small Communist Party. After the Army rebelled, the government provided arms to political and union militias who made up the Loyalist side in the Civil War.

Insurgents. The revolt against the government was led by officers of the Spanish Army and the Civil Guard, supported by large landholders and by the Falange (a fascist party) and by a small group of Monarchists. The supporters of the Popular Front government called the other side "Insurgents."

The country was in turmoil, due to strikes, attacks on the clergy and churches, and demands for autonomy from the Basque-speaking provinces in the north and the Catalan-speaking region of the northeast. The February 1936 elections put the Popular Front in power, a coalition of parties of the left.

The Popular Front included liberals, a large but divided Socialist Party, and a small but determined Communist Party. The Socialist Trade Union, the *Union General de Trabajadores,* or UGT, was quite powerful. On the other side, in the National Front, were the *Monarchists*, a fascist party called the Falange, and several smaller conservative parties. The *Nationalist* front represented the Church, large landowners, and the Army.

Following Spanish politics was difficult for outsiders, and for many in Spain as well. A coalition of parties in the center made up a third, but quite a small bloc of deputies to the Parliament, or Cortes. Another huge group that did not participate in the elections at all, probably two million in strength, included a variety of anarchists.

Even though many parties supported the Popular Front, the government was made up of the liberal politician members of the Front. That government seemed incapable of restoring order, as churches were looted and sectors of the country saw armed groups attacking each other. Strikers and strikebreakers fought, priests, landlords and political leaders of all stripes were assassinated.

Red Words

Monarchists. Among those opposing the Popular Front were several small groups supporting the restoration of the monarchy. These monarchists tended to represent old wealth.

Nationalists. Another term for the Army-led rebels against the Popular Front government, which was a little more neutral in tone than "Insurgents."

Notes on the Left

The unions and political parties in Spain in the mid 1930s represented a kaleidoscope of names. Just keeping track of those on the left was difficult. All went by acronyms. PSUC (*Partit Socialista Unificat de Catalunya*) was the Communist Party of Catalonia; POUM (*Partido Obrero de Unificacion Marxista*) was a Communist Party that took an independent path from the Comintern, with members who thought of themselves as Trotskyists; FAI (*Federacion Anarquista Iberica*) was a federation of anarchist groups; CNT (*Confederation Nationas de Trabajo*) was an anarcho-syndicalist trade union; JSU (*Juventudes Socialistas Unificadas*) was a youth group made up of socialist and communist youth organizations. George Orwell, later famous as the author of *Nineteen Eighty-Four* and *Animal Farm*, came to Spain as a volunteer, joining a POUM military unit. He found the names tiresome and exasperating.

With the selection of the Popular Front government, Army generals plotted a takeover of the government. Many of the leading officers had been posted to outlying or colonial provinces to hamper such plotting. General Francisco Franco was in the Canary Islands, and General Mola was in Morocco. Even so, they planned a coup.

Vignettes

In the *Cortes* or Spanish Parliament, the deputies debated the threat of rebellion that swept the country and the threat of counterrevolution that simmered in the Army. Calvo Sotelo, a monarchist, said that the only way to bring order to Spain was through a strong regime, with private property protected by the state against unruly strikes, but regulated in the national interest. Hugh Thomas, in *The Spanish Civil War* (1961), quoted Sotelo's speech to the Cortes as follows: "This State," declared Sotelo, "Many may call Fascist; if this be indeed the Fascist State, then I, who believe in it, proudly declare myself a Fascist."

The Parliament broke into howls of opposition and support. He went on to say that the Army would remain loyal, even it meant rising in behalf of Spain against anarchy. That suggestion of a military revolt brought another storm of outcry.

Calvo Sotelo was answered by the woman delegate, Dolores Ibarruri, known as "*La Pasionaria,*" or the passionflower. A dedicated communist, she stated that the fascists were gangsters, and controlled by a Fascist International, operating out of Hitler's Germany and Mussolini's Italy.

The lines had been drawn.

The Army vs. the Government

June and early July 1936 witnessed a series of murders and assassinations of political leaders. On July 13, 1936, Calvo Sotelo, the leading representative of the Falange and fascist point of view, was assassinated, most thought on orders from Casares Quiroga, the leader of the government.

Red Words

Republicans. By a strange twist, those supporting the Republic were the most radical parties. Thus in Spain, the term "Republican" that Americans associated with a conservative party, became a designation for the Loyalist parties of the Popular Front.

Over the next few days, military units planned their uprising, and the government gradually acceded to demands from the left unions, which urged distribution of arms to workers' militias to defend the Republic. In the chaos that followed, more churches were burnt. Armed militias fought against garrison troops, and pro-*Republican* officers set up summary courts to try and execute rebel officers. In some regions, Army troops arrested the authorities of the civil government. In others, stalemate set in. In some towns in Andalusia, armed anarchist gangs rounded up members of the middle class and clergy, and executed them.

By the end of July 1936, Spain was divided into alternating zones of control. In Morocco and extreme south of Spain, in Cadiz, the Nationalist Insurgents were in command. Central Spain and the Mediterranean provinces up to the French border were in Republican hands, loyal to the Popular Front government. The north and west of Spain were in Nationalist hands, except for the northern coast along the Bay of Biscay, in which the Basques supported the Republican government.

Notes on the Left

If you prefer algebra to politics, the following equations can help keep the sides clear:

- ◆ Loyalists = Republicans = Popular Front
- ◆ Insurgents = Nationalists = Falange + Monarchists
- ◆ Falange = Fascist
- ◆ Popular Front = Socialists + Communists + Anarcho-Syndicalists

And the anarchists fought on the Popular Front side, without ever running for office or joining the government!

Within the Republican regions, the militias established fuller control. In location after location, besieged Civil Guard or Army garrisons were surrounded, sometimes starved into submission, then captured and shot.

Meanwhile, in the Nationalist regions, all political activity was suppressed. Left-wing newspapers were closed. Those who had been active in trade unions, or even those who had voted for Popular Front candidates, were shot. Stories of atrocities abounded, some invented by communist writers, but others verified by independent commissions. Victims on both sides were shot in front of their families or had to dig their own graves; women were raped and mutilated; mass executions were common. Responsible estimates of the number of political executions in the Nationalist areas exceeded 40,000.

Vignettes

A mystery surrounds the death of the Spanish poet García Lorca, during the chaos of the early Spanish Civil War. Lorca took refuge with another poet and close friend, Luis Rosales. Even though Rosales had a brother who was a Falangist, Lorca was taken and shot by the military. However, the exact time and place of his death remained a mystery, and his grave was not located. Various theories and rumors suggested that Lorca might have been killed in a brawl, or in revenge by another jealous poet.

Foreign Interventions

From the beginning of the Civil War in Spain in the summer of 1936, both sides sought help from abroad. Giral, the new Prime Minister of the Republic, sent a telegram to Léon

Blum, the Popular Front Prime Minister of France, asking for help. General Franco, leader of the Insurgents, sought help from Italy and Germany.

In July, a meeting of the Comintern in Moscow urged support for the Republican side in Spain, and the issue was placed on the agenda for a meeting of the Comintern in Prague, Czechoslovakia. Even without the issue of ideology, Russia had geopolitical reasons to support the Popular Front in Spain. If the fascist-leaning Nationalists won in Spain, France would end up with hostile fascist powers on three sides, in Germany, Italy and Spain. France would in turn be relatively powerless to act as a counterweight to Hitler's Germany, and Germany threatened Russia.

> ### Notes on the Left
>
> Nationalist General Mola bragged that, in addition to the four columns of troops he had advancing on Madrid, he had a secret "Fifth Column" of supporters secretly waiting inside Madrid to rise in favor of Franco. It was a propaganda ploy, for there was no organized group of Insurgent supporters. Later, however, the Nationalist supporters within Madrid did organize into a "Fifth Column." The term caught on in international usage. Hemingway wrote a short play called the "Fifth Columnist."
>
> Thereafter, the term came to mean a secret group of underground cells, full of traitors, waiting for the moment to rise. In an ironic twist, common in political history during and after World War II, the term "Fifth Columnists" was often used to describe potential rebels of the left, rather than the right, as Mola had used the term.

On the other hand, Stalin appeared reluctant to provide direct military help to Spain or use his influence through the Spanish Communist Party to create a Soviet Spain. Perhaps he was concerned that such a development would alarm France and Britain, or that it would be hard to control at such a distance from the Soviet Union.

Without wanting either a communist victory or a complete communist defeat, he channeled limited support through other communist parties to Spain. Jacques Duclos, leader of the French Communist Party, and Palmiro Togliatti, head of the exiled Italian Communist Party, both went to Spain to provide leadership.

Russia eventually provided arms, money, aircraft, gasoline, and other supplies. In addition, the communist parties of Western Europe sent thousands of volunteers.

Fascists Help Franco

Germany, too, saw the geopolitical importance of Spain. Hitler decided, after the first requests from Franco, that the German Luftwaffe should provide assistance to the Insurgents. He looked forward to the day, with a Falangist victory, when the Western Mediterranean would be under the control of pro-Nazi fascist powers. Germany immediately provided Junkers transport aircraft, Heinkle fighters, pilots and ground support crews. All of these proved indispensable.

In Portugal, the regime was already organized along fascist lines, under Dr. Antonio Salazar. Portugal provided air-transit rights to the German aircraft, sanctuary for Nationalist refugees, and an arms-purchasing agency in Lisbon. The Spanish Loyalist ambassador remained a virtual prisoner in his embassy in Portugal. Eventually, about 20,000 Portuguese fought on the Nationalist side.

Italy provided over 50,000 troops, who fought effectively on the Insurgent side, helping to ensure the defeat of the left.

Britain, Canada, and the United States React

Ideology and ideological influence were perhaps the most important for the Communist International. The war attracted a host of intellectuals, mostly in support of the Popular Front government. Among the most notable of those writing in English were George Orwell, Ernest Hemingway, Stephen Spender, and John Dos Passos.

So many writers went to Spain, either as volunteers in the International Brigades or as journalists, that readers soon had access to many personal insights and views of the war. The war became the background and subject of hundreds of articles, stories, and books. The most well-known literary works of the era in the English language were Ernest Hemingway's *For Whom the Bell Tolls*, George Orwell's *Homage to Catalonia*, and Graham Greene's *The Confidential Agent*.

Through the writings of dozens of authors and through advertisements and propaganda by associations set up to provide humanitarian aid, the Spanish Civil War became a cause that fired the imaginations of a whole generation on the left in the Western democracies.

The Loyalists had several things going for them in their appeal to the United States and Britain. The Popular Front government had been legally elected, and the Nationalists, even though they claimed to be fighting to restore law and order, were in fact in rebellion against the government. So those on the left were in the position of supporting constitutional government against unconstitutional rebellion. Furthermore, the Popular Front represented a selection of parties of the left. So even if one were not a Communist Party member, but rather a socialist or simply a sympathizer with the goals of socialism, support for the Loyalists made sense.

Civil War with a Civil War

However, as the war went on, the Communist Party in Spain was able to direct the distribution of Soviet and Comintern aid, and began to take over the Loyalist side. As the Loyalists were driven back, a "civil war within a civil war" broke out in Barcelona, in which the communists broke up the Trotskyite POUM, destroying their headquarters, arresting and shooting the officers and men of the POUM 29th Division and men in anarchist units. The infighting among the factions of the left caused some members to lose faith in the cause.

Voices

George Orwell noted in his 1938 memoir of the war, *Homage to Catalonia*, that he was shocked when the armed forces of the POUM, the Trotskyist Communist Party, were suppressed by the Soviet-supported Communist Party in Barcelona. He had supported the POUM and served in their 29th Division. After the communists decided to rout out the Trotskyite POUM, Orwell realized that he could be arrested and possibly shot:

> It was a queer situation we were in. At night one was a hunted fugitive, but in the daytime one could live an almost normal life. Every house known to harbour POUM supporters was—or at any rate was likely to be—under observation, and it was impossible to go to a hotel or boarding house, because it had been decreed that on the arrival of a stranger the hotel-keeper must inform the police immediately. Practically this meant spending the night out of doors.

Later, after being interrogated by the communist police about his Trotskyite affiliation, Orwell was touched when a police officer shook hands with him. He wrote in *Homage to Catalonia*:

> It sounds a small thing, but it was not. You have got to realize what was the feeling of the time—the horrible atmosphere of suspicion and hatred, the lies and rumours circulating everywhere, the posters screaming from the hoardings that I and everyone like me was a Fascist Spy .... It was like publicly shaking hands with a German during the Great War .... It was good of him to shake hands .... I have the most evil memories of Spain, but I have very few bad memories of Spaniards.

International Brigades

In Britain, France, Belgium, the United States, and Canada, thousands from parties of the left volunteered to fight for the Loyalists. They were organized in International Brigades, totaling about 40,000, although the number at any one time did not exceed about 18,000. Another 5,000 foreigners fought in Spanish Loyalist units. About half of the volunteers served in noncombatant roles, in medical services, or other auxiliary units.

There were seven International Brigades, each with three or four battalions. As far as possible, those in each battalion spoke the same language. The English-speaking battalions were in the XV Brigade. The XV Brigade included the British 2nd Battalion. The 3rd Battalion of the XV Brigade was made up of the Lincoln Battalion, including Americans, and the Mackenzie-Papineau Battalion, including Canadians and some Americans. The volunteers called the Canadian Battalion the "MacPaps."

Volunteers for the Nationalists

Very few individual international volunteers came to the Nationalist side, although the troops sent by Germany, Italy, and Portugal were all officially called volunteers. The Nationalists did get about 600 volunteers from Ireland in the "O'Duffy Brigade," and groups of right-wing volunteers from France, from anti-Soviet Russian exiles, and from several Eastern European countries. America sent no volunteers to the Nationalists, and Britain sent less than a dozen.

Military and Financial Aid to Loyalists

The amount of financial aid and military aid from France and the Soviet Union to the Loyalist side has been difficult to calculate, but reliable estimates put the Soviet and Comintern aid to a total of about $400 million. The French government provided about 200 aircraft to the Loyalists.

The Germans made estimates of the Soviet aid to the Loyalists, sent by sea, based on intelligence reports. Altogether, they estimated that the Loyalists received 242 aircraft, 731 tanks, 29,000 tons of ammunition, and 28,000 tons of gasoline by ship. In addition, Comintern and Soviet aid arriving by land across the French border included another 200 tanks, 4,500 tons of ammunition, and 14,000 tons of fuel.

The only government besides the Soviet Union and France that sent aid to the Loyalists was Mexico, which provided some $2 million in supplies and aid. Another $2 million was raised by left-wing and communist groups in the United States, for humanitarian assistance.

Vignettes

Only a few of the Canadian and American volunteers had served in the military before going to Spain, and in the spirit of equality, most enlisted men did not salute officers. However, as discipline on the Loyalist side picked up, a communist clenched-fist salute became required. One member of the Lincoln Battalion remembered:

> The Americans took to the new discipline slowly, feeling their way. Some at first refused to salute at all. Others, better aware of its purpose, did so cautiously, raising the right arm with the hand clenched loosely, not taut in a fist, barely higher than their shoulders. It took the gracious explanation of one of the Spanish soldiers to convince the Americans. "*Hombre*," he said, "it isn't a sign of deference, nor has it got anything to do with superiority or inferiority. It's just courtesy, *hombre*, like when you meet a friend in the street. You kiss him on both cheeks, no? Or you clasp his hand. Well, in the army your hands are dirty or you haven't shaved for a week, no? So you salute. Understand?" The ingenious explanation pleased many of the men. Slowly the salute was adopted.

—Edwin Rolfe, *The Lincoln Battalion* (1939)

The Bitter End

The warfront moved slowly over the two and half years between July 1936 and March 1939. After terrible sieges, Republican-held Barcelona fell to the Nationalists in January 1939, and Madrid fell in March 1939. Hundreds of thousands of soldiers and civilians fled from Barcelona across the French border.

During the siege of Madrid, food supplies fell to the point of starvation, and relief agencies in Canada, Norway, Denmark, the United States and France sent in aid. At one point, in a propaganda display, the Nationalists "bombed" Madrid with food supplies.

In the last days of the war, dissension between the communist commanders and other units in Madrid resulted in another "civil war within a civil war." The communist leaders argued for a fight to the end against the Nationalists, while the other Loyalists sought to negotiate a settlement.

Although the communist forces were defeated in this mini-civil war within Madrid, the issue of how to surrender to the Nationalists became moot a few days later, when the frontline Loyalist soldiers realized that the Nationalists would win. Most Loyalists simply walked away from the lines, and the forces of Franco and his German and Italian allies took control of the country by the end of March 1939.

Many, but not all of the survivors of the International Brigades, escaped by ship or overland through the border with France. A few were imprisoned and never heard from again. According to the Nationalist's own reports, they had conducted over 200,000 arrests of civilians during the course of the war. With the Nationalists in tight control of information after their victory in 1939, the fate of many civilian and military prisoners was never learned.

Cracks in the Popular Front

The civil wars within the Spanish Civil War that took place in Barcelona and on a smaller scale in Madrid came as a shock to many on the left who supported the Popular Front government of Spain. For communists and others on the left in Britain, Canada, and United States, support for the Loyalists had represented a way of challenging fascism.

The international community turned its attention to the growing crisis between Germany and Poland. Suddenly, in August 1939, diplomatic negotiations between Germany and the Soviet Union brought to an end the underlying anti-fascist coalition represented by the Popular Front tactic.

The Least You Need to Know

- The Spanish Civil War broke out when the Army tried to overthrow the elected Popular Front government.

- The Popular Front supporters were known as Republicans or Loyalists, and those on the Army's side were known as Nationalists or Insurgents.

- Within the Republican side, the Communist Party sought to exercise control, winning power in Barcelona.

- The Popular Front received thousands of foreign volunteers to fight in International Brigades.

- The Spanish Civil War disillusioned some on the left about working through a Popular Front with communists.

Chapter 12

The Soviet Union in World War II

In This Chapter

- ◆ Soviet foreign policy in the 1930s
- ◆ The Nazi-Soviet Pact
- ◆ Germany invades the Soviet Union
- ◆ The great struggle
- ◆ The Soviet victory and the postwar division of Europe

By the late 1930s, the communist experiment in the Soviet Union appeared to be on the verge of collapse. Stalin's efforts to convert the country into a modern industrialized society by seizing control of the economy and forcibly collectivizing agriculture had largely ended in chaos. The Russian Communist Party itself was decimated by Stalin's purges in which hundreds of thousands had been imprisoned, exiled, or executed at the hands of the dreaded secret police.

The Soviet Union was also isolated internationally. The regime's revolutionary propaganda had made it a pariah state during much of the 1920s and early 1930s. Although the Soviet Union was somewhat successful in normalizing its relations with Western nations by the mid 1930s, most still viewed the country with grave suspicions. After Adolph Hitler came to power in Germany in 1933 and openly called for the destruction of the Soviet Union, many Western observers relished the possibility that the Nazi and Bolshevik regimes would go to war and obliterate each other in the process.

However, the Soviet Union disappointed such critics, surviving World War II and emerging from the conflict stronger than it had ever been. By the late 1940s, it was one of the two global superpowers, along with the United States. Soviets claimed direct or indirect control over most of Eastern Europe and a significant portion of the rest of the world as well. In this chapter we unravel the story of how this remarkable change came about.

Soviet Foreign Policy in the 1930s

To a large extent, Soviet foreign policy in the 1930s took a backseat to domestic concerns. Stalin could not afford any foreign conflicts at a time when he was focused on carrying out the sweeping internal changes in the Five-Year Plan and the agricultural collectivization program (see Chapter 8, "Stalin and the Purges"). In November 1933, the Soviet Union took a major step toward being accepted into the international community when the United States formally recognized the Bolshevik regime as a legitimate government. Up until that point, successive conservative U.S. administrations had refused to acknowledge communist rule.

After Franklin Roosevelt's victory in the 1932 presidential elections, however, the United States and the Soviet Union were able to come to a settlement in which Stalin promised to refrain from communist propaganda in the United States in return for the establishment of normal diplomatic relations. In the following year, the Soviet Union agreed to join the League of Nations. The United States, by the way, never did join that organization. Soviet diplomats began taking part in international conferences dealing with issues such as collective security and trade agreements.

Notes on the Left _____

In the early 1930s, Japan began seizing large sections of China, including the province of Manchuria that lay directly on the Soviet border. This resulted in tensions between Japan and the Soviet Union. One particularly difficult issue was the question of the Chinese Eastern Railway, which had been built by Russia during the Tsarist period. Despite official communist policy that rejected all forms of imperialism, the Soviets insisted that they still owned the railway. In 1935, the Soviet Union and Japan reached a compromise in which the Soviets agreed to sell their shares in the railway in return for 170 million Japanese yen. However, this agreement only temporarily reduced the underlying tensions between the two countries.

With the rise of Nazi Germany in the West and an aggressive and nationalist Japan in the East, the Soviet Union found itself trapped between two potential enemies. In 1936, Stalin's worst fears were realized when Germany and Japan entered into an Anti-Comintern Pact directed specifically against the Soviet Union. In the following year, fascist Italy also joined the Pact, and the Soviet Union appeared increasingly isolated.

Stalin had scant success in building better relations with Western democracies in order to counteract the threat from the Anti-Comintern Pact. He directed the Comintern to abandon its long-standing policies that prohibited communist parties in the West from cooperating with less radical groups and participating in the political process. Although communists did join Popular Front anti-fascist alliances in several countries, this rapid reversal did little to make Western governments less suspicious of Soviet intentions. When civil war broke out in Spain in 1936 (see Chapter 11, "Spanish Civil War: Loyal Communists and Rebel Conservatives"), the Soviets found themselves largely acting alone in defending the democratically elected republican government.

Stalin began to believe that Western countries were perfectly happy to let Nazi Germany attack and overthrow the Soviet Union. His fears seemed proven when France and Great Britain began to embark on a policy of *appeasement* in which they acquiesced to almost every demand made by Hitler. When Hitler proclaimed that Germany would began expanding its army and re-militarizing its border with France, both of which were a clear violation of the Treaty of Versailles that had ended the First World War, the West refused to intervene. Nor did France and Great Britain act when Germany unified with Austria in March 1938, although this was again a violation of the Treaty of Versailles. The so-called *Anschluss*, or unification with Austria, made Germany the largest and most powerful country in Europe.

Red Words

The policy of **appeasement** was based on the completely erroneous and unfounded hope that Nazi aggression would dissipate and war could be prevented if other countries accepted Hitler's demands. Many people in the West believed that Germany had been treated poorly by the Treaty of Versailles, so some of Hitler's moves seemed somewhat justified. When Nazi Germany announced it was rebuilding its military in violation of the treaty, Western leaders neither had the political will or the popular support to intervene. Likewise, Nazi demands to incorporate ethnic Germans from Czechoslovakia into Germany seemed to be a legitimate claim to some observers and certainly not something worth fighting over. However, from the perspective of Stalin and many communist sympathizers in the West, appeasement appeared as nothing less than a policy of encouraging the Nazi regime to continue its aggression toward the East in the hopes of starting a war between Germany and the Soviet Union. A handful of conservatives such as Britain's Winston Churchill, who despised both the Nazi and communist regimes, also spoke out against appeasement.

The crowning moment came in September 1938, when British Prime Minister Neville Chamberlain and French Premier Edouard Daladier met with Hitler in Munich and agreed to allow Germany to occupy the Sudetenland region in Czechoslovakia, an area largely inhabited by ethnic Germans. The British cooperated in pressuring Czechoslovakia to agree to German demands. Stalin was not consulted, even though the dismemberment of Czechoslovakia brought Nazi control closer to the Soviet borders.

Voices

In a speech given in March 1939, shortly after Germany annexed all of Czechoslovakia, Stalin bitterly complained about the behavior of Western democracies:

> Or take Germany, for instance. They [France and Great Britain] let it have Austria, despite the undertaking to defend its independence; they let it have the Sudeten region; they abandoned Czechoslovakia to her fate, thereby violating their obligations; and then they began to lie vociferously in the press about "the weakness of the Russian army, the demoralization of the Russian air force, and riots in the Soviet Union, egging on the Germans to march further east, promising them easy pickings, and prompting them: Just start a war on the Bolsheviks, and everything will be all right." It must be admitted that this too looks very much like egging on and encouraging the aggressor.

The Nazi-Soviet Pact

The West's decision to abandon Czechoslovakia prompted a major reversal in Soviet foreign policy. Hitler quickly reneged on his promise not to engage in any further expansion, when Germany occupied the remaining portion of Czechoslovakia in March 1939. Finally convinced that Hitler could not be stopped peacefully, France and Great Britain began negotiating with the Soviet Union in hopes of creating a military alliance against Germany. But it was far too late, and the negotiations made little headway.

Instead, in August 1939, Germany and the Soviet Union stunned the world when they announced that they had signed a mutual nonaggression pact. The agreement was the result of secret negotiations between German foreign minister Joachim von Ribbentrop and his Soviet counterpart V. M. Molotov. In the space of a few hurried meetings over several days, the two mortal enemies agreed to set aside their differences and pledged not to attack one another. On September 1, 1939, a week after the agreement was announced, Germany invaded Poland and started the Second World War.

The Nazi-Soviet Pact was mutually beneficial to both Nazi Germany and the Soviet Union. It allowed Hitler to go to war with Poland and the West without having to worry about fighting the Red Army as well. Although Stalin had little reason to trust Germany, the Pact did give the Soviet Union time to build up its own military defenses.

Vignettes

Born in 1890, Molotov joined the Bolshevik Party at a young age and took part in the October 1917 revolution. He was a supporter of Stalin and survived the murderous purges in the 1930s to become Soviet foreign minister in 1939 shortly before negotiating the Nazi-Soviet Pact. After Germany attacked the Soviet Union, he played a key and prominent role in building the Soviet alliance with the West.

He also maintained close ties with communist anti-German resistance groups operating in occupied countries throughout Europe. One of the many homemade weapons used by such groups were glass bottles filled with gasoline and plugged with a rag that could be set alight and thrown at German troops. These became known as "Molotov cocktails."

However, the agreement was more than a temporary truce between two formerly hostile nations. The Nazi-Soviet Pact included many secret provisions, most of which were not widely known until after the defeat of Germany at the end of the Second World War. Under these provisions, the Soviet Union was allowed a free hand in territories along its immediate borders in return for Stalin's promise not to intervene when Germany attacked Poland. Stalin used these secret protocols to embark on his own program of aggressive expansion.

Stalin and Nazi foreign minister Joachim Von Ribbentrop were all smiles after signing a treaty of non-aggression (Nazi-Soviet Pact) between the Soviet Union and Germany in August 1939. Stalin was much less cheerful when Germany broke the treaty and invaded the Soviet Union two years later.

(National Archives)

The Division of Poland

One of the secret provisions of the Nazi-Soviet Pact was a plan to divide Poland between Germany and the Soviet Union. Shortly after Germany attacked, Soviet troops also invaded Poland and occupied almost half of the country. Poland disappeared, and Germany and the Soviet Union now shared a common border. The Soviets occupied their new Polish territory until Germany attacked a year and a half later.

In the spring of 1940, more than 14,000 Polish army officers and intellectuals were killed and buried in mass graves near the city of Katyn. The Soviet Union later blamed the massacre on German troops. However, subsequent research revealed that the massacre was carried out by Soviet troops during their occupation of Poland, and in the post-Soviet era, the Russians admitted and offered an apology for this atrocity.

The Winter War with Finland

In the winter of 1939–1940, Stalin also attempted to expand into Finland in order to protect the Soviet Union's northern border, especially around the key city of Leningrad (originally called St. Petersburg and then Petrograd, the city had been renamed by the communist regime after Lenin's death). Soviet negotiators pressed Finland to cede strategic territory, but Finland refused. Stalin ordered the Red Army to attack in November 1939, believing that the vastly larger and better-equipped Soviet forces would quickly overwhelm the Finns.

The Russo-Finnish, or "Winter," War didn't go well for the Soviet Union at first. Despite their numerical superiority, the Red Army was badly led and poorly prepared for the harsh winter conditions. Finnish troops won a series of remarkable victories and inflicted huge losses on the Red Army. However, the Red Army eventually wore down their opponents, and Finland capitulated in March 1940. The experience demonstrated the critical need for Soviet military reforms. As a result, Stalin replaced most of the senior officers.

Occupation of the Baltic States

The three small countries of Latvia, Lithuania, and Estonia occupied a strategic position along the Baltic Sea. Eager to increase the buffer zone between the Soviet Union and Germany, Stalin took advantage of the Nazi-Soviet Pact to move against the three countries. In June 1940, Soviet troops invaded and occupied all three countries.

Notes on the Left _____

The Baltic states of Latvia, Lithuania, and Estonia had originally been part of the old Russian Empire. After the Bolshevik Revolution in October 1917, all three had declared themselves independent. At the Treaty of Brest-Litovsk signed in early 1918, the new Bolshevik regime recognized the independence of the Baltic states; however, most Bolshevik leaders believed that this was only a temporary measure.

The Baltic states included a sizeable population of ethnic Germans, many of whom were sympathetic to the Nazi regime after the rise of Hitler in the 1930s. When Germany eventually invaded the Soviet Union in the summer of 1941 and occupied the Baltic states, it found many supporters among ethnic Germans and local nationalists who initially saw the German troops as liberators.

After the defeat of Germany, the Baltic states were reoccupied by Soviet troops. They remained part of the Soviet Union until its breakup in the early 1990s.

The German Attack on the Soviet Union

The Nazi-Soviet Pact gave Germany the freedom to move its armies against the West without having to fight the Soviet Union at the same time. In a series of lighting attacks in the spring of 1940, German troops defeated and occupied Belgium, Holland, Denmark, Norway, and France. Over the next year, German armies won additional victories in the Balkans and Greece. Germany also allied itself with Romania, Hungary, and Bulgaria. By the summer of 1941, all of Europe, with the exception of Great Britain, and the neutral countries of Switzerland, Sweden, Spain, and Portugal was under its control. And even the four neutrals tended to be cooperative with the Nazi regime.

On June 22, 1941, the conflict that everyone had long been expecting finally began when Germany invaded the Soviet Union with an army of more than 200 divisions. Code-named Operation Barbarossa, the German invasion involved a massive assault across the entire expanse of the Soviet Union, from Leningrad in the north to Odessa in the south. The communist regime found itself in a desperate struggle for its existence.

German Advances

The initial German attack came as almost a complete surprise, despite repeated warnings to Stalin that such an attack was imminent. He suspected that British agents planted many of the warnings to provoke a conflict. Stalin feared a war with Germany before the Red Army was ready, and ordered his front-line commanders to avoid any possible confrontation with German troops along the border. Much of the Soviet officer corps had been decimated during Stalin's purges in the late 1930s (see Chapter 8), and most of the remaining senior officers were better known for politically supporting Stalin than for their military expertise. On top of that, the reforms that had started in response to the Red Army's poor showing during the war with Finland in 1939–1940 had not yet been completed.

<table>
<tr><td>

Vignettes

The warnings that Germany was about to attack the Soviet Union came from many sources. Communist workers in Sweden and Poland reported that the Nazis were building up their armies along the Soviet border. A few weeks before the invasion, Germany also evacuated its embassy in Moscow and ordered all German ships to leave Soviet ports. However, Stalin refused to take any steps in response. The Soviet Union even continued to deliver supplies of petroleum, manganese, chromium, and other critical materials to Germany, as it had promised under the terms of the Nazi-Soviet Pact. Soviet-supplied materials were used to manufacture many of the weapons carried by German troops when they attacked the Soviets in June 1941.
</td></tr>
</table>

As a result, Soviet troops provided almost no resistance to the initial German attack. By the end of the year, German armies had pushed over 1,000 miles into the Soviet Union, encircled the city of Leningrad, and were within sight of Moscow. More than two million Soviet soldiers had been killed or captured. Only the advent of winter slowed the German advance and prevented the complete collapse of the Red Army.

Notes on the Left _____

The German siege of Leningrad began in August 1941 when German troops succeeded in cutting off the city from the rest of the Soviet Union. However, the arrival of winter opened up a new supply line when the lakes surrounding the city froze over and the Soviets were able to drive supply trucks across them. The siege lasted for another two years, during which hundreds of thousands of its inhabitants died from famine and disease.

The German pressure picked up again in the spring of 1942. Although the front lines north from Leningrad to Moscow had stabilized, German forces were able to push deep in the south toward the key city of Stalingrad. However, there the attack stalled. At its furthest point during the fall of 1942, the German advance had conquered almost one third of the Soviet Union.

Stalingrad

The battle of Stalingrad during the winter of 1942–1943 became the decisive turning point in the war. The city occupied a strategic position along the Volga river and was a major industrial and transportation center. German forces began besieging Stalingrad in September 1942. Despite throwing all available troops into the campaign, the Germans were not able to capture the city, as Soviet forces put up a bitter resistance in house-to-house and factory-to-factory fighting.

By December 1942, the Germans had exhausted themselves and had gone on the defensive in the face of large Soviet counterattacks. Since Hitler had ordered that no German troops should retreat, the German forces in Stalingrad continued to try to resist rather than pull back to more defensible positions. By February 1943, the remaining German troops had been surrounded, and more than 200,000 German soldiers were killed or forced to surrender. It was a crushing blow to German military prestige, but the Soviet victory had come at the cost of hundreds of thousands of their own casualties.

The Soviet Counteroffensive

The German defeat at Stalingrad marked the beginning of a long, bloody campaign as the Red Army regrouped, rebuilt its strength, and began driving the German forces back. Although the German army won a majority victory in the summer of 1943 in the battle of Kursk, the tide had clearly turned. By the end of 1943, German forces were in retreat all across the Eastern front.

Notes on the Left

Throughout 1942 and 1943, Stalin begged his American and British allies to invade Western Europe and reduce the German pressure on the Soviet Union. American and British military leaders insisted that they were not yet sufficiently prepared for such an operation. It was not until the Teheran Conference in November 1943, where Stalin met with British Prime Minister Winston Churchill and American President Franklin Roosevelt, that the Western allies finally promised to undertake an invasion sometime during the following year.

However, Stalin continued to suspect that America and Great Britain were deliberately stalling in order to allow Germany to inflict as much damage on the Soviet Union as possible. The long delay in opening up a second front did little to reduce Stalin's fears that the West was determined to end communist rule in the Soviet Union.

The United States and Britain were fighting a two-front war, with large forces engaged in both the Pacific and South East Asia against Japan and in Europe against the Nazis. In particular, the American commitment to the Pacific with its heavy demand for naval assets retarded American ability to support a European invasion until ships, aircraft, and troops were adequate to deliver and supply an invasion force. Stalin, of course, had only one front and he always seemed to forget that the United States and Britain had two.

The Soviet advance continued in early 1944 and drove the Germans back even further. When the Allies opened up a second front by landing in Normandy in June 1944, the German military was forced to fight two enemies at the same time. Over the next six months, Soviet troops succeeded in retaking all of the territory that had been lost to Germany during the first years of the war. They also advanced into Finland, Bulgaria, Romania, and Hungary, and forced those Germany allies to surrender.

In January 1945, Soviet forces crossed into Germany itself for the first time in the war. The final battle for Germany was as brutal a campaign as the German advance into the Soviet Union had been. Although in disarray, German forces put up a desperate resistance to delay the Red Army as long as possible. However, Soviet troops entered the outskirts of Berlin in late April 1945. Hitler committed suicide shortly afterward, and on May 7, 1945, Germany surrendered unconditionally.

The Keys to the Soviet Victory

The Soviet Union survived its desperate struggle with Nazi Germany for two main reasons. The first was that Stalin explicitly drew on the deep-rooted patriotism of Russians, who were determined to resist the German invasion at all costs. Despite Stalin's murderous campaign against his own people during the 1930s, few Russians could contemplate turning against him when the future of Rodina—the motherland—was at stake.

Stalin also took steps to bolster support from many elements of Soviet society. For example, although communist policy officially denounced all forms of religion, Stalin made many concessions to the Russian Orthodox Church during the conflict, and the Church repaid him with vocal support for the war effort.

Vignettes
Stalin's role in leading the Soviet Union to victory was widely celebrated throughout the country. During his early rise to power, Stalin had initially taken steps to remain behind the scenes and keep out of the limelight. Once firmly in power, however, he encouraged popular admiration, using public relations devices to convert from a behind-the-scenes manipulator to a well-loved celebrity. With the defeat of Germany, Stalin's "personality cult" came to a climax. During his birthday celebrations in 1949, an image of his face was projected into the sky over Moscow. Schoolchildren staged parades in which they carried thousands of posters showing Stalin leading the Red Army to triumph. Government publishing houses printed more than 700 million copies of his writings. Like Hitler and Mussolini before him, Stalin used the mass media and what Americans saw as "Madison Avenue" advertising techniques to build his power.

Most Russians were fighting to defend their country, not necessarily to defend communism. However, Stalin always made sure to link the two and in that way, the "Great

Patriotic War," as the conflict with Germany became known, was heralded as much as a victory for communism as a victory for Russia. Moreover, the Soviet cause was greatly aided by Hitler's fanaticism. In some parts of the Soviet Union, including the Baltic states and the Ukraine, the German invasion was even welcomed at first. For many nationalists in these areas, the arrival of German troops signaled a chance to throw off the yoke of communist rule from Moscow. But the brutality of the German occupation convinced most of the population that, however bad it might have been, communist rule was certainly preferable to the Nazis.

Furthermore, the Soviet Union won the battle for production. Although German forces succeeded in seizing a huge portion of the country during their initial advance, the Soviet Union's industrial power was not as severely undermined as it might have appeared. Soviet troops followed a scorched-earth policy as they retreated, destroying anything that would aid the Germans, while entire factories were dismantled and moved to the east away from the German threat. The Soviets could also draw upon significant amounts of Western aid delivered under the *Lend-Lease program.*

Red Words

The **Lend-Lease program** was initially implemented by Franklin Roosevelt in March 1941 to send vital supplies to Great Britain. The program allowed for the easy purchase of American goods by granting extensive credits to the British government. After the U.S. entered the war in December 1941, the Lend-Lease program was extended to the Soviet Union as well. By the end of the war, the Soviet Union had received more than 11 billion dollars worth of supplies, including 34 million uniforms; 14 million boots; 400,000 trucks; and 50,000 jeeps. Americans ferried aircraft from factories in the States to Alaska, where Soviet pilots picked them up.

Although appreciated by the Soviets, the aid program did generate some hard feelings as well. Many of the first American and British tanks and planes shipped to the Soviet Union were vastly inferior to the Soviet's own models. Soviet military leaders suspected that they were being given junk in order to make sure that the Red Army would not become too powerful. And the goods sent under the Lend-Lease Program were not gifts, but were technically on loan.

The Soviet-planned economy, which had proven so difficult to implement during Stalin's Five-Year Plans in the 1930s (see Chapter 8), was ideally suited for the demands of total war. Communist officials had the tools to convert the entire Soviet economy to serve the needs of the Red Army. Soviet factories in the east produced huge numbers of weapons, tanks, and planes. While most were not as technically advanced as the equipment used by the German army, they were dependable and cheap to make. The German panzer units developed considerable respect for the Soviet's powerful and numerous T-4 tanks. With its virtually unlimited manpower, the Red Army was able to wear down the German forces through a bloody war of attrition.

Soviet Foreign Policy and the Postwar Division of Europe

During the war with Germany, the Soviet Union had little choice but to ally itself with America and Great Britain. Stalin developed a working relationship with Churchill and Roosevelt, and the "Big Three" met several times. The West provided military aid to the Soviet Union, and Stalin in return toned down his communist rhetoric and ceased the Comintern's political activities in the West. But Stalin never really trusted his allies. Throughout his wartime negotiations, he pressed for concessions that would greatly expand Soviet power in the postwar era.

Teheran and Yalta

The first meeting between Stalin, Roosevelt, and Churchill took place in November 1943 in the Iranian city of Teheran. The most important decision made at the meeting was the West's promise to open up a second front in Europe by invading France sometime during the following year. Churchill wanted to invade the Balkans, which would have given the United States and Great Britain considerably more influence in Eastern Europe after the end of the war. However, Stalin pushed for an invasion of France, and Roosevelt supported him.

Voices

Roosevelt and Churchill always recognized that the Soviet Union would have to be allowed considerable influence over Eastern Europe. Stalin insisted that the German invasion had demonstrated the need for a buffer zone along its western borders to protect the Soviet Union from attack. In a separate meeting with Stalin in October 1944, Churchill had drafted a preliminary plan for dividing the Balkans into Soviet and Western spheres of influence. Handwritten on a small scrap of paper, the plan called for the Soviets to have 90 percent control of Romania and 75 percent control of Bulgaria. Britain would have 90 percent control over Greece. Other countries, such as Yugoslavia and Hungary, would be split 50–50. Churchill remarked to Stalin, "Might it not be thought rather cynical if it seemed we had disposed of these issues, so fateful to millions of people in such an off-hand manner? Let us burn the paper." Stalin replied, "No, you keep it."

In February 1945, the Big Three met again in the Soviet resort city of Yalta. This conference essentially decided the postwar fate of all of Eastern Europe. The allies agreed to divide Germany into four occupation zones, each to be administered separately by the Soviet Union, America, Great Britain, and France. Roosevelt also asked the Soviet Union to join the war against Japan within three months of Germany's defeat.

Roosevelt and Churchill agreed to territorial changes in which the Soviet Union would retain large parts of what had been Poland, which in return would be given parts of what had been Germany. They also pushed for a Soviet promise to hold free elections in Poland to determine its eventual government. Stalin agreed, as long as the Poles elected a government that would be favorable to the Soviet Union. With Soviet troops firmly in control of all of Poland, and most of Eastern Europe as well, there was very little the Western allies could do to force anything more from the Soviet Union.

The Postwar Division of Europe

The end of the war found Soviet troops occupying most of Eastern Europe from Poland to Bulgaria. Stalin naturally desired that the postwar regimes established in these countries be favorable to the Soviet Union. In many cases, local communist groups had been the most active and most successful in resisting the German occupation. However, the issue of what was to happen to Eastern Europe had been set aside during the conflict, while the Allies were concentrating on the defeat of Germany. But once Germany had surrendered, the question began to create serious tensions between the West and the Soviet Union, and the wartime alliance quickly began to deteriorate.

Churchill, Truman, Stalin. Meeting at Potsdam in July 1945, the Allies planned the postwar division of Germany, but the tensions among them were starting to show. Here, Truman chats with Churchill to his right, leaving Stalin cut off from the discussion.

(National Archives)

At the first postwar meeting, held in Potsdam in July 1945, the mood was very different than that at Yalta. Roosevelt had died several months earlier, and the new American President Harry Truman was much more suspicious of the intentions of the Soviet Union. Although Truman demanded that Stalin hold elections throughout Eastern Europe, Stalin refused since this could not guarantee Soviet security. For his part, Stalin distrusted the American announcement that it planned to keep troops in Europe for the foreseeable future. He was also angered by an American decision to end the Lend-Lease program that had supplied huge amounts of U.S. aid to the Soviet Union.

Notes on the Left

The meeting in Potsdam occurred at the same time as the Americans were carrying out their first test of the atomic bomb at their secret site in Los Alamos, New Mexico. News of the successful test was brought to Truman, who decided that he had to tell Stalin about the new weapon. Stalin showed almost no reaction. He had already found out about the bomb program through his spy network, but he kept a poker face.

Over the next few years, Stalin ensured that pro-Soviet communist regimes would be established in all the countries under the control of the Red Army. In 1946, communists seized power in Bulgaria, in a bloody coup that killed thousands of opposition leaders. In 1947, the provisional government of Poland held elections, resulting in a landslide victory for the communist party. The West charged that the elections had been rigged but could do little to change the outcome. Hungary, Czechoslovakia, and Romania all formed communist governments in 1947 and 1948.

Finally, in 1949, the Western Allies agreed to end their military occupation of Germany and merged the British, American, and French zones into a new Federal Republic of Germany. In response, the Soviets established the German Democratic Republic in their occupation zone. Europe was divided down the middle between Soviet-dominated and communist-ruled countries in the East and American-supported and democratic nations in the West. The Cold War had begun.

Expansion of Soviet control during and after World War II.

Seized in 1945

Communist Bloc countries with dates of communist seizure of power

Baltic States occupied in 1940

Soviet border 1919 to 1945

Territory gained under Nazi-Soviet Pact in August, 1939

Territory gained during war with Finland in 1939-1940

"Iron Curtain"

The Least You Need to Know

- ◆ Stalin engineered a complete reversal in his foreign policy shortly before the war by signing the Nazi-Soviet Pact.

- ◆ The war between Nazi Germany and the Soviet Union was a brutal and bloody conflict in which more than 20 million Soviet citizens were killed.

- ◆ Although the war created a temporary alliance between the Soviet Union and the West, there remained deep mistrust on both sides.

- ◆ The Second World War ended with a victory for the Soviet Union that saw its troops firmly in control of most of Eastern Europe.

- ◆ Stalin used his military success to establish communist regimes throughout Eastern Europe, which led to a collapse of the wartime alliance with the West.

Part 4

Communist Expansion and the Cold War

In this part, we follow how Soviet arms and secret police established communist parties in most of Eastern Europe. In a couple of places, Yugoslavia and China, local Marxists won their own fights without much help from Russia. From the United States and Britain, it suddenly looked as if the tough-minded Soviet communists had taken over about a third of the world and were aiming to take the rest. The activities of American communists now seemed very un-American, and we take a balanced look at the so-called McCarthy era.

Meanwhile, the Soviets had problems of their own. Yugoslavia and China both wanted to go their own way, and trouble started brewing in the "satellites" of Czechoslovakia, Hungary, Poland, and a few other places.

Chapter 3

Satellites In (and Out of) Orbit

In This Chapter

- ◆ Satellites and nations
- ◆ Conformity and deviation
- ◆ Bulgaria: in orbit
- ◆ Romania: a dangerous game
- ◆ Albania: the wayward wanderer

In this chapter, we look at how the Soviet Union worked to expand the area ruled by Communist Parties through the region that the Red Army liberated from the Nazis at the end of the Second World War. We look at how the Soviets were able to set up friendly regimes in several countries, right away after the Second World War. In addition to the control over the republics of the Soviet Union, communists gained firm control in Bulgaria, Romania, and Albania. At first, these "satellites" appeared to stay in pretty close orbit, but as time went on, two of the regimes maintained tight control over their populations while deviating from Soviet policies and control. So if you ever wondered about how communism got a foothold in the Balkan section of the world, you'll learn that here.

Party Politics or Russian Policy?

To outsiders, particularly leaders in Britain and in the United States, the use of Soviet power to support communist governments in Eastern Europe very soon appeared to be a case of Soviet empire-building, although nominally local communist parties reflected the proletariat of their own nation. Leaders like Harry Truman in the United States, Winston Churchill in Britain, and others in the West had good reason to see the development of communist-influenced or communist-controlled governments as a symptom of Soviet expansion rather than as spontaneous expressions of local revolutionary socialist ideas.

Through the 1930s, the Comintern had laid down the rules for foreign communist parties, and when foreign leaders did not quite follow Moscow's orders, they were demoted. A few would be brought to the Soviet Union where they would get low-level jobs, be imprisoned, or even liquidated. Any Comintern-related communist party was answerable to Moscow. This was not an empty or false charge by rabid anti-communists, but the official requirement set out in the original charter of the Comintern in 1920.

During the 1930s, some of the communist parties in Eastern Europe had been completely run from Moscow. In case after case, party functionaries from one country served on the central party committee in another country. Germans and Hungarians, for example, served on the Romanian party central committee. This was a point that Romanian communists later used in their internal party politics. In a way, before the Second World War, it did not matter to anyone in the West exactly who served on such committees, because the communist parties in these countries were miniscule. But when the parties started getting power in the 1940s, to Truman and Churchill it certainly seemed that the Russians were using these comradely groups to build close allies. And it was true.

How It Looked to Stalin

Following World War II, the Soviet Union focused on rebuilding war damage and resettling millions of displaced people. Although Stalin started a crash program to build a nuclear weapon, the monopoly on nuclear power was held by the United States from 1945 through 1949. At any moment, the Western powers might turn on the Soviets to destroy communism, he feared. To maintain a buffer and extend the power of the Soviet Union, Stalin kept occupation troops in the Eastern European countries that the Red Army had liberated from the Nazis. Russian troops were stationed in a broad swath, from Bulgaria in the south through East Germany and Poland in the north.

The fear that the Americans and British would work to undermine Soviet control was not entirely unfounded. Soviet agents in Britain, notably Donald Maclean and Kim Philby, leaked information to the Russians about American and British efforts to aid anti-communist resistance in Albania and even in the Ukraine, one of the Soviet Republics.

Tipped off by Philby, police and military put a stop to these operations, arresting and later shooting American-funded agents as soon as they landed on the beaches of Albania or crossed the borders into Soviet territory.

Speeches by Churchill and Truman, and the testing of atomic bombs by the United States in 1946 at Bikini atoll in the Pacific, with films of the tests released to the public, looked to Stalin like a set of threats. The actual measures in support of resistance groups, coupled with Stalin's notorious suspicion of the West and his expansionist goals, set off the Cold War (see Chapter 15, "The Communist Party and the Cold War").

Tactics

In the period 1945–1947, the Soviets sought to convert their military occupation power in Eastern Europe into longer-lasting control. At first, the local communist parties in Eastern Europe found a place in the governments established by the occupying Soviet troops, working in coalitions with other parties of the left. In two of these countries, Bulgaria and Romania, the communist parties had early success in taking power, while it took a little longer in other countries.

The Party had several instruments of control, although the members of the parties were supposed to think of control as "discipline." Each party was run by a central committee, or politburo, that in theory spoke for the whole party. In turn, the party was supposed to represent the proletariat. When the party took control of a country, the proletariat and the party together were supposed to represent the nation. Democratic centralism was centrally controlled, but hardly democratic in the British or American sense of the word.

This idea of democratic centralism, developed by Lenin and refined over the years, in effect meant that each communist party had a small group at the top that would take power and then run the country. That group, like Lenin and his inner circle, could use the instruments of state power to ensure that things worked their way, eliminating those who disagreed. Thus, tight party control could be established and backed up by police, a controlled press (owned and operated by the party or the state), and if need be, by the military. Just as in fascist Italy or Nazi Germany, such regimes aspired to "total" control and came to be known as "totalitarian."

Baltics and Balkans

A word on geography. It is awfully easy for Americans and Canadians to confuse Baltics and Balkans, especially if you don't have family members from either region. The Baltic countries lie on the Baltic Sea, northeast of Poland, and between Finland and Russia. They include Latvia, Lithuania, and Estonia.

To find the Balkan Peninsula, however, you have to go down the map to Southern Europe and look to the countries just to the north of Greece. In World War II, the countries of the Balkan Peninsula or "the Balkans" included Yugoslavia, Albania, Bulgaria, and Romania. Yugoslavia itself was a federation of six smaller republics, all independent countries now in the early years of the twenty-first century (see Chapter 18, "Yugoslavia: A Separate Road").

Soviet Republics

For the republics within the Soviet Union, the totalitarian system was in place by the end of World War II. The Baltic countries (Latvia, Lithuania, and Estonia) had been forcibly joined to the Soviet Union in 1939 after the pact between Stalin and Hitler, becoming republics within the Union in 1940. The three Soviet Baltic republics had large Russian-speaking populations, and large emplacements of Soviet troops. The same could be said of the other larger, non-Russian republics of the Soviet Union, specifically Ukraine, Belorussia, Kazakhstan, and the Central Asian and Caucasus republics. Altogether, by the post–World War II period, there were 15 republics in the Soviet Union. Despite some rumbles in the Baltics and the Ukraine, it was not too difficult to use a combination of espionage, local secret police, and the rest of the apparatus of party and state control to keep them in line. But for the satellites in Eastern Europe, it was a bit tougher.

Bulgaria—A Stalinist Regime

Bulgaria, lying on the Balkan Peninsula just to the north and northeast of Greece, is a country about the size of Tennessee. It was an ally of Germany in World War II; Russian troops defeated the Germans there in 1944. Bulgarian-born Georgi Dimitrov, former head of the Comintern, became leader of the Fatherland Front, a coalition of anti-Nazi groups during the War. Dimitrov was secretary general of the central committee of the Bulgarian Communist Party. He was also Stalin's long-time personal friend, and they had often appeared in public together.

At the time the Russian army came into Bulgaria in 1944, the country's Communist Party claimed about 25,000 members, although opponents' estimates put their number at about 8,000. The Soviets installed a coalition government with 4 communist ministers (or, as Americans and British would say, "cabinet members") and 12 from other parties on the left in the Fatherland Front.

One by one, between 1944 and 1947, noncommunist members of the government were purged. The key to control was the fact that the Russians installed a communist in the Ministry of Interior that controlled the police. Within six months after the Soviet army moved into Bulgaria, the Ministry of Interior arrested over 10,000 people and executed over 2,100. In October 1946, the Fatherland Front won with 78 percent of the vote.

Even so, a popular vote of 22 percent for opponents showed considerable guts in the face of arrests and executions.

Bulgarian Backgrounder

Before World War II, the communists in Bulgaria had operated under the name of the Labor Party, and did fairly well in certain elections. In 1932, for example, the Labor Party captured a majority of the seats in the city council of Sofia, the country's capital. However, the Communist Party itself operated underground, and remained very loyal to the Comintern, with many Bulgarian communists living in Moscow. It is estimated that about 600 Bulgarians held jobs in Soviet Union government positions in the 1930s.

In 1947, a new Bulgarian constitution was announced and Georgi Dimitrov emerged as the nation's leader. He remained in charge until his death in Moscow in 1949. His body was embalmed by the same man who had preserved the body of Lenin, and a special mausoleum was constructed in Sofia to house the corpse over the next decades. Despite Bulgaria's apparently strong loyalty to the Soviet cause, there were difficulties even here.

Vignettes
In 1947, the Bulgarian Deputy Premier Traicho Kostov received official congratulations from the Bulgarian Communist Party on his birthday. Two years later, in December 1949, he was hanged as a spy for Yugoslavia and as a foreign agent who had conspired with the Americans. At his trial, he openly denied an earlier confession he had signed in police custody, but was executed anyway. After his execution, a final "revised" confession was published admitting his guilt. In 1967, again on his birthday, 18 years after his execution, the official Communist Party newspaper once again hailed Kostov as a brilliant fighter for communism. By then, it was too late for Kostov.

Purges and Counterpurges

Dimitrov was replaced by Vulko Chervenkov, known as the "little Stalin" of Bulgaria. His dirty work was carried out by Minister of Interior Anton Yugov, but soon Chervenkov dismissed Yugov for not being vigilant enough. In the mid 1950s, Chervenkov had to resign and Yugov took over; in the early 1960s, Yugov himself was purged by the central committee of the Party. Yugov got off better than some others did, living comfortably in a nice house with a chauffeur and a gardener in the late 1960s.

The issues that led to these rounds of purges and reversals, however, were not signs of popular pressure. Rather, the policy shifts appeared to emanate from shifts in Kremlin policy, some of them over the issue of how to industrialize. Traicho Kostov, the ruthless Minister of Interior and effective head of the Party in the period from 1944 to 1947, was himself purged and executed in December 1949. His actual crime appeared to have been an attempt to sell Bulgarian tobacco on the international market, in competition with Bulgarian tobacco sold through a joint Russian-Bulgarian company. However, rather than charging him with excessively serving Bulgarian economic interests over those of the Russians, he was charged with ideological deviation and treasonous behavior.

In a sense, Bulgaria represented the sort of country that lots of people in the West imagined all communist regimes to be: loyal to Moscow, not showing much shift in politics, with all dissent and civic discussion repressed, and following Moscow in lockstep. Of all of the satellites, Bulgaria probably came closest to the imagined stereotype in the West.

In the period from the late 1940s through the mid 1950s, Bulgaria under Chervenkov became the model Soviet satellite in Eastern Europe. Yugoslavia broke with the Soviet Union in 1948 (see Chapter 18), and Bulgaria was happy to join in anti-Yugoslav pronouncements. Bulgaria even began to claim that Macedonia, one of the federal republics of Yugoslavia, should really be known as "Western Bulgaria." Bulgaria broke off diplomatic ties with the United States in the most intense Cold War period, 1951–1960.

Notes on the Left

In 1948, Yugoslavia and the Soviet Union parted company. Although the causes of the split were not clear to outsiders, it appeared that Josip Broz Tito, the leader of the communist regime in Yugoslavia, was acting independently of Moscow, trying to incorporate Albania into the Yugoslav Federation. Other moves, such as uniting with Bulgaria, were also apparently in the works. When Stalin got wind of these attempts to increase the Yugoslav power base, which were being arranged without first consulting Moscow, he was enraged. Yugoslavia had a strong army, discouraging any thought of military invasion, but Moscow urged Yugoslav communists to seek a new leader. However, Tito's control of his party and bureaucracy could not be cracked. The Yugoslav-Soviet split became quite permanent, and affected the policies of neighboring countries who could now prove their loyalty to Moscow by denouncing Yugoslavia.

The Bulgarian government moved quickly in collectivizing agricultural production, following the pathway set by the Soviet Union. By 1950, Bulgaria had 44 percent of all farmland either in state farms or collectives, more than any other satellite country at the time. By 1957, Bulgaria announced that all private farms had been eliminated, although farmers were actually able to retain small plots on which they raised huge amounts of food and dairy products for private sale. That particular fact did not get much publicity, but was figured out later by outside analysts.

Bulgaria traded almost exclusively with other countries in the *Communist bloc*. Before the war, only about 12 percent of Bulgaria's foreign trade had been with those nations, but by 1951, over 90 percent was within the bloc. Gradually, however, in the 1950s and 1960s,

Bulgaria began a program of wider trade with the West. By the late 1960s, about one third of the country's foreign trade was with nonbloc countries.

Red Words

The term **Communist bloc** changed meaning depending on what countries were in favor with the Kremlin. In the 1950s, "bloc" countries included the Soviet Union, East Germany, Poland, Czechoslovakia, Hungary, Romania, Bulgaria, and Albania. In Asia, China, North Korea, and Mongolia were also in the bloc. In the United Nations, the Soviet Union had been able to obtain two General Assembly seats for member republics of the Soviet Union: the Ukraine and Belorussia (Belarus).

A Satellite in Orbit

Todor Zhivkov emerged as the Bulgarian strongman in 1954, and for the next 35 years continued to maintain Bulgaria as a tightly controlled communist state. Until he was ousted in 1989, Bulgaria remained the Soviet satellite with the closest ties to the Soviet Union, with a party that followed Soviet shifts quite religiously. Even in strictly administrative questions, like a Soviet emphasis on decentralized planning that began in 1964, Bulgaria was quick to follow along. Outsiders debated whether Bulgaria was genuinely faithful to the Soviets, or simply a subdued and subservient satellite, or a mixture of both. It was clear that, from the Soviet perspective, Bulgaria was a solid ally and loyal to the vision of communism that emanated from Moscow.

Romania

Romania (or Rumania, as it is sometimes spelled) had to give up chunks of territory during and after World War II. What was left over was about the size and shape of the American state of Oregon. On its northern border, sections of land known as Bukovina and Bessarabia were ceded to the Soviets. The two Soviet republics, Moldova and Ukraine, benefited as a consequence of the 1939 Nazi-Soviet Pact. The Germans gave the Russians a free hand to annex what they liked there, and on June 26, 1940, the Soviets presented the Romanians with an ultimatum for the lands. Most of the new lands were annexed to the Moldovian Autonomous Soviet Republic, and in August 1940, the status of Moldova in the Soviet Union was raised to a full member republic.

Germany then helped out its ally Hungary by transferring 16,000 square miles of Transylvania from Romania to Hungary. And in the south, the Germans forced Romania to give up another piece, south of the Danube River, known as southern Dobruja, to Bulgaria. Altogether, Romania lost over a third of its territory and five million citizens by these transfers.

As elsewhere in Eastern Europe, such losses of borderlands remained a sore spot, sometimes making Romania a less than ideal satellite from the Kremlin viewpoint. With strong territorial grievances against its neighbors Ukraine, Moldova, Bulgaria, and the Soviet Union itself, it was hard to be a warm-hearted comrade.

During World War II, Romanian forces fought on the German side, temporarily retaking Bessarabia, pushing back the Russians to Odessa, and committing atrocities in the part of Russia they occupied. These memories soured relations between Romania and the Soviet Union in the postwar period.

Furthermore, the language of Romania is closer to Italian and Spanish than it is to any of the Slavic languages of some of its neighbors, so its cultural link to Russia was never as strong as that of countries such as Czechoslovakia or Bulgaria.

The King's Coup

Romanians staged a coup that threw out the pro-Nazi regime on August 23, 1944, in which the local Communist Party played a significant role. The coup was organized, oddly enough, by the ruling monarch, young King Michael, who collaborated with a coalition of the Communist, Social Democratic, National Peasants', and National Liberal parties. The new, pro-Allied government welcomed Russian troops and turned its army against Germany.

The coup and the abrupt change of sides by Romania allowed the Russian Red Army to move quickly and push the Germans back to Bulgaria, Yugoslavia, and Hungary. Later, Romanian communist historians played up the role of their party in the coup, while the Soviet historians for a while claimed that the liberation of Romania was almost entirely the work of the Russian Red Army. Which version of the coup's history one accepted became an indicator of one's precise position in Romanian communist politics in later years.

The Russians played on the territorial issue, promising to get the Transylvanian lands back from Hungary, which was finally achieved in a peace treaty in 1947. The net loss of land and territory for Romania was about 20 percent of the prewar land and about 15 percent of the population.

According to the scrap of paper on which Churchill scribbled his agreement with Stalin, the Soviet Union was to have 90 percent preponderance in Romanian affairs. In effect, Britain agreed to let the Russians do what they liked in Romania. In early 1945, before the fall of Berlin, the Soviet Deputy Foreign Minister, Andrei Vishinski, called on the King and told him to dismiss the current government. Within a month, with a million Soviet troops in the nation, the new government was established, headed by Petru Groza, a leader of the "Plowmen's Front," communist party.

> **Vignettes**
>
> When Andrei Vishinski called on King Michael in February 1945, he spent two hours presenting an ultimatum that described exactly what sort of government the Russians expected the Romanians to establish. He gave the king a list of cabinet officers he expected to see in office the next day, pounding the table. When Vishinski stormed out of the room, he slammed the door so hard that the plaster cracked on the wall. King Michael was not amused. Eventually, however, he accepted a government that satisfied the Russians.

With a Little Help from My Friends

The Groza government, through the use of the secret police, began a series of arrests and purges. Then, on December 30, 1947, the king was forced to abdicate, and a new constitution was established, declaring Romania a people's republic.

Since Romania had been an Axis power in World War II, the Soviets took capital goods in payment of war reparations. Although officially set at $300 million in 1938 prices, some estimates put the final tally of equipment and supplies transferred to the Soviets at about $2 billion in 1950 values.

Soviet economic exploitation of Romania took several other forms. The manufacturing, mining, and lumber economy was organized in 16 joint Soviet-Romanian firms, each controlling a sector such as crude oil, chemical, or timber. After 1953, the Romanians purchased back the Soviet half of these "Sovroms" at greatly inflated prices, although the Soviets held their share in the oil and uranium Sovroms until after 1956.

Romania remained a somewhat docile satellite until the mid 1960s, when the country adopted an explicit policy of "Romanianization," which meant a cultural shift away from Russian culture. Although pronounced and well noted by communists and noncommunists outside of Romania, the shift was never sharp enough to justify a military invasion by the Soviet Union. The deviation, such as it was, was strictly controlled from the top by two strong dictators, Gheorghiu-Dej and later, Nicolae Ceausescu.

Gheorghiu-Dej

The Romanian Communist Party had been characterized in the 1920s and 1930s by the fact that many of its key members were non-Romanians, and that for years it operated from Moscow. A smaller wing of the Party had operated underground and in Romanian prisons. There was a "Muscovite" wing and a "home" wing of the Party. In October 1945, a leader of the "home" group, Gheorghe Gheorghiu-Dej was selected as secretary general of the Party. The "Dej" part of his name came from his hometown. It was part of his style to emphasize his roots in Romania. The Muscovites and the home wing continued a behind-the-scenes struggle for power, blaming each other for ideological mistakes. In 1952, Gheorghiu-Dej succeeded in purging the Party's central committee of the Muscovites.

Notes on the Left

Romanian communist politics remained haunted in the post–World War II period by conflicts between those who had worked in Moscow, the "Muskovites," and those who had operated in Romania, the "home wing." A leader of the Muscovites was Ana Pauker, known in the West as "Red Ana." After being imprisoned for five years in Romania, she was released to Moscow under a prisoner-exchange agreement in 1939. Gheorghiu-Dej, while being interned in Romania, conducted an in-prison coup, expelling Moscow-trained Stefan Foris from the Party on the grounds he was a police spy. Foris was later killed on instructions from both Dej and Pauker in 1946. Those who had stuck it out under internment through World War II tended to follow Gheorghiu-Dej, while those operating in exile in Moscow tended to follow Pauker, in the postwar competition for control of the Party.

A Separate Foreign Policy

Historians have had trouble unraveling the dark internal politics of Romanian communism in its early days. Some believe the fight between the faction led by Ana Pauker and the one led by Dej was simply a personality clash. Others see it as a sign of a deeper Russian/Romanian division. Even if the Muscovite/home factions had deeper implications, however, Romania remained a tightly controlled totalitarian state, with few signs of departure from the Kremlin-dictated lines of foreign policy for years.

However, in the 1960s, when China began to rival the Russians for leadership of the communist world, Romania took a very careful "neutral" stand between the two communist superpowers. For a period, the Romanians offered to be honest brokers between the two powers, mediating the China/Soviet Union differences.

Gheorghiu-Dej played a careful balancing act through the early 1960s, constantly making his independence of the Soviet Union known in little ways. However, Romania remained economically dependent on trade with the Soviet Union, and Dej's political deviation was one of announced neutrality in the Sino-Soviet split and a slight opening to the West.

Notes on the Left _____

Troubles between China and the Soviet Union began to simmer, coming to a head in 1960, when the Chinese announced that the Soviet Union was no longer the correct interpreter of Lenin's message! The Soviet Union withdrew technicians from China, and henceforth, the two great communist powers increasingly disputed ideological questions. Although the lines of debate seemed obscure to outsiders, Chinese and Russian agents overseas supported different factions of communist parties, until by the mid 1960s, there were definite Maoist and Soviet alignments.

The Soviets charged the Maoists with a version of leftist deviationism close to Trotskyism that sanctioned world revolution, while the Chinese charged the Soviets with pursuing traditional Russian imperialism under the guise of Leninism. To noncommunist observers in the West, both charges had the ring of truth. As with the Soviet-Yugoslav split of 1948, the positions on the Soviet-Chinese split of 1960 could be a test of satellite loyalty.

Dej to Ceausescu

Dej died on March 19, 1965, and the Romanian Party selected Nicolae Ceausescu to succeed him as party leader. Relatively young, at age 47, Ceausescu had the difficult task of building a personal following while at the same time decrying the prior *personality cult* that had grown up around Dej.

Red Words _____

Personality cult, or cult of personality, became negative words in the world of communist discussions in the late 1950s and the 1960s. Since Stalin had built power around himself in the Soviet Union using the tools of propaganda and secret police, his successors, particularly Nikita Khrushchev, claimed that such an approach was bad policy. For a few years, leaders of other communist regimes who wanted to build a personal strong position were in a bad spot. They claimed to be relying on collective leadership, rather than one-man rule, but at the same time they had to build up a loyal following. Khrushchev himself was later accused of trying to establish a cult of personality.

Ceausescu continually spoke of "collective leadership" while at the same time building up his own power as a strongman or leader of the ruling group. Together with his wife, he began a campaign of clamping down on the emerging youth culture, even starting a no-smoking campaign. Ceausescu strengthened his hand with a number of reshuffles within the Party. He demonstrated a more dramatic break with the Dej regime when he began shifting Romanian foreign policy from neutrality in the Chinese-Soviet split back to a pro-Soviet position in the late 1960s. Oddly enough, by showing loyalty to the Soviet Union, he could demonstrate his independent power. Just one more of those paradoxical twists that came from life in Eastern Europe!

Ceausescu continued the policy that showed Romania's independence in a number of ways. For example, he opened relations with West Germany in 1967, departing from the policy of other Soviet satellites. Romania opened several trade deals with Israel, again a policy not in line with the other countries of Eastern Europe.

Notes on the Left

One problem not resolved in many of the communist nations was the issue of *succession of power*. Several strongman leaders ruled for life, much as monarchs:

Joseph Stalin	Soviet Union	1924–1953
Josip Broz Tito	Yugoslavia	1944–1980
Enver Hoxha	Albania	1945–1985
Kim Il Sung	North Korea	1949–1994
Mao Zedong	China	1949–1976
Todor Zhivkov	Bulgaria	1954–1989
Fidel Castro	Cuba	1959–Present
Nicolae Ceausescu	Romania	1965–1989

Although Romania remained in orbit, its orbit was not nearly as stable as that of Bulgaria. Both Romanian dictators, Dej and Ceausescu, demonstrated that a communist regime by the 1960s did not have to remain loyal in every respect to Moscow. The very fact that they ruled as powerful strongmen in their own country was a measure of their independence.

Albania

In Chapter 18, we will explore the deviation of Yugoslavia from the lines laid down by the Soviets in 1948. And in Chapter 19, "China's Second Revolution and the Sino-Soviet Split," we'll detail the disputes between the Chinese communists and the Soviets that surfaced in the 1960s. But for now, to follow the story of Albania, we just need to keep in mind the fact that Yugoslavia split with the Soviets in 1948, and that China denounced the Soviets in 1960. Little Albania played these debates for all they were worth.

Albanian Background

Albania, the poorest country in Europe and the smallest of all the communist satellite countries, seized on both the Yugoslav-Soviet division of 1948 and the Chinese-Soviet division of 1960 to head out on its own pathway. The unique history of Albanians and their geographical position helps explain this satellite that acted more like an asteroid or comet. Traditionally governed by clans, and the only largely Muslim country in Europe, Albania was primitive by comparison to even underdeveloped Bulgaria and Yugoslavia. It had practically no industry and it sent its young people abroad for higher education.

Albanians, from early in the twentieth century when their nation was formed as a separate country, always felt abused by their neighbors and by the major powers. Although taken over by Italy in 1938–1939, Albania actually gained territory during World War II. When Germany dismembered Yugoslavia, it officially attached the Kosovo province of Yugoslavia, inhabited by ethnic Albanians, to Albania.

Before World War II, the communist groups in Albania represented small, internal factions amounting to no more than discussion groups, and consisting of no more than a few hundred members. Yugoslavia was able to weld these groups into a single movement, sending agents to organize resistance to the Italians and Germans. On November 8, 1941, the Albanian Communist Party was set up under Yugoslav instruction and support. Until March 1948, the Albanian Party could be regarded as an extension of the Yugoslav Party.

Of Communists and Kings

As the British supported resistance movements against the Nazis, they sent aid to the Albanian communist partisans linked to Yugoslavia, rather than to the royalists supporting King Zog of Albania. National Liberation Movement selected the Albanian communist leader, Enver Hoxha, as its secretary general and commander of its army. In May 1944, the National Liberation Movement declared itself the government of Albania and denied permission for return of exiled King Zog. After the Allied conquest of Italy, the British sent interned noncommunist Albanians stationed there back to Albania, where the Hoxha regime promptly executed them.

Proletariat Dictatorship Without Any Proletarians

Without intervention by any major Allied forces or the Red Army, Albania secured its liberation from the Axis in November 1944. The communist partisans took power, in the name of the proletariat. Of course, in a country with almost no factories, impoverished farmers, and devastated by war, there was not really any proletariat. In effect, in 1944,

Albania emerged as a "satellite" or client state of Yugoslavia. However, the restoration of Kosovo back to Yugoslavia did not sit well with the Albanians, even with Albanian communists who had taken power with Yugoslav support.

From Moscow to Beijing, with Love

When Yugoslavia got in trouble with Stalin in 1948, the anti-Yugoslav faction in Albania saw its chance. Suddenly, by declaring loyalty to Moscow, Albania got "promoted" from being a satellite of a satellite, to being a direct satellite of the Soviet Union. Over the next few years, using techniques of political division, terror, and control of the state, Enver Hoxha emerged as the undisputed leader of the small nation. By 1955, he solidified the position he had held since 1944–1945.

Albania's shift to supporting China in 1960 apparently grew out of a fear that if the Soviet Union began to enter a period of détente with the West, the Russians might improve their relations with Yugoslavia. If that were to happen, the Kremlin might expect the Albanians to once again become friendly with Yugoslavia and the Yugoslavs might then revive the idea of taking over Albania.

After discussing possible foreign aid arrangements with the Soviet Union in 1960–1961, the Albanians made it clear that they would accept aid from the Chinese. Chinese technicians began to replace Russian ones, and Hoxha had a few pro-Soviet leaders exposed as plotters in a scheme to overthrow him. A show trial held in a movie theater eliminated Soviet-trained admiral Sejko and his "collaborators."

Back to Clan Rule

Later Hoxha conducted a true, old-fashioned purge, using the techniques developed by Stalin to get rid of pro-Russian and pro-Yugoslav remnants. Of 31 members of the 1948 central committee, 14 were liquidated and another 8 were forcibly retired. The surviving 9 were all personally loyal to Hoxha. In the enlarged central committee that supported Hoxha in the 1960s, many were related to each other as in-laws, cousins, or spouses. The traditional system of clan government seemed to exist behind the trappings of a communist regime.

By the early 1960s, Albania had become something quite unique in the communist world, a Chinese satellite in Europe. Albanian policy statements followed the language of Beijing. Albanians, like the Chinese, continued to accuse the Soviet Union of using communism to advance the cause of Russian imperialism, or to complain of Soviet-American world domination. Hoxha died in 1985, after ruling his country for 40 years.

The Least You Need to Know

♦ Three of the countries of the Balkan Peninsula each represented a different type of satellite, with Bulgaria the most loyal to the Soviets, Romania making independent statements, and Albania going completely out of the Soviet orbit.

♦ Each of these three countries of the Balkan Peninsula saw *really* long-term regimes by strongman dictators: Todor Zhivkov in Bulgaria: 35 years (1954–1989), Nicolai Ceausescu in Romania: 24 years (1965–1989), and Enver Hoxha in Albania: 40 years (1945–1985).

♦ Enver Hoxha took Albania from being a satellite of Yugoslavia, through a period of loyalty to Russia, to becoming a Chinese satellite by the early 1960s.

♦ Territorial claims against neighboring regimes in each case remained sources of disunity among these countries.

Mao Zedong and the Communist Revolution in China

In This Chapter

◆ Origins of the Chinese communist movement

◆ Guerrilla armies against the Japanese

◆ Mao Zedong's life and thought

◆ The communists seize control

◆ Life under the new regime

The spread of communism throughout Eastern Europe after the Soviet Union's victory in the Second World War (see Chapter 12, "The Soviet Union in World War II") greatly disturbed many Western observers. However, as momentous as these events were, the communist takeover in China in 1949 was even more troubling. With almost one third of the world's population, the prospect of a communist-ruled China was a terrifying image. Communism appeared to be on an unstoppable march, and the need to find some way of hindering its further expansion led directly to the undeclared hostilities known as the Cold War (see Chapter 15, "The Communist Party and the Cold War").

This chapter explores the origins of the communist movement and the role of its charismatic leader Mao Zedong (Tse-Tung, old spelling). It examines how the Chinese Communist Party emerged as a dominant political force after years of protracted struggle against both internal and external enemies. It also describes how Mao Zedong eventually seized power after the Second World War, as well as his efforts to impose communism on the world's largest country.

The Old Regime in China

During the first decades of the twentieth century, China was a country in serious decline. As was the case with its northwestern neighbor, Tsarist Russia, China experienced grave difficulties and tumultuous social upheaval as it struggled to modernize. In theory, the country was ruled by the Manchu dynasty that had come to power in the late 1700s. By the late 1800s, however, the dynasty had lost its hold over large parts of the country as foreign powers, including the United States, Germany, Great Britain, France, and Japan, had seized many of the major port cities and established colonial enclaves. In 1900, popular resentment against foreign occupation erupted into the Boxer Rebellion in which Chinese Buddhist monks trained in the martial arts attacked foreigners throughout the country.

From Empire to Republic

Although the Manchu dynasty made efforts to implement reforms following the Boxer Rebellion, these did little to stave off the continuing political crisis. In 1911, a revolution led by the Chinese nationalist leader Sun Yat-sen overthrew the regime and established a new republican government. However, the country remained deeply divided. The new regime had grave difficulties in asserting control, especially over local military officials in the south and along China's frontier provinces. Internal fighting among republicans, supporters of the old Manchu dynasty, and opportunist military leaders who wanted to start their own ruling dynasties plunged the country into civil war.

The early 1920s were another difficult time for China. In the absence of any effective central government, much of the country fell into chaos. Local *warlords* who commanded their own private armies set themselves up as petty rulers over large areas of the country, including the imperial capital of Beijing (Peking, old spelling). In the north, the Russian Civil War spilled over into Mongolia and across the borders into China itself. Foreign powers continued to maintain a stranglehold over many of the major port cities.

Red Words _____

The Chinese **warlords** were, for the most part, high-ranking officers in the old Chinese Imperial Army or local provincial governors. With the collapse of almost all central authority following the revolution in 1911 and the overthrow of the Manchu dynasty, the warlords took advantage of the chaos to establish their own fiefdoms over much of China. Ruling through their control over large and often well-equipped armies, many of the warlords amassed huge personal fortunes. In many cases, they were also supported and funded by the Japanese, who wanted to encourage disunity in China in order to make their own territorial expansion easier. The fight against the warlords by the Kuomintang nationalist government that was established in 1924 took many years, and in some remote areas lasted well into the Second World War.

Vignettes

The last emperor of China, Henry Pu Yi, came to the throne as an infant in 1908. Only six years old when the Manchu dynasty was overthrown, he lived much of his early life held in seclusion at the enormous royal palace in Beijing, known as the Forbidden City. He was eventually allowed to leave in 1924, and spent much of the late 1920s enjoying a playboy lifestyle. After the Japanese occupation of Manchuria in the early 1930s, he became the puppet emperor of the newly created region renamed by the Japanese as Manchukuo. At the end of the Second World War, Pu Yi was captured by the Russians and accused of being a war criminal. Following the Chinese communist victory in 1949, Pu Yi was handed over to the new government, which imprisoned him until 1959. Pardoned by Mao Zedong, Pu Yi spent the last years of his life working as a gardener, before dying in 1967.

The Kuomintang

In 1924, however, Chinese nationalist forces coalesced around the Kuomintang movement (Chinese for "National People's Party"). Based in the southern city of Canton and headed by Sun Yat-sen, the Kuomintang promised to establish a new regime based on three principles: nationalism, democracy, and social progress. After Sun Yat-sen's death in 1925, the movement was taken over by his chief military advisor Chiang Kai-shek. Over the next several years, Chiang Kai-shek led a series of successful military campaigns against the warlords and restored order to parts of central and northern China.

In 1928, Chiang Kai-shek was finally able to recapture Beijing (or "Peking" in an older spelling) and declared himself ruler of a new nationalist government. Despite this announcement, much of the country still remained under the control of other Chinese groups or foreign powers. The Kuomintang government spent much of the next decade fighting its internal foes, including the Chinese Communist Party, as well as trying to resist Japanese expansion into Chinese territory.

The Kuomintang and the Chinese Communist Party

The relationship between the Kuomintang and the Chinese Communist Party was a complex one. Although the two movements were to become mortal enemies, they had initially formed a close alliance. In 1923, Chiang Kai-shek traveled to the Soviet Union to solicit support for the Chinese nationalist movement, and he also studied military organization with the Bolshevik Red Army. Representatives from the Chinese Communist Party also attended the first Kuomintang congress in 1924, where they voted to support all of the policies. For the next several years, the two groups cooperated closely to achieve their common goal of removing all vestiges of foreign occupation in Chinese territory.

Obstacles to Communist Growth in China

In part, this initial period of cooperation stemmed from the weakness of the Chinese communist movement. China, on the surface at least, appeared to be a very stony and infertile ground, ill-suited for the sowing of communist ideas. Although there were large numbers of industrial workers in the major cities, there was no socialist tradition that communism could feed upon. And the vast majority of Chinese were rural peasants who knew little and cared less about such ideology.

Moreover, Marx's writings were not translated into Chinese until the early 1900s. While some Chinese intellectuals were familiar with Marxism, especially those who had studied in the West, most were heavily influenced by traditional and conservative Confucian beliefs that emphasized obedience to the state and the family. China was hardly a breeding ground for revolutionary beliefs.

A national Chinese communist party was not formally organized until 1921, when it held its first meeting with the help of representatives from the Soviet Union's newly created Comintern (see Chapter 8, "Stalin and the Purges"). The founding congress was only comprised of 57 members, one of whom was Mao Zedong, the future leader of the movement. The Party as a whole was also relatively small at first. By 1924, there were only 500 formal members, although the Party would work hard and successfully at building a mass movement over the next few years. The Party only had any significant following in a few key cities, such as Shanghai and Canton. The alliance with the Kuomintang movement, therefore, gave the Chinese Communist Party at least some limited influence over the development of nationalist policies.

Vignettes

Like most of the other Chinese communist leaders, Mao Zedong came from a relatively prosperous background. Mao's father was a yeoman peasant farmer and a grain merchant, wealthy enough to send his son to be educated. Born in 1893 in the province of Hunan, Mao attended local schools before moving to Changsha in 1912 to begin his advanced education. There he became exposed to the radical and nationalist ideology, stirred up by the 1911 revolution against the Manchu dynasty.

Mao first learned about Marxism and the recent Bolshevik Revolution in Russia during a visit to Beijing in 1918–1919. He returned to Changsha and worked briefly in a laundry before becoming director of a primary school. He maintained contacts with other student activists and in 1921 helped organize the first meeting of the Chinese Communist Party. For the next six years he worked as a Party administrator and cooperated closely with the Kuomintang during its alliance with the Chinese communist movement. During this period, he was primarily concerned with helping to end all forms of foreign imperialism in China.

Mao Zedong. Mao assumed leadership in the Communist Party in the 1930s and led it to victory in 1949 after a long civil war against Chiang Kai-shek's Kuomintang movement.

(AP/Wide World Photo)

However, the Party also cooperated with Kuomintang because they were ordered to do so by the Bolshevik government in the Soviet Union. Eager to promote a strong and stable China that could help protect its eastern borders from foreign intervention, the Soviet

Union provided considerable military and financial aid to the Kuomintang. Soviet advisors, such as Michael Borodin, helped train Kuomintang troops and reorganize the Kuomintang's administration along the lines of the Bolshevik Party. Any possibility of conflict between the Kuomintang and the Chinese communists would undermine the effort to unify China as a friendly power, so the fledging Chinese Communist Party was instructed to ally themselves with Kuomintang movement.

Notes on the Left

The Bolshevik decision to support the Kuomintang rather than the Chinese Communist Party was in some ways a strange one. Soviet leaders recognized that the Kuomintang was a bourgeois, middle-class movement rather than a truly socialist one. However, most Soviet leaders argued that China was a special case. Marx himself had been generally dismissive of the possibility for communism to take hold in Asia, blaming an "oriental mentality" that made individuals too submissive to the state. Many of the Bolshevik leaders shared this sentiment.

Stalin, for his part, also insisted that the Soviet Union should support the Kuomintang, maintaining that the most import goal of Soviet foreign policy should be to protect the one country where communism had staged a successful revolution. The Kuomintang seemed far more likely to create a strong, united, and friendly China, which Stalin argued was more important to the Soviet Union than promoting the spread of communism. Nonetheless, this policy would become one of the major ideological disputes between Stalin and Trotsky.

Growth of the Chinese Communist Party

Although uncomfortable with the arrangement, Mao Zedong and other Chinese communist leaders agreed to follow Moscow's orders. In 1925–1926, the Chinese Communist Party played an important part in organizing popular revolts against the hated foreigners who controlled the important port cities of Canton and Shanghai. The Party grew rapidly as a result, and by 1927, its membership had risen to almost 60,000. But, the Kuomintang also benefited from the rise in nationalist fervor, which it used to help launch a series of military campaigns that succeeded in extending its hold over more of the country. Several prominent communists took up positions within the Kuomintang government. The Communist Party didn't challenge the Kuomintang's leadership and continued to accept the role of junior partner.

However, the underlying tensions between the Kuomintang and the Party could not be covered up forever. In their effort to attack the foreign factory owners who exploited Chinese workers and the foreign landlords who charged exorbitant rents, the

Communist Party could not help but reveal that it was equally hostile to Chinese factory owners and Chinese landlords. Unfortunately, it was these groups who provided much of the support to the Kuomintang. The meteoritic rise of the Chinese Communist Party also worried Chiang Kai-shek, who became concerned that its growing popularity might undermine the prominent position of his own movement as the focal point for Chinese nationalism.

Kuomintang Internal Coup

In 1927, Chiang Kai-shek suddenly struck against his former allies. He organized a coup among the more conservative Kuomintang leaders and forced the movement to purge its more radical members. The Soviet advisors were ordered to leave the country, and Kuomintang troops attacked Chinese communist groups, labor unions, and left-wing student organizations throughout the country, killing thousands of potential communist supporters. Much of the Chinese communist leadership died in the bloodbath, and the remainder led by Mao Zedong fled to more remote areas of the country.

The Chinese Communist Party Discovers the Peasantry

Up until its break with the Kuomintang in 1927, the fledgling Chinese Communist Party had acted more or less as a traditional communist movement. The Party was most active in urban areas, where it sought to build a following from disaffected industrial workers. However, the Kuomintang attack that almost destroyed the Party forever forced Chinese communists to alter their behavior radically. Most important, the Party abandoned its focus on industrial workers. Brutalized by the Kuomintang suppression, and later by the invading Japanese, Chinese urban areas would not became a center for communist activity until the movement's final victory more than two decades later. Instead, Chinese communism would depart from all of its Western counterparts and develop strong roots in the Chinese peasantry.

Retreating with a handful of followers, Mao Zedong established a rural base of operations in the remote region of Kiangsi in central China. At this time, Mao was not yet head of the Chinese Communist Party, although he was one of its most important leaders. However, he broke sharply with the remaining members of the Communist Party leadership over their future strategy. Heeding the orders of Soviet agents, other communist groups made a desperate effort to recapture some of the cities where the movement had once been strongest. All of these efforts were bloodily repulsed, and by 1930, the only viable center of communist activity was the Kiangsi group headed by Mao.

Voices

As the son of a peasant farmer, Mao had always been enamoured with the revolutionary potential of China's peasant masses, who had played a key role in previous revolutionary upheavals during the nineteenth century. In March 1927, shortly before the Communist Party was attacked by the Kuomintang, he reported on a visit to his native Hunan province and urged the Party to consider expanding their efforts to attract peasant support:

> All talk directed against the peasant movement must be speedily set right. All wrong measures taken by the revolutionary authorities concerning the peasant movement must be speedily changed. Only thus can the future of the revolution be benefited. For the present upsurge of the peasant movement is a colossal event. In a very short time ... several hundred million peasants will rise like a mighty storm, like a hurricane, a force so swift and violent that no power, no matter how great, will be able to hold it back. ... They will sweep all imperialists, warlords, corrupt officials, local tyrants, and evil gentry into their graves.

Appeal to the Peasants

Mao set out to attract peasant support primarily through a program of radical land reform. As he argued, "The people are the sea; we are the fish. As long as we can swim in that sea we will survive." In the case of China, this "sea" could only mean the vast peasant classes that made up most of the Chinese population. He sent agents to every village in the Kiangsi region to carry his message and organize local communist cells. He also built an organized and highly trained military force that, unlike soldiers throughout most of the rest of China, worked to protect the peasantry rather than exploit them. Finally, he developed a strategy of guerrilla warfare that capitalized on the communist troops' good relations with local peasants, to engage the Kuomintang forces in hit-and-run operations rather than direct confrontation.

These tactics were very successful, but the Kuomintang forces were too powerful and began to isolate and surround the communist enclave in Kiangsi. By 1934, Mao began to fear that his movement would become cut off from the rest of China and came up with a radical and completely unexpected solution. He proposed to abandon Kiangsi and move the Party's headquarters to the even more remote province of Yuan, a region that lay thousands of miles to the north along China's border with Mongolia. On October 15, 1934, Mao led his followers and troops on an epic journey that would become known as "the Long March."

The Long March

The Long March cemented Mao as the undisputed leader of the Chinese Communist Party. The decision to leave Kiangsi was bitterly opposed by a group of Soviet-trained communists, known as the Bolshevik Twenty-Five. In some regards, they were right, for the campaign itself was an undisguised catastrophe. Of the 80,000 people who left Kiangsi, less than 10,000 reached their destination of Yuan a year later. The victims of the harsh conditions and the endless battles with Kuomintang troops and local warlords included two of Mao's children and his brother. And Yuan was a much poorer prospect for becoming the movement's base than Kiangsi had been. The province was stricken by poverty, backward, and home to a population of merely 600,000.

However, Mao's leadership during the Long March earned him the devotion of all who accompanied him. By the time the remnants of the Party arrived in Yuan, Mao had emerged as the clear head of the movement. His ability to avoid the countless traps and overcome the numerous obstacles the Party faced during its 6,000-mile-long and tortuous journey through the Chinese hinterland gave him a reputation of having a charmed life. In later years, the image of Mao as a prophet leading the party to its sanctuary in Yuan would play an important role in developing his personality cult. And although the Party had been decimated during the Long March, what remained was a hard corps of disciplined followers who set out to build a stronghold for the movement that would eventually seize control of the entire country.

The Struggle Against the Japanese

The one great advantage of Yuan was its isolation. Removed from the Kuomintang's incessant pressure, the Chinese Communist Party had time to reorganize and rebuild. Following the model he had developed in Kiangsi, Mao set out to garner support from the local peasant population and reconstruct the weakened Chinese Red Army. By 1937, he had turned Yuan into an unassailable fortress capable of resisting the Kuomintang. In the same year, however, China went to war with Japan, and Mao and Chiang Kai-shek agreed to a tacit, if often fragile, truce in order to resist the foreign invaders.

Japan Attack on China

The Japanese launched their attack on China after putting years of growing pressure on the Chinese nationalist government to agree to widespread concessions. The invasion came along two fronts. In the north, where Japan had already seized the Chinese province of Manchuria in 1931, Japanese forces marched toward Beijing and conquered large parts of the country. In addition, Japanese troops also seized many of the chief Chinese port cities and pushed inland all along the coast. The Kuomintang capital of Nanjing (Nanking, old spelling) was taken in December 1937, with enormous loss of life after Japanese troops sacked the city.

Notes on the Left

The war between China and Japan (1937–1945) was the culmination of a long period of Japanese expansion into the Asian mainland dating from the early 1900s. In 1915, Japan had forced the new Chinese government to accept a lengthy list of demands that gave Japan great influence over the northern Chinese region of Manchuria. At the Treaty of Versailles that ended the First World War, Japan also secured the rights over the old German colonies in China, despite the fact that China had also been on the Allied side. In 1931, Japan moved to annex Manchuria, which was renamed Manchukuo, and placed the last member of China's old Manchu dynasty on the throne as a puppet emperor.

The undeclared war in 1937 began after China refused to accept an additional list of Japanese demands that would have given up control over most of northern China to Japan. Chiang Kai-shek was initially reluctant to enter into open conflict with the Japanese, but in December 1936, he was kidnapped by other Kuomintang leaders and persuaded to resist any further concessions. The outbreak of hostilities prompted the United States to condemn the Japanese actions and embargo oil shipments, moves that would eventually lead to the Japanese attack on Pearl Harbor and the U.S. entry into World War II.

After these initial defeats, however, the war in China bogged down into a lengthy battle of attrition in which both Kuomintang and the communists used guerrilla tactics to delay the Japanese advance. After the Japanese attack on Pearl Harbor in December 1941, the Americans and the British both sent large amounts of supplies to the Kuomintang and urged Chiang to launch a more vigorous attack against the Japanese occupation forces. However, Chiang was reluctant to engage his forces openly against the Japanese and preferred to build up his defensive positions around the new Kuomintang capital in Chongqing (Chungking, old spelling).

The People's Liberation Army

Mao's communist troops, on the other hand, led a much more successful military campaign. The People's Liberation Army, as the communist forces were known, conducted numerous operations against the invaders and inflicted heavy losses. With the sudden collapse of the Japanese army toward the end of the war, communist forces advanced to occupy much of the northern part of the country, including Manchuria. At the time of the Japanese surrender to the Allies in August 1945, China was divided between the communists in the north and the Kuomintang in the south. The long truce that had lasted throughout the conflict collapsed as both sides struggled for complete control over the country.

The Communist Victory

The battle between the Kuomintang and the Communist Party between 1945 and 1949 represented the culmination of more than twenty years of struggle for the future of China. Although Chiang continued to be heavily backed by the United States, and also signed an alliance with the Soviet Union, Mao had much wider support among the Chinese population as a whole. The communist military campaigns against the Japanese, in comparison to the Kuomintang's more limited efforts, earned Mao considerable popularity among many nationalist groups. Mao was also able to draw upon a much more dedicated and disciplined army of followers.

The Civil War Resumed

Fighting between the two factions broke out almost immediately after the Japanese surrender. In late 1945 and early 1946, the United States attempted to broker a new truce, but the civil war soon resumed. The conflict remained a stalemate until the end of 1947, but the Kuomintang forces began to disintegrate early in 1948. Many of the best nationalist troops had been lost during the campaigns of the previous two years, and Chiang found it difficult to find and train new recruits. Mao, on the other hand, could draw on an almost inexhaustible supply from the Chinese peasants who flocked to his cause. The economy in the Kuomintang-controlled areas began to collapse, and many of its provincial leaders either collaborated with the communist forces or defected outright.

Chinese Communist Victory

By early 1949, the Kuomintang forces were in full retreat across the country. After a tentative effort to negotiate a cease-fire with the communists failed, in July 1949 Chiang Kai-shek began plans to withdraw from the mainland and evacuate the remnants of the Kuomintang government to the island of Taiwan.

The following month, the United States announced it was ceasing all aid to the nationalists. On October 1, 1949, the Chinese Communist Party officially proclaimed the formation of the People's Republic of China, with Mao serving as chairman of its central administrative council.

Notes on the Left _____

The communist victory in China created a furor in the United States (see Chapter 16, "Communists in the U.S. Red Scare"). Conservative groups blamed communist sympathizers for having "lost China" to the red menace and launched a witch hunt to root out suspected communist agents in the State Department and other government offices. The issue also played a major role in convincing President Truman to intervene in South Korea after it was invaded by communist North Korea a few months after the formation of the People's Republic of China (see Chapter 15, "The Communist Party and the Cold War").

However, there was relatively little the United States could have done to prevent a communist takeover in China. By the end of 1947, it had already given more than $2 billion worth of aid to the Kuomintang, and in early 1948 sent another $400 million in military equipment and supplies. But this aid had almost no impact on the rapidly collapsing Kuomintang army. In fact, large amounts of American supplies were actually sold to communist forces by corrupt Kuomintang officials. The only possible options for the United States would have been using the atomic bomb, as some anti-communists suggested should have been done, or launching a massive military intervention that would have resulted in huge American casualties.

Domestic Reforms and Foreign Crises

Although his victory had been 20 years in the making, Mao proceeded very cautiously in implementing any radical transformation of Chinese society during the 1950s. After decades of foreign invasion and civil war, China was in desperate need of peace and stability in order to rebuild its shattered economy. As an official party slogan put it, the initial goal was "Three years of recovery and ten years of development."

Establishing Control

During the first years following the formation of the People's Republic of China, the communist regime focused on cementing its hold over the country, particularly in the urban areas. The new government established order and built up an administrative structure in which the Communist Party retained firm control over local governments. The regime also instituted a purge of all suspected Kuomintang sympathizers in which hundreds of thousands were arrested and imprisoned.

However, Mao made no effort to eradicate all forms of capitalism in China. While adamantly opposed to any imperialist exploitation of Chinese workers, he allowed local, as opposed to foreign, Chinese, factory owners and merchants relative leeway in helping the economic recovery. The Communist Party's official policy was, in fact, to aid this segment of Chinese society achieve the level of bourgeois development that Marxist ideology suggested had to precede a final socialist revolution.

Voices

In a speech given only a few months after the formation of the People's Republic, Mao summarized the Communist Party's approach to the Chinese middle-class:

The whole Party should try earnestly and painstakingly to make a success of its united front work. We should rally the national bourgeoisie and the petty bourgeoisie under the leadership of the working class and on the basis of the worker-peasant alliance. The national bourgeoisie will eventually cease to exist, but at this stage we should rally them around us and not push them away. ... Many of them were our enemies before, but now that they have broken with the enemy and come over to our side, we should unite with them .... It is in the interest of the working people to unite with them. We need to adopt these tactics now.

Land Reform

In the countryside, Mao made good on his promise to institute a complete land reform. Although much had already been accomplished in the areas that had been under communist control during the 1930s and 1940s, land reform was quickly extended throughout the country. Under the program, all elements of the old landlord class were removed and their holdings redistributed among local peasants.

However, unlike Stalin's campaigns against the kulaks in the 1930s (see Chapter 8), Mao made no effort to liquidate the class of richer peasants who farmed their land using hired labor. In fact, these peasants were specifically excluded from the land reform program since they accounted for a significant portion of China's agricultural productivity.

Korea

The communist government's political and economic reforms were relatively successful. In its foreign affairs, however, the regime struggled through a series of crises. The first followed almost immediately on the heels of the communist victory in 1949. Inspired by Mao's success, in June 1950, the communist government of North Korea launched an invasion of South Korea in order to unite the country under communist rule (see Chapter 15).

The invasion prompted a U.S.–lead military intervention. When American troops succeeded in driving North Korean forces back across the border and began advancing toward China, Mao ordered the People's Liberation Army to counterattack. Hundreds of thousands of Chinese "volunteers" poured into North Korea, and the conflict dragged on until an armistice was signed in 1953. Mao had demonstrated his determination to never allow foreign forces to threaten China again, but war cost thousands of Chinese casualties, including one of Mao's sons.

The Taiwan Question

In 1955, conflict between China and the United States broke out again, this time over the question of Taiwan. Although the People's Republic had been recognized as the legitimate government of China by most of the international community, America refused to do so. Instead, the United States continued to support the Kuomintang government in exile that had taken over the island of Taiwan.

The Chinese Communist Party, on the other hand, insisted that Taiwan was an integral part of China. In early 1955, communist and Kuomintang forces began fighting for control of two small offshore islands lying between Taiwan and the mainland. Fearing a communist invasion, the United States sent naval forces into the region. Mao was forced to back down, but the communist regime maintained its claim over Taiwan and tensions in the region remained high.

Notes on the Left

The small and unique country of Tibet occupies the strategic intersection between China and India high in the Himalayan Mountains. The region is deeply religious and for centuries has practiced a traditional form of Buddhism in which the country's ruler, known as the Dalai Lama, was selected by monks who believed that he was the reincarnation of the former ruler. Under the old Manchu regime, Tibetans had peacefully accepted considerable Chinese influence over their country in return for local autonomy in choosing their own form of government.

The Chinese Communist Party, however, had long insisted on complete Chinese control over the region. Following the Chinese invasion in 1959, Tibet became a cause célèbre for many in the West, who accused the Chinese of genocide in their efforts to stamp out Buddhism in the country. The issue remains a highly contested one in the twenty-first century.

Tibet

In their efforts to complete the unification of China, in 1953 the communist government moved to occupy the neighboring country of Tibet in 1953. In an agreement signed in 1951, Tibet had already agreed to allow the new regime considerable influence over its defense and foreign affairs as long as the deeply revered Tibetan religious leaders retained autonomy for internal matters. However, this arrangement was insufficient to meet Mao's insistence on complete control throughout every part of what he defined as being Chinese territory.

Mao put additional pressure on Tibet, and in 1959, fighting broke out between communist troops and the Tibetan populace. The religious leader of Tibet, the Dalai Lama, fled into India as invading elements of the Red Army occupied the country.

The Least You Need to Know

- ◆ Communism came very late to China and did not start developing any sizeable following until the early 1920s.

- ◆ The Communist Party was not initially aided by the Soviet Union, which preferred to support the Kuomintang nationalist movement headed by Chiang Kai-shek.

- ◆ Mao Zedong rejected the model of the Soviet Union and other Western communist movements and instead based Chinese communism on support from the vast peasantry population.

- ◆ During the Second World War, the Chinese Communist Party was far more successful than the Kuomintang in fighting the Japanese invasion of China.

- ◆ Despite American aid to the Kuomintang, Mao emerged victorious in the Chinese civil war between 1945 and 1949, and the Kuomintang retreated to the island of Taiwan.

- ◆ After the communist victory, Mao moved slowly in transforming China into a communist society, but the regime became embroiled in a series of international conflicts relating to questions of Chinese nationalism and various territorial claims, including Taiwan and Tibet.

Chapter 15

The Communist Party and the Cold War

- ◆ Cold and hot wars
- ◆ American strategies to stop communism in Europe
- ◆ Strategies to spread communism
- ◆ Military alliances and weapons
- ◆ Spies, bombs, and rockets

After World War II, Stalin took up the task for which he had once denounced Leon Trotsky, spreading communism from one country into a world movement. The United States emerged from World War II as the most powerful noncommunist state in the world, and immediately took up the cause of stopping communist ideas from spreading. The result was the Cold War.

The Cold War was so named because, in contrast to the air, ground, and naval battles of World War II, the conflict between the Soviet Union and the United States did not take the form of a hot war involving such battles. Divided over ideology and challenging each other for influence across the planet, the two nations never came to a full-blown hot war against each other.

Instead, both nations worked through political and revolutionary groups, fought several major wars and many minor conflicts through support of allies and intermediaries, lined up alliances made up of like-minded nations, and confronted each other across international borders, often marked by barbed wire and guard towers. In this chapter we look at the origins of the Cold War and the alignments of nations that made up the two sides. We also examine a few episodes in the early Cold War and take a look at the atomic spies who helped the Soviet Union develop a nuclear weapon.

Cold War, Sometimes Hot

The Cold War began in 1946 and lasted until 1989. On one level, it was a conflict between the ideology of communism confronting the loosely organized ideas of the free-enterprise capitalist system. However, the division was more complex in some ways. On the whole, those nations that sided with the Soviet Union during the Cold War had regimes organized along the lines developed by Karl Marx and Vladimir Lenin, and the governments that sided with the United States preserved largely free-enterprise systems. An uncommitted Third World included many developing nations, some of whom had established Marxist or socialist regimes. Although the Cold War did not lead to a major armed conflict between the United States and the Soviet Union, twice during the period, the United States and some of its allies went to war against nations that were part of the pro-Soviet bloc, with governments dominated by the Communist Party.

Korea and Vietnam

In Korea in 1950–1953, the United States and 15 other allies fought against a harsh communist dictatorship in North Korea that sought to conquer South Korea. In Vietnam in 1964–1973, the United States, together with a few allies, fought to prevent a communist takeover of South Vietnam. In the case of Korea, the communist military takeover was stopped; in the case of Vietnam, following a long and difficult struggle, U.S. forces withdrew after a fragile cease-fire agreement. Two years later, the communists succeeded in taking over South Vietnam and unifying the country under a Marxist-Leninist regime.

Vignettes
On March 5, 1946, Winston Churchill, the former Prime Minister of Great Britain, got up to make a speech, titled "The Sinews of Peace," at a small college in Fulton, Missouri. Calling on the English-speaking countries, equipped with atomic weapons, to unite against communism, he said: "From Stettin in the Baltic to Trieste in the Adriatic, an iron curtain has descended across the Continent."

Winston Churchill's phrase, "iron curtain," stuck in people's minds and for decades, Americans, Canadians, and the British called the countries of Eastern Europe that were run by communist governments Iron Curtain countries.

Declaration of a Cold War

Stalin responded to Churchill, accusing him of issuing a call to war. Communism, said Stalin, was normal in Europe, and followed the law of historical development. The March 5 speech by Churchill and Stalin's response captured the division that had emerged in Europe following World War II, and it was often remembered as the beginning or the "declaration" of the Cold War.

Truman Doctrine and Marshall Plan

In response to Russian support of pro-communist guerrilla forces fighting in Greece, on March 12, 1947, President Harry S. Truman announced to Congress a policy soon dubbed the Truman Doctrine. Truman promised $400 million in military and economic aid to both Greece and Turkey to oppose communist-supported rebellions in the two countries. He explained to his advisers that he "scared hell out of the American people." He described the Soviet Union's regime and the communist governments and rebel groups it supported as totalitarian, representing a challenge to freedom.

This military side of Truman's policy to stop the growth of communism in Europe was soon coupled with an economic plan. Secretary of State (and former U.S. Army General) George Marshall urged European nations to set up a long-term economic program with American aid. In June 1947, at a conference in Paris, French officials sought to convince the Soviet Union to join in an evolving organization for economic recovery of Europe. After considering whether to participate, the Russians decided that the plan would require giving up sovereign decisions over economic policy, and they chose not to join in.

The economic plan became known as the Marshall Plan. It channeled billions of dollars to Europe over several years, and made German recovery part of a system of joint Western European recovery. Behind the recovery plan was the concept that thriving economies with near-full employment would not provide fertile ground for the planting of communist ideas. If the standard of living of Western Europe climbed, Truman and his advisors believed, Marxist parties would have a hard time winning converts.

Truman often spoke of the Truman Doctrine and the Marshall Plan as two sides of the same strategy, one side military and the other economic. Both were intended as specific policies to stop the spread of Soviet Union influence and support for communist ideology.

The X Article and Containment

In what became known as the "X" article, George Kennan, a State Department expert on Russia, presented his views. The article was published in the July 1947 issue of the prestigious journal *Foreign Affairs*. Kennan did not sign his name, and the article appeared with the mysterious X instead of the author's name. In 1946, he had sent a long telegram to Washington from Moscow, outlining his views, and the "X" article was a public restatement of what he had said in that telegram.

Red Words

Containment was a concept developed by U.S. State Department expert on Russia George Kennan. He suggested that, like a disease, communism had to be "contained" behind what Churchill had called the "iron curtain."

Kennan used psychological language, suggesting that the Russian government traditionally had a neurotic view of world affairs. When communist ideology became mixed with Oriental secretiveness and Russian insecurity in the mind of Stalin, the West confronted a dangerous situation, Kennan claimed. He suggested that the United States would have to take the lead in "*containing*" the Soviet Union, thus preventing the expansion to the West. Kennan also suggested that the United States should try to work toward bringing democracy to the satellite countries of Eastern Europe.

Comintern to Cominform

By the fall of 1947, the lines of the Cold War division of Europe were clear. On one side, there were communist-dominated governments of Eastern Europe friendly to the Soviet Union, and on the other the Western democratic regimes, organized financially in the Marshall Plan, with Western Germany promising to be built into a key part of that system. Reacting to the American steps as threats, the Soviet Union called for a special meeting of the Eastern European communist parties, in Poland in September 1947. There, the chief Kremlin spokesman Andrei Zhdanov called for the formation of a new international organization to advance the cause of communism. The result was the Cominform, or communist information bureau, to be headquartered in Belgrade, Yugoslavia. In addition to the parties of Eastern Europe, the communist parties of France and Italy joined the Cominform.

In some ways, the Cominform resembled the Communist (or Third) International or Comintern, the association of world communist parties established in Moscow in 1919 and disbanded in 1943, during World War II. The Cominform could be used to secure socialist solidarity and help ensure that local communist parties around the world answered to the decisions taken by the CPSU. One of the first acts of the Cominform was to help organize labor strikes in 1947 in France and Italy. The Cominform was disbanded in 1956.

Voices

"Two opposite political lines have crystallized. On one extreme the USSR and the democratic countries aim at whittling down imperialism and the strengthening of democracy. On the other hand the United States of America and England aim at the strengthening of imperialism and choking democracy .... There arose two camps—the camp of imperialism and anti-democratic forces, whose chief aim is an establishment of world wide American imperialist hegemony and the crushing of democracy; and an anti-imperialist democratic camp whose chief aim is the elimination of imperialism ....

"In these conditions the anti-imperialist democratic camp has to ... agree to a common platform to work out its tactics against the chief forces of the imperialist camp, against American imperialism, against its English and French allies, against the Right Wing Socialists above all in England and France. To frustrate those imperialistic plans of aggression we need the efforts of all democratic and anti-imperialist forces in Europe."

—*Cominform Manifesto*, October 5, 1947

German Issues

An early conflict between the communist government of the Soviet Union and the non-communist governments of Western Europe, that could have blown up into a Third World War, developed in Germany. At the end of World War II, the four major powers that had defeated Germany worked out plans for occupying and controlling Germany. They divided Germany into four zones. The Eastern zone was occupied by Soviet troops, while the three Western zones were parceled out to the United States, Britain, and France.

German Zones

The capital of Germany, Berlin, was located inside the Eastern, Soviet zone. In order to provide the Western allies with partial control of the capital city, Berlin itself was divided into four zones. In the three Western zones of Berlin, about 2.4 million Germans lived in a pocket that was governed by the Western democracies, surrounded by the Soviet Zone.

In 1947, the British and Americans began to economically unite their two zones in Germany, and the French joined in. Then in 1948, the three Western powers announced that they were establishing a self-governing federal government out of their united zones.

Blockade of Berlin

On April 1, 1948, the Russians responded to the unification of Western Germany by restricting military supplies moving from the western part of Germany through the Russian zone to Berlin. In the West, progress toward setting up a new currency and a new government went forward, and the Western powers soon extended the new currency to West Berlin. On June 24, Stalin ordered the stoppage of all surface traffic through the Russian zone to Berlin, beginning the Berlin Blockade.

Berlin Airlift

The United States responded with the Berlin Airlift, flying in over the Russian zone and delivering some 13,000 tons of food and fuel supplies to Berlin. Truman sent several B-29 bombers to Britain, that had been converted to carry atomic bombs. This move was seen as a threat to use nuclear weapons if the Airlift airplanes bringing food into Berlin were shot down.

NATO and WTO

On April 4, 1949, the United States, Canada, and the nations of Western Europe organized the North Atlantic Treaty Organization (NATO). The purpose was to assure the Western Europeans that, if the Soviet Union sought to take over any one of the countries by military force, the rest of the members of the alliance, especially the United States, would come to aid the victim. The original signatories of NATO were Belgium, Canada, Denmark, France, Greece, Iceland, Italy, Luxembourg, Netherlands, Norway, Portugal, Turkey, the United Kingdom, and the United States of America. In 1955, Western Germany joined the alliance.

In response to NATO admitting Western Germany, the Soviet Union organized the Warsaw Treaty Organization (WTO), more commonly known as the "Warsaw Pact." The original members were Albania, Bulgaria, Czechoslovakia, East Germany, Hungary, Poland, and Romania. Each of these countries had a regime dominated by a communist party, and each of the parties and the governments at first followed the Soviet Union's positions in international affairs.

NATO military planners anticipated that the Soviet Union and the Warsaw Pact nations might attack through Germany. NATO organized military and naval exercises and training among its armed services so that they would use identical equipment and be prepared to fight a Third World War effectively, should the Cold War turn into a hot one.

The nations of the communist bloc included the *satellites* of Eastern Europe, organized in the Warsaw Pact together with the Soviet Union and the Asian communist states. From time to time later in the Cold War, individual nations in Africa, Asia, and even Latin America developed governments dominated by communist parties. Sometimes Western analysts regarded such regimes as part of the bloc.

Weapons of War

One of the major reasons the Cold War seemed so dangerous was the possibility that it would change into a true hot war over some particular crisis. The Berlin Blockade and the Airlift which relieved the blockade was one such crisis, but by June 1949, that issue appeared to have been at least temporarily resolved when the Kremlin lifted the blockade.

Red Words

In the years following World War II, the Soviet Union established military-backed communist regimes in a number of countries of Eastern Europe. The countries were so tightly controlled at first by Moscow-directed parties and secret police that journalists in the West began to call them **satellite** nations, using the image from outer space in which satellites rotate in orbit around a planet.

The Russian Bomb

However, later that summer, the American leadership and public received a new shock. In August 1949, the Soviet Union detonated a nuclear device in its first full-scale test of such a weapon. The bomb that the Soviet Union's scientists had designed was exactly like the one that Americans had tested four years before at Alamogordo, and identical to the second one dropped on Japan at Nagasaki on August 8, 1945.

American defense analysts and planners had anticipated that the Soviets would develop such a weapon, but most had estimated that they would not be able to make one for several more years. When in February 1950, Klaus Fuchs, one of the scientists who worked on the American bomb, confessed that he had spied for the Soviet Union and helped provide them with details of the secret design, shock waves ran through the U.S. media and government.

The Kremlin's Atom Spies

The spy rings were separate from each other, and usually Soviet agents of the KGB and the military intelligence wing, the GRU, were careful to prevent communication among different cells containing the individuals who provided information. For that reason, it took years to identify individuals who were sometimes only shown in the records by code names. As the stories began to come out, however, Americans were impressed by what author Rebecca West popularized as a "New Meaning of Treason," motivated by ideology.

Notes on the Left _____

With the defection to Canada of a code and cipher specialist at the Soviet Embassy in Ottawa in 1945, the Canadians, British, and Americans began to learn that the Soviet Union had operated an extensive wartime espionage network in their countries. Igor Gouzenko turned himself in to the Royal Canadian Mounted Police in September, fearing that he might be going home to the Soviet Union and preferring life in the West. Although he did not have specifics as to the identity behind code names, his revelations were sufficient to begin investigations.

Among the spies were several that were among a new breed. Rather than professional spies, they were ordinary civilians, some scientists and technicians, who were motivated to support the Soviet Union out of their political beliefs in communist ideology. Canadian Alan Nunn May, German Klaus Fuchs, and the American couple, Julius and Ethel Rosenberg, all conducted espionage for the Soviet Union because of their ideological commitment, neither as professional spies nor as traitors for money.

As the general public in Canada and the United States learned more and more about the extent of Soviet espionage, that knowledge fed fear and suspicion of American and British Communist Party members.

Notes on the Left _____

Klaus Fuchs, a communist refugee from Nazi Germany, had worked for the Kremlin's espionage network precisely because of his ideological commitment. After graduate study in physics in Britain, he took an assignment with the Manhattan Engineer District to help design the atomic bomb. At Los Alamos, New Mexico, he wrote up extensive notes on the research progress for transfer to the Soviet Union. He refused to take money for his work, and when his controller pressed a small amount on him, he donated it back to the Soviet Union.

Nuclear Arms Race

With the Soviet development of a nuclear weapon, the balance of power shifted. Immediately after the two nuclear weapons had been dropped on Japan in 1945, Stalin realized that, in order to oppose the United States, the Russians would need their own weapon. He poured resources into the already existing program and put the notorious and ruthless head of the KGB, Lavrenti Beria, in charge of the weapon development program.

Hydrogen Bombs and *Sputnik*

Following the 1949 detonation of a weapon designed along the lines of what they had learned from espionage, the Russians worked on new designs and larger weapons. By 1953 and 1954, they began to develop hydrogen or thermonuclear bombs, many times more powerful than the early atomic bombs.

In 1957, the Soviet Union successfully put a small satellite in orbit, *Sputnik* (meaning "fellow traveler" in Russian). The launch of the satellite demonstrated to the world that the Soviet Union would soon be able to develop intercontinental ballistic missiles (ICBMs). By 1960, the Soviet Union had demonstrated a successful ICBM.

If the Soviet Union could mount a hydrogen bomb on an intercontinental missile, the Russians would have the capability of launching a surprise attack on U.S. cities that could effectively destroy them. This capability moved the Cold War to a new level of tension between the communist regimes of the Warsaw Pact and NATO.

Missile Gap

When John F. Kennedy ran against Richard Nixon in the U.S. Presidential election of 1960, Kennedy suggested that the Eisenhower administration had allowed a "missile gap" to develop. The United States had not yet successfully tested an ICBM. Furthermore, American espionage inside the Soviet Union was not sufficient to determine the exact number or placement of weapons.

Following the Russian downing of a U-2 spy plane over Soviet Union's territory on May 1, 1960, the United States discontinued such flights. A planned system of photo satellites that would return information about the Kremlin's weapons was not yet in place. Thus, although the Eisenhower administration suspected that Kennedy's charges of a missile gap were inaccurate, they had no definitive information to disprove the charges.

Nikita Khrushchev

By 1960, the leader of the Soviet Union was Nikita Khrushchev. Born in a small Ukrainian village in 1894, he dropped out of school at age 14 to become a metal worker. During the 1930s, he took an active part in the purges, and rose through the ranks of the Party to a position of leadership. He was known as a frank-speaking man of the people as well as a determined and committed communist.

Despite hints at a thaw in the Cold War and his condemnation of Stalin, Khrushchev kept a tight rein on the parties of Eastern Europe. Khrushchev ordered the suppression of an uprising against Soviet control in Hungary in 1956. In 1961, he directed the construction of a wall to separate the eastern and western sections of Berlin. The Berlin Wall, intended to slow down the exodus of East Germans to the West, became a symbol of the Cold War itself.

Notes on the Left

At the Twentieth Congress of the Communist Party of the Soviet Union in February 1956, Khrushchev denounced Stalin's "cult of personality." Khrushchev had emerged as the party leader soon after the death of Joseph Stalin in 1953. Compared to Stalin, at first it appeared that Khrushchev would take a softer line toward the capitalist states, and toward the United States in particular. Perhaps, Americans hoped, there would be a "thaw" in the Cold War. However, Khrushchev's regime was in some ways a continuation of harsh Stalinist positions.

The construction of the Berlin Wall in 1961 provided a powerful symbolic image of the distance between the communist bloc and the West. American President John Kennedy, on platform to left, visited the wall in 1962 to show that the United States would stand by its ally West Germany.

(National Archives)

In the following chapters we'll examine the efforts of the Soviet Union to keep control of the communist parties and the communist regimes of Eastern Europe through the Cold War years, and to expand its influence to the "Third World."

The Least You Need to Know

♦ The Cold War was a power struggle between the communist nations led by the Soviet Union and the Western democracies led by the United States.

♦ The Truman Doctrine and the Marshall Plan were devised by the Americans to prevent the spread of communist ideology in post–World War II Europe.

- The communist parties of the Soviet Union and Eastern Europe joined in the Cominform, together with those of Italy and France.

- In response to NATO admitting West Germany as a member, the communist regimes of the Soviet Union and Eastern Europe organized the Warsaw Pact.

- The Soviet Union's nuclear weapons were developed with the help of a new generation of undercover agents, motivated by their ideological commitment to communism.

- The Soviet communist regime challenged the United States in the Berlin Blockade (1948–1949) by developing nuclear weapons and long-range missiles in the 1950s and by building the Berlin Wall in 1961.

Chapter 16

Communists in the U.S. Red Scare

In This Chapter

- ◆ Communist Party internal problems
- ◆ The FBI and the Party
- ◆ Courts and the Party
- ◆ Professional and political anti-communists
- ◆ Senator Joe

In this chapter we see that, when Americans seemed to most fear the Communist Party, the Party was already on the rocks. In the late 1940s, when communist parties made great strides in gaining power in Eastern Europe, the Communist Party of the United States went through one crisis after another. We cover the fact that the crises of the Communist Party in the United States began before and continued after the political storm created by Joseph McCarthy, the junior senator from Wisconsin. Despite the fact that he played a small part in the American anti-communist drive of the period between the 1940s through the 1960s, the whole movement is remembered as "McCarthyism."

Internal Splits in the CPUSA

Membership in the CPUSA had suffered in 1939–1941 because, after years of officially denouncing the rise of Hitler and fascism in Europe, Stalin entered an agreement with the Nazis in August 1939 to share with Hitler the dismembering of Poland at the beginning of the Second World War. Communist parties around the world were told to stop criticizing Hitler and Nazism.

> ### Notes on the Left
>
> On August 23, 1939, Joachim von Ribbentrop, the Foreign Minister of Nazi Germany, met with V. M. Molotov, the Foreign Minister of the Soviet Union. The two agreed to a treaty that promised that the Soviet Union would not oppose Hitler's move into Poland, and the Nazis would recognize Soviet power in Latvia, Lithuania, and Estonia. Called the German-Soviet Nonaggression Pact, the treaty made it very difficult for Jewish Communist Party members and many others in Britain, Canada, and the United States to stay in the Party.
>
> Suddenly, communism became "the god who failed" for those who joined the Party as anti-Nazis. Ironically, the "nonaggression pact" opened the door to one of the most sordid aggressions in the twentieth century, the Nazi and Soviet dismemberment of Poland.

After the June 22, 1941, invasion of the Soviet Union by Germany, the Communist International once again suddenly changed its official line. Parties in the West were urged to support the fight against fascism and membership began to come back.

Dissolution of the Comintern

In 1943, Stalin dissolved the Comintern, or the Third International, as a gesture toward the Western Allies, particularly the United States and Great Britain. Those countries had disliked the presence of communist parties within their own countries that had taken orders from Moscow under the Third International. By dissolving the Comintern, Stalin seemed to bow to the Allies' concern that their own citizens not have divided loyalties.

Formation of a Nonparty Association

In the United States, in 1944, the Communist Party was at its all-time peak of membership, estimated at 80,000. Membership had grown during the war. In that year, the Party dissolved, and its leader, Earl Browder, reorganized it as the "Communist Political Association." This followed the idea that the Comintern was dissolved and the parties were independent.

However, Moscow's support for the concept of the parties going in independent directions was very short-lived. As tensions between the Soviet Union and the British, Canadian, and American governments grew in 1945–1946, the Soviet Party once again sought direct control over the parties in the West.

The Duclos Letter

The new line was announced through an article (called a "letter" in America) published in France by the French communist Jacques Duclos, in the journal *Cahiers du Communisme*. Duclos condemned "Browderism," which meant, he asserted, collaboration with American capitalism, and "opportunism." Browder was guilty of right wing *deviationism*, Duclos made clear. The Duclos "letter" was a signal that Browder and his independent approach to the party was out of favor with Moscow, and a heads-up to other members to arrange a change in the American Communist Party structure.

Red Words

According to the official line of the Communist Party as set forth through the Third International (1919–1943), and by Stalinists in the period from 1944 to 1953, there were two types of **deviationism**. Those like Trotsky, who deviated to the left and advocated world revolution were known as left-wing sectarians or left deviationists. Those like Earl Browder, who deviated to the right by advocating cooperation with the capitalist powers were known as opportunists or right-wing deviationists. As the Soviet party sought to control international communism, Moscow condemned those "deviating" either to the left or the right of the Soviet line.

Browder Out, Foster In

Following the Duclos letter, the Communist Political Association in the United States met, and the leadership took a vote. With only Browder disagreeing, the group reorganized as the Communist Party, and Browder was suspended from office. Later, the Party expelled him.

Under the new leadership of William Z. Foster, the Party began to closely adhere to the positions of Stalin and the Soviet Union's foreign policy. Through the next years, as the United States and the Soviet Union contested for power in Europe, Foster kept the official line of the Party, through its publications, closely in line with that of the Soviet Union.

Voices

"The masses in Europe are again striking at the root evil that is producing the ever-more disastrous series of devastating world wars, economic crises, and tyrannous governments, namely the monopoly controlled capitalist system itself. They do not accept the stupid notion, current in some American political circles, to the effect that the capitalist system is a sort of divinely ordained institution which can do no harm .... Instead, they are trying to abolish the real evil, the capitalist system ...."

—William Z. Foster, *The New Europe* (1947)

With Foster in charge, the CPUSA began to agitate strongly through all its publications against many aspects of U.S. foreign policy. As tensions rose between the Soviet Union and the United States over European issues, it became apparent that the Communist Party of the United States closely sided with Moscow, not with Washington.

Furthermore, revelations regarding espionage for the Soviet Union during World War II by members of the Party further demonstrated to U.S. and Canadian authorities that Communist Party members in the United States had divided loyalties. Some of the spies were self-confessed, while others were exposed through detective work, including the gradual decoding of secret Soviet communications.

J. Edgar Hoover, Anti-Red Crusader

The rhetoric employed by the leaders of the anti-communist "crusade" in the United States in the later 1940s fed a public hysteria. Among those most strident in their attacks on American communists was the Director of the Federal Bureau of Investigation, J. Edgar Hoover. In addition to testifying to Congress about the menace of communism as he saw it, Hoover published a popular attack on the Party, *Masters of Deceit*. That work mixed factual data about the Communist Party with an exaggerated view of the nature of its underground activities and the extent of the communist network of cells in the United States.

Voices

"The Communists have been, still are, and always will be a menace to freedom, to democratic ideals, to the worship of God, and to America's way of life .... Communism in reality is not a political party. It is a way of life—an evil and malignant way of life. It reveals a condition akin to disease that spreads like an epidemic and like an epidemic a quarantine is necessary to keep it from infecting the Nation."

—J. Edgar Hoover, in testimony to Congress, 1947

U.S. Government Crackdown on the Party

As a consequence of the growing loyalty issue, during the administration of Harry Truman, the U.S. Justice Department began to enforce a 1940 piece of legislation, the Smith Act. Under this act, it was illegal to belong to an organization advocating the overthrow of the United States government. Other laws provided further tools. The 1940 Hatch Act barred both Nazis and communists from government activities. In 1940, the Voorhis Act required groups with foreign affiliations to register with the government, a piece of legislation specifically directed at the CPUSA.

Hoover went beyond speeches and published attacks, and employed these legal tools to crack down. On July 20, 1948, he served arrest warrants on Eugene Dennis, the General Secretary of the CPUSA, and on 11 other members of the Communist Party National Committee. The charge was conspiring to teach and advocate the violent overthrow of the United States government, outlawed under the 1940 Smith Act. The Smith Act had been briefly invoked in 1941 to arrest several leaders of the Trotskyite Socialist Workers Party.

It was difficult to make the case against Eugene Dennis and the rest of the Communist Party leadership, as they had not taken any overt acts, such as stockpiling weapons, which would indicate that they were actually planning a violent overthrow. Rather, Hoover relied on linking revolutionary literature, some drawn from the writings of Marx and Lenin, to the positions of the Communist Party members. Testimony from ex-Party members and FBI informants demonstrated that these texts had been used in classes. In the atmosphere of growing international tension between the United States and the Soviet Union, these charges seemed to carry weight.

The Dennis trial became a noisy affair, because the Party was able to rally supporters to demonstrate outside the courthouse and to organize petitions. Rather than defending the First Amendment right to use any literature they chose in classes as protected speech, the Party claimed the works they studied did not really advocate violence. With contempt of court citations, witnesses refusing to testify, and demonstrations outside the building, the trial dragged on for 11 months. The Party leaders were finally found guilty.

When the case was reviewed by the Supreme Court in 1951, the Korean War had already broken out and the nation was at its peak of concern over the communist threat. In a six-to-two vote, the Supreme Court upheld the conviction of Dennis and the others.

Still more legislation in the period provided tools for the government to break up the CPUSA. In 1950, the Internal Security Act, and in 1954, the Communist Control Act passed Congress and allowed for arrest of party members.

By 1956, Hoover had been able to arrest about 150 local and state leaders in New York, California, Maryland, Massachusetts, and other states under one or another of these statutes. Some were not convicted, and some adopted the free-speech defense, that some-times worked, under a slightly more liberal group on the Supreme Court by the late 1950s.

> ## Voices
>
> Justices William O. Douglas and Hugo Black did not agree with the conviction of the Communist Party leadership for violation of the Smith Act in 1951. In their dissenting opinion written by Justice Douglas, he was more concerned about the free speech issue than about the danger to national security posed by the Communist Party. Douglas waxed sarcastic. The Party, he said, "was the best known, the most beset, and the least thriving, of any fifth column in history."

Liberal Opposition to Political Persecution

Many liberals who had not joined the Party but were sympathetic with some of its goals were shocked at the U.S. Justice Department using federal legislation to arrest people for their political affiliation. To many, it seemed an invasion of the constitutional rights of individuals, including the right of free speech and the right of association. Some of those who supported freedom of conscience, however, tended to argue for the rights of *fellow travelers* to speak their minds, rather than for the rights of dedicated party members or party *cadres*, as Justice Douglas had done.

> ## Red Words
>
> In the 1940s, those who tended to support some of the ideas of the Com-munist Party, but who did not join the Party, were known as **fellow travelers,** said to be traveling the same path. On the other hand, paid members of the Party who worked to recruit new members, took positions of leadership, or worked for Party publications, were regarded as **cadres** of the rank and file of the Party.

The Party in Hiding and Decline

Nevertheless, the legislation and the arrests stood up in court. The Supreme Court upheld convictions under the 1940 Smith Act in decisions in 1951. The Smith Act made it a crime to advocate the overthrow of the U.S. government, and many political leaders in both major political parties in the early 1950s agreed that advocating the overthrow of the gov-ernment was a greater threat to the constitution than the arrest of those who advocated it.

During the period from 1951 to 1955, much of the leadership of the Democratic Party as well as the Republican Party endorsed the effort to suppress the Communist Party.

As a consequence, in the early 1950s, a few cadres of the Party went *underground,* operating a system of secret couriers. With Stalin's death in 1953, and the emergence of Khrushchev as leader of the Soviet Union by 1955, the CPUSA began to abandon its system of underground communication. However, with the events of 1956, including Khrushchev's denunciation of Stalin and the suppression of the Hungarian uprising later that year, the American Communist Party dissolved.

Red Words

When a Communist Party member concealed his or her membership, either to avoid arrest under the Smith Act or to conduct an illicit activity such as espionage for the Soviet Union, he or she was said to be operating **underground.** Of course, this did not mean that they always took the subway, but only that they concealed their activities.

Hoover Resorts to Covert Methods

J. Edgar Hoover was more convinced of the danger of American communism than some of his superiors in the Justice Department. When the Supreme Court began to reject a few cases in the mid and late 1950s, he decided to resort to means other than arrest to help break up the Party.

At that point, Hoover instituted a covert program, not revealed until the 1970s, known as Cointelpro. This program involved unauthorized surveillance, political sabotage, and disinformation designed to hasten the breakup of the CPUSA. Hoover also employed illegal wiretaps and break-ins. Some of the material his agents uncovered would be leaked to sympathetic journalists and politicians.

Political Opponents of Communism

There had been earlier popular drives against radicals and their political allies in the twentieth century. During the 1920s, in response to several bomb attacks by anarchists and to the affiliation of socialists and IWW members with antiwar groups in World War I, there was an early Red Scare.

During the 1930s, the newspaper publisher William Randolph Hearst had attempted to revive concern about communists through his extensive chain of daily newspapers. However, in the political atmosphere of the 1930s, Hearst appeared to lose credibility with liberals by his attacks on communists more than win over support to his cause.

Through the 1930s, a variety of other conservative politicians tried to arouse public concern about the presence of communists in the United States, sometimes as a guise or technique to winning support for other political goals such as opposition to the labor movement or social reforms. Some of the most vociferous anti-communist spokesmen had been former members of the Party or fellow travelers who were disillusioned and turned against it.

"HUAC" and Its Hearings

The Congressional committee that brought public attention to the presence of Communist Party members in a variety of American institutions was the House Committee on Un-American Activities. To make its acronymn pronounceable (and a little insulting), the press always called it the "House Un-American Activities Committee," or HUAC (pronounced *Hew-Ack*). The Committee drew much adverse publicity and often, like the Hearst press in the 1930s, appeared to draw sympathy for those it exposed. For many Americans, it seemed the Committee simply sought to damage the careers of people who had once been members of the Communist Party, using the power of the government in a back-handed way to suppress freedom of expression. For others, however, it seemed the Committee exposed the extent of disloyal networks in the United States.

Many witnesses refused to answer questions about their political beliefs, on the grounds that all of their views and their former expression of those views were protected by the First Amendment to the U.S. Constitution.

Hollywood Ten

The most notorious group brought before HUAC were 10 former members of the Communist Party active in the Screen Writers Guild. This group, the "Hollywood Ten," were called before HUAC in October 1947. Many of the ten used their testimony to attack the investigation itself, and to try to expound their political beliefs. Federal marshals immediately arrested several. The House of Representatives cited them for contempt of Congress and they were tried and convicted early in 1948. The Supreme Court refused to hear their cases, and they served six months in prison for their behavior.

Soon, those called to testify before HUAC and other congressional committees about their political beliefs stopped attempting to use a First Amendment defense. Instead, they started to use the Fifth Amendment to the Constitution, which includes, among other rights, the right to refuse to testify against oneself. Many witnesses were "taking the Fifth," stating, "I refuse to answer that question on the grounds that it might tend to incriminate me." While those who refused to answer about their own activities on Fifth Amendment grounds escaped arrest for contempt, many of them ended up being blacklisted by employers' associations.

Notes on the Left

The Hollywood Ten, members of the Screen Writers Guild, testified before HUAC in October 1947. The ten were Alvah Bessie, Herbert Biberman, Lester Cole, Edward Dmytryk, Ring Lardner Jr., John Howard Lawson, Albert Maltz, Samuel Ornitz, Adrian Scott, and Dalton Trumbo. Lawson told the Committee: "It is absolutely beyond the power of this committee to inquire into my association in any organization."

When asked whether he was now or ever had been a member of the Communist Party, Ring Lardner Jr. said that he could answer the question but would hate himself in the morning for it. For those statements and others like them, the Hollywood Ten were arrested and imprisoned for contempt of Congress. The Supreme Court upheld their convictions. At a meeting at the Waldorf-Astoria Hotel in New York, the Association of Motion Picture Studios decided to fire the ten writers, and then all refused to hire them, constituting a "blacklist." The ten were unable to work at their craft after that, although several of the writers worked successfully under pseudonyms.

Professional Anti-Communists

Benjamin Mandel had been a teacher in the New York City schools who was forced out of the Party with the purge of Trotskyites in 1929. Eventually Mandel helped HUAC and later the Senate Internal Security Subcommittee as a staff aide. J.B. Mathews was a minister who had supported many communist causes as a fellow traveler, and like Mandel, he turned against the Party. He worked with the Hearst press to develop factual exposes of Party activities. Together with the Catholic priest Fr. John Cronin, these men represented a group of professional anti-communists.

Vincent Hartnett was a television producer who helped compile the entertainment blacklist, *Red Channels*. The professional anti-communists knew each other and exchanged information, supplying details to investigators and working to prevent employment of those they accused of pro-communist activities.

Other committees, with less success in winning popular interest, exposed communists and fellow travelers among labor union leaders and in a wide variety of civil rights organizations and nonprofit groups. At one point, *Red Channels* even regarded support of the Consumer's Union as a suspicious activity. But there were more serious issues as well.

Notes on the Left

There were several blacklists of those suspected of being communists or fellow travelers. In 1950, three former FBI agents and a professional anti-communist put together a blacklist called *Red Channels*. Their pamphlet specified former Party members, those who had been supporters of some communist causes, and others, totaling a list of over 150 names. Included were many who made careers in television, on stage, as writers, or who returned to films when the anti-communist hysteria had died down. Among some of the better-known on the *Red Channels* list were Leonard Bernstein, Oscar Brand, Aaron Copland, José Ferrer, Ruth Gordon, Shirley Graham, Lillian Hellman, Judy Holiday, Langston Hughes, Gypsy Rose Lee, Burgess Meredith, Zero Mostel, Pete Seeger, Artie Shaw, William Shirer, Howard K. Smith, Louis Untermeyer, Orson Welles, and Betty Winkler.

Some on the list had been open members of the Communist Party for various lengths of time, or as fellow travelers had supported various left causes. For many on the list, employment opportunities declined for a few years, but by the early 1960s, the effectiveness of the list declined. However, a few individuals had their careers permanently ruined, and a few even lost their jobs because their names simply resembled those on the list.

Some of the victims of *Red Channels* accused the blacklist of becoming an instrument for extorting money. By paying a fee, those listed could enter a process that could clear them and remove their names.

Espionage Cases

In the early 1950s, a number of major investigations and trials continued to keep public attention focused on the issue of communism and whether or not it represented a threat to the American way of life. In addition to Hoover's direct attack on the Party leadership, revelations of espionage activities of Party members drew concern.

Whittaker Chambers and Alger Hiss

Former Commmunist Party member and writer for *Time* magazine Whittaker Chambers created a national stir when he denounced Alger Hiss as a former spy. Hiss had been a rising young political star of the Franklin Roosevelt administration in the New Deal and had served in the State Department in World War II. When Chambers came forward with his allegations in 1948, Hiss served as director of the prestigious Carnegie Endowment for International Peace. Hiss denied the charges brought by Chambers and also denied he had ever met Chambers.

At first, many observers scoffed at Chambers's evidence. However, the young congressman, Richard Nixon who served on HUAC, decided that Chambers told the truth, and

Nixon persisted in investigating the details of Chambers' allegations. Eventually, Hiss was caught in a number of contradictions, including revelations that he had rented an apartment to Chambers, provided him with a car, and that his wife had typed a number of classified documents to be provided to the Soviet Union.

Vignettes
In order to provide proof of his charges, former communist Whittaker Chambers had preserved copies of many of the documents that he had passed from Alger Hiss to his Soviet controller when he worked as an agent. He later moved microfilm copies of the documents to his farm in Maryland, where he concealed them in a pumpkin in his garden. When investigators demanded that he provide evidence of the truth of his charges, he led them to the garden and brought out the microfilms. The press had a heyday in describing Chambers's production of the "Pumpkin Papers." Among the documents that Chambers gave as evidence were several from the State Department that had been retyped on a typewriter once owned by Hiss.

Although Hiss continued to deny the charges and claimed that he had been falsely accused and framed, in 1950 the courts found him guilty of perjury in his testimony to Congress over the charges. Hiss served a seven-year sentence for the perjury charges. The claimed espionage had been conducted during time of peace, and the statute of limitations made it impossible to bring criminal charges of espionage against Hiss.

Julius and Ethel Rosenberg

A case that became even more controversial than the Hiss case was that of Julius and Ethel Rosenberg. They had been members of the Communist Party in the late 1930s, and they had dropped out of the Party during the Second World War. However, a string of evidence led to them, showing that they had acted to provide classified information to the Soviet Union during the War.

Using evidence from the defection of a Russian code specialist Igor Gouzenko at the Russian embassy in Ottawa, Canada, and material decoded from the secret transmissions by the Soviet consul in New York to Moscow during the war, the FBI became convinced that they had identified a key spy who had worked on the atomic bomb project during World War II. As noted in Chapter 15, "The Communist Party and the Cold War," this spy, Klaus Fuchs, had been a young communist and physics student who escaped Nazi Germany, fled to Britain, and then worked on the British and American effort to build an atomic weapon. By 1949, Fuchs was back in Britain.

When British intelligence agents confronted Fuchs with the charges that he was suspected as a spy, he broke down and confessed. The British convicted Fuchs of violating the

Official Secrets Act, with a 14-year sentence. He only served for several years before being traded for a British spy caught in the Soviet Union.

Meanwhile, the FBI tracked down Fuchs's contacts in the United States. The trail brought the FBI to a network of former Communist Party members, including David Greenglass, Ethel Rosenberg's brother. When the FBI confronted Greenglass, he confessed, and in exchange for leniency, identified others in his cell or ring of amateur spies. He pointed to Julius Rosenberg, his brother-in-law, as the person who had recruited him to spy for the Kremlin.

Convicted in 1951 of espionage in time of war for having spied for the Soviet Union, Julius Rosenberg and his wife Ethel were executed in 1953.

(National Archives)

Julius and Ethel Rosenberg were arrested in 1950 and brought to trial for espionage in time of war, a capital offense. They continued to deny any participation in a spy network, but were convicted and then executed in 1953. Because of their refusal to confess, many Americans believed they had been persecuted for their political beliefs. The FBI and the Justice Department did not reveal all the sources of their information, as they did not want to show the degree to which they had cracked Soviet codes. Furthermore, they hoped to track down other agents.

The harsh sentence of death for the Rosenbergs, compared to four years served in prison by Alger Hiss and the nine years served in prison by the physicist Klaus Fuchs, who had provided valuable nuclear weapon plans to the Soviet Union, struck many as a serious miscarriage of justice.

On the other hand, between 1950 and 1953, the United States was engaged in war in Korea against the communist government of North Korea. The revelations of espionage by former American communists during a hard-fought war against a Communist regime suggested to many that the charges of disloyalty by Hoover, Nixon, and others were well founded.

Joseph McCarthy Gets an Idea

Joseph McCarthy was a young Republican senator from the state of Wisconsin. He had no national reputation at the beginning of 1950. However, on February 9, 1950, he gave a speech in Wheeling, West Virginia. He charged that the U.S. State Department was riddled with communists and he held up a piece of paper that he claimed had a list of their names. Because no transcript of his speech was made, various reports disagreed as to the number of communists he said worked in the Department.

Whether there were over 200 or some 57, he claimed that the Secretary of State knew about the presence of the Party members who were working and making policy in the Department. There was no list. McCarthy's speech, his first on the issue of communism and loyalty, came two weeks after the conviction of Alger Hiss and after a well-received address by congressman Richard Nixon based on his handling of the Hiss Case. McCarthy's baseless charges soon became known as *McCarthyism*.

Red Words

Within a month after Joseph McCarthy made his speech accusing the U.S. State Department of being full of communist agents, Herblock, the cartoonist for the *Washington Post*, had coined the term, **McCarthyism.** A cartoon showed a towering column of barrels of mud, with a bucket of mud about to fall from the top. Soon, the word became a synonym for unfounded charges or mudslinging.

Later, when McCarthy began to win over some believers to his charges, the term "McCarthyism" took on a meaning of militant patriotism. However, the word survived in history books as a code word for crude defamation of character and thoughtless attacks on civil liberties.

With a series of crude attacks, bullying tactics, and public speeches that offended more polite opponents, McCarthy soon won a popular following. He seemed to revel in his irreverence. Early in 1950, a lady reporter asked him when he had first discovered communism. Unabashed, McCarthy replied, "Two and a half months ago."

Over the period from 1950 to 1954, McCarthy conducted many committee hearings of a Senate subcommittee on conduct of the government, browbeating witnesses, dominating radio and television news, and staying on the front pages of newspapers. In the end, he offended too many people with his unfounded charges, and was censured by his fellow senators in a vote of 67 to 22 on December 2, 1954.

Voices

The Senate Resolution censuring Senator Joe McCarthy pointed out that he had accused a highly respected committee investigating his behavior as being "attorneys in fact" of the Communist Party. By making these and other charges, the censure motion said, McCarthy "acted contrary to Senatorial ethics and tended to bring the Senate into dishonor and disrepute, to obstruct the constitutional processes of the Senate, and to impair its dignity; and such conduct is hereby condemned." McCarthy said later, "I wouldn't exactly call it a vote of confidence."

Senator Joseph McCarthy dominated public consciousness with his attacks on supposed communists in government positions. Despite all the attention his committee hearings and his newspaper interviews brought, he did not uncover any evidence of espionage or subversive activity. His period in the limelight was just short of five years, from February 1950 through December 1954. Students of history have since tended to speak of the "McCarthy Era."

However, attacks on the Communist Party by professional anti-communists, by HUAC, and by the FBI were well underway in 1947, three years before McCarthy "discovered" communism, and they continued, with diminished fervor, into the early 1960s. The FBI continued its covert attack on the Party and former Party members through Cointelpro into the 1970s.

The Least You Need to Know

- The Communist Party of the United States was weakened by internal dissent after World War II.
- As the Cold War between the Soviet Union and the United States intensified, the loyalty of American communists came increasingly under question.
- FBI Director J. Edgar Hoover took the lead in arresting Party leaders and using undercover means to break up the Party.
- In both the House and Senate, investigations exposed the presence of communist cells in government, unions, and Hollywood.
- Senator Joseph McCarthy joined the campaign against American communists after it was well underway, and he was discredited before the campaign ran its course.
- Because of McCarthy's newsworthy tactics, his name became attached to the whole anti-communist drive and the "era" in American history.

Trouble in Paradise

In This Chapter

◆ Rise of communist governments in Eastern Europe

◆ Rumbles, riots, and rebellion

◆ Control by the Soviet Union

◆ Varieties of Eastern European communism

In this chapter we see how the Soviet Union established political control in the countries of Eastern Europe following World War II. In particular, we look at Eastern Germany, Poland, Hungary, and Czechoslovakia. In each of these nations, Marxist-Leninist parties eventually established control in the years following World War II. These parties acted as instruments of the Soviet Union, working through the NKVD, later known as the KGB. The communist parties in Eastern Europe moved to solidify control and soon became more repressive. The landmark date for the increase in repression was the September 1947 formation of the Cominform, with a tough speech by Andrei Zhdanov from the Soviet Union spelling out the Soviet view of the Cold War.

Even within tightly controlled regimes, there were plenty of indications that the masses and many leaders wanted to preserve their independence, to develop their own versions of communism, or to abandon communism entirely. So, while many in America, Canada, and Britain believed that the

"Soviet bloc" was a powerful, monolithic system firmly controlled out of Moscow, there were quite a few cracks in the system. There was plenty of trouble in paradise.

Veteran Leaders

Many of the communists who would dominate national parties in various Eastern European countries in the early post–World War II years had met at the Seventh Congress of the Communist International, held in 1935. That Congress was attended by party delegates from 65 countries. True to the Comintern line, these members had rejected both Trotskyiste leftist deviationism and right-wing opportunism. However, as we have seen, the parties adopted the line that they could cooperate with other political parties of the left, some that they had previously condemned as social fascists.

China had been represented at the 1935 meeting by Mao Zedong. The German party sent Walter Ulbricht, Ernst Thälmann, and Wilhelm Pieck. Italy sent Antonio Gramsci and Palmiro Togliatti. Czechoslovakia was represented by Klement Gottwald. The United States Communist Party sent William Z. Foster. Bulgaria was represented by Georgi Dimitrov, who also served as the leader of the Comintern.

One by one, some of the leaders from the 1930s established control of the post-war parties and much of the leadership of the satellite governments in the post-war era came from this cadre of leadership. Some of them continued the Popular Front technique of working with other parties. They all, except Tito's communists in Yugoslavia (as we'll see in Chapter 18, "Yugoslavia: A Separate Road") needed help from the Soviet Union.

East Germany

When the Soviet Union invaded Germany at the end of World War II, Walter Ulbricht and the other leaders of the German Communist Party returned to Berlin with the Russian troops. Ulbricht immediately set to work trying to rebuild the German Communist Party (KPD). Despite the fact that the USSR also supported a variety of small left-wing parties, it was difficult to set up a left-dominated government. For one thing, most communists and social democrats had simply been exterminated under the Nazi regime. Another difficulty was that in the Soviet zone of occupation, the communists and social democrats merged in a new party of unity, but in the western zones controlled by the other allies, the social democrats opposed any merger with the Communist Party.

After the Cominform denounced Yugoslavia in 1948 (described in Chapter 18), and after the Berlin Blockade of 1948–1949, the German Party transformed into a more strictly Leninist party, rather than one representing both the social democrats' and the communist point of view. Even so, when the East German regime was organized in 1949, it was called the German Democratic Republic, not a "people's republic."

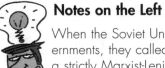

Notes on the Left _____

When the Soviet Union assisted communist parties in Eastern Europe to establish governments, they called themselves people's republics. The phrase was a code word for a strictly Marxist-Leninist regime that would govern as a single-party state. The people, organized through a communist party, would exert allegedly democratic rule. The one exception among the satellite countries of Eastern Europe was the creation of the German Democratic Republic (abbreviated DDR in German). The constitution resembled that of other multi-party democracies, such as the Weimar Republic (1919–1933) in Germany and democracies in Western Europe.

Rumbles in the Streets

Ulbricht and his associates soon emerged as hard-line Stalinists. Popular resistance to the tough regime emerged on June 16, 1953. At that time, about 300,000 workers out of a total workforce of some 5.5 million went on strike. The immediate cause of the strike was a cut in pay and an increase in work product quotas. Soviet military forces, with tanks, brutally suppressed the strike that had broken out in 274 locations. After 21 deaths, the strike petered out.

Ulbricht blamed the strike and uprising on outside agents from the West. Even if this were true, the German workers had many legitimate grievances. Ulbricht tried to calm the situation by conceding that the strict economy measures had been too hasty.

Keeping the Lid On

Meanwhile, the secret police increased surveillance and East Germany seemed securely in the communist camp. One continuing problem in the German Democratic Republic through the next forty years was the fact that disaffected individuals "voted with their feet," going to West Berlin, and then emigrating to West Germany.

Hungary

A step-by-step takeover took place in Hungary. Matyas Rakosi worked through a coalition of several parties, including the Smallholders, Peasant, and Social Democrats. These groups suppressed the conservatives, then, the communists worked with the Peasant Party to annihilate the Smallholders. Combining bribery, blackmail, exile, prison sentences, and executions, the communists emerged in control by 1949, using the *salami tactic.*

Red Words

In November 1945, the Communist Party of Hungary obtained 17 percent of the vote. By 1947, using fraud and intimidation, they received about 22 percent. Rakosi's tactic of piecemeal elimination of the opposition became known as the **salami tactic,** no doubt calling up the image of slicing up a stick of salami in order to devour it.

Hard- and Soft-Line Sharing

By May 1949, the People's Front for Independence in Hungary had a single list of candidates and took over full control of the government. Rakosi became known as a *hard-line* leader, clamping down on anyone suspected of an anti-Stalin position within the Party. However, as things changed in Moscow following Stalin's death in 1953, Rakosi had to share power with his *soft-line* rival, Imre Nagy.

De-Stalinization: Bad Luck for the Stalinists

Unfortunately for Rakosi, Soviet Party Chairman and Premier Nikita Khrushchev denounced Stalin's "cult of personality" at the Twentieth Party Congress in February 1956, and the hard-liners were suddenly out of favor. At first, only those who had attended the closed session of the congress knew about the denunciation. But the long-time leader of the Italian Communist Party, Palmiro Togliatti, released a copy of Khrushchev's speech. The release caused a sensation in communist parties in Western Europe, among analysts and journalists in the West, and of course, it created a lot of confusion in Eastern Europe.

Red Words

In the emerging communist governments in Eastern Europe after World War II, party members tended to divide between those who insisted on closely following the Soviet model, generally regarded as Stalinists or **hard-line** members, and the **soft-line** members who considered a more liberalized economic model with some ideas borrowed from capitalism and the West. In Hungary, Rakosi was a hard-liner, while Imre Nagy was a soft-liner.

"De-Stalinization" was, like so many events in communist history, a paradoxical situation. For those who were hard-liners and most used to adhering closely to the line laid down in Moscow, Khrushchev's speech was particularly difficult. In effect, he was ordering them to confess that slavishly taking orders from Stalin had been a mistake! Finding a pathway through that minefield of ideas required some very fancy footwork. Before we examine the effect of de-Stalinization in Poland, Czechoslovakia, and Hungary, let's take a look at the power line-ups in each.

Poland

Although Bulgaria, Romania (see Chapter 13, "Satellites In [and Out of] Orbit"), and East Germany settled into a pattern of hard-line Stalinist rule in the late 1940s, the process of establishing a communist regime in Poland was more complex and more difficult.

Poland Betrayed

Poland had been dismembered, cut in half during 1939–1940 when Germany invaded from the West and the Soviet troops rolled in from the East. A Polish government in exile in London broke off relations with the Soviet Union in 1943, after news leaked out of Poland that Russian forces had massacred close to 15,000 Polish intellectuals, military officers, and political leaders in the Katyn forest.

In 1944, when the Jews of Warsaw attempted an uprising against the Nazis, the Soviet Red Army stood by and watched the Nazi massacre of the Warsaw resistance fighters. Neither of these actions endeared the Soviet Union to the Poles, and it was very difficult for a Soviet-dominated Polish Communist Party to win many adherents.

Polish Reds

In January 1942, a new party, the Polish Workers' Party (PPR), was founded by two communists, but support for the Party diminished after the suppression of the Warsaw uprising. The German Gestapo tried to stamp out the remnants of the Party, yet the organization survived the war. Barely. Estimates numbered the membership in the thousands, not in the hundreds of thousands.

Borders and Coalitions

When the Soviet Union began to transfer government from their occupation forces to local Poles in 1944, they established a Union of Polish Patriots and a Polish Committee of National Liberation that incorporated the small PPR. Following agreements between the Soviet Union and the Western Allies at Yalta, a government including representatives from the London government and the Soviet-supported groups was established on June 28, 1945.

Britain and the United States recognized the new government. Following other four-power agreements at a conference in Potsdam, later in the summer of 1945, the Polish border was readjusted. Parts of eastern Poland were ceded to the Ukraine, while parts of Germany were ceded to Poland.

Polish Muscovites and Polish Natives

In Poland, even the small PPR was divided, somewhat along the lines of other Eastern European parties. Here the Stalinists or hard-liners were known as "Muscovites," and the soft-liners were known as "Natives." As the Party grew in the post-war period and maneuvered for power, the Muscovites got the key government positions.

In 1947, a rigged election led to key London members of the coalition fleeing the country. Then the Muscovite wing began to suppress the Natives within the PPR. Wladislaw Gomulka, the head of the Natives, was imprisoned on charges that he suffered from "right-wing bourgeois nationalism."

The workers in the city of Poznan led a demonstration over economic issues. Here, unlike the events in Eastern Germany, the result was an agreement by Khrushchev in Moscow that Wladislaw Gomulka could be selected as first secretary of the Polish Party. Gomulka took over in October 1956.

To outsiders, these changes in the Polish regime seemed insignificant. However, in Poland and in Eastern Europe more generally, it seemed that Khrushchev had signaled a new openness to some form of national communism, rather than the old system of domination from Moscow. But how much did Khrushchev really mean it?

The Czech Case

Between World War I and II, the Communist Party in Czechoslovakia had been relatively strong. After World War II, communist Czechs actually did fairly well in free elections. In 1946, for example, the Party had about one million members, and it gained 114 seats out of 300 in a Constitutional Assembly. In contrast to Poland and Eastern Germany, the Russians were fairly well liked in Czechoslovakia.

Perhaps all these reasons accounted for the fact that the Soviet Union did not pressure Czechoslovakia to immediately adopt a communist regime. Taking a wait-and-see attitude, the Kremlin may have expected that a friendly regime would be voted into power without any of the manipulation that took place in the other satellites.

What changed Stalin's mind was a decision made by the Czech cabinet on July 4, 1947, to seriously consider joining the Marshall Plan. Stalin summoned several members of the Czech cabinet to Moscow and gave them a dressing-down. The Czech leader Klement Gottwald, himself a communist, said he had never before seen Stalin so furious. The Czechs were ordered to reject the Marshall Plan, and they hastily agreed. However, their attempt to act independently had signaled Stalin that the Czechs could not be trusted to check with him first.

The Czech Coup

The communist coup d'etat in 1948 in Czechoslovakia was easily arranged. The communist minister of the interior began firing police officials who were not communists and replacing them one by one. The noncommunist members of the government resigned, and a new government was formed with all the key positions held by communists and a wing of the social democrats who worked with them. Jan Masaryk, a noncommunist Czech patriot well-known in the West, was foreign minister. He was the son of Thomas G. Masaryk, one of the founders of Czechoslovakia. He did not resign, but on March 10, 1948, he was found dead in a courtyard. Suicide or murder? "Defenestration in Prague" meant being thrown out of a window, a favorite method of execution there for hundreds of years. Both Thomas and, later, Jan apparently suffered the same fate.

The Slansky Trial

In country after country in Eastern Europe in the 1950s, those who dissented from the official line were tried on charges ranging from espionage to treason, and many were executed. The purge trials in Czechoslovakia were perhaps the most notorious.

In 1951, Victor Slansky, a long-time loyal Czech Stalinist, was tried and purged. Ironically, Slansky himself had advocated that the Party should hunt down traitors. "We must be all the more vigilant," he said, "so that we can unmask the enemies in our own ranks, for they are the most dangerous enemies." In July 1951, Slansky was awarded the Order of Klement Gottwald for the Building of Socialism. He was at the peak of his career.

Through 1950 and 1951, dozens of Czech communists who had lived in the West, who were Jewish, or who had shown evidence of bourgeois leanings were arrested. KGB specialists in torture would be delegated to work with the local police to extract confessions from the arrested. Several pointed out that Slansky had appointed them himself. In November 1951, Slansky admitted his own "errors" to the Party's Central Committee. A dossier of information, including Slansky's self-admission of errors, was taken to Moscow, where Stalin reviewed it. Stalin insisted that Slansky be immediately arrested before he escaped to the West.

When Slansky was brought to his *show trial*, the prosecutor had memorized a series of questions, and Slansky had memorized the answers. Once, the prosecutor slipped up and asked the wrong question, but Slansky, sticking with his memorized script, answered the question that should have been asked! On November 27, 1951, Slansky and 13 others were found guilty of treason, espionage, sabotage, and military treason. Slansky and 10 others were executed on December 3, 1951.

Red Words _____

Show trial. In the Soviet Union and in the satellite nations of Eastern Europe, Communist Party members who were purged were placed on public trial. The trials became somewhat ritualized, with capital charges and explicit confessions elicited through replies to questions from a state prosecutor. The trials served as instruments of power and as means of preventing deviation from the correct line.

Czech Repression

Despite the fact that the coup in Czechoslovakia was relatively bloodless, the brutality of the Stalinist regime that came into power there soon became notorious and showed that, while political/democratic methods had been used to take power, the result was a totalitarian state. Arrests, torture, purges, show trials, and a tough secret police that seemed to echo the worst excesses of Stalin's police state in the 1930s fed anxieties in the West. But, after Stalin's death in 1953 and after the de-Stalinization urged by Khrushchev in 1956, the possibility of dissent in all the satellites seemed to increase.

Hungary Resists

Across much of Eastern Europe, the process of de-Stalinization was difficult. Too many hints that Moscow would accept variation from its policy would be dangerous. But too strict a regime that continued with purges would not appear to conform to Khrushchev's attempt to put distance between his regime and that of Stalin. It was tough for local communists in Eastern Europe to show that they were independent of Moscow (as Moscow instructed they should be) without sounding like they were drifting outside the Marxist-Leninist camp. Not too many could carry off the balancing act.

In places like Hungary, Stalinists made it very difficult for the Soviet Union to try and mend their fences with Yugoslavia and to maintain leadership with the communist parties in Italy and France. Parties in the West took very seriously the concept of national deviation or separate paths to a Marxist-Leninist state.

Nagy and the New Course

The issue came to a head in October 1956 in Hungary. Between 1953 and 1955, Prime Minister Imre Nagy had taken steps that showed a "New Course" for the Party in Hungary. He permitted peasants to leave cooperatives, and he reduced the influence of the security services. He also suggested some plans for rationalizing the nation's economic policy, which had concentrated on developing heavy industry while neglecting the consumer.

Nagy suggested working toward more trade with the noncommunist West would be useful. But in 1955, Stalinist Rakosi forced Nagy out of the government and into prison. A spontaneous uprising in 1956 started in Hungary to call for Nagy's return.

Partly inspired by the emergence of Gomulka in Poland, as the leader of the Native wing of the Party there, and believing that Khrushchev's announcements at the Twentieth Party Conference in 1956 showed that Moscow would tolerate new changes, Hungarians took to the streets. Perhaps many believed that, as in Poland, street demonstrations would create pressure to move away from the hard-line regime.

Nagy emerged as prime minister again in October 1956. In a short-lived regime the Hungarians started to stake out a national path.

Voices

Imre Nagy, head of the short-lived government of Hungary during 1956, was a "New Course" communist. He wrote:

> The party's economic policy must be so directed as to increase the forces of production and to develop the people's economy in a proportionate and planned way .... Proportionate developing of agriculture ... will ensure the realization of the basic law of socialism (raising the standard of living) .... The party's economic policy must be founded on the principles of proletarian internationalism and the pursuit of a lasting peace, peaceful coexistence, and economic competition of different systems. Furthermore, trade agreements between the two systems (communist and capitalist) must serve the improvement of international division of labor as well as the expanding of the socialist world market.

Rakosi Out, Nagy In

Matyas Rakosi had governed Hungary under a strict Stalinist regime from 1947 until 1953, but was replaced by Imre Nagy in 1953. Rakosi remained head of the Party and removed Nagy from office in 1955. In 1956, following Khrushchev's denunciation of Stalin, Rakosi stepped down to be replaced by Erno Gero, also known as a Stalinist. Following the street demonstrations on October 23, 1956, the Soviet Union agreed to replace Gero with Imre Nagy.

In the fall of 1956, as part of the liberalization in Hungary, Prime Minister Nagy lifted restrictions on the formation of multiple political parties, released from prison a Catholic bishop, Cardinal Mindszenty, and then announced plans to withdraw from the Warsaw Pact that had been established in response to the formation of the North Atlantic Treaty Organization. The New Course was suddenly becoming a reality. The steps down the path were too much for Moscow.

Janos Kadar, in touch with the Kremlin, established a separate government in Eastern Hungary. Supported by Russian tanks, Kadar returned to the capital, Budapest, to overthrow the Nagy regime in November 1956. When Nagy was forced out of the government, he was not imprisoned. He was an old-time Muscovite and could not yet be killed without permission from the Kremlin.

Hungarian Uprising

In response, the Hungarian people conducted an uprising against Soviet domination. Workers and students armed themselves and fought the Russian forces briefly, in hopes that aid would come for their cause from the West. However, at that time, the United States faced a presidential election, and the British and French were engaged in a short war against Egypt to prevent the Egyptian nationalization of the Suez Canal.

The Hungarian uprising was brutally suppressed. Over 200,000 Hungarians, including many of the *freedom fighters*, fled to Western Europe and the United States. The Soviet Union tricked Nagy into capture, and later exiled him and many of his government to Romania. Nagy was brought back to Hungary in 1958, secretly tried and hanged in Budapest.

> **Red Words**
>
> When Hungarian youth and workers fought to prevent the Soviet reestablishment of control in 1956, Western media dubbed them **freedom fighters**. Within the Soviet bloc, the rebels were seen as reactionary agents, but in the West, they were hailed as heroes.

Kadar remained in power in Hungary for the next 32 years (1956–1988). Despite the role he played in repressing the uprising and in bringing in Soviet forces, even Kadar introduced some liberalizing reforms. But Hungary remained part of the Warsaw Pact. Later, some of the reforms introduced in Hungary, such as "market socialism," influenced policies in the Soviet Union.

Prague Spring

Despite repression of popular uprisings in Germany, Poland, and Hungary, and the continuation of a strict hard-line regime in Bulgaria and Romania, some of the communist parties of Eastern Europe continued to show reform tendencies. In Poland, Gomulka represented the national or native wing and remained in power. In Hungary, Kadar, even though he had suppressed the Nagy regime with the aid of the Russians, represented a type of reform communist. Even in East Germany, where the secret police were the most notorious in their system of informers and thought control in Eastern Europe, Walter Ulbricht appeared to keep an ear to the ground for popular discontents.

The evolution of dissent in Czechoslovakia did not center on any single charismatic figure, but rather seemed to grow from many spokespeople within the party, reaching a climax in the "Prague Spring" of 1968. The activities and writings that emerged from Czechoslovakia in early 1968 sounded very different from earlier dissenting voices in Germany, Poland, and Hungary.

Novotny Out, Dubcek In

In 1967, Alexander Dubcek replaced Antonin Novotny as Secretary General of the Czech Communist Party. Within the Party, dissent against Novotny had focused on some of Novotny's neo-Stalinist failures, and the Party leadership selected Dubcek as a moderating influence.

Action Program

By March and April 1968, Czech discussion within the Party became more and more open and public. In a statement called the Action Program, the Party announced that if their ideas did not represent the potentiality of the society, the Party's ideas had to be altered. Intellectuals began to argue that open discussion and the participation of masses of work-ers, artists, intellectuals, scientists, and others in the political life of the country would benefit Czechoslovakia.

Two Thousand Words

The Prague Spring spokesmen believed in opening up the political process to a broad base. It sounded like democracy the way the term was used in Britain, Canada, and the United States. Not only members of a narrow, top-down controlled communist party should participate in the civic life of the country, but everyone should have that right, claimed the spokesmen of Prague Spring.

Ludvik Vaculik wrote a piece that summed up the sentiment and that captured the sense of a new beginning in springtime, called "Two Thousand Words." He said, "This spring, as after the war, we have been given a great chance. We have once again the opportunity to take a firm grip on a common cause …."

In the Soviet Union, the leadership was not ready for quite so much variation from the approved party line. After maneuvering military forces near the Czech border, and after several tries at high-level meetings, a group of Warsaw Pact forces invaded Czechoslo-vakia and dismissed the Dubcek government on August 27, 1968. A repressive regime was installed, and many of the intellectuals who had contributed to the ferment of discussion emigrated to Vienna, Austria, where they formed a sort of opposition-in-exile over the next decade.

> **Voices**
>
> Zdenek Mlynar, a Czech intellectual, thought of himself as a reform communist, but some of his ideas seemed very close to those common in Western democracies. In 1968, he wrote:
>
>> In general it has been suggested here that more than one kind of political organ must be created. The political system which is based on this principle is called a *pluralist system*, and it would therefore be true to say that an experiment is going on in Czechoslovakia to create a pluralist system for which there is at present no real analogy among the socialist states.
>
> He did not like the idea of multiple parties, but he thought perhaps a two-party state, like that of Britain, might be appropriate for Czechoslovakia.

Poland Boils Over

Late in 1970, Edward Gierek replaced Wladislaw Gomulka in Poland. Although Gomulka had represented a Polish version of communism, he had remained on the good side of the Soviet regime through the 1950s and 1960s. Popular discontent with his regime simmered, largely over economic distress. Gierek hoped to reinvigorate the sluggish Polish economy with loans from Western sources.

Solidarity at Gdansk

However, the economic crises continued, and in 1976, Gierek severely repressed a series of strikes. In the late 1970s, a group of intellectuals in Poland began working with workers' groups. Problems came to a head in the summer of 1980 with a series of strikes that produced a dramatic standoff between the government and workers at the Gdansk shipyards.

Many observers in both Eastern and Western Europe were surprised when the government gave in to the workers' demands at the Gdansk strike. The key change was that the government accepted a spontaneously formed union, Solidarity, as the representative of the shipyard workers.

Over the period from 1980 to 1981, Solidarity began to act more like a national party, rather than like a trade union. Even though it appeared that Solidarity's leader, Lech Walesa, sought to take over the government, the specific goals that Walesa and Solidarity announced were strictly limited.

> **Voices**
>
> The Solidarity leaders claimed they had a "self-limiting revolution." Even though their demands were specific, their rhetoric was pretty tough. In a 1981 statement, "Who Are We and What Are Our Aspirations," Solidarity announced:
>
> > Our union emerged from the rebellion of Polish society touched by the experience of over three decades of violations of human and civil rights, from the rebellion against ideological discrimination and economic exploitation. It was a protest against the system of exercising power. What all of us had in mind were not only living conditions, although we lived poorly, worked hard and very frequently in vain; history has taught us that there is no bread without freedom. What we had in mind were not only bread, butter, and sausage, but also justice, democracy, truth, legality, human dignity, freedom of convictions, and the repair of the republic.

Jaruzelski Clamps Down

Late in 1981, General Wojciech Jaruzelski took control of the Polish Party and the government. He shut down Solidarity, imposed martial law, and imprisoned many Solidarity leaders. The repression worked for a while, but by the end of the 1980s, when changes swept through Eastern Europe again, Jaruzelski worked out a power-sharing agreement with Solidarity.

Rebels and Resisters

In East Germany, Poland, Hungary, and Czechoslovakia, the effort to impose a political framework dictated out of Moscow worked for over forty years. The communist parties took power by cleverly working with other parties of the left and then betraying their alliances. But shifts in Moscow made life difficult for the leaders.

Here and there, popular uprisings reflected economic and political dissent; intellectuals, even those dedicated to the Party, rankled at being kept on a short leash. Show trials and repression only fed a simmering discontent. The de-Stalinization, announced by Khrushchev in 1956, threw another variable into the mix. Stalinists were discredited, but anyone who took seriously the concept of complete independence from Moscow, as appeared the case in Hungary and Czechoslovakia, encountered not just a rap on the knuckles, but a military invasion. So ideas could simmer, but not take the form of true independence. The discontent was ready to surface when Moscow suddenly loosened its hold in the late 1980s.

The Least You Need to Know

◆ Communist parties gained some power in Eastern Europe following World War II using Popular Front alignments, betrayal of their left allies, and the application of brute force.

◆ After the Cominform was established in 1947, the communist parties solidified their control by eliminating their temporary allies from the regimes.

◆ Tension between hard-line Stalinists and soft-line moderates resulted in power shifts in East Germany, Poland, Czechoslovakia, and Hungary.

◆ Hard-line regimes relied on military force and KGB agents from the Soviet Union to help maintain their power.

◆ Popular uprisings and support for liberalization that followed de-Stalinization were suppressed by military force in Hungary in 1956 and in Prague in 1968.

◆ Between 1946 and 1988, communism in parts of Eastern Europe remained riddled with dissent and the ferment of ideas.

Chapter 18

Yugoslavia: A Separate Road

In This Chapter

- Tito's rise to power
- Partisans, Chetniks, and Ustashe
- In and out of the Cominform
- A new type of socialism: self-management
- The ethnic powder keg

In this chapter we look closely at the one country in Europe that set up a communist regime independently of the Soviet Union, Yugoslavia. The unique history of that country and its Communist Party made it the first communist regime to rebel successfully and openly against control from Moscow. Under the leadership of Marshall Tito, Yugoslavia not only stopped taking instructions from the Soviet Party in 1948, but began to develop a series of unique ways of managing the economy, leading to a ferment of new ideas.

Since workers selected their own management and shared the profits, the resulting arrangement smacked of syndicalism or the ideal of producer cooperatives. Yugoslav communist intellectuals developed several lines of criticism of communist government and society. We look at how Milovan Djilas knocked the self-enriching style of communist bureaucrats, and we review how young critics in the *Praxis* group considered the psychological and human side of living in a controlled socialist state. Unfortunately for the peoples of Yugoslavia, their deep-seated inter-ethnic hatreds continued to simmer, ready to blow the Yugoslav powder keg apart.

A Divided or United Land?

Yugoslavia was created as a modern nation at the end of World War I. The League of Nations redrew the boundaries of Europe, and created this new country out of several provinces of the Austro-Hungarian Empire, combined with the former small states of Serbia, Macedonia, and Montenegro. The inhabitants spoke several languages: Slovenian, Serbo-Croatian, Albanian, Hungarian, and Macedonian (which was close to Bulgarian).

Although Serbo-Croatian was a single language with two dialects, the Croats used the Roman alphabet for writing, while the Serbs used the Russian-style Cyrillic alphabet. Furthermore, Croats and Slovenes were Roman Catholics; Serbs and Macedonians were Orthodox Christians. Muslims, Roman Catholic Croats, and Orthodox Christian Serbs populated one of the provinces, Bosnia-Herzegovina. In fact, World War I started over the assassination of members of the Austro-Hungarian royal family by militant Serbs in Sarajevo, the capital of Bosnia. A look at the map will show how the kingdom of Yugoslavia (1919–1941) was assembled out of the separate national groups and provinces.

1919–1941 and 1945–1990 showing constituent republics.

Yugoslav Federal Republic

The League of Nations established Yugoslavia and a constituent assembly set it up as a parliamentary monarchy. As that monarchy developed, however, it was dominated by Serbs, leading to underground anti-Serb movements in some locales. King Alexander was assassinated in 1934 on a visit to Marseille, France, and for the next few years, Prince Paul served as regent for young King Peter.

The Communist Party

The Communist Party of Yugoslavia (CPY), like the other communist parties, had its origins out of former socialist parties at the end of World War I. The CPY participated in the elections to the constituent assembly, and won fairly large support in some regions, ending up the third largest group in the assembly, with 58 seats. However, as the Party adopted radical positions, it was outlawed and its members ejected from parliament. The CPY was behind the 1934 assassination of King Alexander. Meanwhile, the Party was wracked by factionalism. Since many CPY members lived in exile in the Soviet Union, they were caught up in the purges there. At least 100 leaders of the CPY were executed or sent to the gulag under Stalin. It was a standing Balkan irony of the 1930s that Stalin killed more Yugoslav communists than had the royal government of Yugoslavia.

Vignettes
Josip Broz was born in 1892, the son of a Croatian father and Slovenian mother. After four years of elementary school, he went to work at age 12 as a locksmith in Zagreb. A bit of a ladies' man, he learned several languages, living in Germany, Czechoslovakia, and Austria. He took dancing lessons in Vienna and as a youth enjoyed the cafés and theaters of that cultural capital. He served in a Croat regiment of the Austro-Hungarian army in World War I, rising to the rank of sergeant-major. He was captured on the Russian front and stayed there through the years of the revolution. He returned to Croatia with a Russian wife and a faith in communism in 1920. Broz came back to Yugoslavia as Tito.

Josip Broz adopted the conspiratorial name "Tito" and emerged as a party functionary in the CPY during the 1920s. He served briefly as secretary of a local branch of the metal-workers union in Zagreb. His mixed Slovene-Croatian ancestry, his knowledge of Russian and German languages, and his background as a worker and soldier all helped solidify his position as secretary of the Zagreb section of the CP, on the payroll of the Comintern. In the late 1920s, there were only about 250 members of the Party there, and only about 3000 in the whole country. Arrested by the Yugoslav government for membership in an illegal organization, Tito was lucky enough to be in jail in the period from 1928 to 1934.

It was a stroke of luck for a couple of reasons. On the one hand, it kept him out of the gruesome infighting that divided the Party in the period. In addition, in prison he met a brilliant intellectual, Moshe Pijade, who schooled him in some of the finer points of Marxism-Leninism. He graduated from prison with a clean political record (from the Comintern point of view), a solid worker background, and bright prospects for a future career in the Party. He moved to Moscow, and kept his head down, somehow avoiding the purges there that wiped out most of his colleagues. The CPY shrank from some 60,000 members to less than 6,000 as an underground party.

By the period 1938–1939, Tito was appointed by the Comintern as the secretary general of the CPY. At the time, he did not control much, living in a small room in the Hotel Lux in Moscow where the Comintern paid the rent for the collection of foreign communists living in exile or working for the Comintern.

One advantage for Tito that came out of the purged and shrunken CPY, was that, as he began to build up the Party for Yugoslavia, he did so from scratch. Among his early recruits were men who later emerged as important in Yugoslav communism: Alexander Rankovic from Serbia, Edvard (or Edward) Kardelj from Slovenia, and the Montenegrin Milovan Djilas. By October 1940, Tito had reconstituted the CPY with workers and intellectuals, and with a central committee all on Comintern payroll as professional revolutionaries.

The Little Axis

On March 25, 1941, the Yugoslav government signed the Tripartite Pact that allied Germany, Italy, and Japan. Earlier, Hungary, Romania, and Bulgaria had signed aboard in what journalists called the "Little Axis" and Yugoslavia appeared to be following suit. However, within two days, a military coup overthrew the Yugoslav government, deposed the regent Prince Paul, and installed young King Peter. Ecstatic crowds of anti-German Serbs flowed into the streets with chants of "Better war than the pact! Better death than slavery!" Actually, it comes out easier to chant in Serbian: *"Bolje rat nego pakt! Bolje grob nego rob!"* It even rhymes!

The CPY had a problem, however. The Hitler-Stalin Pact was still in effect. Comintern policy between September 1939 and June 1941 was clear: Do not oppose the Nazis. Tito and his henchmen (and henchwomen) kept quiet, although they later falsely claimed to have taken the lead in the demonstrations against joining the Axis.

Meanwhile, the Croats saw a chance to get out from under Serb domination. When Germany invaded Yugoslavia and bombed Belgrade on April 6, 1941, Croat units of the Yugoslav army simply surrendered or went home, glad to see the Germans arrive to throw out the hated Serb regime.

Germany cut Yugoslavia up like a piece of cheese. The Dalmatian coast was taken away from Croatia and given to Italy. In compensation, the Croats got to control Bosnia-Herzegovina. The Kosovo province of Serbia was sliced off and appended to the Italian puppet-state of Albania. Slovenia and Croatia were declared independent and allied with the Axis. The Vojvodina province of Serbia was handed over to the Axis-allied Hungarians. The remaining rump state of Serbia was set up as a protectorate under German control.

In Croatia, the local military, the Ustashe, loyal to the Germans, began slaughtering Serbs, and in both Croatia and Bosnia, ended up killing about 750,000 people, including some 25,000 Jews.

The CPY continued to lay low during the German conquest, since the Comintern line dictated that Germany was an ally. However, on June 22, 1941, Hitler's forces invaded the Soviet Union, and within days, the CP line began to change. *Grandfather* ordered Tito to fight the Axis, working with other anti-fascist forces.

Red Words

During World War II, communications from the Comintern to the Communist Party in Yugoslavia constituted both military and political orders from Stalin, who had turned 60 in 1939. The code word for the Comintern at the time was appropriately **Grandfather.**

Chetniks and Partisans

Supporters of the defeated Serbian monarchist government were known as Chetniks, and since they resisted the Nazis, Grandfather's orders meant that Tito should work with the Chetniks. However, for several months, radio communication between Moscow and Tito's central committee broke down. Tito's lieutenants organized military units, led by veterans of the Spanish Civil War, known as Partisans, and soon the Partisans launched into pitched battles against both the pro-Nazi Croat Ustashe and the pro-Allied Serb Chetniks. Tito specifically wanted the resistance to Germany to be dominated by the Communist Party, and looked forward to the time when bourgeois and monarchist elements of the resistance would be eliminated.

Notes on the Left

As if Yugoslav politics were not twisted enough, a further complication came with British aid to the resistance. Britain (a parliamentary monarchy with conservative Winston Churchill as Prime Minister) began to send aid to Tito's Partisan communists, and at the same time, Moscow sent aid to the Chetniks, the forces of the defeated Kingdom of Yugoslavia. The British liaison officer, Fitzroy Maclean, later wrote a couple of books about his adventures in Yugoslavia.

Although Tito apologized to Grandfather for not getting his marching orders straight, the Partisans continued to fight against not only the Germans, the Italians, and the pro-Nazi Ustashi, but against the monarchist Chetniks. All of these crosscurrents suggested how difficult it would be to hold together the Yugoslav nation. Perhaps the fights between Partisans and Chetniks showed some of the origins of Tito's independence from Moscow.

Tito's resistance army grew huge. He commanded 80,000 Partisans in December 1941. By July 1942, there were 150,000 Partisans, and by December 1943 there were 350,000. At the end of the war, in March 1945, when the Partisans converted into the People's Liberation Army as a regular force, there were 800,000 troops, the largest communist army in Europe aside from that of the Soviet Union. Later, when service as a Partisan tended to help one's career in Yugoslavia, about 1, 500,000 claimed they were veterans. Some may have been exaggerating.

With the defeat of the Germans, Italians, Ustashe, and Chetniks, Tito was the undisputed leader of the country. Although the Soviet Red Army asked permission to cross through Vojvodina, and although many Yugoslavs served in the Soviet Red Army for a brief period, the country had been liberated by Yugoslavs, not by Russians.

The Cominform

The Soviet Union officially shut down the Comintern in 1943, as part of the effort to stay on good terms with Britain and the United States. However, as the Cold War began, and as Truman announced his doctrine to provide aid to Greece in its fight against communist insurgents, Stalin decided to re-institute a system of international control of communist parties. The role of Yugoslavia in the new organization, the *Cominform*, is, like much of Yugoslav history, unique and quite peculiar on the surface.

Red Words

Cominform was the Communist Information Bureau, established following a meeting in September 1947 at the town of Szklarska Porêba in Poland. The first function of the Cominform was to make sure that the communist parties of Eastern Europe adhered to the interests of the Soviet Union, and that they got rid of signs of pro-American or pro-capitalist leanings.

During the period from 1945 to 1947, Tito's regime clamped down on all resistance, establishing totalitarian control that imitated that of Stalin in the Soviet Union. Meanwhile in the Soviet Union, Andrei Zhdanov took the lead in ensuring that dissenters and those exposed to foreign influence (such as soldiers who had served in Europe) be repressed. Tito's regime appeared to out-Zhdanov the Russians. He shut down newspapers, set up a prison camp on an island in the Adriatic Sea, and made sure that no other political parties attempted to organize.

Voices

At the organizing meeting of the Cominform in Poland in 1947, Andrei Zhdanov, the Russian, made clear the new policy was specifically aimed at the United States:

America's aspirations to world supremacy encounter an obstacle in the USSR, the stronghold of anti-imperialist and antifascist policy, and its growing international influence, in the new democracies, which have escaped from the control of British and American imperialism, and in the workers of all countries, including America itself, who do not want a new war for the supremacy of their oppressors. Accordingly, the new expansionist and reactionary policy of the United States envisages a struggle against the USSR, against the labor movement in all countries, including the United States, and against the emancipationist, anti-imperialist forces in all countries. (As quoted in Gale Stokes, *From Stalinism to Pluralism.*)

In contrast to other Eastern European countries such as Poland, Hungary, and Czechoslovakia, in which communist parties at that time worked in collaboration with other parties, Tito's regime was a tough, one-party Stalinist-style outfit. Thus, when the Cominform was established in September 1947, Tito's regime was to be the model for how the other Eastern European countries should behave. The Cominform newspaper was based in Belgrade, the Serbian and Yugoslav capital.

Cominform Expels Yugoslavia

Almost overnight, however, things changed. The paradox was that Tito had such tight control over Yugoslavia that he was not a good model for how to exercise firm control from Moscow. Tito apparently planned a few steps that irritated Stalin at the time, including appending Albania to the Kosovo province of Serbia, and merging Bulgaria into Yugoslavia as a seventh republic. Without clearing these ideas with Moscow, Tito even got the Albanians to agree to his troops moving into their country. Negotiations with Bulgaria went along fairly well, although the communist leaders there preferred to have equal status with all of Yugoslavia in the new federation, not just with the constituent republics like Serbia, Croatia, and the rest. Dimitrov, the Bulgarian communist and former head of the Comintern, suggested a Balkan federation that would include Yugoslavia, Bulgaria, and Romania. When, through his intelligence agents and some Albanian communists who did not relish the idea of being folded into Yugoslavia, Stalin heard that these moves were afoot, he summoned Tito to Moscow.

At one point, Stalin may have liked the idea of a communist-ruled Balkan federation, but as Tito began to take his own concrete steps to achieve the concept, Stalin apparently saw Tito as a rival for power in the Marxist-Leninist world. As we have seen, Stalin did not tolerate rivals or competitors for very long. Tito's independence, his full control over Yugoslavia, and his repeated assertion that the attainment of a communist state in Yugoslavia was achieved without any help from the Red Army added up to insubordination.

For a few months, the two totalitarian powers jockeyed for control, using their secret police. Tito's political police, the UDBA, eventually rounded up 12,000 pro-Soviet individuals, while pro-Yugoslav individuals in Bulgaria, Hungary, and Albania were arrested and tried for various crimes. Through early 1948, there were several public signs that trouble was brewing. In March 1948, Moscow withdrew military advisers from Yugoslavia and then protested against rumored statements that Moscow sought to dominate the Cominform. The Communist Party of the Soviet Union accused the Yugoslav Communist Party of "Bernsteinism," that is to say, peaceful absorption of socialist ideas into capitalist systems. Even more serious, Moscow charged Belgrade with being pro-American.

As Tito and Stalin exchanged letters, Tito used the question of support for the draft letters as a litmus test of loyalty to himself. When two members of the central committee balked at his tough language, he had them arrested and sent to his concentration camp, Naked Island (or, in Serbo-Croatian, Goli Otok), in the Adriatic.

The final and formal expulsion of Yugoslavia from the Cominform took place with a resolution passed on June 28, 1948. The Cominform resolution urged loyal Marxist-Leninists to "replace" the current leaders of the Yugoslav Party. Of course, since Tito had firm control over the army, the secret police, and the Party, there was no way such a replacement would happen.

Always a dapper dresser, Josip Broz Tito, here on the right, meets with a visiting U.S. naval officer. Such contacts only tended to confirm Moscow's suspicion that Tito could not be trusted to toe the line.

(National Archives)

Yugoslavia's Brand of Communism

Following the expulsion of Yugoslavia from the Cominform, the rest of the world hardly knew what to make of the situation. The Soviet position was that Yugoslavia was now collaborating with the capitalists. Americans hoped Yugoslavia would join the West, but were disappointed to learn that Yugoslavia insisted on maintaining a fully socialized economy. Every industry remained under state ownership, with the noted exception of tailors and watchmakers. Over the period from 1948 to 1950, there was little change in the internal economic system, as state-controlled enterprises continued to try to reach goals established in an ambitious Five-Year Plan.

Then, in 1950, Yugoslavia abandoned Stalinist models and moved in a new direction that some observers thought was based on syndicalism. The two architects of the system were Edvard Kardelj and Milovan Djilas. Factories and shops remained "socially owned," but instead of attempting to manage the enterprises through state-appointed administrators, the country shifted to a system of elected workers' councils that took over management. At the same time, Tito reached out to the West. American foreign aid to Yugoslavia came to $600 million between 1949 and 1955, with another $588 million in military aid in the same period.

The system that emerged was peculiar, with such strange phenomena as strikes and disputes over profit rates of outfits such as power companies. Furthermore, the system kept changing, with a trial and error search for an alternative to the West's private capitalism, and to "state capitalism," which is what the Yugoslavs began to call the Soviet system.

Over the next three decades, Yugoslavia continued to experiment with varieties of worker management councils, local self-government, direct democracy, and a socialist market economy. In the rhetoric the country adopted, certain words took on negative connotations, including statism, authority, and centralism. Much of the language Yugoslav communists used shocked outsiders, both in the Soviet system and in the West. Yugoslavs were interested in reducing taxes, maximizing profits, and reducing state intervention in the economy. Conservatives in Britain and Republicans in the United States had exactly the same ideas. At the same time, some of the Yugoslav communist ideas sounded like a mix of the more radical concepts of anarcho-syndicalism, Robert Owen's cooperativism, and Proudhon's advocacy of an end to private property.

On June 26, 1950, the government turned factories over to the workers, for management of production. The system was imposed from above, but not at all based on the Soviet model. Marx had anticipated that, with socialism, the state would "wither away," and Milovan Djilas and Edvard Kardelj focused their policy on the withering away of the state. Self-management was to become the main instrument of building of socialism. Since neither Marx nor Lenin had said much of anything about self-management, the solution was a form of creative Marxism, and the creative application of theory. The result could be called either capitalism without capitalists or socialism without the control of society. To make workers' council control a reality required a real transfer of power and controls into the hands of the councils. And that is exactly what happened.

Notes on the Left

After 1950, in every enterprise in Yugoslavia (including factories, retailers, schools, and even government agencies) a workers' council was elected by secret ballot. The council ranged in size from 15 to 70 members. The members had two-year terms, with one half renewed every year. The council would rule by majority vote, electing a board of five or more, including a director who would be responsible for day-to-day management. The position of director was advertised, and candidates were interviewed both by the local government and workers' council of the enterprise. The workers' wages were tied to the profitability of the enterprise. At first, about half the base profit was turned over to the state, but the rest was available to the enterprise for reinvestment or distribution.

The Yugoslav system was amended and modified with new sets of laws passed in 1952, 1954, 1958, and 1961, giving the enterprises power to operate in the market. By the end of the 1950s, councils planned production, marketed products, bought raw materials, decided on employment, made agreements with foreign firms, invested funds, and distributed profits.

Despite lots of inefficiencies, per capita income increased, while the variety and choice of goods in shops improved, leading to a consumer civilization. New elites began to emerge, with a tenfold increase in university faculty and students. Visitors from other Eastern European countries stared at the shop windows in amazement. One measure of prosperity was automobile ownership. There were 8,500 privately owned cars in 1952; 274,000 in mid 1967, and the numbers began to increase by 50,000–100,000 per year after that.

Despite such improvements in the life of the people, there remained lots of disparities and problems. Yugoslavia reported high unemployment and emigration. The figures were surprising, since other socialist countries refused to admit that unemployment was even possible, and did all they could to suppress emigration.

Some Free Thinking

The constant change in Yugoslavia and the dynamic search for a new path to socialism did not mesh too well with the continued totalitarian style of political control. Eventually, voices of dissent began to emerge. The most noteworthy was that of Milovan Djilas, who spoke out against the extravagant lifestyle of some of the leaders in Yugoslavia. Djilas, who saw the workers' councils as a concrete step toward the withering away of the state, gave articulate expression to the critique of a strong, centralized socialist state.

Djilas

Tito expelled Djilas from the CPY, and Djilas then compiled his thinking into a book, *The New Class*, published in 1956 and 1957. Widely read in the West in translation, the book created quite a stir. He argued that government officials in socialist states who managed the economy had all the trappings of property ownership. That is, they could use, enjoy, and dispose of material goods. In effect, socialist officials became the new class of exploiters. It sounded very much like Orwell's critique in *Animal Farm*, when the pigs became almost indistinguishable from the human farmers they had overthrown!

Voices

"The new class instinctively feels that national goods are, in fact, its property, and that even the terms *socialist, social* and *state* property denote a general legal fiction. The new class also thinks that any breach of its totalitarian authority might imperil its ownership. Consequently, the new class opposes *any* type of freedom, ostensibly for the purpose of preserving 'socialist' ownership. Criticism of the new class's monopolistic administration of property generates the fear of a possible loss of power."
—Djilas, *The New Class* (Harcourt Brace, 1957)

Djilas directed his criticism at the bureaucrats in the socialized economies of the Soviet Union and the other Eastern European countries, and not at the directors of enterprises hired by workers' councils in Yugoslavia. His book and ideas meshed quite properly with the emerging system of self-management that he had helped establish. Nevertheless, his criticism of state bureaucrats did not go down very well with the bureaucrats in Tito's own regime, and Djilas was jailed for writing the book. As an outcast of the system, Djilas continued to write and criticize communist regimes, becoming the first well-known *dissident* in the West. Other dissenters or dissidents, less well-known than Djilas, began to show up in the cafés and beer halls surrounding the flourishing Yugoslav universities.

Red Words

Beginning in the 1950s, intellectuals in Eastern Europe and the Soviet Union who criticized the flaws in the communist regimes came to be known as **dissidents**.

The *Praxis* Group

A group of Yugoslav social thinkers published the journal *Praxis* in Zagreb, in the years 1964–1974. Published in Serbo-Croatian and translated into Western European languages, *Praxis* soon had an influence throughout Europe. The thrust of the journal was to try to create socialism with a human face, arguing that modern socialist states, like capitalist societies, created large impersonal systems. Whether these systems were corporations or bureaus, the nature of modern economic enterprise required that certain basic human values be sacrificed to routinized tasks, authority structures, impersonal communication, and anonymous relationships. All modernizing societies, these thinkers argued, faced similar problems of alienation and self-estrangement.

Socialism had its own problems. As Djilas had argued, state management led to a new class, which could be as exploitative as the worst type of capitalist. As the management of enterprises was turned over to the producers with small groups run on democratic principles, it was inevitable that minorities would have a right to express themselves. In Yugoslavia, the official Communist Party was uncomfortable with the fact that minorities bred factionalism that could lead to the emergence of multiple parties, working against the principles of Leninist discipline. Suppression of dissent and factionalism caused a backlash. When students rebelled in favor of democracy in 1968, occupying university buildings in Zagreb, Sarajevo, and Belgrade, the government clamped down further. Those intellectuals who had been advocating *praxis* were targeted by the government as having inspired the student uprising.

Red Words

In the 1960s in Yugoslavia and in Western European Marxist groups, the word **praxis** took on a special meaning. Work in large capitalist and socialist enterprises often tended to be alienating because of its boring and routine nature, and the necessarily hierarchical structures of complicated organizations. By contrast, "praxis" represented the ideal that the inner nature of practical tasks should be self-fulfilling and a means to self-expression. A parallel development in business theory developed in America at the same time, focusing on the concept of participatory management and the pursuit of excellence. However, in Yugoslavia, the advocates of praxis became blamed for feeding discontent with the system.

The government did not quite know what to do with these freethinkers who spoke their minds. After firing a number from government and university positions, the state subsidy for their journal was finally cut off. The official Yugoslav League of Communists criticized the praxis group as "anarcho-liberals." But the praxis advocates claimed that they simply represented a return to the ideas once advocated by Marx, and that they, like other good communists of the era, rejected the rigid ideas of Stalinism.

The Powder Keg

Despite the signs of dissent and the ferment of ideas that accompanied workers' council management and the attempt to wither away the state, Tito kept a firm hand on the country. Beneath the surface, however, old issues remained.

Religious and Ethnic Divisions

The religious and ethnic divisions of the country were suppressed, and many Croats, Bosnians, and Slovenes felt that despite Tito's personal biethnic background, the regime was Serbian-dominated. Tito endorsed the repression of Albanians living in Kosovo.

The federal nature of the republic meant that separate hierarchies of administrators did not blend together. That is, Slovenes ran Slovenia, Croats ran Croatia, and so forth. Belgrade was not only the capital of Yugoslavia, but was also the capital of Serbia, and the federal administration had only token numbers of Slovenes and Croats.

When Tito tried to assert a uniform Yugoslav culture or a single Yugoslav point of view, the non-Serbs worried that those words would simply provide an excuse to make the Serb culture dominant. "Yugoslavism" appeared to be another name for Serbism.

A Centralist Decentralizer

Even for Yugoslavs, it was difficult to understand the politics that simmered below the surface. After the expulsion of Djilas, it seemed that Edvard Kardelj was the advocate of decentralization, while the head of the UDBA security service, Alexander Rankovic, was for a stronger central regime.

Paradoxically (and perhaps typical of the country), Kardelj dogmatically pushed, from the center, the principle of decentralization. Meanwhile, Rankovic insisted that some decisions had to be made centrally, but his centralism seemed practical, rather than doctrinaire. Underlying this division, Rankovic and his closest supporters were all Serbs, while Kardelj was a Slovene. So Rankovic's advocacy of centralism seemed to some a cloak for further Serbianization of the country, while Kardelj's centrally imposed insistence on decentralization might mask ethnic separatism.

Who Watches the Watchers?

The power struggle between these two points of view came to a showdown in 1966, when Rankovic was discredited for placing electronic bugs not only in his opponents' offices and homes, but in Tito's own living quarters. Despite Rankovic's claim that it was army intelligence, not the security services that had planted the bugs, his outfit got the blame. This little in-house dispute, that Tito resolved by throwing out Rankovic, showed that behind the two personalities of Kardelj and Rankovic, the deep ethnic and religious divisions of the country continued to simmer. Inside and outside Yugoslavia, analysts wondered whether the decentralized and divided federal republic would be able to hold together, once Tito passed from the scene. He remained in power until his death in 1980. He had served as leader of the country for 34 years. In the Balkans, only Enver Hoxha of Albania ruled longer, for 40 years.

The Least You Need to Know

◆ Communist Partisans defeated the Nazi occupiers, resulting in a strong, one-party communist state in Yugoslavia in 1945.

◆ The Yugoslav system of workers' council management and profit sharing was completely unlike socialism elsewhere.

◆ Despite the totalitarian system, arguments over decentralized economic control and the power of bureaucrats produced some of the most articulate critics of communism in Milovan Djilas and in the *Praxis* group.

◆ Tito ruled the ethnically divided country for 34 years, suppressing separatist tendencies that always threatened to break the Yugoslav federation into its component republics.

Chapter 19

China's Second Revolution and the Sino-Soviet Split

In This Chapter

- ◆ Mao's efforts to radicalize Chinese society
- ◆ Mao's struggles with opponents within the Communist Party
- ◆ The Cultural Revolution attacks bourgeois values
- ◆ Tensions within the communist bloc and the Sino-Soviet Split
- ◆ China after Mao's death

A decade after Mao came to power in 1949, China's communist regime had made great strides in rebuilding the Chinese economy ruined by years of foreign invasion and civil war. The communists' ambitious program of land reform had broken the power of the old landlord class and distributed millions of acres to China's poorer peasants. Taiwan still remained in the hands of Mao's mortal enemies, the Kuomintang Party headed by Chiang Kai-shek, and was likely to remain so given the United States' continuing support for Chiang. Foreign powers still held two small colonial enclaves in Hong Kong and Macao, controlled by the British and the Portuguese respectively. But the rest of the country was firmly in communist control.

However, for Mao and many other of the senior communist leadership, China appeared to be at a crossroads. The Party had made great progress, but it had really not yet begun the process of transforming China into a communist society. Now that China had been freed from foreign domination and the Party's internal enemies had been wiped out, the time was ripe to complete this transformation.

China's second revolution that began in the 1950s was a revolution from the top down, led and directed by Mao. It radicalized all of Chinese society and thrust it into social turmoil that set peasants against workers, parents against their children, and older communists against their younger colleagues. This chapter examines the impact of this second revolution on China and its relationship with the Soviet Union and with the rest of the world.

Agricultural Collectivization and the Great Leap Forward

Mao's proposed second revolution in China represented a combination of social and cultural changes. The social changes were easier to achieve than the cultural ones. The pace of agricultural and industrial development in China had to be accelerated in order to hasten China's social transformation toward the creation of a communist proletariat. Mao reckoned that this development could proceed quickly, in fact far more quickly than most of his fellow communists thought was possible. However, the cultural changes required in order to install a communist mentality on the population were more difficult to achieve. Mao recognized that he had to overcome the innate conservatism of traditional Chinese society, as well as resistance from within his own Party.

Agricultural Collectivization

The effort to transform Chinese society along communist lines began with the drive for agricultural collectivization. The first tentative steps toward this goal were taken in 1953 with the announcement of a five-year plan that greatly increased state control over economic planning in order to increase industrial development. The plan also called for the modest goal of organizing about one third of China's peasants into agricultural collectives by the end of the decade. After an internal debate within the Party over the pace of collectivization, the timetable was sped up with the more ambitious aim of completing collectivization within a few years.

On the whole, the collectivization program was a great success. With the exception of some scattered resistance, particularly in the south where the Party's hold on the countryside was not as well-entrenched, most Chinese peasants embraced the program. By the end of 1957, almost the entire rural population of four to five hundred million people had been organized into one of 500,000 collectives. Each collective contained around 250 families who farmed their holdings as a unit. Communist officials based in the villages supplied general guidance and offered technical advice.

Notes on the Left

China's experience with collectivization was markedly different from what happened in the Soviet Union. During the collectivization program in China, Mao did not face the scale of resistance Stalin had faced. Although there were some reports of sabotage, most Chinese peasants accepted the orders to combine their farms together and work them jointly. In part, collectivization in China was more successful because of the Chinese Communist Party's large-scale support among the peasantry. While the Bolsheviks were an urban movement, communism in China had developed its strongest roots in the countryside (see Chapter 14, "Mao Zedong and the Communist Revolution in China"). In addition, and unlike Stalin, Mao did not have to contend with a large and powerful group of middle-class peasants. Most Chinese peasants were still extremely poor and backward, which made the promise of increased development through collectivization much more enticing.

The first years of the program were chaotic, as the new collectives struggled to develop a system for allocating responsibilities and distributing state-supplied assets, like seed crops and tractors. But the transformation did not create nearly as many economic problems as some of the communist leadership had feared. It did not bring the economic benefits that others had hoped for either, but most of the Party saw the program as a great triumph in bringing China closer to communism.

The Hundred Flowers Period

Mao attributed the speed with which China's peasants had accepted collectivization as a sign of their "immense enthusiasm for socialism." He also seemed to have believed that the vast majority of the Chinese population shared this enthusiasm and desired to push forward as quickly as possible. Paradoxically, the one group that seemed to resist such a rapid transformation of Chinese society was a cadre of communists within the Party itself. Mao had been forced to overcome considerable internal opposition to his collectivization plans from communist leaders who feared the economic dislocation that might follow. Much of the Party's hierarchy seemed unwilling to accelerate any faster down the road toward reorganizing China along completely communist lines.

Mao's solution was to announce a general relaxation of censorship rules in order to encourage more open debate both within the Party and across society as a whole. Known as the "hundred flowers movement," this new policy was formally launched at the Communist Party annual congress in 1956. The guiding slogan was to be "Let a hundred flowers bloom, let a hundred schools of thought contend." Mao himself started the process by acknowledging that the Party had made many mistakes, including the liquidation of hundreds of thousands of "class enemies" in the first years after seizing power in 1949.

Mao's goal in inviting such public criticism had a couple of aspects. First, he hoped to regain the support of the Chinese intelligentsia and educated classes, many of whom had grown disenchanted with the regime when its promises of a more democratic society failed to materialize. Mao also hoped to revitalize the communist movement. By allowing more criticism of the government, he was warning his own Party members that they could not let themselves become a complacent bureaucracy and allow their revolutionary fervor to slip.

Notes on the Left

Mao's criticism of bureaucracy stemmed from his analysis of what had occurred in the Soviet Union. According to Mao, the Russian Communist Party had developed into a stratified and rigid organization, far removed from the revolutionary will of the masses. Soviet party bureaucrats made economic decisions based on the need to follow rational economic principles rather than pursuing ideological goals. Bureaucrats were agents of a centralized state apparatus and were often primarily concerned with maintaining their position. Mao's most serious objection was that bureaucrats don't make revolutions, they make policies. As such, they were unlikely to have much enthusiasm for any radical transformation of society, and Mao feared that the Chinese communist movement was following the same path of its Soviet counterpart.

A hundred flowers may be pretty to look at, and a hundred schools of thought pleasant to hear, but Mao made sure that his was the only voice that counted. The period of openness did encourage many to speak out against the government. And while this had the desired effect of shaking the Party out of complacency, such criticism could not be allowed to continue. In 1958, he suddenly reversed himself and announced that China was threatened by counterrevolutionaries who had abused their new freedoms. He warned that such "poisonous weeds" would have to be rooted out. In the resulting backlash, Mao also instituted a purge of the Party itself, in which more than a million members were publicly rebuked or removed from their positions and sent to the countryside to be "re-educated" with agricultural labor.

The Great Leap Forward

Having secured his position as head of the communist movement, Mao then set out to complete the transformation of China by turning to its industrial sector. The first Chinese five-year plan that begun in 1953 had called for modest steps toward developing China's industrial base. However, the country suffered from several challenging problems that limited the pace of industrialization. The first was the difficulty of finding adequate capital needed for creating the kind of large-scale development projects that featured prominently in the Soviet Union's five-year plans (see Chapter 8, "Stalin and the Purges"). Second, China lacked the technological skills that were needed to follow a Soviet-style approach to industrial development.

Mao's solution to both these problems was a radical and unorthodox one. Rather than proceeding along Soviet lines, he proposed turning to the one asset China had in abundance, its teeming masses of people. Inspired by the success of agricultural collectivization, he believed that the revolutionary zeal of the peasantry could achieve rapid industrialization overnight. In 1958, he announced that China would embark on a "Great Leap Forward," in which industrialization would be brought to the countryside in the form of thousands of small-scale enterprises using simple technology and employing human capital in place of machinery. His utopian vision held that any obstacles to this goal could be overcome through hard work, dedication, and the unstoppable expression of popular will.

The plan also called for a radical change in the social organization of rural China, one that undermined much of what had been achieved during collectivization. Rather than seeing the backwardness of the Chinese peasantry as an obstacle, Mao argued that this was a great advantage, in that the peasants would be eager to embrace a new way of working. With the help of millions of Party officials and technical experts dispatched into the countryside, villages throughout the country were rapidly organized into communes.

All private property was forbidden. Steel foundries and production lines were set up in backyards and worked by teams of villagers assigned to a "production brigade." Communal dining halls and nurseries were set up to free Chinese women from domestic chores and allow them to devote more time to agricultural labor. Larger groups of peasants were mobilized almost like army units and pressed into work on huge development projects.

The Great Leap Forward was more than an elaborate and ambitious variation of China's previous five-year plan. At its heart, Mao's program envisioned a return to the revolutionary values that had won communism its original victory in China. In much the same way he had stirred the masses to action during the war against Japan and the Kuomintang (see Chapter 14), he now called upon the peasants to "militarize" in a new war against the forces of nature that held back China's development. Workers and peasants were extolled to throw themselves into battle to achieve the final communist victory. At the cost of greatly upsetting the communist generals who ran China's formal military, the People's Liberation Army, he advocated the widespread arming of the peasantry and the formation of local militias. He envisioned that the network of rural communes would lead to a new communist consciousness, making any formal party organization unnecessary.

Party Opposition

Such ideas were deeply disturbing to many groups within the Communist Party. At one point, Mao even threatened to abandon the Party and raise a new army from the peasantry to overthrow the government unless it agreed to all of his plans. However, opposition to the Great Leap Forward program intensified when it disintegrated into an unimaginable economic disaster. Even those who shared Mao's vision found their faith withering in the face of an almost complete agricultural collapse. Many of the backyard industrial enterprises were unworkable, and that aspect of the program was soon abandoned. Many of the large development projects collapsed as well after the Soviet Union withdrew technical advisors, and peasant enthusiasm proved inadequate to make up the difference.

Notes on the Left

The Soviet Union's decision to pull its technical advisors out of China was the result of a growing friction between it and its communist neighbor to the east. The move had a dramatic impact on Mao's plans as thousands of technical experts were withdrawn from the country overnight. Soviet advisors were ordered to clean out their offices and take all blueprints and technical drawings with them. Construction at many sites had to be stopped, and factories and power plants that were already built had to be shut down when the Chinese found they could no longer buy any spare parts. Mao did not forget this "Soviet treachery," and the events were a major cause of the serious rise in Sino-Soviet tensions that would occur within a few years.

Famine

Worst of all, the effort to convert peasants into industrial workers had a calamitous effect on agricultural production. Although the official target for the 1958 harvest was 375 million tons of grain, little more than 200 million tons were actually produced. Beset by droughts and other natural disasters, output dropped even further in 1959 and 1960. China was plunged into a famine that claimed somewhere between 15 million and 30 million lives. It would take almost two decades for China's per capita grain production to return to the level achieved before the Great Leap Forward.

By the end of 1960, Mao had little choice but to abandon his grandiose plans. The result was a great personal embarrassment to him, but it was a worse blow for the Party as a whole. The debacle of the Great Leap Forward drove a deep wedge between the Chinese peasantry and the Party and created a legacy of bitterness that would affect the communist government for years. It also greatly contributed to the declining relationship between China and the Soviet Union. Mao soon faced a significant internal opposition from within the Communist Party that threatened to unseat him as leader of the country.

Mao's Cultural Revolution

The collapse of the Great Leap Forward left Mao on the defensive in his struggle with more moderate factions in the Chinese Communist Party. He warned that these elements did not represent true communism, but rather a resurgence of bourgeoisie that had disguised themselves as party members. But in the wake of China's economic crisis, he could not afford to try to move more vigorously against his internal opponents.

The mainstream Communist Party bureaucracy, headed by Mao's chief critics Liu Shaoqi and Deng Xiaoping, reasserted its hold on the government. In mid 1959, when the true cost of Mao's plans was becoming apparent, Liu led a successful challenge to Mao and replaced him as chairman of China's central government committee. This made Liu the new head of state in the People's Republic of China, although Mao retained the even more important post of chairman of the Communist Party itself.

Vignettes

Liu Shaoqi and Deng Xiaoping had been prominent leaders in the Chinese Communist Party since the 1920s. However, both had become members while students outside of China. Liu, who was born in 1898, joined in Moscow where he was studying with the Bolsheviks. Deng, on the other hand, was a student in Paris when he decided to enlist. Both Liu and Deng were also pragmatists who were more concerned about finding practical solutions to China's problems than following a particular ideological path.

Their role in blocking Mao and ending the Great Leap Forward was to cost them dearly later. Mao marked them as his greatest enemies and the personification of everything that had gone wrong with China's communist movement. During the Cultural Revolution launched in 1966, Liu and Deng would be labeled as the "number one capitalist-roader" and "number two capitalist-roader" respectively. Both would be purged from the Party. Liu died shortly afterward, and Deng was exiled to work in a tractor factory before being reinstated to the Party in the mid 1970s. Following Mao's death in 1976, Deng would eventually become leader of China until he retired in 1989.

Nonetheless, Liu and Deng moved quickly to dismantle many of the programs that had been implemented during the Great Leap Forward. Most of the rural communes were broken up or scaled back in size, and economic reforms introduced a limited level of free market profit motivation in order to increase production.

Liu and Deng also moved to rebuild the Party apparatus, bringing back many of the rightist officials who had been dismissed under Mao's orders during the late 1950s. These steps had the result of increasingly centralizing political power in the higher level Party organizations and reinforcing Mao's fears that the Party was becoming a bureaucratic state.

Personality Cult as Political Tool

However, Mao still held a great deal of influence over large segments of the Communist Party rank and file, although his reputation had been badly damaged by the debacle of the Great Leap Forward. In 1963, he attempted to regain his control over the Party apparatus by implementing a "socialist education movement" to indoctrinate the Party and remove the threat of a communist bureaucratic class that he so despised.

The socialist education movement emphasized many of the themes that Mao had been articulating since the late 1950s, especially regarding the importance of maintaining a revolutionary spirit among the masses. And although Mao's personality cult had already started to develop before this, he took steps to encourage a younger generation of communist supporters to see him as "The Great Helmsman" who had single-handedly led the Party to victory.

> **Notes on the Left** _____
>
> Mao's personality cult would evolve into ludicrous extremes during the Cultural Revolution. The Red Guards marched in the millions carrying enormous portraits of him. Posters containing his sayings were plastered on walls and buildings through China. Sacred shrines with elaborate murals depicting his life were set up all over the country. Children were told to greet their teachers with shouts of "May Mao live ten thousand times ten thousand years." Mao legitimized this by claiming there was nothing wrong with a personality cult, as long as the person being lionized was correct in his thinking and truly devoted to the revolutionary cause. He, of course, believed that both applied to him.

Mao also had another important trump card up his sleeve, his control over China's military forces, the People's Liberation Army (PLA). Though his relationship with the PLA had suffered during the excesses of the Great Leap Forward, it was still under the direction of Mao's personal protégé Lin Biao. Working with Lin, Mao moved quickly to regain the support of the PLA and ensured that all its leading officers were firmly in his camp.

During the early 1960s, Mao encouraged the PLA to play a greater role in China's domestic affairs, including having PLA officers assigned to work with local Party cadres. The socialist education movement emphasized that the Party should emulate the PLA's discipline and the revolutionary zeal.

Launching the Cultural Revolution

In 1966, at the age of 72, Mao launched his last and most dramatic attempt to radicalize China. Known as the Great Proletarian Cultural Revolution, the effort was a direct attack on his enemies in the Communist Party hierarchy. Using his influence over the Chinese masses and the PLA, Mao attempted to bring all of China into a state of *permanent revolution* that he hoped would end China's slide into communist bureaucracy. His political struggle within the Party became recast as a class war that pitted the revolutionary masses against the more moderate members of the Party, labeled by Mao as bourgeois counter-revolutionaries. The resulting social upheaval would throw China into chaos for most of the next decade.

Red Words

Mao's notion of **permanent revolution** was similar in many ways to Leon Trotsky's theory of permanent revolution. In fact, many of Mao's communist critics, especially those in the Soviet Union, accused him of being a follower of Trotsky. However, Mao always denied this charge, and there were some important theoretical differences. Trotsky argued that the revolution in the Soviet Union had to be permanent in two senses. First, although Russia was a backward country, the workers could seize power directly and jump quickly from a bourgeois into a socialist revolution. Second, the revolution could not be successful unless it spread throughout the world.

Mao's notion of permanent revolution accepted the first of these ideas, but not the second. Moreover, Mao took Trotsky's theory a step further. According to Mao, revolutionary progress had to be a continuous and uninterrupted process that always involved elements of class struggle. His saw his role as driving the masses forward to ever higher levels of political consciousness by bringing them into conflict with their class enemies, and he defined these enemies as anyone who resisted this process, which included many of his opponents within the Communist Party.

Red Guards

The Cultural Revolution began in the spring of 1966 in the form of attacks by Mao's supporters against a minor author who had written an allegorical play criticizing Mao's policies during the Great Leap Forward. The attacks became increasingly strident and soon developed into a more general campaign against all "anti-socialist" intellectuals and against "right-wing" opportunists within the Communist Party.

Groups of students organized themselves into bands of "Red Guards," devoted to protecting Mao from his supposed enemies and stamping out all "old ideas" and "bourgeois values" that still infected China. These old ideas became defined as anything that did not conform to Mao's beliefs. In August 1966, Mao assumed the symbolic leadership of the movement when he addressed a crowd of one million student supporters in Beijing and encouraged them to continue. The campaign against old values soon degenerated into a confused, indiscriminate, and violent attack on all aspects of traditional Chinese culture. Although much of the resulting turmoil centered on the cities, millions of Red Guards also flooded into the countryside, destroying homes, museums, ancient monuments, and religious sites throughout China.

Most of the Red Guards were extremely young. Here a female member of the Red Guards wears a typical "uniform" of a simple peasant jacket with a badge showing "The Great Helmsman."

(National Archives)

Quotations of Chairman Mao

Holding Mao's Little Red Book of political sayings, which they claimed contained all knowledge and learning that anyone required, they destroyed works of art, ancient manuscripts, recordings of Western music, and religious artifacts. The Red Guards also attacked intellectuals throughout the country, forcing them to endure public humiliations, such as shaving their heads or confessing their crimes on placards that they wore around their necks. Many were driven to suicide.

" " Voices

Mao's Little Red Book, officially titled *Quotations from Chairman Mao*, was a collection of sayings taken from his writings over the previous four decades. The army initially published it in 1964, and more than a billion copies were printed over the next few years. The sayings were organized around different themes, such as "The Party," "Revolutionary Heroism," "Methods of Thinking and Methods of Work," and "Building our Country through Diligence and Frugality." The sayings included such passages as:

In the world today, all literature and art belong to definite classes and are geared to definite political lines. There is in fact no such thing as art for art's sake, art that stands above the classes, art that is detached or independent of politics.

We should rid our ranks of all impotent thinking. All views that overestimate the strength of the enemy and underestimate the strength of the people are wrong.

It is man's social being that determines his thinking. Once the correct ideas characteristic of the advanced class are grasped by the masses, these ideas turn into a material force which changes society and changes the world.

Purging Opponents

In 1967 and 1968, the Cultural Revolution took a more political turn. Mao used gangs of Red Guard members against his opponents within the Communist Party. Liu Shaoqi and Deng Xiaoping were both purged from the Party, as were hundreds of thousands of their supporters. In a manner reminiscent of Stalin's purges in the 1930s (see Chapter 8), most were made to suffer through public show trials in which they pled guilty of being foreign agents or counter-revolutionaries dedicated to sabotaging China's new society. Red Guard units also attacked local communist organizations throughout the country, and in many locations these conflicts evolved into pitched battles that were only suppressed by the use of military troops.

By 1969, however, the campaign had succeeded in destroying all of Mao's opponents, leaving him as the undisputed leader in China. He instructed the Red Guards to cease their attacks and called upon the army to restore order. In all, more than 400,000 people are suspected of having been killed during the chaos, although exact figures may never be known. Mao's victory had come at an enormous cost in human lives and dealt a crippling blow to China that would reverberate throughout Mao's remaining years, and past his death in 1976.

The Sino-Soviet Split

One of the legacies left by the Cultural Revolution was a foreign crisis that would affect China's international relations for the next two decades. By the late 1960s, the growing friction between China and the Soviet Union erupted into a full-blown state of hostility.

Roots of the Split

There were many causes for the Sino-Soviet split. In part, the tension between the world's two most important communist countries had its roots in the early history of the Communist Party in China. During the 1920s, the Soviet Union was far closer to Mao's archenemy Chiang Kai-Shek and continued to support Chiang's Kuomintang movement until shortly before the communist victory in 1949 (see Chapter 14). Although Stalin was quick to recognize Mao once he came to power, the Soviet Union had also recognized the Kuomintang as the legitimate government of China only a few years earlier.

There was also an important ideological division between Mao and the Soviet Union that became most apparent after Stalin's death in 1953. When Khrushchev embarked on his aggressive de-Stalinization campaign in 1956 (see Chapter 17, "Trouble in Paradise"), Mao took this as a personal affront. Up until that point, he had been praising Stalin as one of the greatest communist leaders in the history of the movement.

Moreover, Khrushchev's attack on Stalin's personality cult and dictatorial behavior could be equally applied to Mao's leadership in China. For his part, Mao argued that Khrushchev had allowed the Soviet Communist Party to degenerate into precisely the kind of bureaucracy that Mao was struggling against in China. During the Cultural Revolution, Red Guards made this point eloquently when they held repeated demonstrations outside the Soviet embassy in Beijing.

Competition for World Leadership

This ideological difference spilled over into China's foreign policy when it found itself competing with the Soviet Union for leadership of the communist movements in the Third World. At the Bandung Conference in 1955, Chinese foreign minister Chou En-Lai proposed China as model for a "third path" that Third World countries could follow if they wanted to avoid choosing sides between the United States and the Soviet Union.

Although China lacked the wherewithal to act as a truly global superpower, it did gain significant influence over communist movements throughout Asia, Africa, and even on the Soviet Union's doorstep through its close ties with Albania (see Chapter 13, "Satellites In [and Out of] Orbit").

Border Issues

On another level, however, the tension between China and the Soviet Union was a direct result of long-standing border disputes between the two countries. The 5,000-mile frontier was loosely defined in places, and there were numerous territorial disputes, ranging from Mongolia to Manchuria. A significant portion of the Soviet Union's armed forces were deployed along the border, and there were numerous clashes between Soviet and Chinese troops. After China exploded its first atomic bomb and joined the ranks of the nuclear powers in 1967, the Soviet Union found itself trapped between potential enemies on both its eastern and western borders.

Two years later, hostilities between the Soviet Union and China exploded into a full-scale conflict when large numbers of Soviet and Chinese forces battled each other along the Ussuri River in northern Manchuria. For a time, it appeared as though the Third World War would not start in Europe, as most expected, but in Asia.

The Split Viewed by Others

The Sino-Soviet split had profound implications for the communist movement throughout the world, and for the relationship between the West and the two great communist powers. Communists everywhere now had two models to choose from, and the battle between Maoists and non-Maoists outside of China raged on through the 1970s and into the 1980s.

For Western policy makers, on the other hand, the image of communism as a monolithic worldwide movement had been shattered forever. The Sino-Soviet split revealed that there were deep divisions within the movement that could be exploited. The most famous example was Richard Nixon's astonishing visit to China in 1972, when he did much to repair long-standing disputes that had divided the two nations since the end of the Second World War. This led to the United States' recognition of the communist regime as the legitimate government of China in 1979. And although the two countries would continue to have an uneasy relationship, American foreign policy would move away from the simplistic ideological stance that characterized it during the early years of the Cold War.

The deepening tensions between the Soviet Union and Communist China became dramatically visible when Mao Zedong allowed American President Richard Nixon to visit China in 1972. Here Nixon reviews a parade of soldiers from the People's Liberation Army.

(National Archives)

The Death of Mao and Struggles for Succession

In the last years of his life, Mao largely retired from public life, although his struggle with internal enemies was far from over. The most important of these was the clash with Lin Biao, Mao's former protégé and head of the Chinese armed forces. At one point, Lin had been named as Mao's designated successor, but he fell victim to the aftermath of the Cultural Revolution. Lin had been one of the most avid supporters of the Red Guards during the late 1960s.

When Mao called a halt to the Cultural Revolution in 1969 and began the slow process of rebuilding the Party, he clashed with Lin over a number of issues relating to the Party's future organization and the role of the PLA. Although many of the details about this conflict are still unknown to outsiders, Lin appears to have tried to stage a military coup against Mao in late 1971. According to later reports, he attempted to flee to the Soviet Union when the coup failed, but died in a plane crash, along with his entire family.

The Gang of Four

Lin's death left Mao without any appointed successor, and the issue of who was to take over after Mao's death was a pressing concern in the mid 1970s after Mao became increasingly ill. One possibility was Zhou Enlai (Chou En-Lai, old spelling), China's foreign minister. However, Chou was ill himself and died in 1975. Another group of would-be claimants coalesced around Mao's wife, Jiang Qing, and included several of the most left-wing members of the Party's leadership. Known as the Gang of Four, this group seemed poised to assume power when Mao died after a long illness in September 1976.

Vignettes
Jiang Qing had originally been an actress before she joined the Party and married Mao in 1938. Almost 20 years younger than he was, she remained in the background until the late 1960s, when she became deputy director of the Cultural Revolution committee. Responsible for some of the worst attacks on traditional Chinese culture perpetuated by the Red Guards, Jiang remained a powerful figure in China throughout the early 1970s. Her bid to take over after Mao's death in 1976 was ended when she and her supporters were arrested and condemned to death for their role in the Cultural Revolution. Her sentence was later commuted to life imprisonment, and she died in 1991.

Deng Again

However, the Gang of Four's plans were disrupted by the resurgence of the more moderate wing of the Party. After almost 30years of Mao's rule and having gone through the tumultuous events of the Great Leap Forward and the Cultural Revolution, the moderates in the Party weren't inclined to support any continuation of Mao's policies. After a brief but bitter political struggle, the Gang of Four was arrested in October 1976 and sentenced to death for numerous crimes. Mao's position as head of the People's Republic was taken over by Deng Xiaoping, Mao's old enemy who had been purged during the Cultural Revolution but reinstated to the Party shortly before Mao's death.

Under Deng's leadership, the communist government implemented numerous economic and social reforms during the late 1970s and early 1980s. Although the Party retained absolute control over political affairs and moved quickly to crush any internal opposition to communist rule, it did greatly reduce government controls on economic activity and sought to promote rapid development in the country.

The Least You Need to Know

♦ Ten years after his initial victory, Mao embarked China on a second revolution that would complete its transformation into a communist society—the program of agricultural collectivization was relatively successful, but his plans for an overnight industrial revolution in the "Great Leap Forward" were a complete disaster.

♦ Mao greatly feared that the Chinese Communist Party would lose its revolutionary zeal and become a stagnant bureaucracy unless it devoted itself to leading the masses forward in a state of permanent revolution.

♦ The Cultural Revolution was Mao's last effort to radicalize Chinese society and remove the threat that he perceived as coming from his opponents within the Communist Party.

♦ The Sino-Soviet split in the late 1960s and early 1970s helped end the West's image of communism as a worldwide, monolithic movement and opened up new possibilities for international diplomacy.

♦ The last years of Mao's life were characterized by an open struggle to determine who would lead China after his death.

Part 5

From Advance to Retreat

In this part we see how communists in China and the Soviet Union vied for control of the world movement, and fought in Asia, Africa, and Latin America to win power, linking their fights with local aspirations for independence, development, and an end to poverty. But at the same time that communists won in a few locations, problems in the Soviet Union came to a head. As the Soviets tried to modernize their system, they began to unravel the tight control established in earlier years. We look at the breakup of the Soviet Union and the end of communist regimes in Eastern Europe. While some Americans liked to brag that they won the Cold War, a closer look suggests that the communists lost it. By the twenty-first century, there were only a few remnants of communist regimes around the world.

20

National Liberation and Communism in the Third World

In This Chapter

- ◆ Communism's appeal to independence movements
- ◆ Communist parties in the Third World
- ◆ Cold War tensions become hot conflicts
- ◆ The United States' involvement in Vietnam
- ◆ Communism on America's doorstep in Cuba

In the years after the Second World War, communism appeared to be on the march, not just in Eastern Europe and China (see Chapters 13, "Satellites In [and Out of] Orbit," and 14, "Mao Zedong and the Communist Revolution in China"), but around the world. As Western nations struggled to maintain their hold on a vast network of colonies that had been seized during the late nineteenth century, some of the fights took on the appearance of an ideological battle between democracy and communism. In Asia, Africa, and America's own backyard in Latin America, the United States and the Soviet Union fought proxy wars using local forces. The postwar conflict between the United States and the Soviet Union may have remained undeclared in Europe, but in the jungles of Vietnam or the plains of Africa, it was anything but cold.

This chapter looks at why communism gained an influence in the Third World. We focus on a few of the places where it led to the formation of communist regimes and check out why this influence remained limited despite Western fears of the global spread of communism.

Communism in the Third World

Up until the Second World War, communism was largely a Western phenomenon. Marx's writings were based on his observations of social change in Europe and the United States during the nineteenth century (see Chapter 2, "Marx and Engels"). Despite claims to represent a global movement, almost all members of the First and Second Internationals came from Western countries and were primarily concerned with Western problems. Even though Lenin developed a theory that tied the problems of capitalism to the West's colonial expansion over the rest of the world (see Chapter 6, "The Russian Revolution"), the communist movement made little popular headway outside of Europe, Russia, China, and the United States until the 1950s and 1960s.

Notes on the Left

One of Lenin's most important contributions to Marxist thought was his outline of the economic basis of imperialism. Lenin believed that Europe's dramatic nineteenth-century colonial expansion was fueled by a crisis in capitalism, an idea suggested by British economist J.A. Hobson. Hobson maintained that capital owners in the West needed to find new places where they could make investments that would command high profits. Lenin refined Hobson's arguments, claiming that this process represented a final stage of capitalism. According to Lenin, the ever-decreasing level of profits was bound to continue, and when capitalism ran out of places to exploit, the system would collapse. The fact that this capitalism didn't collapse was only one of the many flaws in Lenin's analysis, but Marxist-Leninist theory became a powerful ideological tool in the struggle to liberate countries from colonial control.

The initial success of Japan and Germany over the colonial powers during World War II dealt a crippling blow to their rule. When the West called upon their colonies to help defend them from Germany and Japan, the implicit understanding was that many of the colonies would be rewarded for their loyalty. The United States granted independence to the Philippines in 1946, and Great Britain did the same for India and Pakistan in 1947. India had long been the crown jewel in Britain's overseas possessions. World War II had taken an enormous financial and military toll on the West, and few European nations had the will or the resources to resist colonial demands for independence.

Independence movements throughout the *Third World* were primarily focused on achieving political and economic national liberation. However, many of the movements borrowed elements from Marxist-Leninist ideology to justify their demands for self-determination. Communist theory, as refined by Lenin, offered a stinging critique of European colonial rule. In addition, the fight for independence in many colonies was also a fight against certain local native elites who had benefited from colonial rule. Claiming to be Marxists could also be shrewd. In the postwar world divided between East and West, the only place to turn for aid was the communist bloc. The Soviet Union, and to a lesser extent China, pitched in to support Third World independence groups, looking for influence and allies.

Red Words

The term **Third World** itself grew out of the postwar conflict between communism and the West. At the Bandung Conference in 1955, a group of 29 newly independent African and Asian countries met in Indonesia to discuss possibilities for mutual aid and cooperation. These nations identified themselves as the "Third World" in an effort to demonstrate that they were not politically or ideologically aligned with either the West or with the Soviet Union. Instead, they sought to find their own path between the two. However, most countries found it difficult to stick to a third way and ended up aligned with one of the two global superpowers.

Of course, it was a bit ironic for Third World independence leaders to turn to a Western ideology to justify claims for getting out from under Western rule. For the most part, rulers in the newly independent countries understood that irony. Only a handful of countries actually formed communist regimes that strictly followed a Moscow-style interpretation of Marxism. Most implemented policies that were only vaguely socialist in nature, including widespread state controls over the economy and efforts to nationalize foreign-owned investments.

For the West, however, ideological fine points became lost in what appeared to be a bigger struggle between democracy and communism. And, it was the Third World where much of this struggle was played out. Those Third World governments that aligned themselves with the West got American and other Western support, though many were neither democratic nor even particularly interested in a capitalist free-market economy. But when any country accepted massive Soviet or Chinese aid or instruction, the West usually branded it as communist, regardless of policy details.

Asia: Empires in Disarray

Communism developed its strongest influence in the Third World in Asia, and it was Asia where the ideological conflict between East and West led to large-scale warfare. The Japanese advance into Southeast Asia during 1941–1942 resulted in the conquest of most of the British, French, and Dutch colonies, from Burma through Indonesia, as well as the American territory of the Philippines. After the war, colonial powers found it very difficult to retain their hold on the region in the face of considerable local opposition. In Burma and Vietnam, local communist groups had already been organized to lead the resistance against Japan. After the end of the war, these groups continued to push for independence.

Mao Zedong's victory in China in 1949 provided a material boost to the strength of these movements (see Chapter 14). In an effort to forestall a communist takeover, Western countries did grant independence to most of their colonies in the region. However, internal fighting continued as communist guerillas redirected their efforts against the new Western-supported regimes. During the 1950s, the struggle became war.

Korea: A Land Divided

The first skirmish in the West's war against communism occurred in Korea. Since 1905, Korea had been a colony of Japan. After the Soviet Union declared war against Japan, its troops occupied most of the northern half of the country, while Japanese forces in the south surrendered to the United States. Korea divided along the 38th parallel, with a communist administration in the north and a pro-Western government in the south. According to postwar agreements, plans were made to hold a referendum to decide on Korea's future. In June 1950, however, North Korea invaded South Korea in an effort to unify the country by force.

Notes on the Left

The United Nations was only able to coordinate the defense of South Korea because of a tactical blunder by the Soviet Union. Under the terms of the UN charter, the Soviet Union, along with Britain, France, China, and the United States, held a veto over all UN Security Council resolutions. China was still represented by the nationalist government in Taiwan. In June 1950, the Soviet ambassador to the UN boycotted the Security Council deliberations in protest over its refusal to recognize the new communist regime in China. In the absence of the Soviet delegate, the United States was able to get a mandate from the Security Council to legitimize its actions in Korea, and forces from more than a dozen other UN countries assisted. The Soviet Union never made the same mistake again, and all other military efforts against communist movements in the Third World were carried out as independent operations not sanctioned by the United Nations.

The initial United Nations' counterattack was successful in preventing a North Korean victory. When UN forces continued their advance into North Korea, however, communist China intervened with hundreds of thousands of its own troops (see Chapter 14). The war dragged on for three years before an armistice agreement in 1953. The settlement put the line almost exactly where it had been before the war.

Korea remains divided in 2002, and a more formal peace treaty never replaced the armistice agreement. The Democratic People's Republic of Korea, in the north, is one of the few orthodox and hard-line communist regimes still remaining in the world. Kim Il Sung, who first became premier of North Korea in 1948, ruled the country until his death in 1994. The regime maintained close ties with the Soviet Union and followed a similar economic policy of forced agricultural collectivization and investment in heavy industries. Despite numerous economic setbacks, including a series of devastating famines in the 1990s, North Korea always devoted an enormous portion of its budget to military spending and never renounced its claim to all of Korea.

Malaysia: A British Victory

During the Second World War, Japanese forces overran Malaysia, as well as other European colonies in Southeast Asia. A British colony since the nineteenth century, the country was initially made up of several different territories and ethnic groups, cobbled together under a British colonial administration. After the Second World War, British efforts to organize a new country in Malaysia proved difficult, and in 1948, a communist movement began among the large groups of ethnic Chinese living there.

The communist insurgency lasted for 10 years, and was finally suppressed by large numbers of British troops. The communist guerrillas used terrorist tactics against the urban centers, while the British responded by forcing more than 500,000 Chinese to resettle in fortified areas. However, the guerrilla campaign pressured the British to accelerate the independence process. In 1957, Malaysia became an independent member of the British Commonwealth. Although communist-led outbreaks continued into the 1960s and 1970s, the movement never seriously challenged the new Malaysian government.

Indonesia: Leader of the Nonaligned

A former colony of the Netherlands, Indonesia is a chain of islands lying between Malaysia, Australia, and the Philippines. The country gained independence in 1949, but the new regime headed by Achmed Sukarno faced vast problems in ruling over the world's fourth most populous country, made up of more than 100 large islands and many more small ones, and one that included numerous ethnic and religious groups. Although he was one of the first supporters of the Third World nonaligned movement, Sukarno made many overtures to the communist bloc during the 1960s to gain political support for territorial claims in New Guinea and Malaysia.

In 1965, the Indonesian Communist Party attempted to seize the country by force. The Indonesian military suppressed the uprising and the military and ethnic mobs murdered tens of thousands of communist supporters. Much of Indonesia was thrown into chaos for the next several years until General Raden Suharto, head of the Indonesian army, assumed control of the government. Suharto remained in power until 1998, when a democratic reform movement convinced him to step down and allow free elections for the first time.

Indo-China: Southeast Asian Cauldron

The French colonies of Indo-China include the present day countries of Laos, Cambodia, and Vietnam. During the Japanese occupation of Indo-China in World War II, an effective nationalist movement, known as the Viet Minh, coalesced around the Vietnamese Communist Party headed by Ho Chi Minh. In 1945, Ho declared an independent Vietnam republic, but the move was not recognized by the French who tried to establish a regime headed by the heir to the Vietnamese imperial family that had ruled the country before the French occupation in the late nineteenth century.

> ### Vignettes
>
> Born in 1890, Ho Chi Minh (born Nguyen That Thanh) left Vietnam for France in his early 20s. He became involved in the French socialist movement and tried to gain support for colonial independence in Vietnam. Ironically, Ho was initially a great admirer of the United States. At the Treaty of Versailles that ended World War I in 1918, he attempted to meet with American President Woodrow Wilson to argue that Wilson's emphasis on the principle of self-determination in Europe should apply to Europe's colonial possessions. Although unsuccessful, Ho continued to admire much about the United States, and he modeled the declaration of independence for Vietnam in 1945 after America's Declaration of Independence written 169 years earlier.
>
> During the 1920s and 1930s, Ho traveled to the Soviet Union and China, where he studied guerrilla tactics and party organization. He returned to Vietnam during World War II and raised the guerrilla army that ended French colonial rule. Ho served as president of North Vietnam from its creation in 1954 until his death in 1969. When North Vietnam finally united the country under communist rule in 1975, the old South Vietnamese capital of Saigon was renamed Ho Chi Minh City.

The conflict between the two proposed governments of a newly independent Vietnam broke out into a military struggle in the early 1950s. The campaign spread throughout the country, but the Viet Minh forced a large contingent of French troops to surrender at the battle of Dien Bien Phu in 1954. The defeat was a major blow to French military prestige and accelerated the French decision to abandon much of its colonial empire. The French met with Ho Chi Minh at the Geneva Conference in the same year, where both sides agreed to divide the country along the 17th parallel, with Ho Chi Minh ruling the north and a French-sponsored administration in the south.

Under the agreement signed in Geneva, both North and South Vietnam pledged to hold free elections to determine the fate of the country. However, with the support of the United States, the new South Vietnamese government refused elections, fearing Ho's popularity would sweep a communist regime to power. Over the next several years, several opposition groups in South Vietnam began protesting for reforms and an eventual unification with the North. One protesting group was a communist movement named the Viet Nam Cong San, more widely known as the Vietcong. The Vietcong responded to the resulting military crackdown with a guerrilla campaign, getting heavy support from the communist regime in North Vietnam.

By the early 1960s, the conflict developed into a full-blown war, and increasing numbers of American troops and military advisors were sent to help the South Vietnamese government. In 1964, after North Vietnamese torpedo boats clashed with American naval vessels that were supporting clandestine raids on the North in the Tonkin Gulf, President Lyndon Johnson announced that the United States would take whatever steps necessary to prevent a communist victory in South Vietnam. These steps included a bombing campaign of North Vietnam and the dispatch of several hundred thousand American troops to fight alongside the South Vietnamese forces.

In early 1968, the Vietcong launched a major offensive during the Vietnamese Tet religious holiday. The offensive took the Americans by surprise and succeeded in capturing many South Vietnamese cities and, for a brief period, even occupied the American embassy in the capital of Saigon.

The Tet offensive was eventually repulsed, but the communist achievements contributed to American popular opposition to the war. However, the campaign also decimated the indigenous Vietcong movement in South Vietnam. From 1968 onward, the war entered a new phase of more open intervention by North Vietnamese forces infiltrating into the south.

In an effort to reduce the movement of North Vietnamese troops, the United States intensified its bombing campaign in the north. The war spilled over into the neighboring countries of Cambodia and Laos, both used by North Vietnam for supply lines to the south. Cambodia and Laos fought civil wars and eventually fell to communist groups, the Khmer Rouge in Cambodia and the Pathet Lao in Laos, both supported by North Vietnam.

Most of the Vietcong who participated in the January 1968 Tet Offensive were killed or captured, like the one shown here. However, the communist assault was very successful in demonstrating that the United States had a long, difficult fight ahead of it in its war against communism in Vietnam.

(National Archives)

Cambodian Tragedy

The experience of Cambodia was one of the most tragic outcomes of the Vietnam War. Granted independence by France in 1954, the new regime headed by Prince Norodom Sihanouk attempted to keep the country neutral during the conflict in Vietnam. In 1970, however, Sihanouk was deposed in a military coup, and the country fell into civil war with fierce fighting among several different groups supported by outside forces. These included the Cambodian communist movement known as the Khmer Rouge (or "Red Cambodia").

Headed by Pol Pot, the Khmer Rouge emerged victorious in 1975 and formed a new regime. Pol Pot advocated an extreme version of communism that rejected all forms of Western influence, including such technological innovations as the motorcar, modern medicine, and even eyeglasses. He also argued that the only legitimate form of society was an agrarian, peasant structure. Over the next three years, the Khmer Rouge emptied the Cambodian cities and drove millions into the countryside where they were forced to work in agriculture. They also killed all suspected members of the Cambodian upper classes, which included anyone who was not from a peasant or worker background. An estimated million and a half people died during the genocide.

The Khmer Rouge's excesses greatly embarrassed their former North Vietnamese backers, and the new communist government of Vietnam invaded Cambodia in 1978 and deposed Pol Pot, who escaped into the countryside with large numbers of his followers. Throughout the 1980s, Cambodia suffered through a continuous civil war as various factions, including the Khmer Rouge and supporters of Prince Sihanouk, fought the Vietnamese and vied for control of the country. The conflict was ended by a peace treaty signed in 1991 and a new coalition government headed by Prince Sihanouk was formed. However, fighting with the Khmer Rouge continued until Pol Pot's death in 1998.

Communist Victory in Vietnam

The American presence in Vietnam continued during the late 1960s and early 1970s. After increasing domestic opposition to the war in the United States, the administration of Richard Nixon decided to scale down the size of the U.S. involvement while negotiating a settlement. With the departure of the last American troops in 1973, the South Vietnamese regime quickly began to collapse. In April 1975, North Vietnamese troops entered Saigon, and the country was formally united under communist rule, after more then a decade of fighting. In total, over 58,000 Americans died in the war, while North and South Vietnam together suffered almost 1.5 million casualties.

The new communist regime in Vietnam focused its initial efforts on rebuilding the country. However, its moves to implement broad economic controls and its continued political repression prompted hundreds of thousands of refugees, often referred to as "boat people," to flee the country over the next decade. In the late 1970s, communist Vietnam invaded neighboring Cambodia to remove its communist leader Pol Pot, whose murderous rule had plunged the country into chaos. These actions and border disputes led to a major rift with China, and the two communist countries fought a brief war during the early 1980s.

By the end of the 1980s, Vietnam backed away from communist economic policies and allowed reforms to encourage economic growth and attract foreign investment. These changes continued during the 1990s, although they were not accompanied by political reforms. The regime did reach out to the United States to try to settle outstanding issues relating to the war, including the question of Americans missing in action, the "MIAs." In 1995, the United States recognized the communist regime as the legitimate government of Vietnam.

Africa and the Middle East

Africa and the Middle East were also drawn into the postwar conflict between East and West for global supremacy. However, communism never gained as much influence in the region as it did in Asia.

While many of the newly formed countries in Africa and the Middle East embraced socialist policies that made the West uncomfortable, only a few regimes openly declared themselves to be Marxist. Nonetheless, the area became embroiled in the Cold War, as both the United States and the Soviet Union sought influence in the region. At times, this competition erupted into armed clashes, but in most cases it took quieter forms.

The Middle East: Clash of Cultures

Communism had trouble gaining a foothold in the Middle East. Marxism's emphasis on a secular interpretation of history and its open hostility toward religion made any efforts to organize a communist movement difficult in a region where the vast majority of people were devout Muslims. The Islamic world was far more comfortable expressing demands for social justice in a religious idiom than adopting communist ideology that focused on the inescapable struggle between bourgeoisie and proletariat.

However, Arab nationalists in the 1940s and 1950s did borrow elements of socialist thought in their efforts to reform and unify Middle Eastern society. The *Ba'ath Party* that came to power in both Syria and Iraq represented a combination of nationalist and social-ist ideology. Likewise, Gamal Abdel Nasser, who ruled Egypt between 1952 and 1970, implemented a radical program of land reform and emphasized state control of economic planning in a system of Arab socialism. None of these three socialist regimes could be considered Marxist, although all developed strong ties with the Soviet Union.

Red Words

The **Ba'ath Party** (from the Arabic for renaissance) was a secular reform move-ment founded in Syria in the early 1950s. It had two major goals. First, it aimed at uni-fying the Arab world thus ending the internal ethnic and religious fighting that it saw as having allowed Western imperialism to gain such power in the region. Second, it emphasized social reform along socialist lines with extensive state controls over eco-nomic activity.

The Ba'ath Party came to power in Syria in the late 1950s and led the country into a short-lived union with Egypt that collapsed in 1961, after less than 3 years. The Party, now headed by Hafez al-Assad, remains in power in Syria in 2002. In 1963, the Ba'ath Party seized control in Iraq, and has been led by Saddam Hussein since 1979. The authoritarian regimes in both countries have moved away from initial socialist princi-ples espoused by the movement's founders and are now more focused on nationalist issues.

The only truly Marxist regime in the Middle East was in Yemen, a small country next to Saudi Arabia at the southern tip of the Arabian Peninsula. After several years of fighting in the 1960s, the southern half of the country won its independence from Great Britain in 1967 and renamed itself the People's Democratic Republic of Yemen. The northern part remained a separate state, the Yemen Arab Republic. South Yemen adopted a radical

Marxist ideology and signed a treaty of friendship with the Soviet Union in 1979. However, the regime suffered from internal political problems and fought numerous border clashes with its neighbors. In 1990, it reunited with North Yemen.

Africa: Ethiopian Marxists

Several African nations saw sizeable communist movements during the 1950s and 1960s. These included South Africa and Rhodesia, where the Communist Party joined the fight against the apartheid system set up to maintain white rule. As with the Middle East, however, only a small number of African countries ever declared themselves to be Marxist.

Ethiopia formed a communist regime under Colonel Mengistu Haile Mariam in the mid 1970s. Mengistu replaced Ethiopia's aging emperor, Haile Selassie, who had reigned since 1930. Although Mengistu was more of an authoritarian military ruler than a devoted communist, the country did adopt a Marxist-based constitution in 1987. However, despite pressing social problems highlighted by a devastating famine in the 1980s, the Mengistu regime's primary emphasis was on nationalistic issues relating to Ethiopia's territorial claims against Somalia and efforts to suppress a separatist movement in Tigré and Eritrea. With the collapse of the communist bloc in the late 1980s (see Chapter 22, "Reds in Retreat: The Collapse of Communism in Eastern Europe"), Mengistu lost his international backing and was toppled by a coalition of rebel groups in 1991.

Angola and Mozambique: Portugal's Forgotten Empire

Communist movements had the most success in the former Portuguese colonies of Angola and Mozambique, which were not granted independence until the mid 1970s. Portuguese efforts to maintain their control over these territories gave rise to several competing nationalist movements, including the communist Movimento Popular de Libertacao Angola (MPLA) and the Mozambique Liberation Front (Frelimo). Following a military coup in Portugal in 1974, both countries were granted independence and formed Marxist regimes.

Neither, however, had much success in creating a stable government, suffering numerous economic problems and conflicts with internal resistance movements. The Frelimo government in Mozambique abandoned its communist ideology in the early 1990s and eventually agreed to hold elections. In Angola, the MPLA regime became embroiled in a long conflict with the anti-communist União Nacional para Independência Total de Angola (UNITA). MPLA received help from Cuban troops, while UNITA got massive funding from the United States. After an UN-brokered agreement in the late 1980s, Cuba agreed to withdraw its forces from Angola and the MPLA agreed to hold free elections. However, fighting between the MPLA and UNITA continued throughout the rest of the decade.

Notes on the Left _____

The civil war in Angola during the 1980s was a classic example of the Cold War being fought by proxy armies on an isolated battlefield. The MPLA was founded in 1956 and from the beginning received aid and support from the Soviet Union. After coming to power in 1975, the new regime also reached out to Cuba for military assistance, and several thousand Cuban troops fought alongside MPLA forces in its conflict with UNITA.

Established by Jonas Savimbi in 1966, UNITA also fought against the Portuguese occupation, but broke with the MPLA in 1975. UNITA launched a guerrilla campaign against the MPLA regime that received significant aid from the United States and South Africa. During the 1980s, Savimbi was widely praised by American President Ronald Reagan as an anti-communist hero, alongside the Contra movement in Nicaragua (see the following section, "Continuing Latin American Crises") and the mujaheddin in Afghanistan (see Chapter 21, "Cracks in the Iron Curtain: Crisis and Reform in the Soviet Union"). Although certainly an anti-communist, Savimbi's democratic credentials were less impressive, and in 1992 he refused to accept results of elections held in Angola and launched a new guerrilla campaign against the government.

Latin America and the Cuban Revolution

The evolution of communism in Latin America differed from that in other parts of the Third World. In the first place, the movement had far older roots stretching back to before the First World War. Most Latin American countries had developed viable socialist parties during the late nineteenth century, comparable to their counterparts in the United States and Europe. After the Russian Revolution in 1917, many of the more radical socialist groups joined the Third International and formally renamed themselves communist parties (see Chapter 7, "Lenin and the Communist Regime"). During the 1920s and 1930s, the communist movement in Latin America largely followed the orders coming from the Comintern, as was the case with the European and American communist parties. However, the movement remained very limited in strength, with maximum membership of a few thousand supporters in most countries.

However, communism remained a minor political influence in Latin America until the movement was suddenly vitalized by the success of Fidel Castro's revolution in Cuba in 1959. Cuba had long been closely aligned with the United States. Its dictator, Fulgencio Batista, enjoyed good relations with successive American presidents and had close ties to American companies with Cuban sugar industry holdings. In overthrowing Batista, Castro demonstrated that a communist revolution was possible despite American political and economic influence in the region.

Vignettes

Born in 1926, Fidel Castro joined the opposition movement against the dictatorship of Fulgencio Batista in Cuba in the early 1950s. After being exiled from the country for his role in an unsuccessful coup attempt, he and a small band of 11 followers landed in southwestern Cuba in December 1956 and launched a rural guerrilla movement. From these tiny beginnings, Castro's movement steadily grew in strength, until it toppled Batista in 1959.

The charismatic Castro was initially heralded as a progressive reformer. Many American observers pointed to Castro's love for baseball as proof that he could not be anti-American. In 1961, however, Castro announced he was a Marxist, and tensions with the United States increased. Despite numerous attempts to remove Castro, including the ill-fated Bay of Pigs invasion in December 1961 and several assassination plots, he remains firmly in power in Cuba in 2002.

Fidel Castro's close ties with the Soviet Union created great concern for U.S. officials. Here he is hugging Soviet premier Nikita Khrushchev. U.S. fears were proven valid when the United States discovered that Castro had allowed Soviet nuclear weapons to be based in Cuba.

(UPI Photo)

Cuba Si, Yankee No

The rise of a Marxist regime so close to American shores represented a major challenge to the United States. Its opposition to Castro became open hostility after he declared Cuba to be a Marxist state and moved to nationalize all American-owned assets in the country. The United States broke diplomatic ties with Cuba in January 1961 and implemented a trade embargo that continued into the twenty-first century. In December 1961, the United States also launched a poorly planned invasion of the country at the Bay of Pigs using groups of Cuban political exiles. Later, Castro allowed Cuba to be used as a base for Soviet ballistic missiles aimed at the United States, and the resulting crisis in 1962 brought the world close to a nuclear war.

The Castro regime maintained close ties with the Soviet Union throughout the 1960s. Castro implemented numerous social reforms, but he showed little inclination to grant any form of political liberty. Despite numerous efforts to encourage economic development, Cuba remained heavily dependent on Soviet aid and without the support of communist bloc sugar purchases, the Cuban economy would have faced severe difficulties.

Castro earned the enmity of most governments in Latin America, and the great admiration of communist movements throughout the region, when he began efforts to export revolution to other parts of Third World. In 1962, the Organization of American States, at the urging of America, excluded Cuba from membership, and most member countries broke off diplomatic relations with Cuba, facing communist movements of their own. In 1967, Che Guevara, one of the 11 followers who landed with Castro in 1956, was killed in Bolivia while leading a communist insurgency against the conservative regime. In 1973, the democratically elected Marxist president of Chile, Salvador Allende, was overthrown and killed by an American-supported military coup, after he began a nationalization program which threatened American investments.

> ### Notes on the Left _____
>
> The Shining Path in Peru, also known as the Tupac Amaru Revolutionary Movement, was founded in 1970 as a breakaway group from the mainstream communist party in Peru. Its strongest support comes from the rural highlands in central Peru. Unlike most other communist movements in Latin America, the Shining Path aligned itself with China, adopting a Maoist ideology that it deemed more applicable to Peru's largely rural and peasant population. During the 1980s, the movement launched a terrorism campaign against the Peruvian government, including successful attacks on urban centers. Peru implemented martial law in 1992. Although many of the Shining Path's leaders were captured during the military crackdown, it still operates in the rural parts of the country. Over the 1980s and 1990s, thousands of people died in the conflict.

Continuing Latin American Crises

During the 1970s and 1980s, other Latin American countries struggled with social turmoil and political unrest. In some cases, such as Argentina, military regimes seized power and instituted severe repression in which all left-wing movements were considered to be communist, no matter what their political orientation. In others, such as Peru and Colombia, communist guerrilla movements challenged the existing governments and plunged the countries into periods of civil war. The United States intervened throughout the region to offer support to regimes that declared themselves to be anti-communist.

American intervention against pro-communist regimes in Latin America became controversial in the United States. Open and then clandestine U.S. support for the Contra movement opposing the left-wing Sandinista regime that had come to power in Nicaragua in 1979 became one of the heated issues in American politics in the early and mid 1980s. A brief U.S.–led invasion in October 1983 to eject a pro-communist regime in Grenada also caused a stir in the United States.

With the collapse of the Soviet Union in the early 1990s and the end of the Cold War, many communist movements in Latin America lost ground. However, in 2002, communism remains a prominent political force throughout the region, and there are still communist guerrilla movements in Peru and Colombia. The one remaining communist regime in Cuba made no efforts to abandon its official ideology, although the country suffers from grave economic difficulties in the face of a continuing American trade embargo and the loss of its communist backers in the Soviet Union.

The Least You Need to Know

- Communism in the Third World was closely tied to national liberation movements attempting to win independence for former colonies.
- Communism made its strongest inroads in Asia, which became the front lines in the Cold War battle between East and West.
- Outside of Asia, only a small handful of countries ever formed communist governments, although many countries adopted socialist principles.
- Of all the communist movements in the Third World, the rise of Fidel Castro in Cuba represented the most powerful challenge to the United States.

Chapter 21

Cracks in the Iron Curtain: Crisis and Reform in the Soviet Union

In This Chapter

- ◆ The Soviet Union during the 1970s and 1980s
- ◆ Foreign policy and the invasion of Afghanistan
- ◆ The need for reforms
- ◆ Mikhail Gorbachev comes to power
- ◆ *Perestroika* and *glasnost*

For almost three decades after the end of the Second World War, the Soviet Union had reigned supreme as one of the two global superpowers. With its influence extending from East Germany to Mongolia, and from the Arctic Ocean to Africa, the Soviet Union was arguably one of the greatest empires in history. It had led the world into the Space Age with the launching of the first satellites. And its message of an idealized communist future struck a powerful and poignant chord with millions around the world.

By the late 1970s, however, the Soviet Union started to face serious internal problems. Its long-running struggle with the United States was taking a severe economic toll as the Soviet Union tried to keep pace with Western technological advances and consumer culture. The massively cumbersome and overly bureaucratic structure of government that had been established during the Stalinist era was beginning to show signs of age. Relations with its neighbors and allies suffered a number of critical setbacks, and internal opposition to the communist regime was growing.

The Soviet Union was in desperate need of reform. This chapter examines how the Communist Party in the Soviet Union responded to the challenges it faced during the 1970s and 1980s. It also shows why these attempts at reform ultimately failed.

The Economic Crisis

Generally high levels of growth marked the early 1970s in the Soviet Union, at least in the industrial sector. For the first time in its history, the communist regime could point with pride to the fact that the Soviet Union outproduced the United States in several key areas, including steel, oil, coal, wool, cement, and tractors. However, this growth disguised severe structural problems that raised troublesome questions for government leaders.

Consumer Goods

Most Soviet consumer goods were noticeably inferior in quality to those available in the West. Soviet economic planning was heavily focused on questions relating to general industrial development, but little attention was paid to what the Soviet consumers actually wanted or desired. Large piles of some commodities remained unpurchased on the shelves of government stores, while others were all but impossible to find. By the 1970s, the Soviet standard of living was certainly vastly improved over what it had been two decades earlier, but the gap between what Soviet citizens had and what they expected was growing at an alarming rate.

Voices

Soviet citizens often made jokes about the poor quality of goods available to consumers. According to one, "A teacher was discussing the story of Adam and Eve. At the end of the class, the teacher asked the students who Adam and Eve were. One student answered, 'they must have been Russian because they didn't have any clothes, a house, or a car, and they thought they were in paradise.'" Another story has a communist leader visiting a collective farm and asking about the harvest. The workers responded, "The harvest was so good that we have a pile of potatoes reaching up to God in Heaven." After being scolded that God and Heaven did not exist, the workers replied, "That's all right, neither do the potatoes."

Agriculture

The Soviet agricultural sector still suffered from grave problems. A crop failure in 1972 forced the Soviet government to make huge grain purchases from abroad, including the United States, to avoid widespread food shortages. This was followed by another weak harvest in 1975. Moreover, the agricultural collectives that had been forced upon the rural population by Stalin in the 1930s (see Chapter 8, "Stalin and the Purges") were ill-suited to carry out investments in new crops, fertilizers, or other agricultural improvements.

Despite four decades of living with the collectives, many agricultural workers still preferred to tend their own small plots rather than work on the collective-owned fields. Output from these individual plots accounted for almost half of the Soviet Union's domestic food supply.

Corruption and Crisis

The Soviet Union's economic problems worsened in the late 1970s and became overwhelming by the early 1980s. Industrial growth slowed significantly, and the economy as a whole stagnated. Corruption and waste within the state-controlled economy were rampant, despite efforts to weed out inefficient managers and dishonest officials. Soviet planners quickly abandoned any hope of achieving the ambitious goals laid out in the five-year plan announced in 1981.

The agriculture sector continued to suffer. Production actually fell in successive harvests from 1979 to 1983, and government officials faced the disquieting notion that the Soviet Union could no longer feed itself without foreign imports. And, although industrial output did grow, it lagged far behind what was occurring in the West. Communist leaders could still argue that the Soviet Union produced more tractors than any other nation in the world. But they were loath to recognize that gross domestic output across the economy as a whole was slipping below that of West Germany and Japan—ironically, the two countries that the Soviet Union had helped defeat during the Second World War.

On top of this, the increasing demand for consumer goods remained largely unsatisfied. More Soviet citizens than ever before owned the basic consumer durables that people in the West had long taken for granted. In 1980, 86 percent of Soviet homes had a refrigerator and 74 percent had a television, in contrast to 32 and 51 percent in 1970. But the price of these goods compared to average Soviet salaries had reached the point that many Soviet citizens in the 1980s actually had less spending power than before.

Food and Energy Supply

As food began to be in increasingly short supply, the long lines of people standing in front of empty stores became legendary. Most urban centers suffered from severe housing shortages that forced many Soviet families to live in small, cramped apartments. There were widespread environmental problems, especially in industrial regions, and Soviet doctors voiced concerns about the growing public health issue. Perhaps most troubling to communist officials was the fact that the unregulated, black market was becoming an increasingly important part of the Soviet economy.

Notes on the Left

The Soviet Union had long relied on close economic ties with its satellite system of Warsaw Pact countries. In 1949, Stalin established the Council for Mutual Economic Assistance (known as Comecon) to coordinate economic policies among all the Soviet satellites. The result of these policies was often to ensure that goods produced in East Germany or Czechoslovakia were sold cheaply to the Soviet market. Likewise, during the 1970s, countries in Eastern Europe were forced to pay greatly inflated prices for the Soviet oil that they all relied upon for their energy needs.

As favorable as this system was for the Soviet Union, however, it was a double-edged sword for the Soviet economy. During the 1980s, Eastern Europe's own economic woes made it impossible for the Soviet Union to solve its own difficulties by exploiting trade arrangements with other members of the Warsaw Pact. On the contrary, Soviet leaders were far more worried about the threat that these economic problems posed to the communist regimes in Eastern Europe. Accordingly, they had little choice but to try to help by supplying cheap goods and raw materials.

By the mid 1980s, the Soviet Union was trapped in an economic and financial crisis. The investment needed to modernize the country could only come from Western sources, but the Soviet foreign debt in 1985 was already 15 times what it had been in 1970. Most of the economies of Eastern Europe were only able to continue functioning because of significant Soviet subsidies. Soviet military expenditures, which already amounted to around 20 percent of the country's budget, had skyrocketed after the invasion of Afghanistan and the resumption of an arms race with the United States (see the following section). The country was on the brink of bankruptcy.

Rising Foreign Tensions

The 1970s began hopefully enough for the Soviet Union with the opening of a more congenial relationship with the West in general, and with the United States in particular. Known as the policy of *détente*, both the United States and the Soviet Union sought to move away from direct confrontation with one another and toward some sort of common understanding. In 1972, both signed a major arms control agreement for the first time since the development of the atomic bomb, and the Strategic Arms Limitation Treaty (SALT) represented a significant lessening of threat of nuclear war.

Red Words _____

The policy known as **détente**, from the French for "relaxation," did not indicate a major ideological shift on the part of either the United States or the Soviet Union. Détente represented a goal of reducing international tensions by abandoning the open hostility that had characterized U.S.–Soviet relations for most of the period after the Second World War and finding ways to come to a mutual accommodation with one another.

Détente Runs Down

In the same year, the Soviet Union also normalized its relations with West Germany. In a major reversal of its official policy since the beginning of the Cold War, the Federal German Republic agreed to accept the division of Germany and recognized East Germany as a separate state. In 1975, this diplomatic victory was followed by an international agreement signed in Helsinki, in which all signatories resolved to accept the frontiers of the Soviet Union established at the end of the Second World War.

However, the period of better relations with the West was short-lived. In the late 1970s, a civil war broke out in neighboring Afghanistan between the pro-Soviet communist government and a variety of ethnic and Islamic opposition forces. Fearful that the conflict might spread across the border into its territory, the Soviet Union sent troops into the country in December 1979. The move was widely denounced by most Western governments and by many other countries around the world.

Afghanistan: The Soviet Union's Vietnam

The Soviet invasion of Afghanistan invited many comparisons to the American war in Vietnam (see Chapter 20, "National Liberation and Communism in the Third World"). In both cases, a global superpower was attempting to win victory over small, but dedicated resistance groups that fought a guerrilla campaign. Both conflicts evolved into long and protracted proxy wars, with the opposing superpower aiding local groups in their fight against outside military intervention. When casualties began to mount and each war dragged on with no clear end in sight, both countries experienced considerable domestic upheavals as opposition to the war became widespread. And both conflicts ended in the eventual defeat of America and the Soviet Union, demonstrating the limitations of being a global superpower.

However, there are some notable differences. The issue in Vietnam, at least from the American perspective, was the ideological battle between capitalism and communism. Afghanistan was very different. The Afghanis who opposed the communist regime were drawn from a complex mix of ethnic groups and Islamic movements, most of which were equally opposed to the United States. Only a few months before the Soviet invasion of Afghanistan, a similar Islamic movement had overthrown the American-supported regime in neighboring Iran. Soviet leaders certainly understood the dangers of duplicating what had happened to the Americans in Vietnam, but their more pressing concern was to prevent such Islamic movements from moving across the borders into the heavily Islamic regions of the Soviet Union such as Chechnya, Uzbekistan, and Tajikistan.

Afghan Quagmire

The Soviet invasion of Afghanistan proved to be a terrible mistake. The original goal was simple. As had been the case during previous interventions, such as in Hungary in 1956 or Czechoslovakia in 1968 (see Chapter 17, "Trouble in Paradise"), the aim was to present a show of force that would quickly overcome all opposition to the Soviet supported regime. Unlike these earlier actions, however, the campaign in Afghanistan was not short or decisive. The conflict soon turned into a bloody military campaign, as local resistance fighters, known as *mujaheddin*, or "holy warriors," fought the Soviet invaders using guerrilla tactics. Although the size of the Soviet occupation force would eventually grow to more than 100,000 soldiers, the Soviet Union was unable to maintain control over most of the country outside of the urban areas.

The war in Afghanistan became an enormous financial burden as the fighting continued for years, not ending until the Soviet withdrawal in the late 1980s. It also resulted in more than 14,000 Soviet casualties and caused deep divisions within Soviet society, as many soldiers returned from Afghanistan feeling embittered and disillusioned about their service to the communist cause. The war also exposed severe problems within the Soviet military establishment and made it far more difficult to count on the Red Army as an instrument in maintaining Soviet control over Eastern Europe.

The Afghanistan invasion also destroyed any chance of continuing the policy of détente with the West. The United States' public and vocal condemnation of Soviet actions was soon followed by active support for the Afghanistan mujaheddin. In the summer of 1980, the United States also led a boycott of the Olympic Games that were held in Moscow and announced an embargo on much needed grain shipments to the Soviet Union.

> ### Vignettes
>
> The failure of the 1980 Summer Olympic Games, held in Moscow, was a considerable embarrassment for the Soviet Union. The Games had originally been envisioned as a major diplomatic coup for the Soviet regime that justified their considerable expense. After the Western-led boycott, however, the Soviet Union was left presiding over a hollow shell of the Games. Four years later, the Soviet Union retaliated by boycotting the 1984 Summer Games held in Los Angeles.

Dealing with Reagan

With the election of the avowedly anti-communist Ronald Reagan to the American presidency in the same year, relations between the two countries quickly returned to their old status of outright hostility, in which Reagan repeatedly referred to the Soviet Union as "the Evil Empire." Reagan also announced that the United States would begin a significant military buildup that threatened to drag the Soviet Union into another arms race at a time when its economy could hardly afford any additional military expenditures. In 1983, Soviet relations with the West were further damaged when Soviet fighter planes shot down a civilian jet that had crossed into Soviet airspace from South Korea, killing all 269 passengers.

Political Uncertainties

The Soviet political leadership in the 1970s and early 1980s was poorly suited to deal with the country's pressing problems. During most of this period, Leonid Brezhnev led the country. Brezhnev was a Soviet hard-liner who stressed the need for military intervention to protect the Soviet hold on Eastern Europe. During the Soviet intervention in Czechoslovakia in 1968, he formalized this policy as the "Brezhnev Doctrine," which asserted that the Soviet Union had the right to intervene in the internal affairs of any Soviet satellite whose communist regime became unstable. Brezhnev was also intolerant of any internal criticism directed at the Soviet leadership and moved quickly to suppress dissident groups.

Vignettes
Leonid Brezhnev was born in 1906. Like most members of the Communist Party's inner circle, he was a professional politician, having joined the Party in 1931 and steadily moved up through the Party hierarchy. He became secretary of the central committee under Stalin in 1952, and was later named to the Politburo in 1957. After the fall of Nikita Khrushchev in 1964, he became general secretary of the Party. Brezhnev initially ruled in conjunction with Alexei Kosygin, but soon emerged as the most important figure in the Soviet Union. He ruled the country until his death in 1982.

Resisting Change

By and large, Brezhnev resisted almost every real effort to change the Soviet system. He did allow token gestures. When the Communist Party Congress in 1976 voiced concerns about the country's agricultural crisis, he responded by replacing the government personnel responsible for the crisis and allowing more freedom to the managers of collective farms. A new constitution announced in 1977 appeared to reflect calls for changes in the political system, especially regarding the relationship between Russians and various ethnic groups who were actually a majority in many of the Soviet Union's border regions.

However, Brezhnev did not move on any more substantive economic or political reforms. The Soviet system as a whole became increasingly rigid and unresponsive to the wishes of the Soviet population. Communist Party membership increased dramatically during the Brezhnev years. But the special privileges granted to Party members drove a wedge between the Party and the general population. The massive government administration stagnated into a complacent and corrupt system run by career bureaucrats, known as *apparatchiks*, who grew ever more isolated from ordinary citizens.

During the 1960s and the early 1970s, the deeply imbedded problems had been disguised by growing prosperity. But as economic difficulties mounted, problems became more visible. Despite widespread complaints about mismanagement and corruption, little seemed to change. Many Soviet citizens, not just the occasional dissident, complained that the country was being run by an aging group of hard-line communist fossils who were completely insulated from the realities of life in the Soviet Union.

Notes on the Left

The Soviet Union, like other Marxist-Leninist regimes, lacked any clear and defined mechanism for regulating changes in political leadership. After Stalin came to power in the late 1920s, he instituted a sweeping purge of all other Party members who might challenge his rule (see Chapter 8). The transfer of power to Khrushchev after Stalin's death, and again when Brezhnev replaced Khrushchev in 1964, was less bloody. But, the choice of new leadership was determined by complex political maneuverings among various well-established factions within the Politburo and the Communist Party Central Committee.

In theory, such choices were confirmed by a vote in Supreme Soviet, which included representatives selected from all parts of the Soviet Union, but generally this amounted to little more than providing a rubber stamp for the decisions that had already been made. Such a system created an atmosphere in which significant political changes or radical shifts in government policies became all but impossible. These flaws became all too apparent during the succession crisis after Brezhnev's death in 1982, when the Soviet Union struggled through a three-year period of rigid administration under Andropov and Chernenko before the more reform-minded Mikhail Gorbachev finally emerged as the country's new leader.

The Last of the Old-Timers

Brezhnev, who turned 76 in 1982, did little to change this perception. Yurii Andropov, the 70-year-old former head of the KGB, replaced Brezhnev, but lasted less than a year and half as leader of the Soviet Union, before dying himself. His replacement, Konstantin Chernenko, was also in his 70s and had the reputation of being another hard-liner and a long-time supporter of Brezhnev. Chernenko's tenure at the helm of the Soviet state was even shorter than Andropov's, and he died in March 1985. Over the space of three years, the Soviet Union was led by three different premiers, each almost indistinguishable from the others.

Vignettes

The careers of Yurii Andropov and Konstantin Chernenko were very similar to that of Brezhnev. Andropov was born in 1914. Like Brezhnev, he spent his entire life working as a Communist Party official. He served as Soviet ambassador to Hungary from 1954 to 1957 and played a major role in overseeing the Soviet military intervention in 1956. He was appointed head of the KGB in 1967 and ran that organization until becoming head of the Communist Party following Brezhnev's death in 1982.

Chernenko followed a similar path, although he was more of a minor functionary than a dominant political leader. Born in 1911, he joined the Communist Party at a young age and rose slowly through the ranks to become a member of the Central Committee in 1971 and a member of the Politburo in 1978. His choice to become the head of the Communist Party after Andropov's death was largely determined by the fact that he was one of last prominent members of the Brezhnev generation still alive.

Mikhail Gorbachev Comes to Power

Chernenko's death in March 1985 opened the way for Mikhail Gorbachev to assume leadership of the Soviet Union. At the age of 54, Gorbachev was significantly younger than any of the Soviet premiers who immediately preceded him. Although the Bolsheviks had seized power almost 70 years prior to Gorbachev's elevation to the position of the Communist Party General Secretary, he was the first Soviet leader to have actually been born after the October Revolution. Ironically, he was also to be the last leader of the Soviet Union.

Gorbachev represented a new, younger generation of communist leadership that had been blocked from achieving power by the presence of older, entrenched elites, such as Brezhnev and Andropov. As Soviet citizens joked, "Gorbachev does not need to be supported in the Kremlin, he can walk in unaided by himself." Moreover, unlike earlier Party leaders, Gorbachev was also a trained professional and a university graduate who had earned degrees in law and economics. Despite the daunting problems faced by the Soviet Union, his ascension to power seemed to offer the first chance of real reform for the Soviet Union.

Gorbachev's first efforts to promote change were, in fact, modest efforts carried out under a so-called program of "acceleration." The concept espoused by the Kremlin was that the Soviet Union's basic economic structure was sound; all that was needed was some fine-tuning of the small details. For example, he pointed to alcoholism as a major cause of the

Soviet economic problems and launched a major anti-drinking campaign. A new five-year plan announced in 1986 raised wages and allowed for a variety of limited financial incentive programs to encourage production and minimize inefficiencies and waste.

However, Gorbachev's initial reform efforts had mixed results. He had a hard time imposing reform on the well-entrenched Soviet bureaucracy and mid-level Communist Party administrators. And the anti-alcoholism campaign actually backfired as the drop in alcohol consumption hurt state revenues and contributed to the Soviet government's growing financial difficulties. In 1986, Gorbachev announced a new program of wider reforms.

Perestroika and *Glasnost*

Gorbachev's more sweeping reform policies became known by the two catchwords of *perestroika* and *glasnost*. The first of the two was a program of economic liberalization to allow a freer market that would be more responsive to consumer demands. While not any kind of move to abandon communist principles altogether, perestroika did imply a shift away from a completely planned economy and toward a mixture of socialist and capitalist elements. Citing comparisons with the New Economic Policy implemented by Lenin in the 1920s (see Chapter 7, "Lenin and the Communist Regime"), Gorbachev announced that perestroika was aimed at rebuilding the Soviet economy.

The accompanying policy of glasnost was a relaxation of censorship rules to allow more discussion and open debate within Soviet society. It included a loosening of the government's control over publishing houses and ending the decades-old practice of jamming foreign news services that were being broadcast into the country. Journalists who worked for the state-run television channels were permitted to produce stories about the failure of government services or allegations of local corruption. And the government allowed frank discussions about issues such as the status of ethnic minorities and historical wrongdoings carried out in the name of communism, which would have been unimaginable only a few years previously.

Red Words

Perestroika means "reconstruction"; it was a policy of making the Soviet economy more decentralized and opening it up to a limited degree of capitalist-style management and profit motivation. **Glasnost** is the Russian word for "openness"; it reflected a willingness to permit more popular criticism of the communist regime's historical and current mistakes.

Although representing a significant departure from policies of Brezhnev and his immediate successors, Gorbachev's reforms were not such a great or radical transformation of the existing order. Gorbachev was a committed supporter of the communist movement, and his policies were more an effort to reform the system from within than overturn it completely. Many of the problems he attempted to tackle could only be solved through a much more dramatic and thorough transformation than was possible without abandoning communism altogether.

Gorbachev's Foreign Policy

While Gorbachev's domestic reforms enjoyed limited success, his foreign policy reforms seemed far more fruitful. Recognizing that the Soviet Union simply could not afford to embark on another arms race with the United States, he set out to repair the damage that had been done to U.S.–Soviet relations over the previous five years.

As a first step, he removed foreign minister Andrei Gromyko. Known as "Grim Grom" by the Western diplomatic corps, Gromyko had served as foreign minister since 1957, and it is little wonder that the Soviet Union's relationship with the West seemed trapped in a recurring pattern of hostility and recrimination.

Gorbachev replaced Gromyko with the far more flexible, and youthful, Eduard Shevardnadze and embarked on an ambitious effort to rebuild the Soviet Union's international reputation. In 1986, he embarked on a "charm offensive" to develop closer ties with Western Europe and reached out to the United States at the Reykjavík Summit to propose new rounds of arms control agreements. He also engineered a Soviet withdrawal from Afghanistan.

Vignettes

Paradoxically, during his first years in office, Gorbachev was in many ways more popular with international audiences than he was in the Soviet Union itself. Unlike earlier Soviet premiers, Gorbachev took great pains to make himself available to Western media. During the Reykjavík Summit in October 1986, images of Gorbachev and his stylishly dressed wife Raisa holding press conferences and being interviewed by journalists did much to dispel the stereotype of the dour and grim-faced communist leader. His visits to the West, including a trip to the United States, witnessed the unprecedented sight of Gorbachev playing to the crowds gripped by what some referred to as "Gorbamania." This widespread popularity in the West was never duplicated among Soviet citizens.

The result was a vastly improved relationship with the West in general, and especially with the United States. Gorbachev came to enjoy a considerable popularity in the West, and international tensions cooled considerably from what they had been in the early 1980s.

Limitations and Failures of Reform

Despite popular adulation in the West, Gorbachev was on far shakier ground within his own country. His ambitious reform program angered many of the more conservative elements within the Communist Party. By the late 1980s, he faced open resistance from many local officials, while there were rumblings of possible coups being planned by hardline elements within the army and the KGB.

At the same time, his reforms seemed to be making little headway toward solving the ever-worsening economic and social crisis. The economic reforms embodied in perestroika could only scratch the surface of the collapsing system. And the willingness to allow public criticism of the government, as preached by glasnost, did not necessarily mean that the government would be able to respond to this criticism. In fact, there was a deepening sense that the Soviet regime was fatally incapable of reform, as evidenced by the disastrous nuclear accident at Chernobyl in 1986.

Trapped between those who believed his reforms had gone too far, and those who wanted them to go even further, Gorbachev could do little but wait and hope that his popularity might buy him enough time to allow the reforms to make more progress. However, he overestimated both the strength of his popular appeal and the possibility of his reforms eventually achieving better success.

As difficulties at home mounted, the regime's hold over Eastern Europe became more tenuous. Toward the end of the decade, Gorbachev faced the prospect of seeing Communist Party control in Eastern Europe collapse unless the Soviet Union launched massive military interventions like those in Hungary in 1956 and Czechoslovakia in 1968. But by the 1980s, the Soviet Union was in no position to do so.

Meltdown at Chernobyl

The nuclear accident at the Chernobyl reactor in the Ukraine may well have been the final nail in the coffin of communist rule in the Soviet Union. The accident was the worst nuclear disaster in history and occurred when engineers started an uncontrolled critical reaction after disabling the emergency control systems. The resulting explosion killed about 100 personnel and firemen at the site and spread radioactive material over much of Europe. However, the Soviet Union did not announce that an accident had occurred until Western scientists began recording massively higher levels of radioactivity.

The accident dealt a terrible blow to the Soviet Union's reputation as a leading technological nation and severely damaged its relations with both Eastern and Western Europe. Just under 10,000 people are estimated to have died during the accident and as result of subsequent exposure to radioactivity, although the exact number may never be known. The economic toll was equally devastating, as much of the agricultural harvest from the

Ukraine had to be destroyed, and the financial costs of repairing and sealing the reactor grew to staggering levels. Under Gorbachev's new policy of glasnost, the Soviet media widely reported on the incompetence and criminal negligence that had allowed the accident to happen.

The Least You Need to Know

- ♦ The Soviet Union's economic prosperity in the 1970s disguised deeply rooted problems that surfaced during the 1980s.

- ♦ The early 1980s were a time of considerably increased international tensions following the Soviet invasion of Afghanistan and the resumption of an arms race with the United States.

- ♦ A hard-line corps of older communist leaders who resisted any attempts at reform was finally removed when Mikhail Gorbachev came to power in 1985.

- ♦ Gorbachev's policy of perestroika was an attempt to move the Soviet economy toward a more mixed capitalist and socialist model, and his policy of glasnost was a more open approach to public debate, including criticism of the government.

- ♦ Gorbachev set out to build better relations with the West and agreed to a number of new arms control deals.

- ♦ Gorbachev's reforms eventually failed because they could not go far enough.

22

Reds in Retreat: The Collapse of Communism in Eastern Europe

In This Chapter

- ◆ Reform and revolution in Eastern Europe
- ◆ Fall of the Berlin Wall
- ◆ The end of communist rule in the Soviet Union
- ◆ New democracies face new challenges
- ◆ A New World Order?

For most of Europe, 1989 was an *annus miraculus*, a "miraculous year," that saw the fall of communism throughout Eastern Europe. Fifty years after Stalin built an Iron Curtain across the continent, the Soviet Union's hold over its satellites disintegrated in the face of overwhelming popular discontent. Communist governments throughout Eastern Europe collapsed and were replaced by Western-style democracies. Despite the reforms instituted by Mikhail Gorbachev, less then two years later, the Soviet Union itself would undergo the same transformation. With a few notable exceptions, the changes were accomplished without much bloodshed.

In this chapter, we look at the fall of communism in Europe and why it occurred so easily in 1989 when all previous attempts at reform had been brutally suppressed.

The Soviet Union Abandons the Military Option

By the late 1980s, the Soviet Union was facing its worst crisis since the end of the Second World War. The reform programs of Mikhail Gorbachev, launched under the twin banners of *perestroika* and *glasnost* (see Chapter 21, "Cracks in the Iron Curtain: Crisis and Reform in the Soviet Union"), had not succeeded in revitalizing the Soviet economy. As the country continued its long slide into economic chaos, Soviet leaders found it very difficult to do anything about the parallel economic problems that were prevalent throughout its satellite systems in Eastern Europe. As popular protests mounted, communist rulers from Poland to Bulgaria turned to the Soviet Union for help, but their pleas for Soviet intervention were not answered.

For the first time since the erection of the Iron Curtain, the Soviet Union faced the prospect of combating widespread popular unrest throughout Eastern Europe. In 1956, Soviet troops had quickly intervened in Hungary to end a similar call for change (see Chapter 17, "Trouble in Paradise"). They had done likewise when Czechoslovakia attempted to reform in 1968, and in 1980 it had supported the communist leader of Poland, General Wojciech Jaruzelski, when he imposed military rule in response to the Solidarity movement.

Voices

In his book *Perestroika and New Thinking*, published in 1988, Gorbachev outlined his views on the need for a new approach to the Soviet military policy:

> The fundamental principle of the new political outlook is very simple: *nuclear war cannot be a means of achieving political, economic, ideological, or any other such goals.* … But military technology has developed to such an extent that even a non-nuclear war would now be comparable with a nuclear war in its destructive effect. That is why it is logical to include in our category of nuclear wars this "variant" of an armed clash between major powers as well.

There are several reasons why Gorbachev and many other senior Soviet leaders did not consider using force to suppress popular challenges to their communist allies. In the first place, Gorbachev sincerely argued that the use of military force to maintain Soviet control over its satellites was contrary to the basic principle of his perestroika reform movement. The call for a new way of thinking within the Soviet Union also meant a new approach toward its relationship with the rest of the communist bloc. On December 7, 1988, he signaled this change in Soviet policy during a speech to the United Nations by unilaterally announcing that 500,000 Soviet troops would be withdrawn from Eastern Europe. At the same time, he informed communist leaders that they would have to solve their own internal problems without help from the Soviet Union.

Notes on the Left

The example of how the Chinese communist government had responded to its own internal problems highlighted the extraordinarily difficult dilemma faced by Soviet leaders. In the late 1980s, China experienced a growing popular movement calling for deep social and economic reforms and the adoption of more democratic institutions in place of the communist regime's tight control over the country.

The popular unrest echoed similar movements in Eastern Europe. Inspired by Gorbachev's visit, large crowds of protestors occupied Tiananmen Square in Beijing in the spring of 1989. After several days, the communist government ordered troops to remove the crowds, killing as many as 1,000 people. The protests, and the subsequent military crackdown, were covered by Western media and produced a storm of international criticism against China. When the Soviet Union faced the prospect of carrying out a similar military action in Eastern Europe several months later, few Soviet leaders had the stomach to follow China's example.

Personal sentiments aside, Gorbachev and other Soviet leaders also recognized that the military option stood a good chance of failing. The army's poor showing during the disastrous invasion of Afghanistan (see Chapter 21) exposed deep flaws within the Soviet military establishment.

Any intervention in Eastern Europe would demand a major mobilization of Soviet forces that were already demoralized and in dire need of reform. It would also leave the Soviet Union dangerously overextended at a time when it faced its own internal unrest, especially from nationalist movements in the Baltic states and in the Central Asian republics. And, whatever its outcome, the military action would be so enormously expensive that it would destroy all hopes of achieving the economic reconstruction that the Soviet Union so badly needed.

Finally, while Gorbachev seriously doubted whether a military intervention would succeed, he had no doubts whatsoever that any such attempt would have serious consequences for the Soviet Union's relationship with the United States. Although Gorbachev had done much to repair ties with the United States, which had seriously declined during the late 1970s and early 1980s (see Chapter 21), deep tensions over such issues as nuclear disarmament still remained. In Gorbachev's view, resolving these issues was more important than maintaining Soviet control over Eastern Europe. In October 1989, shortly before a summit meeting with Ronald Reagan and just as the popular unrest in Eastern

Europe was gathering momentum, he formally announced the end of the Brezhnev Doctrine. (Brezhnev had claimed the right for the Soviet Union to intervene in Eastern Europe whenever communist regimes were confronted by internal opposition.)

A Wave of Revolutions in Eastern Europe

Unable to call upon the Soviet Union for help, communist leaders in Eastern Europe had three options: to cave in, reform, or crack down. They could cave in to protestors' demands, which essentially meant giving up power. As a second choice, they could introduce some limited reforms in hope of riding out the wave of popular unrest while still remaining in control. Or, they could resist all calls for change and institute their own military crackdown. Each country's choice was dictated by its history and by the personalities of its leaders.

The following list documents the collapse of communism in Eastern Europe:

- 1985. Gorbachev comes to power in the Soviet Union.
- December 1988. Gorbachev announces troop withdrawals.
- May 1989. Hungary opens its border with Austria and allows unregulated travel to the West.
- August 1989. After losing heavily in popular elections, the communist regime in Poland steps aside in favor of a new government headed by members of the Solidarity movement.
- November 1989. East Germany opens its borders with West Germany, and crowds of protestors dismantle the Berlin Wall. The communist regime in Bulgaria falls shortly afterward.
- December 1989. The communist regimes in East Germany and Czechoslovakia collapse. After ordering troops to attack protestors in Romania, the communist leader Ceausescu is overthrown and executed.
- January 1990. The Communist Party in Yugoslavia splinters into opposing national groups who cannot agree on the future of the country's administration. Over the next few years, the country itself splits apart in a bloody series of conflicts.
- March 1990. Free elections in East Germany and Hungary result in landslide victories for opposition parties.
- October 1990. East and West Germany are reunited for the first time since the end of the Second World War.
- December 1990. Lech Walesa, leader of the Solidarity movement, becomes president of Poland.

All three strategies were followed during the eventual months, from the fall of 1989 through the spring of 1990. But, the end result was the same in every case. The popular movements were too powerful to contain by granting token reforms, or even by resorting to military force. Once the floodgates of change had been opened, there was little the communist regimes could do other than step aside. By the end of 1990, all communist governments throughout Eastern Europe had been overthrown.

Poland: Solidarity!

Poland was one of the first countries in Eastern Europe to suffer the imposition of communist rule by the Soviet Union. However, the regime had always faced considerable domestic opposition. Since the late 1970s, the communist government struggled to find a way of dealing with the serious challenge to its authority from the Solidarity movement headed by Lech Walesa (see Chapter 17).

Solidarity claimed the support of over 10 million Poles, almost one third of the country's entire population. In December 1981, with the support and backing of the Soviet Union, the communist government headed by General Wojciech Jaruzelski solved the problem by outlawing the movement, arresting Walesa, and placing Poland under martial law.

These steps didn't end popular protests against the regime. In the wake of continuing economic difficulties, the government was forced to contend with a wave of general strikes that crippled the country. In August 1988, Jaruzelski opened negotiations with leaders of the Solidarity movement to look for a compromise solution. The eventual outcome was an agreement to hold a new general election in which one third of the seats in the Polish parliament could be contested by noncommunist parties (up until that point, only members of the Polish Communist Party were allowed to run for office).

The elections held in June 1989 were a humiliating debacle for the Jaruzelski government. The Solidarity movement won a landslide victory and captured every seat its candidates were allowed to contest, except for one. Although the communist regime still held theoretical control over the country, the stunning defeat set off a moral and political crisis throughout the Communist Party hierarchy. After a period of anguished internal debate, the Communist Party stepped aside in August 1989 and allowed a new interim government headed by leaders from Solidarity. It sent a powerful message to protest movements throughout Eastern Europe; for, if the Soviet Union refused to intervene in Poland, it was not likely to intervene anywhere else. After that, the unraveling of control went faster.

Hungary: Opening the Borders

Although communist government of Hungary had been among the less oppressive of those in Eastern Europe, it, too, faced considerable domestic unrest during the 1980s.

In the early 1980s, its leader, Janos Kadar, had allowed some limited economic reforms, including the establishment of small privately owned enterprises such as retail stores and restaurants. In 1988, however, he was ousted and replaced by the more reform-minded Karolyi Grozs, often referred to as the "Hungarian Gorbachev."

Over the next year, the communist regime in Hungary implemented a series of extraordinary moves. In a major about-face, it relaxed controls over discussion of the 1956 Hungarian uprising (see Chapter 17), even though this amounted to a direct attack on the legitimacy of communist rule in Hungary. Long dismissed by communist propaganda as an unsuccessful counterrevolution, the 1956 uprising was now acknowledged as having been a genuinely popular movement in protest against communist rule and Soviet domination.

In May 1989, the regime opened its border with Austria, allowing hundreds of thousands to cross into the West and see firsthand the staggeringly different living standards that most enjoyed. Several months later, the communist government agreed to accept widespread demands for more democratic reforms. It permitted the formation of opposition political parties and announced a general election. When the election was held in March 1990, the Communist Party came in fourth, winning a mere 8.5 percent of the vote. Stripped of any claim to represent the popular will, the regime stepped down, and a new coalition government headed by the Democratic Forum took power.

> ### Vignettes
>
> Hungary's decision to open its borders with the West had profound implications for other communist regimes. It was not just Hungarians who took advantage of the open border. Travelers from throughout Eastern Europe joined the miles-long lines of people and cars waiting to get out. As thousands of citizens from East Germany and Czechoslovakia flooded across the border into Austria, the communist governments in these countries found themselves in the ludicrous position of arguing that they needed to close their borders with Hungary to stop the outflow. Such pronouncements made mockery of claims that their fortified borders with the West were only intended to serve as a deterrent to invasion. Fifty years after it had been erected, the Iron Curtain had begun to collapse under its own weight.

East Germany: Honecker and the Wall

By the fall of 1989, events in Hungary and Poland had begun to produce a powerful ripple effect across the rest of Eastern Europe. Nowhere was this felt more keenly than in East Germany. Erich Honecker, a strong-arm communist leader who made extensive use of the East German secret police, the *Stasi*, to maintain order, had ruled the country since 1971. However, inspired by the success of the Polish Solidarity movement and Hungary's decision to open its borders with Austria, popular protests in East Germany began to shake the foundations of this rigid communist regime.

Red Words

The **Stasi** was among the most notorious of the secret police forces in Eastern Europe. Ever since the establishment of the German Democratic Republic in 1949, the Stasi had used terror tactics to intimidate and suppress internal opposition to the communist regime. The organization also employed a huge network of agents and informants on both sides of the Berlin Wall. This network included thousands of scientists, students, writers, union leaders, and a wide variety of others who were compromised by the Stasi and forced to spy on their colleagues. When the communist regime finally collapsed in November 1989, one of the first targets of the celebrating crowds was the Stasi headquarters building. Protestors invaded the building and joyfully destroyed hundreds of thousands of files containing reports from Stasi informants.

Honecker begged Gorbachev for Soviet aid in suppressing the protest movements. In September 1989, after thousands of East Germans began escaping to the West through Hungary, he also ordered that the East German borders with the rest of the communist bloc be sealed. However, neither step did much to strengthen his regime or weaken the opposition. The fortieth anniversary of the establishment of East Germany as the German Democratic Republic in October 1989 was marked by huge street demonstrations against the communist government.

On November 9, 1989, Honecker caved in and agreed to open the border between East and West Germany for the first time since 1961. As millions of East Germans poured across the frontier, they were met by West German officials who handed them a welcome bag containing a small sum of spending money and a sample of Western consumer goods. In Berlin, crowds celebrated by using sledgehammers and bulldozers to tear down the hated wall that had divided the city for almost 30 years.

By the end of the month, the communist government had collapsed and Honecker fled the country. New political parties quickly emerged, and in March 1990 the country held free elections for the first time since the rise of Hitler in the early 1930s. The victorious Christian Democratic Party pushed for rapid unification with West Germany, which was officially announced in October 1990. A divided Germany, which for half a century had been the most visible symbol of the Iron Curtain and the Cold War, was no more.

Bulgaria and Czechoslovakia: The People Vote

The collapse of the communist regimes in Bulgaria and Czechoslovakia followed closely on the heels of Jaruzelski's surrender to the Solidarity movement in Poland, the Hungarian Communist Party's decision to hold free elections, and the dismantling of the Berlin Wall. However, events in each country took a slightly different path.

In the case of Bulgaria, the revolution came from above, as opposition groups within the Communist Party engineered the removal of Bulgaria's hard-line leadership headed by Todor Zhivkov, who had been in power since 1954. Although he had attempted to implement an imitation of Gorbachev's reforms during the late 1980s, the efforts were far too limited and superficial. Zhivkov was replaced by the much more liberal and reform-minded Petar Mladenov in November 1989, and this removal signaled a sharp break with Bulgaria's communist past. Over the next months, the Bulgarian Communist Party accelerated the process of reform and agreed to allow free elections.

The democratic revolution in Czechoslovakia, on the other hand, came from below. Headed by Milos Jakes and Gustav Husak, who had overseen the purges in Czechoslovakia following the Soviet invasion in 1968, the communist regime at first attempted to suppress the reform movement in 1988 and early 1989. However, the protests grew in size and strength, until crowds of more than 500,000 people began gathering in Prague.

By November 1989, the opposition movement coalesced around the Civic Forum group headed by Czech playwright Václav Havel. Starved of real support from any part of the country, the communist regime collapsed in December 1989 and was replaced by an interim government headed by Havel. In an important symbolic gesture, Alexander Dubcek, who had instituted the last reform movement in 1968, was recalled back to Czechoslovakia to join the government. This bloodless overthrow of a regime that had shown little regard for using force in the past became known as "the Velvet Revolution."

Voices

Václav Havel became the symbolic voice for the protest movement throughout Eastern Europe by his impassioned cry for an ethical revolution to end the harsh and heartless rule that characterized so many communist regimes. In one of his first speeches after assuming the Czechoslovakia presidency, Havel remarked:

> The worst thing that we live in is a contaminated moral environment. We fell morally ill because we became used to saying something different from what we thought. … Concepts such as love, friendship, compassion, humility or forgiveness lost their depth and dimensions. … The previous regime—armed with its arrogant and intolerant ideology—reduced man to a force of production and nature to a tool of production. It reduced gifted and autonomous people, skillfully working in their own country, to nuts and bolts of some monstrously huge, noisy, and stinking machine, whose real meaning is not clear to anyone.

Romania: The People Rise

The last government to fall during the miraculous year of 1989 was Romania. Unlike the other revolutions in Eastern Europe, however, the communist regime in Romania was not overturned in a bloodless coup. Its hard-line ruler Nicolae Ceausescu had been in power since 1965 and was determined not to step aside without a fight. Like the rest of the communist bloc, Romania experienced severe financial problems during the 1980s and suffered a precipitous decline in living standards. Despite this, Ceausescu kept himself and an inner circle of high-ranking communist leadership in remarkable luxury.

Protests against the regime were further inflamed when Romanian secret police attempted to move against prominent members of the minority Hungarian ethnic population. The protests spread to the capital of Bucharest in December 1989, and Ceausescu was forced to flee from the presidential palace by helicopter. After extended battles with secret police troops, the crowds seized the city, and Ceausescu and his wife were captured and executed.

The Collapse of Communism in the Soviet Union

For more conservative elements within the Soviet Communist Party, the events of 1989–1990 were nothing short of a calamity. Suddenly, it seemed, to be "conservative" meant to be loyal to the older, radical vision of Marxism-Leninism. The extensive system of satellite states that Stalin had established as a security zone to protect the Soviet Union's western borders had vanished overnight. Even worse, the success of protests in Eastern Europe gave considerable hope to parallel movements within the Soviet Union.

Gorbachev's Dilemma

Gorbachev was trapped in a dilemma to which he had contributed with his own policies. Overtaken by the remarkable series of events in Eastern Europe, he was unable to go back and recreate the old Soviet system. Nor could he go forward with additional reforms, for he would be blocked by conservative forces from within his own party. The stalemate lasted for little more than a year, but the crisis could not be contained and the communist regime in the Soviet Union succumbed to the same fate as that of its counterparts in Eastern Europe.

The first indication that the Soviet Union itself was on the verge of breaking up was the rise of nationalist protests in the Baltic states of Latvia, Lithuania, and Estonia. Annexed by the Soviet Union during the Second World War (see Chapter 12, "The Soviet Union in World War II"), the Baltic states had long been a thorn in the side of the Soviet government. Following the lead of Poland, Hungary, Czechoslovakia, and other Soviet satellites, nationalist movements in the Baltic states began agitating for the end of Soviet control.

Gorbachev adamantly proclaimed that his decision not to intervene in Eastern Europe did not apply in the case of regions that were formally members of the USSR. However, he could do little to control the protests, which were soon followed by similar movements in the Ukraine, Moldavia, Georgia, Armenia, and throughout the Soviet Union's Central Asian republics.

Notes on the Left _____

The question of nationalities had always been among the most difficult issues for the Communist regime in the Soviet Union. During the Russian civil war from 1918 to 1922 (see Chapter 6, "The Russian Revolution"), the Red Army under the leadership of Leon Trotsky had succeeded in reconquering all of the old Tsarist empire, which had included many non-Russian areas. The Soviet Union eventually became a federal system with 15 separate republics, providing some measure of autonomy for local groups. The Russian Socialist Republic, which stretched from the Ukraine to the Pacific, was by far the largest and most important of the Soviet republics. Although ultimate control rested with the Communist Party of the Soviet Union (CPSU) and the Moscow-based government, each of the other republics had its own communist party as well as its own local government. However, the system was always unwieldy. Tensions, rivalry, and traditional hatreds among the dozens of different ethnic, linguistic, and religious groups that lived within its borders smoldered beneath the surface. In the summer of 1990, these tensions flared to the ignition point.

The Baltics Bolt

Events soon spun out of Gorbachev's control. In the spring of 1990, Lithuania declared itself independent, followed shortly afterward by Latvia and Estonia. Local communist groups in other parts of the Soviet Union started ignoring orders from Moscow and implementing their own political reforms. In May 1990, Boris Yeltsin, who had been removed from the Party by Gorbachev two years earlier, defeated the official Communist Party candidate and was elected president of the Russian parliament. The Communist Party itself, already deeply demoralized, began to dissolve and more than three million members resigned by the end of the year.

Desperate to avoid the impending collapse, Gorbachev tried to institute additional reforms during the summer and fall of 1990. The proposals included an almost complete abandonment of the socialist system and a promise to sell off all state-owned property. Together with Boris Yeltsin, Gorbachev also proposed a radical restructuring of the Soviet federal system to allow much greater autonomy to each of the 15 individual republics.

The Hard-Liners' Coup

These reforms were a last-ditch effort to prevent the complete collapse of communist rule in the Soviet Union. But, the reforms were completely unacceptable to the hard-line, conservative elements of the Communist Party. The official date for the signing of the new treaty that called for a reorganization of the Soviet Union was August 20, 1991. On August 19, a group of communist leaders, including the vice-president and the head of the KGB, staged a coup against Gorbachev, who was vacationing at a resort in the Crimea. Announcing that Gorbachev had been taken ill, the leaders of the coup proclaimed that they were acting to protect the Soviet Union from extremists, mobilized army units, and attempted to occupy the Russian parliament building.

Vignettes

Like many of the reformist leaders throughout Eastern Europe, Boris Yeltsin was a former member of the Communist Party. Born in 1931, he had started out as a construction engineer but switched careers and joined the Party in 1968.

Yeltsin soon developed a reputation for self-promotion and appealing to populist concerns over formal allegiance to Party ideology and policies. In 1985, he was a supporter of Gorbachev and was elected to the Communist Party Central Committee. He also served as chief of the Party in Moscow.

By 1987, however, Yeltsin had begun to fight with Gorbachev over the progress of reform. Taking Gorbachev's glasnost policy a little too much to heart, he also angered many other communist leaders by broadcasting descriptions of the continuing problems with corrupt government officials. Gorbachev expelled him from the Party in October 1987. Yeltsin began an opposition political campaign and was elected president of the Russian Socialist Republic in May 1990. Following his dramatic performance during the coup attempt in August 1991, he oversaw the final dismantling of the communist regime and served as president of the new Russian Federation until his retirement in December 1999. During his last years in office, he was not above using strong-arm tactics against his political opponents and used force to prevent any further breakup of the Russian Federation.

The coup might have succeeded if not for the actions of Yeltsin. Besieged in the parliament building, he called upon the citizens of Moscow to organize protests. Hundreds of thousands joined the crowds around the building and prevented army units from advancing. Many troops also refused to obey orders and proclaimed their allegiance to Yeltsin and Gorbachev. By the time Gorbachev returned to Moscow on August 22, the coup was over and its organizers had been arrested or fled into exile.

The failed coup accelerated the final end of communist rule in the USSR. The Communist Party became completely discredited by its involvement in the attempt to turn back the clock on the reform movement. Crowds celebrated the defeat of the coup by destroying the stature of Felix Dzerzhinsky, the founder of the KGB, that stood outside the infamous Lubyanka prison in central Moscow. On August 29, the Russian parliament suspended all activities of the Communist Party and seized its offices. Shortly afterward, Gorbachev resigned as general secretary of the Party and dissolved its central committee.

Dissolution of the Union

The end of the Communist Party almost coincided with the end of the Soviet Union. News of the coup attempt prompted many of the nationalist-minded republics to declare themselves independent. In December, the Ukraine dealt a final fatal blow to the Soviet Union when it declared independence after a referendum in which 90 percent of the electorate voted to end all ties to the Soviet Union. In December of 1991, the Union of Soviet Socialist Republics officially dissolved, with 11 of the original 15 members agreeing to join a much more loosely organized Commonwealth of Independent States.

An Uncertain Future

The collapse of communism in Eastern Europe and the Soviet Union was heralded by many as a momentous watershed. For most of the twentieth century, the world had been divided in an ideological battle between democracy and communism. The end of communist controlled regimes appeared to represent the dawn of a new era of international cooperation and progress, described by American President George Bush as a "New World Order." But as the inhabitants of Eastern Europe and the former Soviet Union were to soon discover, the new order was neither as progressive nor as peaceful as most had hoped.

Decades of communist rule had left behind a staggering legacy of economic, environmental and social problems that would take years to solve. Moreover, the rapid adoption of free-market principles in formerly socialist nations created new problems as people struggled to understand the vastly different world into which they had been thrust. The economic and financial crisis that had fueled the protest movements in 1989–1991 did not vanish with the fall of communism, no matter how enthusiastically the new regimes embraced democracy and capitalism.

And in some cases, their embrace of democracy was lukewarm at best. Some of the new governments adopted authoritarian rule. Continuing economic problems prevented any rapid rise in living standards that many had assumed would quickly follow the abandonment of communism. For many, there was a growing disenchantment with what had occurred during the miracle of 1989. By the late 1990s, reorganized communist parties throughout Eastern Europe and in parts of the old Soviet Union had begun to gain in popularity and win some electoral success.

Ethnic violence immediately followed the end of communist rule in many places. Communist regimes had eagerly suppressed all political opposition during their reign, but they had also kept an equally tight lid on simmering ethnic tensions. Once the lid was removed, ethnic conflicts erupted throughout the former communist bloc.

In the case of Czechoslovakia, these conflicts were resolved when the country peacefully agreed to split into two nations, the Czech and Slovak Republics, in January 1993. Other regions were not so lucky, however. In Yugoslavia, the complex mix of ethnic, linguistic, and religious divisions—divisions that had been firmly kept in check during the 40-year reign of Tito (see Chapter 18, "Yugoslavia: A Separate Road")—exploded in the early 1990s into a long and bloody series of conflicts worse than anything seen in Europe since the end of the Second World War. Likewise, the former Soviet republics of Azerbaijan and Armenia clashed over territorial disputes, and the new Russian Federation itself became embroiled in a deadly conflict against separatist movements in Chechnya.

What Marx would have condemned and dismissed as a "false consciousness," loyalty to one's tribal, ethnic, and national identity, rather than to one's class interest, turned out to be far more powerful and divisive than anticipated. Communist theory and doctrine had never fully mastered other human realities, including individual economic motivation and the desire for political freedom. But ethnic and national identity had always worked against a monolithic communist regime, and when brute force could no longer be used to hold them down, they erupted, often with ugly violence.

The Least You Need to Know

- ◆ Like the Soviet Union, communist regimes throughout Eastern Europe faced severe economic and political problems during the late 1980s.
- ◆ Under Gorbachev's leadership, the Soviet Union decided that it could not intervene to suppress popular opposition to the communist regimes.
- ◆ In a wave of protests in Eastern Europe that spread from one country to another during 1989, the communist regimes collapsed in the face of growing protest movements.
- ◆ Protests against communist rule spread to the Soviet Union, which became embroiled in a political crisis over the nationalist calls for local independence from Moscow.
- ◆ After a failed coup attempt by Communist Party hard-liners in August 1991, the Soviet Union itself collapsed.
- ◆ The collapse of communism left behind numerous economic problems and ethnic conflicts that continue to trouble much of the former communist bloc today.

Chapter 23

Remnants

In This Chapter

- ◆ The communist governments remaining in the twenty-first century
- ◆ Cuba
- ◆ China, North Korea, Laos, and Vietnam
- ◆ The end of Marxist-Leninist power

In this chapter we take a closer look at the handful of regimes that remained under by a communist form of government at the beginning of the twenty-first century. We'll see that after the end of the Cold War, Marxist-Leninist regimes in Europe and in the former Soviet Union rapidly converted into multiparty states.

Although several of these countries preserved many socialist principles, retaining some of the industrial base under state ownership, none of them used the full system of centralized party control that had characterized the Soviet regime from 1919 until the loosening of control under Gorbachev in the late 1980s. In most of the former Soviet Union and the satellite countries, the communist parties themselves were formally dissolved. Out of more than 185 independent countries in the world at the beginning of the twenty-first century, there were only five nations that still adhered to Marxism-Leninism. As time goes on, that number may diminish, or possibly increase. We'll have to wait and see.

The Five in 2002

Although many countries incorporated some aspects of socialist thinking into their governments and economic systems, by the beginning of the twenty-first century, there were only five that remained committed to the Marxist-Leninist version of socialism known as communism. Each of the five regimes continued to use what outsiders criticized as totalitarian methods to control political life.

So-called democratic centralism continued in five countries to prevent pluralistic democracy as understood in Britain, the United States, and other democracies of the West. The People's Republic of China, the Republic of Cuba, the Democratic People's Republic of Korea, the Socialist Republic of Vietnam, and the Lao People's Democratic Republic, all remained one-party communist states.

The countries that still adhered to the communist version of socialism might at first appear to have little in common. North Korea had always been isolated from the rest of the world, while Vietnam, Laos, and Cuba were former European colonies and quite cosmopolitan by contrast. China was the most populous country on earth, with an estimated 1.2 billion people, while the other four countries were much smaller, with Vietnam at 75 million, North Korea at 24 million, Cuba at 10 million, and Laos at 5 million. Considering the long heritage of Chinese history, stretching back thousands of years, the modern communist regime appears to represent a kind of interlude in the dynasties that have ruled that empire-nation.

Cuba and North Korea had single strongman governments for extraordinarily long periods. Fidel Castro was still in the Cuban seat of power in 2002, after 42 years. Kim Il Sung, who ruled North Korea for 45 years, from 1949 until his death in 1994, was succeeded, as in a monarchy, by his son Kim Jong Il. By contrast, the leaders of China, Vietnam, and Laos had only been in power since the 1990s. Like some other communist regimes, however, both Vietnam and China previously had long-term regimes: Mao Zedong had ruled China from 1949 until his death in 1976, and Ho Chi Minh had governed North Vietnam from 1954 to 1969.

Even more surprising to those who once believed in the unity of the communist world, communist Vietnam fought a war with neighboring communist Cambodia in 1977–1978, as well as a short border war with communist China. As in Eastern Europe, disputes over such issues divided the comrades more than ideology brought them together.

Wars Against the United States

One thing that all of the five communist states that survived in 2002 did have in common was that, at one time or another in the prior five decades, each had been engaged in an armed conflict, directly or indirectly, with the United States. None had been militarily defeated by the United States, and each had emerged from those conflicts with its territory intact. The United States had full diplomatic relations only with two of the nations, China and Laos, although negotiations with Cuba, North Korea, and Vietnam held out hope that their relations would eventually be normalized. Earlier in the book, we've discussed each of these wars, so this is just a reminder of the bare facts if you've already read those parts.

North Korea and China

In the Korean War (1950–1953), the United States defended South Korea against invasion by the communist regime in the North. Fourteen other member countries of the United Nations helped the United States, although American troops represented about one half of those defending South Korea. Beginning on November 26, 1950, communist China sent 200,000 troops to assist the North Koreans, and the war ended with a truce and armistice on July 27, 1953. Although no war had been declared, it was a bloody conflict, with over 33,000 Americans killed in action.

Bay of Pigs

After Fidel Castro's regime successfully established a communist state in Cuba in 1960, the United States supported an abortive invasion attempt. With help from the Central Intelligence Agency and logistical support from the U.S. military, a force of about 1,300 anti-Castro Cubans landed at the Bay of Pigs on April 17, 1961. The Cuban army killed 114 of them and captured another 1,189. Castro was able to use the event as the pretext for arresting about 100,000 suspected opponents of his regime. Although no U.S. troops were involved in the operation, American support in training, funding, and transportation was admitted.

Vietnam

During the Vietnam War, from 1964 through 1973, over 58,000 American servicemen and women were killed in Vietnam. The United States fought to preserve South Vietnam as a noncommunist state against a combination of local communist-led insurgent forces, the Vietcong, and troops from North Vietnam, which had been under a communist regime since 1954. Although the United States bombed North Vietnam extensively, it never committed ground troops to an invasion of the region, out of concern that the conflict would escalate into a world war. At a peace conference in Paris, on January 27, 1973, the United States agreed to stop bombing, and to withdraw its troops, while the Vietcong and North Vietnamese agreed to cease military operations. Once the U.S. forces were out, in early 1975, the Vietcong and North Vietnamese launched full-scale attacks and united the country under a single communist regime.

Laos

In Laos, a coalition government in power from 1960 to 1964 had included the Pathet Lao, a communist-dominated faction. The Pathet Lao left the government in 1964, and with military support from North Vietnam, worked against the U.S. forces and the Lao regime. During the Vietnam War, American CIA and other forces operated extensively in Laos, providing aid to mountain tribesmen to fight against both the Pathet Lao and the North Vietnamese. After U.S. withdrawal from the region, the Pathet Lao was victorious, declaring Laos the Lao People's Democratic Republic on December 3, 1975.

End of Cold War

The Cold War had kept the world in an anxious state from 1946 to 1990, anticipating the possibility of a nuclear war between the nations of the North Atlantic Treaty Organization and the Warsaw Treaty Organization over four decades. With the withdrawal of Soviet armed forces from Eastern European satellites in 1989, and the signing of a series of multilateral treaties in the late 1980s, the number of communist-governed regimes suddenly declined. As discussed in Chapter 22, "Reds in Retreat: The Collapse of Communism in Eastern Europe," in 1989–1993, there were a lot of more or less constitutional changes that converted the communist satellites into multiparty states.

After the events of 1989–1993, none of the former Soviet republics and none of the former communist regimes of Eastern Europe retained a communist government. Once the military and police control weakened, the transformation ran its course.

The unraveling of communist control in Eastern Europe had been set in motion in 1988 by Mikhail Gorbachev's decision to remove military forces from Eastern Europe, and by the Hungarians deciding to open their borders for transit of East Germans seeking to move to Western Europe. The loosening of power produced constitutional and political transformations that brought communist party rule to an end.

Deeper forces were afoot. Discontent, dissent, and dissatisfaction had simmered for years. People resented both the totalitarian nature of the communist regimes and the inability of most of the communist countries to successfully manage the economies of their countries.

There were differences in degree on the issue of political freedom. In East Germany, the Stasi spied on most of the population, suppressing all discussion of political ideas. The only form of protest seemed to be illegal escape from the country "over the wall" or across patrolled borders at the risk of losing one's life. By contrast, in Poland, political opposition took the form of Solidarity—both a union and a political movement. In Yugoslavia and Czechoslovakia, writers and intellectuals continued to voice their discontent with the system, sometimes at home, sometimes from abroad.

In economics, too, there was a range of conditions. Czechoslovakia, Hungary, and Yugoslavia were relatively prosperous compared to Albania and Bulgaria, with more consumer goods and some degree of "market socialism." Despite reforms launched by Gorbachev in the Soviet Union, that country lagged far behind the West, and even behind some of the satellites, in terms of living standards.

The End of the Road?

By 1993, the Communist Party no longer ruled any of these 28 countries (15 former Soviet Republics, and now 13 former satellites). In most of the countries, it had been prohibited or it simply dissolved. The rapid ending of communist regimes surprised many analysts, journalists, and historians. As late as the mid 1980s, very few experts predicted that communist regimes would collapse. When the regimes did collapse, the experts debated why.

Economic Explanations

Conservative critics tended to blame the collapse on the nature of communism itself. They suggested that it was based on flawed theories of human nature and economic behavior. The development of what Milovan Djilas had called a "New Class" of bureaucrats and administrators who acted like wealthy capitalists appeared to confirm that view. The economic crises that mounted in the Soviet Union in the 1970s and 1980s also demonstrated how cumbersome and unworkable the communist regimes had become.

Other evidence of the incapacity of a socialized economy to work as planned could be found in the appearance of extensive private black markets, based on bartering and illegal cash transfers, that made adjustments for shortages. If a market system could not control the demand for goods in short supply through increased prices, then people would find other ways, such as bribes, favors, and private trades, to reward those controlling the goods and services.

Through the 1970s and 1980s, the Soviet Union had failed to catch up with the West in agriculture, consumer goods, energy supply, and all the other measures of a healthy economy. The system simply could not be planned or managed, and it began to come apart. Decentralization was no substitute for the natural play of the marketplace. So went the arguments of those who thought that Adam Smith understood economics better than Karl Marx.

Political Explanations

Marx's theories of history, developed in the nineteenth century, were based on a faith that science would reveal absolute truths. Like Newtonian physics, Marxist social theory presumed a set of immutable laws. If correctly applied, the theory would determine exactly what strategy should be applied at a particular moment in history to move to the next step. Incorrect decisions were not simply variations in opinion—they would be historicaly and flatly wrong, and what the Comintern always called "deviation." These premises accounted for the bitter and intolerant struggles among Marxists and the ruthless imposition of a single approach from party leadership. Comintern policies, Stalin's oppression, and the suppression of dissent throughout the Soviet Union, China, and Eastern Europe all reflected this Marxist-Leninist view that one truth was correct and opposition was incorrect. If you were wrong, you were dead wrong, and sometimes, as a consequence, simply dead.

The characteristic of Western democracies, to agree to disagree and to protect the opponents' rights to voice their views, simply made no sense from a Marxist viewpoint. Such ideas of freedom had developed during the eighteenth century Enlightenment and had been espoused by the Englishman Thomas Paine, among others. Such views were incorporated in the American constitution, in British law, and in the basic law of many other republics and parliamentary democracies. From the viewpoint of Marx, such gentlemanly disagreement was a bourgeois characteristic and had no legitimate role once a scientific understanding of the unfolding of history had been achieved.

A libertarian explanation for the collapse of communism pointed to the fact that Marxist-Leninist regimes only survived through power, intimidation, police spying, and all the other apparatus of totalitarian states. The development of new media of information, such as the photocopier and the facsimile machine, made the suppression of dissent ever more difficult. Evidence for this line of thought could be found in Poland's Solidarity, in the Czech Prague Spring, in the Praxis movement in Yugoslavia, and in the proliferation of underground publications in the Soviet Union.

The suppression of dissent in communist regimes and the bitter struggles over who correctly interpreted Marx that cropped up between Stalin and Tito, and then between Mao and Khrushchev all reflected the same problem of trying to reduce politics to a set of scientific laws. The so-called people's democracies had never been democratic as the term was understood in the West.

Gorbachev's policy of glasnost seemed only to unleash pent-up resentments, rather than to relax them. Ultimately, it was only the power of the Soviet Union's army that kept the lid on dissent. When the economic burden of maintaining military control became too great, the forces of diversity burst their bounds. These were the arguments of those who preferred the political theory of Thomas Paine and Thomas Jefferson to that of Vladimir Ilyich Lenin.

Realpolitik, or Power Explanations

In the United States, advocates of a strong defense argued that the heavy military budget of the United States ultimately made it impossible for the Soviet Union to keep up. The beginnings of expenditures for a space-based defense system (known in the press as the Strategic Defense Initiative, or Star Wars) in the United States threatened to bankrupt the Soviet Union if they sought to keep up. If the competition between the United States and the Soviet Union had all boiled down to an arms race, perhaps the United States simply "won the race."

The survival of Marxist regimes in five countries that had withstood a military conflict with the United States appeared to support the view that communist control had always been a question of military power. Such an explanation appealed to those who worried less about economics or politics, and more about *realpolitik*, the art of international politics based on power, with war as the extension of politics. The nineteenth-century Prussian military writer Karl von Clausewitz had seen it that way, and many modern statesmen and analysts in the West agreed.

Despite some celebration along such lines in the United States, it appeared more likely that communism had not so much been defeated as it had simply collapsed from within. A combination of economic and political discontent required ever more expensive police and military forces to maintain control. While socialism would survive in many forms, the vision of a revolutionary transformation and a dictatorship by the proletariat, guided by a central leadership, as planned by Lenin, had simply proven unworkable. The bubbling discontent of ethnic and national identity that came to the surface once Soviet military power was removed further demonstrated that Marx's followers tended to downplay the importance of national identity as a force in domestic politics and international affairs.

The world in the twenty-first century faced new crises. But the threat that totalitarian regimes based on Marxism-Leninism would dominate the world had diminished, with remnants of the system surviving in somewhat different forms in four countries of the Far East and one in Latin America. As the world moved further and further away from the certainties of the nineteenth-century outlook, the prospect that Marxism would be revived and spread seemed to recede.

The Least You Need to Know

- At the opening of the twenty-first century, Communist regimes survived only in China, Laos, Vietnam, North Korea, and Cuba.
- Communism had not worked economically and did not adapt to change in the Soviet Union.

◆ Communists had very low tolerance for differences of opinion because they believed that all political issues had only a single correct explanation, leading to bitter struggles among communist nations.

◆ Most of those who followed Marx's theories could not accept the fact that ethnic identity and individual pursuit of happiness are far more powerful social forces than are class interests.

◆ Communists had always relied on brute force to remain in power and when the Soviet Union could no longer afford to provide troops for control in Eastern Europe, the system collapsed.

Appendix A

Glossary

anarchist communism   A model for future society that could be created after a sweeping social revolution. Unlike the state communism envisioned by Marx, anarchist communism entailed everything being run by small local communes without any central authority.

anarchists   Anarchists, like socialists, believed that the primary function of the state was to protect private property. With the organization of society in communes, the state would become unnecessary. Anarchists hoped to move to such a state of affairs quickly, and many disagreed with a Marxist program that would require an intermediate step in which the state managed production in the name of the working class.

anarcho-syndicalists   Believed that the dissolution of the state could come through organizing work and production through unions. The American union, the Industrial Workers of the World, reflected these ideas, as did some of the features of Yugoslav communism in the 1950s and 1960s.

appeasement   Actions based on the hope that Nazi aggression would dissipate and war could be prevented if other countries accepted Hitler's demands. From the perspective of Stalin and many communist sympathizers in the West, appeasement appeared to be a policy of encouraging the Nazi regime to continue its aggression toward the East in the hopes of starting a war between Germany and the Soviet Union. A handful of conservatives, like Britain's Winston Churchill, who despised both the Nazi and communist regimes, also spoke out against appeasement.

Ba'ath Party (from the Arabic for "renaissance") A secular reform movement founded in Syria in the early 1950s. It aimed at unifying the Arab world, ending the internal fighting and petty squabbles that it saw as having allowed Western imperialism to gain such power in the region. Second, it emphasized social reform along socialist lines with extensive state controls over economic activity. Two versions continued, one in Syria and the other in Iraq. The authoritarian regimes in both countries moved away from initial socialist principles espoused by the movement's founders and focused on nationalist issues.

Bolsheviks Followers of Lenin who believed that the communist movement in Russia had to be a small, secretive, and highly centralized party. The word "Bolshevik" means "majority" in Russian, but the Bolsheviks were only a "majority" at one early meeting of the Social Democratic Workers Party. On March 8, 1918, the Bolsheviks changed their name to the Communist Party. (*See also* Menshevik.)

bourgeoisie According to Marx, the middle class, or bourgeoisie (in French) tended to side with the owners of capital, fearing that their small holdings of property would be destroyed in a socialist revolution. The adjective is bourgeois, as in "bourgeois sentimentality."

bread and butter unionism The technique advocated by AFL leader Samuel Gompers, former head of the Cigar Makers Union. Gompers focused on staying out of politics and simply negotiating for wage and hour increases along with other job conditions, holding out the strike as a threat when negotiations did not result in gains. Marxists saw such "bread and butter" gains as destructive of a revolutionary spirit, and as outright cooperation with the capitalist system.

Brest Litovsk The treaty known by the name of the town in which it was concluded. The Soviets accepted a humiliating defeat at the end of World War I, including the cession of territory to Germany, Austria-Hungary, and Romania.

cadres In the Communist Party, cadres were paid party workers. While the major parties in most Western democracies had very small paid staffs, the Communist Party employed scores of people on small salaries and paid their expenses. Through the cadres, the party could place paid organizers to work within unions, to establish separate labor unions, organize political parties in particular cities or states, or work in jobs usually held by volunteers in other organizations and clubs.

Cambridge Five Five British subjects active as spies for the Soviet Union in the early Cold War had been recruited while at Cambridge University in the 1930s. The five were Guy Burgess, Donald Maclean, Kim Philby, Anthony Blunt, and John Cairncross.

capital The money invested in equipment, buildings, and land to operate a business. With the industrial revolution of the early nineteenth century, capital became more important. Marx and other socialist critics blamed those who controlled capital, the capitalists, for the social and economic turmoil of the times.

Cheka and **chekists**   The Bolshevik regime under Lenin established a powerful secret police to track down and eliminate political enemies. Known as the Cheka, the organization later evolved into the NKVD and the KGB.

civil society   A number of Czech critics of the communist state in the 1960s and 1970s suggested that cultural organizations completely outside of government and the means of production provided room for free expression. Such organizations made up "civil society" and by focusing interest, energy, and productivity on them, the worst oppressive aspects of modern communist states could be avoided. Building on such organizations would be a pathway toward a more democratic society.

class struggle   Karl Marx and Friedrich Engels developed a theory of history, showing that changes in the means of production had transformed the relationship between social classes. In the nineteenth century, capitalists, the bourgeoisie, and the working class (or proletariat) all had different interests, and the struggle between those classes would define politics. Marx predicted that the class struggle would lead by stages to a bourgeois-dominated society that would then be transformed by revolution into a socialist state in the interests of the proletariat.

collectivization   A Soviet policy that called for land owned by individual peasants to be combined into larger cooperative farms known as a Kholkhoz. Many peasants resisted this process, but by the end of the 1930s, almost all agricultural land in the Soviet Union had been collectivized.

Cominform   The Communist Information Bureau, established following a meeting in September 1947 at the town of Szklarska Porêba in Poland. The first function of the Cominform was to make sure that the communist parties of Eastern Europe adhered to the interests of the Soviet Union and that they got rid of signs of pro-American or pro-capitalist leanings.

Comintern   Short expression for "Communist International." It was the international organization of communist parties that supported the regime in Russia. The Comintern was largely financed and directed by the Soviet Union. During the period from 1920 to 1943, the Comintern controlled, or sought to control, the communist parties of the world. Sometimes the terms "Third International" and "Comintern" were used interchangeably. (*See also* twenty-one conditions.)

commune   Used to describe communal property sharing arrangements in a wide variety of traditional pre-industrial societies. In the nineteenth century in the United States, the term described religious and nonreligious experimental communities that shared ownership in land and the earnings from work.

containment   A concept developed by U.S. State Department expert on Russia George Kennan. He suggested that, like a disease, communism needed to be "contained" behind what Churchill had called the "iron curtain."

cult of personality At the 20th Congress of the Communist Party of the Soviet Union, in February 1956, Khrushchev denounced Stalin's "cult of personality," referring to the excessive hero-worship built up through the use of propaganda techniques and fear that had surrounded Joseph Stalin. Similar personality cults developed around Mao Zedong and other communist dictators.

de-Stalinization In 1956, Nikita Khrushchev denounced Stalin for developing a cult of personality. As the Soviet and other communist parties distanced themselves from the positions taken by Stalin, the process became known as de-Stalinization. However, when some writers appeared to think they could criticize other excesses of communism, they found that de-Stalinization as defined by Khrushchev had strict limits.

détente French for "relaxation," détente did not indicate a major ideological shift on the part of either the United States or the Soviet Union. Both superpowers continued to praise the merits of their own system and criticize that of the other. However, each grudgingly admitted that neither country was likely to achieve outright military superiority in the Cold War. The period of détente lasted from about 1965 to about 1978.

democratic centralism A concept developed by Lenin that was key to the strict discipline he demanded of the Bolshevik party and later communist parties. Under democratic centralism, a central authority would determine the correct policy for the advance of socialism. (*See also* Comintern, politboro, and purge.)

deviationism According to the official line of the Communist Party as set forth through the Third International (1920–1943), and by Stalinists in the period from 1944 to 1953, there were two types of deviationism. Those like Trotsky who deviated to the left and advocated world revolution were known as left-wing sectarians or left deviationists. Those like Earl Browder, who deviated to the right by advocating cooperation with the capitalist powers were known as opportunists or right-wing deviationists. During the period when the Soviet Union controlled international communism, Moscow condemned those "deviating" either to the left or the right of the Soviet line.

dialectical materialism A philosophical principle developed by Karl Marx, applying the concept of dialectic, or development through conflicts and opposites, to the material world. The concept lay at the heart of Marx's vision of history as the playing out of the class struggle.

dissidents Beginning in the 1950s, intellectuals in Eastern Europe and the Soviet Union who criticized the flaws in the communist regimes, came to be called dissidents.

dual unionism The concept advanced by the IWW that workers should organize in revolutionary unions, rather than working through existing trade unions, thus setting up two union structures. William Z. Foster and some other revolutionary labor leaders believed instead in "boring from within," that is, advancing the revolutionary cause from within existing trade and industrial unions.

Eurocommunism In the 1970s and 1980s, some of the communist parties of Western Europe, particularly those in France and Italy, operated more and more independently. Accused of opportunism by some hard-line communists in Eastern Europe, Eurocommunists often cooperated with other parties of the left.

Fabians First organized in Britain in January 1884, the Fabian Society was named in honor of the Roman General Fabius who was known for his strategy of patience and delay in fighting against Hannibal. Fabians supported a gradual transition to socialism in which individuals would still retain private property.

fellow travelers In the 1940s, those who tended to support some of the ideas of the U.S. Communist Party, but who did not join the Party, were said to be traveling the same path, or were fellow travelers.

Fifth Column During the Spanish Civil War, Insurgent General Mola bragged that, in addition to the four columns of troops he had advancing on Madrid, he had a secret "Fifth Column" of supporters secretly waiting inside Madrid to rise in favor of Franco. It was a propaganda ploy, for there was no organized group of Insurgent supporters. Later, however, Franco supporters within Madrid did organize into a "Fifth Column." The term caught on in international usage. The term came to mean a secret group of underground cells, full of traitors, waiting for the moment to rise. After World War II, the term "Fifth Columnist" was often used to describe a clandestine supporter of the left, rather than the right, as Mola had used the term.

First International Established in the period from 1864 to 1872, the First International (also known as the International Workingmen's Association) was a loose organization of socialists and anarchists.

Fourth International *See* Trotskyism.

free love The anarchist belief that people should be able to have sexual relations with whomever they pleased, whether they were married or not. Anarchists argued that morals imposed by the Church and society constrained human freedom.

freedom fighters When Hungarian youth and workers fought to prevent the Soviet re-establishment of control in 1956, Western media dubbed them freedom fighters. Within the Soviet bloc, the rebels were seen as reactionary agents, but in the West, they were hailed as heroes.

front organizations In the United States, the Communist Party worked through numerous affiliated organizations, usually controlled by a few loyal cadres. Opponents on the left, and others familiar with the tactic, called these affiliated groups communist fronts or front organizations.

general strike   A strike across several enterprises, usually in the same city. Thus the strikes in Lawrence (1912) and Paterson (1913) were general strikes in this sense of the word. Internationally, the term usually refers to a strike in which all of the workers in all unionized industries in a city or a whole nation go on strike. Britain saw a national General Strike in May 1926. In the United States, there were such general strikes in Seattle in 1919, and San Francisco in 1934.

glasnost   In 1985, Mikhail Gorbachev announced a policy of glasnost or openness, in which a series of reforms would be discussed. Glasnost represented the end of the Leninist style of central decision-making.

Grandfather   During World War II, communications from the Comintern to the Communist Party in Yugoslavia constituted both military and political orders from Stalin, who had turned 60 in 1939. The code word for the Comintern at the time was, appropriately, Grandfather.

gulag   A Soviet forced labor camp in which prisoners were made to work on development projects such as road building, mining, or timber production. Conditions were so rough that literally millions of prisoners died in the camps. Originally established under the Tsarist regime, the gulag system was greatly expanded during the Soviet era and played an important role in industrializing parts of Siberia and other outlying regions of the Soviet Union.

hard line   In the emerging communist governments in Eastern Europe after World War II, party members tended to divide between those who insisted on closely following the Soviet model, generally regarded as Stalinists or hard line members and the soft line members who considered a more liberalized economic model with some ideas borrowed from capitalism and the West.

industrial union   The industrial union approach was to organize all workers in a particular industry, whatever their craft or trade, into a single union. When the American Industrial Workers of the World began to organize, they aimed for "One Big Union" with separate sections by industry. Later, the Congress of Industrial Organizations (CIO) used an industrial union organizing method.

Insurgents   During the Spanish Civil War, the revolt against the government was led by officers of the Spanish Army and the Civil Guard, supported by large landholders, by the *Falange* (a fascist party) and by a small group of monarchists. The supporters of the Popular Front government called their enemies "Insurgents."

Kremlin   An ancient walled center in Moscow. After Lenin moved the capital of Russia to Moscow in 1918, the Kremlin became the central government office in the Soviet Union. In the rest of the world, journalists and political observers often used the term "Kremlin" as a synonym for the Soviet government as a whole.

Kulaks   Stalin never defined exactly who the Kulaks were beyond saying that they were richer than their neighbors. Some Soviet leaders suggested that a Kulak was any peasant who didn't want his land to be collectivized. Western visitors were stunned to find some so-called Kulaks, supposedly wealthy private landholders, living in what would be seen as abject poverty in any other European country.

left wing   By the mid 1800s, the term left wing was being used to identify political ideologies which called for radical changes in the organization and structure of society. The term originated during the French Revolution of 1789–1799. In the National Assembly, which eventually overthrew the French monarchy, the most radical members tended to sit on the left side of the room while more conservative members sat on the right side.

leftist deviationists   Whenever official communist party doctrine called for cooperation with other parties in the democratic process, as during the Popular Front period (1935–1947), communists who refused such cooperation were accused of leftist deviationism. Trotskyism was treated as a form of leftist deviationism.

Lend-Lease   The program was initially implemented by Franklin Roosevelt in March 1941 in order to send vital supplies to Great Britain. It allowed for the easy purchase of American goods by granting extensive credits to the British government. After the United States entered the war in December 1941, the Lend-Lease program was extended to the Soviet Union as well.

Leninism   V. I. Lenin added many ideas to the basic principles of Marxism. By the 1930s, the term Marxism-Leninism was used to describe the communist version of socialist thinking, in which a vanguard party would seek or hold power in the name of the broader proletariat. (*See also* democratic centralism.)

Lovestoneites   In 1929, Stalin personally ordered the expulsion of Jay Lovestone from the Communist Party of the United States. Lovestone and his followers, the so-called Lovestoneites, continued to make up a small Marxist group through the 1930s, active in unions. The Lovestoneites believed in working within the American system.

machine and tractor stations   One key in collectivization of Soviet agriculture was the establishment of machine and tractor stations to provide modern equipment for the state farms and the collective farms. Since such facilities could be staffed by skilled mechanics rather than peasants, the stations became a means of introducing a modern proletariat to the countryside, and with them, centers for the advancing of party ideology and doctrine.

Marxism   Karl Marx (1818–1883) advocated a view of history and a vision of a socialist future for mankind. His ideas about the establishment of socialism through revolution became incorporated in Bolshevism and Leninism. Some of his ideas about change in history were more broadly adopted by many social scientists, including some in the West who did not support his advocacy of either socialism or revolution.

McCarthyism Herblock, the cartoonist for the *Washington Post*, coined the term, McCarthyism. Soon the word became a synonym for unfounded charges or mudslinging. Later, when McCarthy began to win over some believers to his charges, the term "McCarthyism" took on a meaning of militant patriotism. However, McCarthyism survived in American history books as a code word for crude defamation of character and thoughtless attacks on civil liberties.

Menshevik "Minority" in Russian, the Menshevik branch of the Social Democratic Party were usually more numerous than the Bolshevik or majority group. Unlike the Bolsheviks, Mensheviks did not believe that the path to socialism should be led by a disciplined conspiratorial or revolutionary core. Rather, Mensheviks supported a more political approach and tolerated more division of opinion.

mole In espionage, a mole is a long-time underground traitor, loyal to a foreign government, but living a double life in which he appears to be loyal to his home country. Each of the Cambridge Five was a mole.

nationalists In most common usage, a "nationalist" is someone who believes strongly in the national superiority of his own nation. Nationalists are often conservative defenders of their own nation against foreign or international invasion or even influence. In the 1890s in the United States, a nationalist was a supporter of the ideas of Edward Bellamy, believing that gradual nationalization or government ownership of industry would convert the United States into a socialist utopia within 100 years. In Spain, during the Spanish Civil War, nationalists were the supporters of Franco against the Popular Front government.

new class A term developed by Yugoslav Milovan Djilas to describe the bureaucrats and administrators in state socialist systems who benefited from control over property, similar to wealthy capitalists.

new economic policy A policy announced by Lenin that allowed for some preservation of capitalist structure and capitalist trade while the Soviet Union went through development in the early 1920s.

opportunism Some democratic governments allowed communist parties to operate, and many communist party leaders took the opportunity to develop political careers. When such a policy fell into disfavor in the Kremlin, the practice was denounced as opportunism, or right-wing deviationism.

Owenism Robert Owen advocated a form of cooperative socialism, inspiring consumers' and producers' cooperatives in which profits were distributed to member-customers or member-workers. Cooperativism and Owenism flourished in Britain, Scandinavia, and, to a much lesser extent, in the United States.

Palmer raids In 1920–1921, American Attorney General A. Mitchell Palmer arrested hundreds of anarchists and socialists and had many deported. The raids were later denounced as an invasion of civil liberties, but Palmer intended them to disrupt what he believed were subversive organizations.

perestroika   An attempt to promote change within the Soviet system by loosening, but not removing, the Communist Party's tight control over Soviet society. Advanced by Mikhail Gorbachev in the mid 1980s, perestroika means "reconstruction" and was a policy of making the Soviet economy more decentralized and opening it up to a limited degree of capitalist style management and profit motivation. (*See also* glasnost.)

permanent revolution   A concept advanced by Leon Trotsky, based on two radical departures from traditional Marxism. Backward, feudal countries could jump directly into socialism and bypass the capitalist phase of development as long as they had a disciplined working class movement that was not afraid to seize power. Successful working class revolutions in backward countries could act as a trigger for a worldwide overthrow of capitalism by spreading revolution to more advanced countries. Mao Zedong took Trotsky's theory a step further. According to Mao, revolutionary progress had to be a continuous and uninterrupted process that always involved elements of class struggle. He saw his role as driving the masses forward to ever higher levels of political consciousness by bringing them into conflict with their class enemies. He defined these enemies as anyone who resisted this process, which included many of his opponents within the Communist Party.

personality cult or **cult of personality**   Negative words in the world of communist discussions in the late 1950s and the 1960s. Nikita Khrushchev denounced the cult surrounding Stalin in a speech at the 20th Congress of the Communist Party in 1956. Khrushchev himself was later accused of trying to establish a cult of personality.

Politburo   The central policy-making office in communist Russia. The abbreviation for "political bureau" in Russian, the Politburo was responsible for deciding everything, from foreign affairs to domestic economic policies. Its size varied at different times but was usually made up of around a dozen members, selected by the Central Committee of the Russian Communist Party.

Popular Front or **united front from above**   Announced in August 1935, it meant that the communist parties would work with other groups, labor leaders, and political parties to oppose fascism or the threat of it rising. Popular Front governments took power in France and Spain with minority support from communist parties there.

Prague Spring   In early 1968, in Prague, Czechoslovakia, open discussion of alternate paths to socialism flourished, before being suppressed. The movement was later known as the Prague Spring.

praxis   In the 1960s in Yugoslavia and in Western European Marxist groups, the word "praxis" took on a special meaning. Work in large capitalist and socialist enterprises often tended to be alienating because of its boring and routine nature, and the necessarily hierarchical structures of complicated organizations. By contrast, praxis represented the ideal that the inner nature of practical tasks should be self-fulfilling and a means to self-expression. In Yugoslavia, the advocates of praxis became blamed for feeding discontent with the system.

proletariat   The working class, especially the industrial working class.

propaganda by word   Publishing anarchist pamphlets or making anarchist speeches. Propaganda by deed meant inspiring the masses by attacking policemen, assassinating political leaders, or bombing government buildings.

purge   Because communist parties operated on the principle of democratic centralism in which correct policy was announced and enforced from the top, disagreement with the policy could not be tolerated. Thus party cadres suspected of disagreement were often demoted, dismissed, thrown out of the party, or in extreme cases, executed. Such house-cleaning would be a purge. (*See also* show trial.)

Republicans or **Loyalists**   By a strange twist, those supporting the Republic during the Spanish Civil War were the more liberal and radical parties. Thus in Spain, the term "Republican" that Americans associated with a conservative party became a designation for the Loyalist parties of the Popular Front, including the Communist Party.

revisionism   Advanced by Eduard Bernstein, revisionism was not so much a complete rejection of Marxism as it was a recognition that his philosophical outlook was outdated. Bernstein suggested that reforms were possible by working with middle-class groups with a shared sense of moral responsibility for improving society as a whole. Orthodox Marxists denounced Bernstein as a weak-minded apologist at best and, at worst, a traitor to the working class movement. For pure Marxists, revisionism was a dirty word.

salami tactic   In November 1945, the Communist Party of Hungary obtained 17 percent of the vote. By 1947, using fraud and intimidation, they received about 22 percent. The tactic of piecemeal elimination of the opposition became known as the salami tactic, no doubt calling up the image of slicing up a stick of salami in order to devour it.

satellite nations   In the years following World War II, the Soviet Union established military-backed communist regimes in a number of Eastern European countries. The countries were so tightly controlled at first by Moscow-directed parties and secret police that journalists in the West began to call them satellite nations, using the image from outer space in which satellites rotate in orbit around a planet.

Second International   Formed in 1889, the Second International was an organization of socialists, dominated by followers of Karl Marx. The Second International excluded anarchists from membership, but it broke up in the First World War when socialist legislators in Germany and elsewhere supported the war aims of their separate countries.

sectarian   Small religious groups that break away from mainstream religion are called sects and their members are sectarian.

secular   Ideas or groups that are entirely nonreligious are known as secular. The New Harmony, Brook Farm, and Oneida communities, as well as another two dozen that followed the concepts of Charles Fourier, were secular communes.

show trial   During Stalin's purges of the Communist Party to eliminate opponents, a common practice was to hold a show trial. After a suspect was interrogated, usually with tortures such as sleep deprivation and beatings, he would be placed on public trial, often filmed. At the trials, the accused usually made abject confessions of their "errors," before being sentenced to death or to long terms in prison camps. The show trials stunned communist sympathizers outside the Soviet Union, causing many to drop any affiliation with the Party.

social fascists   In the period from 1928 to 1934, the Comintern accused European and American socialists, labor leaders, and other popular leaders on the left of being social fascists. These groups would falsely promise change, the Comintern argued, with the real purpose of propping up capitalism in its last phases. Since many radical leaders also hated fascism, they found the communist charge of social fascism both hostile and insulting.

socialism   Many different types of thinkers advocated that the benefits of modern productivity be distributed throughout society, not just at the discretion of the private owners of capital. Utopians established communes in the nineteenth century to arrange the sharing of productivity, while Owenites worked through cooperatives. Followers of Marxism believed that such a system could only be established by revolution. Revisionists, like Eduard Bernstein and British Fabians, believed it could be achieved by working through the electoral process. In general, socialist and social democratic parties in the twentieth century followed the Fabian and revisionist approach, rejecting the revolutionary doctrine of Lenin.

socialism in one country   By the 1930s, Stalin focused on building socialism in the Soviet Union, denouncing Leon Trotsky for advocating world revolution.

Soviet   In Russian, the word "soviet" means workers' council or commune. Soviets were local groups of workers and soldiers that formed during revolutionary periods. The term has been used more widely to refer to the Soviet Union.

Stalinism   The regime of Joseph Stalin became known for repression of dissent, a personality cult, and the use of a variety of totalitarian methods. When his methods were emulated in other countries by other communist leaders, they were accused of Stalinism. (*See also* totalitarianism.)

Stasi   Probably the most extensive of the secret police forces in Eastern Europe. Ever since the establishment of the German Democratic Republic in 1949, the Stasi had used terror tactics to intimidate and suppress internal opposition to the communist regime. The organization also employed a huge network of agents and informants on both sides of the Berlin Wall.

Third International   *See* Comintern.

Third World   At the Bandung Conference in 1955, a group of 29 newly independent African and Asian countries met in Indonesia to discuss possibilities for mutual aid and cooperation. These nations identified themselves as the "Third World" in an effort to demonstrate that they were not politically or ideologically aligned with either the West or the Soviet Union.

totalitarianism   First used in fascist Italy in the early 1920s to imply that the total forces of the country were cooperating in a national effort. Later, the term came to refer to the use of all the instruments of state, party, and police power to ensure unswerving obedience to a regime. Totalitarian states, by this definition, included fascist Italy, 1922–1943; Nazi Germany, 1934–1945; Falangist Spain, 1939–1975; the Soviet Union, 1919–1991; and communist regimes in Eastern Europe from the late 1940s through about 1989.

trade union   The American Federation of Labor organized workers by a particular trade or craft. Thus in one large factory, the mechanics and carpenters would each belong to locals of their craft. Trade unionism, like socialism, worked for redistribution of the benefits of productivity to the workers. But most trade unionists sought redistribution on a piecemeal, negotiated basis, rather than through reorganization of the whole economy. American trade unionists tended to reject political activities, but British trade unionists supported it in the Labour Party.

Trotskyism   Leon Trotsky, a leader of the Bolshevik revolution in Russia, was purged from the Communist Party by Stalin and went into exile in 1929. Internationally, he developed small factions of followers who believed that his call for permanent revolution was appropriate. They established a Fourth International of their organizations in 1938.

Truman Doctrine   President Harry S. Truman announced in March 1947 that he would provide foreign aid to Greece and Turkey in order to prevent communist insurgents from seizing power.

Twenty-one Conditions   At the Second Congress of the Communist International in July 1920, the Comintern laid out 21 conditions to which a party would need to agree in order to join the Comintern. The 16th condition required that all decisions of the Comintern Executive Committee were binding on all member parties, thus establishing the principle of democratic centralism on an international basis.

underground   When a Communist Party member concealed his or her membership in the Party, either to avoid arrest or to conduct an illicit activity such as espionage for the Soviet Union, he or she was said to be operating underground.

united front from below   In Comintern language in the early 1930s, a united front from below meant that Communist Party workers should penetrate other parties, like the socialists, and working class groups like labor unions, recruiting members and getting them to join the Communist Party and accept Communist Party leadership and direction.

utopias   In 1516, the British philosopher Thomas More published a fanciful novel describing an ideal society, titled *Utopia*. Since then, idealized, planned societies have been called utopias, and schemes for setting them up have been called utopian.

warlords   High-ranking officers in the old Chinese Imperial Army or local provincial governors. With the collapse of almost all central authority following the 1911 revolution and the overthrow of the Manchu dynasty, the warlords took advantage of the chaos to establish their own fiefdoms over much of China.

Wobblies   In a story that smacked of what we now call an urban legend, the IWW ended up being known as "Wobblies," because of a difficulty in pronunciation. A Chinese American worker was challenged at one of the strikes in the West, and he insisted he was a member of the union. "What union?" his accosters asked. "I-wobble-wobble," he answered. The name stuck, and was used with pride by members of the union thereafter.

Appendix B

Selected Bibliography

Andrew, Christopher. *Her Majesty's Secret Service: The Making of the British Intelligence Community.* New York: Penguin Books, 1987.

Andrew, Christopher, and Vasili Mitrokhin. *The Sword and the Shield: The Mitrokhin Archive and the Secret History of the KGB.* New York: Basic Books, 1999.

Barer, Shlomo. *The Doctors of Revolution: 19th Century Thinkers Who Changed the World.* London: Thames & Hudson, 2000.

Bestor, Arthur. *Backwoods Utopias: The Sectarian and Owenite Phases of Communitarian Socialism in America: 1663–1829.* Philadelphia: University of Pennsylvania Press, 1950.

Brands, H.W. *The Devil We Knew: Americans and the Cold War.* New York: Oxford University Press, 1993.

Brenner, Philip. *The Cuba Reader: The Making of a Revolutionary Society.* New York: Grove Press, 1989.

Bronner, Stephen. *Socialism Unbound.* New York: Routledge, 1990.

Brzezinski, Zbigniew. *The Grand Failure: The Birth and Death of Communism in the Twentieth Century.* New York: Charles Scribner's Sons, 1989.

Buhle, Mari Jo, et al. *Encyclopedia of the American Left*, 2nd ed. New York: Oxford University Press, 1998.

Carver, Terrell, ed. *The Cambridge Companion to Marx.* New York: Cambridge University Press, 1991.

Cliff, Tony. *Trotsky.* 4 vols. Chicago: Bookmarks, 1989.

Cunningham, Valentine, ed. *Spanish Front: Writers on the Civil War.* New York: Oxford University Press, 1986.

Daniels, Robert V. *Trotsky, Stalin, and Socialism.* Boulder, Colo.: Westview Press, 1991.

Deletant, Dennis. *Communist Terror in Romania: Gheorghiu-Dej and the Police State, 1948–1965.* New York: St. Martin's Press, 1999.

Draper, Theodore. *American Communism and Soviet Russia: The Formative Period.* New York: Viking, 1960.

Dubovsky, Melvyn. *We Shall Be All: A History of the IWW.* New York: Quadrangle, 1969.

Dulles, Foster Rhea and Melvyn Dubofsky. *Labor in America, A History*, 4th ed. Arlington Heights, Ill.: Harlan Davidson, Inc., 1984.

Fitzpatrick, Sheila. *The Russian Revolution, 1917–1932.* New York: Oxford University Press, 1984.

Gaddis, John Lewis. *The United States and the Origins of the Cold War, 1941–1947.* New York: Columbia University Press, 1972.

Gill, Graeme. *Stalinism.* New York: St. Martin's Press, 1998.

Gorodetsky, Gabriel. *Grand Delusion: Stalin and the German Invasion of Russia.* New Haven, Conn.: Yale University Press, 1999.

Gottlieb, Roger S. *Marxism, 1844–1990: Origins, Betrayal, Rebirth.* New York: Routledge, 1992.

Guarneri, Carl J. *The Utopian Alternative: Fourierism in Nineteenth Century America.* Ithaca, N.Y.: Cornell University Press, 1991.

Gwertzman, Bernard and Michael T. Kaufman, eds. *The Collapse of Communism.* New York: Times Books, 1990.

Harding, Neil. *Leninism.* New York: Macmillan, 1996.

Haynes, John Earl. *Red Scare or Red Menace? American Communism and Anticommunism in the Cold War Era.* Chicago: Ivan R. Dee, 1996.

Heilbroner, Robert L. *The Worldly Philosophers.* New York: Simon & Schuster, 1980.

Held, Joseph, ed. *The Columbia History of Eastern Europe in the Twentieth Century.* New York: Columbia University, 1993.

Isserman, Maurice. *Which Side Were You On? The American Communist Party During the Second World War.* Middletown, Conn.: Wesleyan University Press, 1982.

Karnow, Stanley. *Mao and China: A Legacy of Turmoil.* New York: Penguin Books, 1990.

———. *Vietnam: A History.* New York: Viking, 1993.

Kaytz, Henryk. *The Emancipation of Labor: a History of the First International.* New York: Greenwood Press, 1992.

Klehr, Harvey. *The Heyday of American Communism: The Depression Decade.* New York: Basic Books, 1984.

Klehr, Harvey, and John Earl Haynes. *The American Communist Movement: Storming Heaven Itself.* New York: Twayne Publishers, 1992.

Klehr, Harvey, John Earl Haynes, and Fridrikh Igorevich Firsov. *The Secret World of American Communism.* New Haven, Conn.: Yale University Press, 1995.

Klehr, Harvey, John Earl Haynes, and Kyrill M. Anderson. *The Soviet World of American Communism.* New Haven, Conn.: Yale University Press, 1998.

Lendvai, Paul. *Eagles in Cobwebs: Nationalism and Communism in the Balkans.* New York: Doubleday, 1969.

Lindesay, William. *Marching with Mao: a Biographical Journey.* London: Hodder & Stoughton, 1993.

Lowe, Peter. *The Korean War.* New York: St. Martin's Press, 2000.

Marx, Karl, and Friedrich Engels. *The Communist Manifesto.* Edited by Samuel H. Beer. New York: Appleton Century Crofts, 1955.

McCauley, Martin. *Gorbachev.* New York: Longman, 1998.

McLellan, David. *The Thought of Karl Marx: an Introduction.* London: Papermac, 1995.

Narkiewicz, Olga A. *Marxism and the Reality of Power: 1919–1980.* New York: St. Martin's Press, 1981.

Nordhoff, Charles. *American Utopias* (Originally published as *Communistic Societies of the United States–1875*). Stockbridge, Mass.: Berkshire House, 1993.

Patterson, Thomas G., and Robert J. McMahon, eds. *The Origins of the Cold War,* 3rd ed. Lexington, Mass.: D. C. Heath, 1991.

Payne, Stanley G. *The Spanish Revolution.* New York: Norton, 1970.

Pearson, Raymond. *The Rise and Fall of the Soviet Empire.* New York: St. Martin's Press, 1998.

Pipes, Richard. *Russia under the Bolshevik Regime.* New York: A. A. Knopf, 1993.

Rees, Tim, and Andrew Thorpe. *International Communism and the Communist International, 1919–1943.* Manchester: Manchester University Press, 1998.

Reis, Edward. *Marx: A Clear Guide.* Chicago: Pluto Press, 1996.

Sakwa, Richard. *Gorbachev and His Reforms, 1985–1990.* Englewood Cliffs, N.J.: Prentice Hall, 1990.

Salisbury, Harrison E. *The New Emperor: China in the Era of Mao and Deng.* Boston: Little, Brown and Company, 1992.

Schrecker, Ellen. *No Ivory Tower: McCarthyism and the Universities.* New York: Oxford University Press, 1986.

————. *The Age of McCarthyism: A Brief History with Documents.* New York: St. Martin's Press, 1994.

Service, Robert. *Lenin: A Biography.* London: Macmillan, 2000.

Short, Philip. *Mao, a Life.* London: Sceptre, 2000.

Smith, Cyril. *Marx at the Millennium.* Chicago: Pluto Books, 1996.

Spence, Jonathan. *Mao Zedong*. New York: Viking, 1999.

Stokes, Gale, ed. *From Stalinism to Pluralism: A Documentary History of Eastern Europe Since 1945*, 2nd ed. New York: Oxford University Press, 1996.

Thomas, Hugh. *The Spanish Civil War*. New York: Harper Brothers, 1961.

Thompson, Willie. *The Communist Movement since 1945*. Oxford: Blackwell Publishers, 1998.

Thurston, Robert W. *Life and Terror in Stalin's Russia, 1934–1941*. New Haven: Yale University Press, 1996.

Watson, William E. *The Collapse of Communism in the Soviet Union*. Westport: Greenwood Press, 1998.

Weinstein, Allen, and Alexander Vassiliev. *The Haunted Wood: Soviet Espionage in America— The Stalin Era*. New York: Random House, 1999.

White, Gordon, and Robin Murray, eds. *Revolutionary Socialist Development in the Third World*. Lexington: University of Kentucky Press, 1983.

White, James D. *Lenin: The Practice and Theory of Revolution*. New York: Palgrave, 2000.

White, Stephen. *After Gorbachev*, 4th ed. Cambridge, Mass.: Cambridge University Press, 1993.

Wolfe, Bertram D. *Three Who Made a Revolution: A Biographical History*, 4th ed. New York: Stein and Day, 1984.

Index